A
COMMENTARY
on the
GOSPEL OF JOHN

The battle of Armageddon is raging within the valley of decision: Jesus, as the Christ of God, on the right, Muhammad as the ultimate prophet of Allah, on the left, Lucifer, as the prince of the New World Order, in the midst. The Book of Revelation now being opened with many other books, describes this battle. This book is but one such of the many.

A
COMMENTARY
on the
GOSPEL OF JOHN

Stanley C. Polski

To order additional copies of this book, contact:
Xlibris
1-888-795-4274
www.Xlibris.com
Orders@Xlibris.com
552918

CONTENTS

AUTHOR'S FOREWORD
THIRD EDITION

The first edition of this commentary was written about 40 years ago. The second edition contains additional comments written over the past 2 years. This third edition adds comments generated in June of this year and such follow in this Foreword. I will deal herein with seven issues: Time, Atheists, Barak Obama, Mammon, Muhammad, Islam and the Lord God of Israel.

John's gospel was written about 2000 years ago, and in that gospel Jesus refers to David, who wrote about 1000 years before Jesus was born. David references the writings of Moses who wrote about 500 years before David and Solomon wrote a number of proverbs and psalms. Moses in his writings refers to events occurring several 500 year periods before he was drawn out of the waters. Moses also wrote of his own life experiences which he enjoyed about 3500 years ago.

Time is a subjective and extremely personal experience. Now what we know of the past and what we know of the future is what we experience and know in the present. Eternity is the reality and time is a derivative notion. A day is as a thousand years and a thousand years is as a day when one spends a day studying what happened over a thousand year interval. But how do we acquire knowledge of a thousand years of events in a day except by the power of words to enlighten us? And who writes the words that are written? How can those not even a hundred years old tell us what happened 13 billion years ago? Or what will happen a million years hence?

Jesus puts the matter succinctly. Before the big bangers came to be, I was.

Our present is always passing and tomorrow is never. Our past is that which we are able to make of it in the moment present. So also the future is what we have power to conceive it to be in that present moment of time we envision it. Thus the given reality is the ever passing present moment in which we enjoy the reality of everlasting life. Thus every living soul writes his biography within himself as his past and future ever grow within the nature of his being. The kingdom of heaven and or the kingdom of hell is within that soul.

All historians are the myth makers of their own present moments.

Alfred North Whitehead remarked that Gibbon's Decline and Fall of the Roman Empire was devoid of dates. Yet when did it fall? From my perspective in this day it is still flourishing. For many others it doesn't exist and has yet failed to come to be. The synchronization of time systems requires the belief in the myths of memory. Add to this the miracles required for any single soul to understand the Roman Empire and one might at least begin to sense the perplexities of the many events inherent in everlasting life. The Jews wait for a savior to free them from the Roman Empire. For many this has already occurred; for some others, this event has yet to come; for many others, this event is shrouded in the mystery of their own spiritual blindness and they care nothing for it. Nevertheless, the Lord God of Israel who created all things, and causes all things to be creative, chose the children of Israel to be with him and He within them. Thus Babylon, Rome, and Jerusalem came to be and the saga of God vs the world is written in the Scriptures of Truth.

The atheists are fools since they preach God does not exist. But the atheists themselves exist and scorn all believers in Christ for their faith. Thus atheists promote and glory in their evolutionary doctrines. They have faith in themselves. And they would have us believe they understand what we cannot comprehend, namely, that they are but the present species of a swirl of cosmic dust which will dissipate into the nothingness from which they came. They believe in everlasting death. Let them enjoy it. It's a pity they delay so long to embrace it. We have no need of them to dissipate their ephemeral existence creating universities of learned illuminati to excrete their brilliance into the black holes of their own cerebral cortexes. Who really needs their creative intellectual crap? Surely they do. These eat their own dung and produce more of the same. They violate the law of conservation of matter. They rival the industrious termites who though small in number create great and hardened hills to house their own matter.

Now is my soul troubled and greatly so.

President Barak Obama is the ultimate jihadist and he is striving to make this America I so greatly love an Islamic Caliphate. Embedded within the tenets of Islam and leavened within the Satanic hypocrisy of the Koran is the lie that those who promote Islam throughout their lives are destined for eternal bliss; and even Allah cannot prevent their entrance into Paradise. Of course, this is pure and unadulterated bullshit. Nevertheless, Obama has sold his soul to entertain this delusion. And this is why he cannot utter one word against Islam, such as "radical Islam". In so doing he would lose his free ticket to Islamic paradise. He also might lose his prized position as the supreme ayatollah of the Democratic Party. This might depress him since even Oprah seems to have dumped him in favor of Hillary.

Nevertheless there are many lesser ayatollahs both foreign and domestic, murderers and Islamic scholars alike, who passionately believe they also are worthy of the same free ticket.

For the poor in spirit America is the nation suffering birth pains to become one within the Kingdom of God. There is war in heaven. A triumvirate comprised of atheists, Mammonites, and the Muhammadan enthralled Moabites war against Jesus as Christ, the Son of the living God. All these have coalesced into the New World Order of Babylon. These all hate the Son of God who would have all learn of him and thereby become the Sons of God. You cannot serve God and mammon and that is why the Mammonites take great pleasure in the mesmerizing spectacles of the world economy. That is why Obama and his clones crave the UK become a nation under the Babylonian State rather than a nation destined for greatness within the Kingdom of God. That is why the hypocritical ayatollah of the Democratic Party lusts to bring peace in the East by inciting war in the West. Nevertheless, the shallow minded stooges of Satanic seduction cannot understand nor comprehend the simplest of metaphors. Lucifer understands, however, and this will piss it off.

However, a mammonite animated world would send orgasmic pleasure impulses down Lucifer's legs. That is why it and its' media motor mouths break for commercials. They don't break bread and look up to heaven. They break for commercials since they need well healed merchants of babble to provide dollars to complement their lack of sense.

Muhammad, by contrast, was expert in traveling merchandise. He was also a brilliant conservationist. He didn't require multiplied gigawatts of electric power plants to produce a mega global arms industry. The Scimitar had minimal effects on global warming.

In this Foreword, I am greatly troubled at this time. It's heart breaking to witness multitudes to choose evil over good. What is so appealing about Islam? I cannot believe so many subscribe to the belief that those who do not submit to Allah, the very God Muhammad created with his sayings accumulated in the Koran, will kill all who do not submit to him, or her, or to it, or to whatever or whoever Allah is? Islam as well as Allah was created by the sayings of Muhammad. The Koran is a mumble jumble of precepts, sayings, commands, and list of characters found in the Jewish and Christian literature of the age in which Muhammad lived.

At best, Muhammad is a profitable plagiarist, and Islam is a best seller. Jesus speaks in parables. Indeed his life, his very living presence, is an unfolding parable. The baskets containing the fragments of bread and fishes, which is as much to say his doctrine and men who have been caught to accept and preach his teaching, is still being distributed to multitudes in the world even to this day. And the fragments are inexhaustible even though only seven and twelve baskets are provided. But then again so also are the leavened doctrines of the Pharisees inexhaustible, although they require multitudes of libraries to house their books. The wise men who still come to Bethlehem, that city of bread, of doctrine, of the words of God, to give the Christ child being born within us therein, that very stable of truth so essential for everlasting life makes us realize Christmas every day. The City of God of Augustine predates the Koran, as does the epistles of John and of Paul. So also the psalms of David, the proverbs of Solomon, the prophecies of Isaiah, the teachings of seven churches, the writings of minor prophets, and a book of revelation compressing two thousand years of life into a few pages.

Gabriel, at least Muhammad's Gabriel, was either ignorant or close mouthed of these truths.

Kill the infidels. And I will provide excruciating pain for them to endure forever. Is this Allah's message, or is it Muhammad's or is Gabriel's or is it Obama's? Could use some forensics here.

Now the Lord God of Israel has the power to destroy both body and soul in hell. This is the reason the fear of the Lord is the beginning of wisdom. Nevertheless those who have given their souls to that great deceiver known as the devil, cannot fear the destruction of that which they do not possess. Thus this world is full of soulless beings who crave to enter within and possess the souls of others since they have lost their own. This is why Obama craves to rule over all with the power of his executive orders. This is also why those who have lost their own souls clone others by injecting their materialistic seminal ideas into those sheep without a sheepfold, and without a shepherd to lead them to find the still waters quickening the pastures of everlasting life. And the hirelings who care not for the sheep will abuse and exploit them as their godless masters direct. The wolves who father Rome devour the sheep with Islamic impunity. They seem to enjoy it immensely.

I am amazed at the colossal stupidity of it all. There is no real flesh and blood Allah and even Muhammad who created this idol of the mind and market place cannot keep his own soul alive.

But what really amazes me is Obama pushing Islam down our throats with his lies, his directives, and ignorance of the Koran. But this is enough for now.

Let all Americans who love the God who blesses America impeach Obama by acclamation.

AUTHOR'S FOREWORD
SECOND EDITION

The first edition of this work was published in 1979. Sold one copy. My daughter bought it. Severely berated me for my comments on women liberators. There is enough in this book to offend many, maybe even all. World population was then two billions plus, now six billion plus. Thus I risk offending billions saith the devil after I dismissed his prior imperative commands.

I wrote the first edition about forty years ago. It is reproduced in this second edition with some typographic changes. It comprises the major portion of this book given in twenty-one chapters. The second edition contains some Preparatory Notes, subtitled, A Chronicle Prolegomena of Barley Loaf Fragments, and the Introductory Notes, subtitled, Sayings Gleaned from a Grass Stained Basket of Fragments of Unleavened Scripture. I wrote these notes over the past two years.

Scholars, given suitable calendars, make much ado about timelines and chronologies. Publishers have concerns about the timing of copyrights, editions, and markets. And legions of scientists have concerns about periods of time extending from yoctoseconds to ages, epochs, periods, eras, and eons. And thanks to the magical processes inherent in the bobbling's of nuclear particles, the Maya calendar has morphed up mya's, 13,777 of them, serially following one after the other with the femtosecond precision necessary for the evolution of my transitory being. So who am I, conceived some eighty plus years ago, reading a book published some four hundred plus years ago, which book is a record of the sayings of a man who lived some two thousand years ago, who spoke of a prophet who wrote of events occurring a few thousand years before he was drawn out of the waters; who am I, I ask, to write these words and have these thoughts? I don't know. However, my Creator has given me a cup to drink full of intoxicating wine, pressed out of the grapes of his very own vineyard. This causes me to envision many things, one of which is the following abstraction, gleaned from the scriptures of truth.

Eternity is the ever present reality, and all times are but derivative notions; there is no past save that which one knows about it in the present. Likewise the future can be no more than one knows of it in the present. The present is the ever moving reality: tomorrow is never. The same metaphysical principle applies to space. Space is the total environment surrounding one who senses and feels it from the standpoint of one's own perspective. Space is infinite and peculiar to each one within it. It is one's own world. As one moves so does one's world move and there is no end to it. On this earth there are billions of worlds colliding, attracting and repelling, one another, the good and evil alike. All writers, as all speakers, write the histories of their own world, and speak the words drawn up from the waters of their own cisterns.

The power of the Word to create is unfathomable. Nevertheless, many men blaspheme God with the words they create, even denying and despising truth itself in order to promote their own glory. The complex organism of an ant is beyond their comprehension. But they explain what occurred billions of years before they came to be and babble on and on and on about their learned ignorance.

The bottom line to the above is that the God who was, even our Creator, being the God who is, is present with us this day even more so than he was with Abraham, Isaac, Jacob in their days. Isaiah, Jesus, and John, that disciple whom Jesus loves, and whose living gospel has provoked this commentary, realize this as living fact. Nevertheless, men who reject God and glut themselves with the fruit of the knowledge of good and evil despise this fact. I leave such to the worlds of their own delusions for the times appointed.

PREPARATORY NOTES
SECOND EDITION

A CHRONICLE PROLEGOMENA OF
BARLEY LOAF FRAGMENTS

7/1/2014 @10:53 PM, Tuesday

Night embraces darkness: the eventide has washed away the evening. I hear the waters breaking upon the sands of time but I cannot see the grains of life emerging within, upon, and amidst these moments of eternity. The beast of these seas emerges as the State whose image, Man, in all his humanity, greatly prophesies the beginnings and ends of all that is, or ever was, or ever shall come to be. A galaxy of innumerable galactic events encased within the skulls of the living dead.

Man and its State bore me through and through.

No introduction, no preface; neither glossary nor lists of acknowledgements, nor summary of events or postscripts of the past can mitigate the pain of tribulation of these few days past. I long for Eve and her touch: and what I get is Obama and his poking fingers.

7/2/2014

Father forgive them for they know not what they do. Nevertheless, that was then, this is now, and many, save not all, know what they are doing, and they do it with gusto, amidst the sorceries of socialism. They pride themselves on their pride: and how might one palliate their hardened hearts? And once they are forgiven, what results? They return again to the Cyclops of their own cycles of confusion. Many fools have evolved into beasts, and morphed Gog into Godzilla, and worship the automatons of anarchy, and infected heaven itself with the merchants of mammon, and the scientific priests of materialism.

Father, we will piss them off further, with words such as these! Nevertheless, it is for their own good: for their bladders are full of adulteries: they love to fuck around with Babylon and her sisters: and full of fornications: for they love their social intercourses with the Nicolaitans who lust to box all of mankind into their worldly systems of hierarchical rule and authority. They love to clone human souls within a particular mechanism of interacting particles ever colliding within the bottomless pits and blackened holes of their own bizarre imaginations. These pride themselves on their power to transform men into machines whereby they program them to fulfill all their godless and anachronistic desires. Lucifer has fallen: but he is still active. So also the luminaries he has cloned for his own benefits.

7/4/2014
A day lost: gone forever. What past of Life is eternally no more?

God! How I hate the godless who nibble at my soul, eat up my Life, and crave to consume my very being by making me as one of their very own!

Why these words? Why their words?

Liars love the lies they conceive, publish and promulgate. The false witnesses of vanity. The One Worlders who strive to rule over all in the place of God. Lucifer's brilliant, academically oriented, universe of fools.

7/13/2014
How many Universities are needed to universalize the universes? Why universalize the universities the Universities create? The questions are a bit rhetorical: nevertheless, the power of deceit embellished within the glittering generalities of Lucifer's generals, even those professors of evolutionary dogmas, enable antichrist scribes to transmit Satan's dogma into the skulls of man. How do I know this?

I experience it daily. Nevertheless, there are other scribes, wise men, prophets and preachers, of courses many, sent into the world by Jesus as Christ, to profess and stream truth into the souls of men.

7/30/2014

The Father, even our heavenly Father, judges no man: but that Spirit has committed all judgement to his Son, born of a woman, conceived by the Spirit of truth to become the Son of sinful man. The flesh and blood reality of this incarnate fact is denied by Lucifer, that fallen star of God's first morning, and his bands of storm trooping illuminati.

We are the sons and daughters of whatsoever fathers us. Satan is prolific and its seed infests the worlds of good and evil alike. Nevertheless we are not all equal: for those that are led by the God of Love, Truth, Beauty, Genius and Joy are led into and become the New Jerusalem. And all this while the blind leaders of the blind fall into the deep ditches of despair wherein they wallow in the bottomless caverns of their very own godless imaginations.

The beast of this sea of multitudes of peoples, of nations, of tongues is the State: and Man is the great false prophet emerging from the dust of the earth, even humanity with all its godless humans, nourishing themselves with the fruit of the tree yielding, indiscriminatingly, knowledge of good and evil.

The statesman, as all men of the State despise the kingdom of heaven and war against the kingdom of God come.

God, even Love in all its power and glory is my heavenly Father: nevertheless by becoming the son in law of man, I have acquired another father.

All this is but a preface to the metaphysical mysteries I needs must explore in order to continue my baptism of fire even as mine own, even our own, heavenly Father desires.

7/31/2014

How quickly has this month come to be and passed away save for twenty-one or so hours left for me to live out within this month of July in this place in which I am now moving along with a host of stars innumerable. All I have is this present moment of eternal life wherein eternity is bound. For what are all things past save that which is contained within the cup of life which I now drink: there is no past save what we make of it in our present: and no future save which we make of it within this present day. Thus past and future are experienced, literally lived out, within the times we know as life eternally present. There really is no more time save those times we create within the twinkling of our eye.

But it's best I rest within a few hours of this eternal day. For I am dead tired even as I am tired of the second death. I endure it, even taste of it, for the times appointed, even as that death passes away.

Life is a living every present reality: Death, a real fiction created by those fools who love to animate the living dead.

The morning has come: the dawning of day has past: and the evening is future, a time of this day yet to come to pass.

The God which is, is the God with us now, even that Lord God which was, the Almighty which is to come. As the poet still proclaims, eternity is full of many acts and hours, and those who inherit everlasting Life enjoy them whensoever they will. For as the Word with us now proclaims, God's will is their will.

But of what does the Word speak? The God of the living, surely not any of the many strange demons of the dead. Even that God who in the beginning created the heaven and the earth: Even in those times before time came to be. And then the earth was without form and void; and darkness was upon the face of the deep. This was the state of the heaven and earth upon which God would work: formless earth: deep void, darkness and waters: such were the elements of Creation. And the spirit of God moved upon the face of the waters. And God said, Let there be light: and there was light.

Now the God who is tells those who have ears to hear what was in the very first day now past. Surely those who have eyes that can perceive this fragment of truth are enlightened thereby.

And God saw the light, that it was good: inclusive also of that light which then was yet to come. And God divided the light from the darkness. God divides that which he wills.

And God called the light Day, and the darkness he called Night. Day and Night are called into being by the division of light from darkness. And the evening and morning were the first day.

In this new age of Satanically inspired statistical stupidities it is essential for those angels among us who have not left their first estates, and who wish to preserve them from the onslaughts of Lucifer's clones, to cultivate some metaphysical insight into the creative processes established by God to foster the growth of the kingdom of heaven within and among the souls of men.

The Word says and thereby the Word creates. Thus men are enlightened: thus Adam participates as the Son of God in the creation. Lucifer, of course, has another agenda. He conspires to rule over all men in the place of God.

The illuminati of the One World Order exalt Lucifer, the prince of the antichrist world, wherein Jesus of Nazareth is crucified on the cross of knowledge of good and evil.

Lucifer blinds men with its brilliance: the result: the blind lead the blind into deep ditches of despair wherein hell is found and the dead are ever busy burying their own.

Nevertheless, this preparatory note does and must have an end. So I'll end it here with a list of ideas, topics, and notions which are to be alluded to in the following Introduction to my Second Edition of a Commentary on the Gospel of John.

Glossary, Acknowledgements, Postscript, Preface; Metaphysics, Symbolism, Parables and Parameters; Reason, The Function of Reason, The Spirit of Truth; Prophecies and Generalities; The Apotheosis of Atheists; Freedom, Education and the Individual; Summarizing the last forty years; The living dead and the living who are dead; The Past and Future living in the Present; The State, The Beast of the Sea, and Leviathan; Man as the Beast of the Earth; Analogies, Metaphors and

Modes of Thought; The eye and electromagnetic disturbances upon the cornea; Auto biographical notes; Man as a Political Animal;

Theories of Quanta; The Religion of Materialism; Learned Ignorance; Statistics and Stupidity; The Theory of Creative Quanta; Massless Quanta; Gravity an electromagnetic phenomena; Space composed of massless quanta; Filling the void; Atomic bombs for all.

Aug 1, 2014 about 12:53 A.M.

I've paused writing to meditate on the Introduction I desire to complete writing, exclusive of typing it out, within the next few days.

The kingdom of Jesus is not of the Old World Order nor of the New World Order nor of the Muslim World; neither is it of the World Council of Churches nor of the World Court of International Law. And most assuredly is not of the spiritually divided United Nations.

From whence then is it? From heaven. But what heaven for there are many heavens? From the heaven God, in the beginning, created.

INTRODUCTORY NOTES
SECOND EDITION

SAYINGS GLEANED FROM A GRASS STAINED BASKET FULL OF FRAGMENTS OF UNLEAVENED SCRIPTURE

I googled Lucifer a little while ago and was enlightened by a wiki response whereby the Latin of Jerome was linked to the Hebrew of Isaiah via the Cyclo (married with the Encyclo) pedias of the Greek. The wisdom and praise coming out of the mouths of those little children who have come to Christ to be taught of God whereby they become the Sons of God is a truth the New Age Illuminati despise.

Jesus of Nazareth, even as Jesus, the Christ, hangs on the tree of knowledge of good and evil crowned with those thorny and heavy matters of the laws of Love, judgment, mercy, and faith, the hypocrites spawned by Lucifer and his professional minions cannot, and care not, to handle. Such despise Love, yet love the New World Order where Lucifer's accomplishments are extolled and meticulously marked, numbered and catalogued in the numerous books periodically perused amidst the stacks constituting the libraries of the dead.

I marvel at the madness of it all.

8/2/2014

It is all a comic book of cosmic proportions. Why do the heathen rage? Cannot the great god of the Arabian wilderness save them? Save them from what? From the consequent perdition of their very own idolatrous conceptions. Where is the great Allah to be found of whom these cowardly gangs of masked murderers scream, rant and rave? Is greatness to be found in the barren cave of scriptural stupidity? The idols of the fallen angelic minds are many: nevertheless Lucifer's Koranic cant has no place within God's kingdom.

8/5/2014

The sherpherds lead the sheep up the highest mountain whereat they might view the unfathomable glory of God. But men who are blind to the wonders of the human eye are ignorant of the heavens a single eye can see. But what is all this to me as I partake in an heartbeat of time of this moment of a vast eternity. Two or three days, or three millennia of temple destruction, comprise a story untold: what more can be said of the living who once were dead?

It is done; but this day is another matter: for another race is yet to be run.

8/7/2014

A glossary is needed: how shall God, love truth, soul, Adam, Eve, wife and woman be defined? How does truth and the lie come to be within the realm of this vast eternity wherein we be what we are? What is flesh and what Spirit?

God is love: and above all things created, love is personal: so says, I acknowledge, Alfred North Whitehead, an angelic intellect of the first estate. Nevertheless, God is best understood in the first epistle of John, wherein in these latter ages, this exhortation is given: Beloved, let us love one another: for love is of God; and every one that loveth is born of God, and knoweth God.

As a postscript to this bit of Scripture written and preached some two thousand years ago in language other than English, I say this: It is as true today, even now in this moment of passing time, as it was then. Nevertheless, all we know of the past is what we know in this present. The Word does not pass away: it Prevails.

A soul is the source of universal love. To whom then shall a man give his soul: And once it is given away what becomes of it?

A Pharisee is one of Pharoah's industrious and self-appointed emissaries. The world is full of Pharisees extoling the glory of Egyptian idolatry and its submission to godless technology. Pyramids of waste are built to entomb the dead carcasses of idolatrous dreamers and schemers who crave to rule over all in the place of God, even that God I know as the Spiritual Lover herself, embellished with the beauty of everlasting life.

The glossary of words is gleaned from the Scriptures of Truth housed within the walls of the New Jerusalem.

The book of life is opened for those who love life, to read.

But who can read all that is written: and who can hear all that ever was said?

How is it that men, who are not able to understand Cain but can comprehend the formation of worlds, galaxies and universes, yet lack compunction to admit the limits God emplaces round their ever expanding egos?

The metaphysical implications of the doctrines of fools made flesh is far too complex for the professors of expansive universities to handle let alone clarity.

Perhaps Allah can illuminate the reality of evil: but Allah is greatly dumb and has bestowed upon his filthy mouthpiece Muhammad via the delusions attributed to a mythical Gabriel, a Koranic assembly of Euphratic babble. Babble on and on and on is Babylon, full of chant, music, and ass elevated aspirations

Who gave birth to Muhammad? Was it Allah? Who gave birth to Allah, was it Muhammad? Who caused the big bang? Was it a blob of femto cubic millimeters of nuclear particles or was it a fantastic convolution of interacting string assemblies yet to be discovered by and for whom the nuclear assemblies of strange particles is not nobly prized?

A thunderous herd of galloping yahoos care not to answer. They pause to add their shit to the Cainanite drama and gallop off into the adventure lands of Disney.

I am weary unto death with the offering and silliness of Cain and its children.

8/17/2014

If I had the power to add a Postscript to this first edition of my life, what would the postscript be? My beginning and ending are finished in this single moment of eternity preset. Eternity is the everlasting reality: time is but a derivative notion.

This introduction to a second edition is sporadically conceived. Thoughts, even as impressions of sensation quickly come, and go away, even before we can create words to capture them. Where do words come from?

Let me preface this second edition with an exhortation for all to expand their understanding of the Creative Power of the Word: even understanding that Word which created, and still is creating, all things.

The metaphysical implications of this bit of universal truth is astonishing.

The symbolism associated with words written, words spoken, words felt and as yet not born, must form a common bond amidst speakers and hearer, writers and readers, performers and audience if communion is to be established and babble curtailed.

The one fundamental sacrament is communion: even the communication of truth: it is both art and science, made one by the essential ingredients of love. Also the effectiveness of parables and parameters is influenced greatly by the quality of the symbols employed.

If we are to reason together we need to understand how reason functions. Being reasonable has a mechanical, almost ritualistic aspect. Calculators and computers are nicely illustrative in their operations of this aspect and function of reason. This leads some fools to believe that computers can think. Fools become unthinking creatures as they divorce themselves from the spirit of truth God so readily provides to those that seek it. Nevertheless, faith is essential: without faith reasons becomes babble.

8/23/2014

Every science has its peculiar logical scaffolding intricately interconnected to provide standpoints, platforms and intricate scaffolds for facilitating the creation of some great work. The parameters used to describe the limitations of the scaffolding are both symbols and ideas. As symbols they may be mechanically manipulated. As ideas, they have realistic limitations.

The scaffolding also is imbued with the idealistic conception of the great work.

Now am I greatly troubled. Even to the point of spiritual paralysis as I find myself immersed in the mire of Luciferian excrement. The temptation to use metaphysics to explain and even justify the processes inherent in Creation is of Lucifer. He desires me to become his clone. And the temptation is ceaseless and comes in a variety of flavors and an awesome array of rainbow coalitions.

There are many sciences which provide the many scaffolds Man requires to create the image of Science the fallen sons of god are creating to enslave men to their erudite power of control. Consequently as I explore the mysteries inherent in their mythological metaphysics I become mired for moments in the mindless mediocrity of their meta-conceptions. I am only exploring: I care not to become part of, or enslaved by, what I discover.

9/3/2014

Knowledge has increased: many run to and fro seeking truth amidst the stacks of the libraries of the dead. Is this ancient prophecy or a modern age generality I herein generate to shed light upon the carcasses of the living dead? The books are open: Hitler is documented ad nauseam. Muhammad has his Koranic sorceries and sayings mortalized by those scribes of antichrist who have sold their souls for Islamic profit. Open the Koran: open Mein Kamph. Open Darwin's Descent of Man. Read the Manifests of Marx.

9/5/2014

Surely there are those among us who take up serpents, lifting them up on high for all the world to see; and drink, any of the many deadly things antichrist scribes pour into our own cup of life, whereby we are not hurt, and thus overcome the souls of Lucifer's Lilliputians.

Those who believe in the Light God sent, and still sends into the world, avail themselves of that power given them by that Light to become the sons of God.

Jesus Christ is that Light. Lucifer despises this fact since they conceive themselves as the light of the morning and as those stars of Babylon who profess the glory of their own self-generated enlightenments. They lust to rule over all with their doctrines created within the darkened caverns of their godless imaginations.

Nevertheless, the son of the morning is ephemeral: extinguished by the Day Star.

9/18/2014

The Sun of righteousness has healing in his wings.

9/19/2014

Who and what then is Lucifer, the fallen son of the morning? And what morning conceives its own son?

The necessity of atheism is an established fact: atheists abound in the world-wide universities of the world. What is atheism that it should clone apostles and priests to tempt men to accept its doctrines? And what are its doctrines?

There is no God? God is not necessary? Thus the scientific lords of this new age, accept, preach, and most assuredly Create their own laws of the universe; and all who do not believe and have no faith in these self-created atheistic doctrines are deemed illogical, unscientific and must be prevented from teaching otherwise those souls the new age lords strive to enslave for their own use. And pray tell what is that use?

Atheists apotheosize themselves. The apotheosis of atheists is a scientific fact, a logical conclusion necessitated by their own evolutionary dogma. Only the fittest survive. Who are the fittest? Those who survive. This is the process, even their law, of natural selection. This is the syllogism of stupidity with which the big bangers console themselves.

10/17/14

Take the internet: cast it into the sea of peoples, multitudes, nations, and tongues: and Google up a catch of a hundred and fifty and three great men. What then, even now, will you do with this great catch?

Do you love these more than Jesus, the Christ of God, even the Spirit of Love herself? Children, decide. Whose doctrine will you feast upon? There are many antichrists, many false prophets who cannot confess that Jesus is come to us in the flesh and blood reality of his own being. These spirits are the fathers of their own lies. They lust to rule over US in the place of God. They hate to hear us called the sons of God, even as they despise the manifestation of Jesus Christ as the Son of God.

Little children who believe in the Word of God, who are taught of Love herself, even the Spirit of Truth dwelling within the mansions of their very own souls, become the Sons of God by eating and drinking the flesh and blood reality of Jesus Christ. The body of his doctrine, even the commandment of everlasting life, even the Word of God sent to us to empower us to understand, and hear, and feel and joy and witness to the kingdom of God growing within and amidst all who love one another.

Nevertheless this is all Ancient Truth albeit in this day we know it as the New Testament: the book of life found within the New Jerusalem.

But liars father their own doctrines leavened with the hypocrisy of their own states of being. The spirit of error is legion and the carcasses of dead swine pollute the sea of Tiberius until the latter reigns of and storms of controversy courses through the Jordan valley into the Dead Sea wherein they are decomposed amidst the salts of Sodom and Gomorrah.

Freedom, education, and the individual are intimately intertwined with the kingdom of heaven found within the fields of each soul's quest for everlasting life. Love is above all things personal: Let us all beware the abstract God, the abomination, even the abominable destroyer, who enters into our souls, even the very temple of our God, to sacrifice therein, even upon the altar of truth, the flesh of swine fattened with the slop of humanity's garbage.

Thus our temple must be cleansed. Nevertheless, the pure in heart see God and need not this cleaning: but for those of us who have nourished our souls with the fruit plucked from the tree of knowledge of good and evil the baptism of truth and the enjoyment of the second death is essential.

How and with what are we educated? We can learn to babble, to lie, to steal, to kill, to destroy, to swindle, to corrupt, and to tax people into poverty and globalize our inanities to the ends of the earth with our learned ignorance.

If you continue in my Word you shall know the truth and the truth shall make you free. If you continue in the words and works of those who father their own lies with political genius and scientific sophistry you will lose your souls and become enslaved by atheists, muslims, anarchists, and any one of numerous mammon driven materialists who have no sensibility to their own godless and idolatrous imaginations.

There is America, God blessed and beautiful: there is African America, enslaved by the merchants of mammon, the idolatries of the world, the atheism of stupidity, the apologists and apostles of Islam, the motor mouths of the media, and the sorceries of socialism.

The State is the beast of the sea: the power by which hell is created, the lie promulgated, and the illuminati enlightened.

I've lived in America and have been presided over by fourteen presidents. They all tax me one way or another into poverty. Why? Taxation is the mechanism by which the servants of mammon enslave the souls of men: the mechanism of social theft by which Caesar's clones extract their tributes to lay at the feet of their worldly idols. Nevertheless, truth is freely and graciously given us by the Creative God of Love we know as our heavenly Father. However, the worldly spoor of bullucks requires trillions of dollars to satisfy the inflationary yens and yuan of the godless.

Thus money doth satisfy all things: and the illuminati create that thing to be so satisfied. They despise the Word and worship the gold, silver, brass, iron and clay image they term Man.

10/8/2014

Thus Man, the political animal, glittered from head to foot with three thousand six hundred threescore and six talents of gold stolen from the treasures of Solomon, is illuminated by Lucifer's worldly minded illuminati as it emerges from the bottomless pit of their evolutionary imagination. Thus have they statistically morphed, even imaginatively engineered, Nebuchadnezzar's dumb dream image into the machine animated, modern era automated, clumsily clanking transformer they term humanity.

10/10/2014

What more can be said: let the dead be raised: let the Lord Our God be praised. Nevertheless, humanity's Man has another agenda.

10/11/2014

Six years after I was born Adolph Hitler culminated his rise to power via executive order. Thus on his orders the liquidation of Czechoslovakia was executed followed by his orders to invade and conquer Poland. And his orders to kill all Jews remain in place even to this very day.

Five yeas after I retired Barack Obama is culminating his rise to power via executive order.

Heads of State are Heads of State. The Beast, even Leviathan with its ten heads of godless power, this commonwealth of hell, lusts to gobble up and devour the children of God. There are many antichrists in this world, Obama being one more pathetic exemplification of this spiritual force.

Make no mistake about the walking, talking dead who run, babble and fly about this wandering star we term Earth. Liars need audiences to sustain themselves in their opulent and vain inanity.

They require the heils of the crowd and the applause of the mesmerized mendicants of mammon, and millions upon millions of plastic cards and quadrillions of electronic transactions to clone the souls of all mankind to evolve into One Colossal Satanic Machine.

Is this an analogy, a metaphor, a model of SS Stupidity? Social sarcasm united with scientific stupidity cause the wicked to prosper within hell, wherein they are trained to reside, to suffer the Malthusian pains of over population.

The Dauntless are medicated by the Erudite. The Concord are enjoying their social delusions as they watch their choice horror films while munching on inflated bags of pop corn. The Amity are tilling the fields with blissful ignorance of locusts, floods, hurricanes, tornadoes amidst crashing aircraft, mortar shells, artillery barrages, flying bullets and impending calamities following broken and oft times exploding pipe lines. Harvest may not follow seed time but homeland security strait from the capitol will provide a pill to alleviate the pain of losing the hunger game. These events lead the Abnegation to issue additional thousands of laws, rules, regulations, statutes and procedures for the edification of the illiterate.

But where are the Divergent? They mastered the art of hyperbolic trajectory and have left the parabolic orbits of the feeble minded.

But now let me in this ever fleeting yet ever present moment of time, set aside the religions of materialism my abundance of learned ignorance, and the statistics of stupidity, and the silliness of pollsters and those who are seduced by polls, and herein set forth and initiate a theory of atomic quanta.

10/24/2014

It is more important for a theory to be useful than truthful—thus did one angel expand the concept of theories. Hell abounds with useful theories—thus am I troubled by setting forth a theory, especially a theory having materialistic implications. The Spirit of Truth, of Beauty, of Love increases the sensitivity of a man's spirit to these troubled feelings, in order to lead righteously those who create many things guided by their theories. Is the theory of atomic quanta true? Is it righteously useful? More importantly let me ask, What has man wrought by the use of his theories?

Let God let me see: for I am vastly ignorant of many matters: especially at this time of the matter with which God created the firmament to divide the waters of the deep.

10/26/14

The firmament is an expansion and God called the firmament Heaven, even the Heaven he made to divide the waters within their very midst. Heaven is in the midst of the waters both above and below.

12/7/2014

God is a Spirit: and they who worship him, must worship him in spirit and in truth. Thus the Spirit created all things: and the Word being the Creator of all things explains all to man. Nevertheless, I am lost in the mind blowing complexity of all things and find myself as lost within the flesh and blood reality of mine own electrified soul. Without Scripture's truth there is nothing save the abyss of blindness reverberating within the pyramids of skulls the lovers of the human races heap up unto themselves.

What now is Death since the living are so full of it? Why is a dung gate essential to the city of truth?

12/8/2014

The Sheep Gate
The Fish Gate
The Old Gate
The Valley Gate
The Dung Gate
The Fountain Gate
The Water Gate
The Horse Gate
The East Gate
The Registry Gate
The Prison Gate

There are many Gates, New and Old, by which men may enter Jerusalem: but only one door.

1/7/2015

And only one Strait Gate.

1/10/2015

This New Testament, this cup which contains the word of my living flesh and blood reality, given me of my heavenly Father, shall I not continue to drink of it? My flesh is enlivened by my blood. Nevertheless, how does flesh and blood create words? Let the world answer. It is the work of the Word which creates the flesh and blood reality of everlasting life. The sons of God are created by the Word, even the living God of everlasting Life. God is a Spirit: so also am I.

1/15/2015

Little children being taught by God become the sons of God who in their own resurrection are like unto the angels. Thus our flesh is the Creation of our spirit once we regain possession of our own soul.

Isaac Newton describes space as the unbounded sensorium of God. Light fills this space. And light can be transformed into bodies: and bodies into light. In the beginning God created the light, and in the continuation of his work, bodies were created from and out of this light. Thus the concept of empty space is devoid of any meaning, a conception created within the bottomless pit of any man's godless imagination. Nevertheless, the void is the empty reality which may be filled with the forms and processes of everlasting Life.

In the beginning the earth was without form and void: what then can we say of the heaven?

2/7/2015

It is God's throne and we live within it, about it, and ever journey around it. It is found within you, about you, and among all that love you even as you love your own self. Heaven is full of rewards, treasures of ancient times, joys of times present, the hope and great expectations of times yet to be. Life is the everlasting reality.

How then shall we live eternally within this unbounded sensorium of God: Let the Spirit of Truth, even the fiery flames of God's Word kindle the lake of fire within us.

7/31/2015

Let us enter New Jerusalem wherein the presence of God is.

8/2/2015

I find it now, within this fleeing moment of time, to grasp the Spirit, difficult. Great aspirations are hard to hold onto with our right hand. What have I within the palm of my hand? A little book of life within which are inscribed fleetingly the many and various courses of my life. From the mountains enveloped amidst the ever penetrating Spirits of heaven, through the valleys and canyons, pastures and plains of earth bound life, into the deepest trenches and pits of hell, wherein the explosive powers of life burst through the mantles of mankind's love of death, the waters of everlasting life courses my soul. Nevertheless the old end inspires a new beginning.

What now have I to do with grasping the hands of the wicked and embracing the doctrines of iniquity? Nothing. Such have fucked the earth with their adulterous conceptions and idolize antichrists and their lovers of godless worldwide dominion.

All liars hate the truth especially that truth we know as the living flesh and blood reality of Jesus Christ, the Son of the Lord God of Israel: Even that God who dwells within his own Son. Nevertheless, even the many multiplied sons of God who yet know not what they shall be, and who forget what they once were, have difficulty in accepting, in their days of tribulation, the flesh and blood reality of their own angelic nature. The feast of tabernacles is a watch and waiting for the coming of the Lord God of Israel. But when that Spirit comes how shall he be received: Each soul in its own miraculous way provides its own conception provoked by this question.

9/21/2015

The New Jerusalem surrounds the earth and therein the light given us of God our Creator is ever found. For those who have eyes hat can see, the perceptions of this truth causes us to realize the reality of the city of God. The old Jerusalem cannot be fully realized save by those who live within the new. The new wine is angelically intoxicating: the visions it provokes are many.

The unbounded sensorium of God is filled with creative quanta. The whole field of particle physics is one such creative quantum. It is a Babylonian masterpiece of spiritual materialism. It hangs on one wall of the many labyrinths found within the museums of the dead.

Now let me put forth a theory of creative quanta. The theory is created on a materialistic foundation of matter, space, and time. For matter let there be a hard indestructible Euclidean sphere of 10 to the -40 meters. Let there be an infinite number of such like particles within Man's concept of empty space, i.e. the heavenly void. Let length and time be dimensional qualities ascribed to the spheres.

Let Man in the Babylonian sense, that is, in the manner of Nebuchadnezzar's image, be immersed within this infinite universe of quanta.

Now Man, even as this atomic theory itself, is a creative quantum, which for the time appointed has its uses for the children of God, even that God we know as Our Heavenly Father.

Man is conceived to sense directions and motions. Thus it can sense right, left, front, back, top, bottom. Or to put more plainly in flesh and blood terms, right hand, left hand, navel, ass hole, head, foot. Thus through a process of abstraction, we derive +x, -x, +y, -y, +z, -z. Now continuing this process of extensive abstraction, Man can cartwheel right, cartwheel left, tumble forward, tumble backward, rotate right, rotate left. Also, it can move in any of the six Euclidian directions specified.

Now the quanta, which are herein described as spheres, can move in any of the six directions and spin in any of the six revolutions. Now the motion of the sphere is a given, as is their existence.

Motion is measured by ratios of length and time. Now there are two types of motion to which the spheres are limited. There is also no motion, which is a convenient zero, although not a nothingness, descriptive of the atomic quanta.

?/?/2016

The space quanta cannot adhere, one to another: but mass quanta can. Both space and mass quanta fill the void.

Creative quanta are the atomic unifying assemblies of such things the worlds of man senses and creates. The motions and ideas provoked, in deed, even created by these creative quanta, which possess both a spiritual and materialistic being, are numerous, and beyond all telling. How a book, a pen, a table, a house, a body, a theory, a nation, a solar system, a galaxy, a universe can have oneness of being in an atomic sense is almost incomprehensible were it not for the very fact truth requires it. The Word is full of it: and I am overwhelmed by the reality of mine own being.

2/8/2016

Creative quanta are the divine elements inherent in the immanent and transcendent natures of our creator, even that God within creating the majesty and glory of all that is without. The Word says, and so it was, and is, and so it shall come to be.

The Word is the Creator. Good and truth are married and become as one within the realm of Love. Nevertheless, the fruit of the tree of knowledge of good and evil infects and plagues the souls of men. Satan is thus conceived, evil and the lie prosper, hell emerges within all nations that forget God, as swine made fat with the intellectual slop of the proud and fallen Luciferian angels, are slain on the altar of truth as a sacrifice to the abominable God they have created.

2/15/2016

It's a paradox of mean proportions that configurations of massless mass quanta impelled into motion by massless space quanta create the creative quantum termed mass. Thus the mass of a man, of an ant, of a galaxy, of a planet, of a sun, moon, or star is understood as a complex unity of velocities, accelerations, energies and processes which create the systems inherent within everlasting life.

The light of the body is the eye which transforms the electromagnetic impulses on the cornea, to enter, via the pupil, into the soul wherein the kingdom of heaven grows. Nevertheless, the eye which is single is the necessary requisite for these heavenly processes: an eye which is evil, however, may be married to vast varieties of adulteries and fornications created by Satan and its children. In this manner, the devil becomes the father of many sinful doctrines. Thus hell is created by those who do just that very thing. The reality of Satan, and its ways, is real: so also is hell. All this is a given: only fools deny this creative fact.

But so what? So let our eye be single. Hell may be interesting, even captivating: but its destruction is inevitable.

One result of developing the theory of quanta illustrates the fact that gravity is an electromagnetic phenomena. Thus, by suitable manipulation of electromagnetic processes, anti-gravity devices may be created. Once this is done, however, the simple processes required to create a vast variety of atomic bombs may potentially be accomplished by all who will crave to do so, fools not excluded. They can easily become as numerous as AK-47's.

Now what?

2/20/2016
    I do not know. The preceding two paragraphs encapsulate my dilemma.

2/26/2016
    Everlasting life is replete with eternal problems. Therefore it's best to continue in the Word and know that truth which empowers us to handle those dilemmas which we hang onto for the times appointed.

The horns of the beast are destroyed with the beast. So why hang on? Death and hell are destroyed by all who love life and the kingdom of heaven. Amen for now.

POSTSCRIPT

The Holy Grail is the New Testament even that cup of life Jesus gives to his beloved. They drink the fruit of the vine, anew with him, in memory of him, in the kingdom of God.

PREFACE

My present wife once startled me by saying, "I know you think you're Jesus Christ." This troubled me somewhat so I was glad to hear her let me off the cross when she added, "You know, Stanley, you are not Jesus." Women, and their God, are amusing. And in this, my wife, whom I greatly love, is not different from those who worship the God of women. Preach a little gospel, and expound a little truth, and women are quick to judge you. Thus images of saints and heretics alike are created. Churches are formed. One woman's Christ is another woman's antichrist. The woman taken out of Adam, and each man is his own Adam, thinks herself wise because she has recently nourished herself with the fruit of the tree of knowledge of good and evil. Thus it comes about that Woman, who was taken out of Man, feels she is as a god because she knows what is good and what is evil. Churches, in the religious sense of that word, are taken out of a part of men and are quickly deceived by the subtle beast of the world into playing the part of a god.

And men who reject the counsel of Jesus and the commandment of the Lord God, are deceived by their own help whom the Lord God made out of them for them. They then eat the fruit of knowledge and think themselves as gods and as wise as God. In truth they are dead to the pleasures of paradise and know it not.

The God of Women is the God of the Church and State who rules by the forces of custom, money, hypocrisy, and pride. But mostly by the spirit of pride, because the kings of pride are many.

In all truth, each man is his own Adam, and Adam is created male and female. Thus the term *man,* in many places in the Word refers to those of us who now happen to be male as well as to those of us who happen to be female.

Today's women liberators are intuitively right and scripturally stupid. They are right because there is nothing more or less superior or inferior about being a male or being a female. They are scripturally stupid because all groups united in some common cause to create yet another organization of men to teach us what is good to know and what is evil to know are an abomination in God's sight. The result is death: God kicks their ass out of paradise and nothing is left for them except the foolish controversies and vain babblings of the world.

Nevertheless, God saves the world with his Word. But what world? for there are many worlds. Your world. John knew this and his gospel is enlightening. It is for this reason I choose to comment upon it.

Beware of those men who love to sit in high places: who love to wear long robes: who love to be called by some title and assume some position of authority over you.

If the Lord God of Israel is your King, the foolishness and pride of men is not your inheritance. We are all God's creatures: yet many worship idols of the mind, of the screen, of the church, of the printed page. The tree of knowledge bears deadly fruit. Eat the butter and honey, which is to say the churned-up milk of the gospel of Jesus and the wisdom of God's Words, before you gaze so longingly upon the tree of knowledge.

Who is Jesus? Where is he? John answers both these questions and others besides. If my wife knew Jesus and what has happened to his image, defaced as it is beyond recognition, she wouldn't embarrass me with wild statements about Jesus: besides, I'm sure he wouldn't feel too comfortable with the comparison himself. He has his life: I have mine: and you have yours. So let's not quibble over the Word: let's use it, consume it, and see what results.

Let's also remember some simple facts: Jesus was in John in a spiritual sense when John wrote his gospel. We have the translated words of John spoken and written in a new tongue, even the English language of the time of King James. English has grown: the Word has grown. Neither John nor Jesus ever claimed it would not.

Again, in a spiritual sense, the words of Jesus and John have come out of me in another tongue. If their words were not within me they could not come out of me. This is true of all who have eaten those words. For good or evil, what a man has within himself, comes out of himself. Words are realities, are things, which come out of the hearts of men as do many other things.

Who is to judge what is good and what is evil? What is true? What is false? What is of the Lord God? What is of that ultimate social computer called Satan?

You are. The valley of decision is real. All of us decide what we believe.

What do I believe? I believe Jesus is the Christ, the living Son of the living God. So do multitudes. But so what? What do I know? I know that to know a man, and Jesus is no exception, one must consume his words and assimilate his doctrines. Jesus is known by his words: part of which John has labored to keep for us.

Scripture is public fact. These commentaries are things done in secret: for even to this 31 day of March, 1977, no one has read them. Will anyone ever read them? Let my God, and not the God of those women I love, decide. Frankly, the world is full of so many books, I question the wisdom of adding yet another. Yet as Pilate once put it, what I have written, I have written.

March 31, 1977
Anaheim, California

PREPARATORY NOTE

The gospel is quoted and my commentary follows. The King James translation is used, numbering and grouping of verses are omitted, but the division into twenty-one chapters is retained. Quotations are blocked and set apart from the text by spaces above and below.

The spirit of John's writing is expanded by implicit references to other scripture, especially to the Book of the Revelation of Jesus Christ given by the Spirit of truth to John for Jesus. References to historical figures and some current world personalities are made only in passing and the reader must look elsewhere for more detailed knowledge of such like great men.

The Word of God includes such works as are found in the fields of science, literature, philosophy, and art. The Word is the key which unlocks the mysteries of death and of hell. As prophesied by Jesus a long time ago, scribes, wise men, and prophets have been sent into the world in order to bring the great works of the gentiles into the city of truth which is that city of the Jews they know as the New Jerusalem. In that city the tree of life is found. One leaf of that tree is the gospel according to John. All this is written in the Lamb's book of life which is being opened today along with many other books.

The commentary is a personal revelation of what I believe and what I have within me. It is also an encouragement to the reader to search for what he has within himself.

INTRODUCTION

In the beginning God created the heaven and the earth. In this ending of the story of Jesus, evolutionists ape Moses and produce from the bottomless pit of their own godless imagination mythological fairy tales concerning the creation of the universe.

In the beginning the Word was with God. In this ending of the story of Jesus' war against the prince of this world, words without wisdom flood the world and except for the ark of scripture, all flesh would have been lost in a sea of wicked dreams.

The tree of knowledge of good and evil grows within a man; and unless God husbands our garden of eternal life, each of us, as Adam, male or female though we be, die because of our unwillingness to allow God to decide what is good for us to know and what is evil for us to know.

No wonder then most men, except for a remnant, are dead to truth, beauty, and love. A man's wife is his spirit: yet, more often than not, our own God-created helpmate, even our own living self, believes the Satanic spirit of the world, rather than the clear commandment given us of the Lord God. Men glut themselves on knowledge and thus lords of mediocrity and princes of confusion and false prophets many are born, and nurtured, and worshipped. We are enslaved by mental midgets and know it not.

God laughs at me each time I express amazement at the foolishness of the world. Yet, in a certain way, it is all so funny that I can sympathize with his reaction. God is a Spirit and we are her created creatures: yet so many intellectual dwarfs band together to mock this simple truth, that I can understand the reign of misfortune which many reward unto themselves. God is not amused at our evil productions, so he destroys them. In the end, God destroys the works of wickedness, and death and hell are cast into a lake of fire. God is a consuming fire, for his Word within us consumes the lies produced by men who worship State and Church and allow themselves to be deceived by Man, and his image. This Man, of which so many Antichrist scribes boast, is the greatest false prophet of all the false prophets of which Jesus prophesied.

In this new beginning of a new heaven, we have unrolled before us the scroll of recorded time in which men decided to work either with or against Jesus, the Christ, the first begotten son of God. The story extends over three and one-half thousand years (or three and one-half days if you read it as God reads it). It begins with the writing of Moses and ends with your decision as to whether you believe Jesus is the Christ, the living son of the living God.

This commentary is written to expand upon what John wrote about Jesus and to show how the words of Jesus live even unto this very moment. The fruit of the vine, harvested in the vineyard of God, is cast into the winepress of his own indignation. Like it or not all of us drink of the cup of experience which God pours out for us upon the table of our mind during this feast day of our life.

The Word of God is at war with the Godless State: the kingdom of heaven grows within us. It is the planting of God, not of Man. Man is an image, the once-dumb image created and worshipped by the ancient kings of the earth, who pride themselves upon their own selves and know not the Lord God of Israel. The image of Man now has a loud and great voice since many little men give voice to it with their own vain and self-important babble.

Nations who refuse to serve the kingdom of heaven growing within each and every one of us are destined for destruction. Those who war against heaven come to earth, war against the Word of God. Such are fools: for they confirm a lie within themselves and live as if there were no God. Thus liars are fathered by their own doctrines: they are nurtured by their own beliefs: they are victimized by others like themselves and they flood the world with lies, hypocritical foolishness, and the words of death. No wonder then the wicked are like the troubled sea whose waters continuously stir up mire and dirt.

As prophesied long ago, Jesus has been handed over to the scribes and chief priests of his own nation: and they in turn, loving more the hypocrisy of the doctrines of men, having kissed him in recognition, allow him to be mocked by Roman law; spit upon with Roman justice; and crowned with those thorny problems of law, justice, mercy, and faith which they themselves refuse to consider.

Jesus Christ is come in the flesh: such is the message of John, the author of the gospel I herein choose to comment upon. Yet the blind cannot perceive that Jesus never left us: they cannot understand that the kingdom of heaven is not only with us today but was enjoyed by many even for more than a thousand years already past: and neither can these same blind know that State, Church, and Man form an evil triumvirate which keeps the souls God has created for his own pleasure from enjoying the kingdom of heaven in earth, which earth is the living flesh and blood of their own bodies.

Decide. Let your yes be yes: let your no be no. Jesus is either the Christ, the living son of the living God, who takes his life up again, and lays it down again, as he receives this commandment from his Father, or he is a self-deceived egomaniac, and his gospel is superstitious bullshit. In this manner, I question myself, and make my own decision. If Jesus is the Son of God, then, surely, his words are important to me. If he is not, then I may dismiss them and welcome the words of the world and its great leaders, and wise men, and prophets, and writers, and comedians. Perhaps Muhammad or Carter or Lenin or Hitler or Castro or General LeMay have something to say which will never pass away: for why should I concern myself with things that decay when searching for an eternal truth? And if these, and such like, have no truth in them, why should I bother with their words at all, for the world abounds with liars and one basket of bullshit is about as useful as another. Surely, I can glut myself with those near at hand and I need not sicken myself by seeking lies in ancient times, and remote places, and weird worlds, and among those who practice strange professions and sell bad advice at a dear price.

But let me end this introduction: it is enough. Read these commentaries or reject them. What is it to me? My God is my judge. Let John himself tell me what he thinks about them; or let him sit in heaven on a throne of dumb silence and ignore the whole matter.

While I have life, there are other things to do and why should I be bound in the confining graveclothes of a disbelieving world? A life of death is tasteless to me and all the unsavory salt of an hypocritical world cannot make it otherwise. If you doubt this, read on: For all that concern themselves with the doctrine of life, and knowledge of good and evil, have a part in the life of Jesus: sinner, angel, devil, hypocrite, chief priest, lawyer, scribe, sons of God, those fathered by the devil, Satan himself, and all others, in a variety of rolls—all play their part in the gospel. The gospel of Jesus is the story of us all: surely, God provides a part for all seasons: and what God provides may be bitter or sweet, yet never useless, for God uses all things well. Judge for yourself.

April 11, 1977
Anaheim, California

CHAPTER 1

In the beginning was the Word, and the Word was with God, and the Word was God. The same was in the beginning with God. All things were made by him; and without him was not any thing made that was made. In him was life; and the life was the light of men. And the light shineth in the darkness and the darkness comprehended it not.

The very nature and beginning of our lives is rooted in the power of the Words of God. Our soul, our house of life, is built with words. Words produce thoughts, dreams, and visions. Words move men to action. Words illuminate fact, cast their light upon fiction, and create that wisdom which enables the living soul to choose the good and reject the evil.

Devils and angels use words to express that which is within them. Words are the power used by statesmen to enslave the souls of men. Words direct the activities of men in law, in war, in prison, in the marketplaces of the world. Words come out of the mouths of teachers and students alike. Words are the coin of the soul, and men make merchandise of other men through the use of words.

A picture, a drawing, a diagram are some of the more elaborate uses of the power of the word to create the life we have within ourselves. Words are both the cleansing spirit of our soul and the blood and flesh of our bodies.

As sons of God we ought to create our kingdoms with words of truth: for the lie ultimately is known for what it is: the evil use of words.

Satan is the evil spirit corrupted by devils through the power of the word. Satan tempts with words, creates with words, enslaves with words. Men create devils with words, and these living spiritual realities are the cause of war, sickness, famine, and death. We have rewarded unto ourselves the fruit of our own iniquity. Hitler is a devil now dead. Nevertheless, his evil spirit is with some even to this day. He is a recent grand example of a fool made king. Every head of state now in the world partakes of the same spirit which infused this devil. There are no statesmen, no men of the state in heaven, for therein God is king, and the petty presidents, premiers, emperors and kings of earth are counted of little worth.

Know all men by the words that come out of their mouths. For men reveal the contents of their souls by the words they speak and the words they write. A man is what he is: a man is either a son of God, or the servant and lover of the world. The world is created by the word: as such it is a thing to be used by the creator of words. And how many evil men have used the power of the lies they father to make of the world a false god? History's tale and the news of this day eloquently testify how evil men glorify themselves and worship to their own hurt the powers of the State, the Church, Mammon, and that prince of the world who usurps through deceit the place of God and his Christ, even Jesus himself, from the throne of the kingdom being built within men.

For the kingdom of heaven is built with the power of the Word. Only fools, who partake of the spirit of Antichrist, deny this truth.

The Word of God is with us and it sits upon the horse of our spirit. Our thoughts, our dreams, our desires: are not these realities the products of the words of our spirit? Surely, our souls, our spirits, our life, and the words of truth within us cannot be separated by the foolish princes of this world who can only touch our body, but cannot enter our soul. Our decision is final. No, is our response to the lies they propagate with their words, lies which have caused them to enter the bottomless pit of their own imaginative blindness. They have an eye full of darkness: there is no light within them. Their darkness is complete. They cannot comprehend the light God sent into the world to give life to the world.

The Word is a creative force. Let us use it righteously: let us witness to the truth of its power: let us choose truth and reject the lie. God is seen by the pure in heart and led of Him.

There was a man sent from God, whose name was John.

God sent John into the world. God sent Jesus into the world. God sent many an angel, such as Isaac Newton, into the world. But men, as men, are idiots. They know not that Brigitte Bardot is an angel of beauty: that Billy Graham is an angel of faith: that Henry Kissinger is an angel of the State: that Pope Paul is an angel of a Whorish Church: and that each man is the angel of his own message. Why? Because stupid, vain, and little men have made of angels things of naught: but their lie cannot stand. For the angels are in their world, even as John was in the world sent there by God.

The same came for a witness, to bear witness of the Light, that all men through him might believe.

The witnesses of God are many in the world. And what is the purpose of that witness except it to be witness of the truth? And what is the truth except Jesus himself, that first begotten Son of God who witnessed to the truth of the nature of God? But every Muhammadan in the world, every Communist in the world, every servant of the State in the world, rejects this witness, and believes not. And why? Because they have been deluded by the Spirit of Man, a false image set up in the world by men who witness that they have nothing of God within them. Consequently, they worship themselves only: and they boast of Man. As if Man, as an image, is not without life. Fools are these: they reject the God of Light and worship the prince of darkness. They are stupid for they themselves give life to their own image: and their image of itself cannot speak. For it is the dumb idol of their own mind.

He was not the Light, but was sent to bear witness of that Light.

God does not send his Word into the world in vain: for it has brought forth the thing He desires. Even the kingdom of heaven come to earth. But worldly men, men not sent by God, cannot see this truth. John knew he was not the Light but only the witness of the Light. But how many men bear witness of the darkness within themselves? They believe not in Jesus: they know Him not. Thus do they witness by the words coming out of their mouths that they have no Light within them. They are angels of confusion. Why be led of them? Surely the children of the light ought not to be led by the men in the world who breathe out of their mouths smoke, confusion, and the spirit of ignorance. Let them be: they are the dead who, left alone, shall quietly bury themselves.

That was the true Light, which lighteth every man that cometh into the world. He was in the world, and the world was made by him, and the world knew him not.

The world is the creation of the word. Our words create our governments, our institutions, our schools, our newspapers, our books, our corporations, our habits, our beliefs, our families, our churches. These, and such like, in their total force, are the world. The world is obviously the creation of the words of all of us. God gave us the power to create the world with the Word. We use God to create even that which God hates: and, as fools, we reject God's desires, follow our own, and enter hell and suffer needlessly. We deceive ourselves by not recognizing that the only world we know is the world we see from the standpoint of our own perspective. Our world is the sum total of our sensory impressions. Some worlds are small: some large: some beautiful: some loathsome. Woe unto those whose world rejects God's kingdom. They are led of themselves and not of God. Their kingdom cannot stand.

Though the world know not God, indeed it cannot, let us know Him. For this knowledge is eternal life.

He came unto his own, and his own received him not. But as many as received him, to them gave he power to become the sons of God, even to them that believe on his name: Which were born not of blood, nor of the will of the flesh, nor of the will of man, but of God. And the Word was made flesh, and dwelt among us, (and we beheld his glory, the glory as of the only begotten of the Father) full of grace and truth.

We have flesh and blood. And to what use do we put our flesh and blood? And who created my flesh, who causes me to have blood? Even my God. Has not God created?

The Word was made flesh: even as we are made flesh. Do we not do the things we desire to do with our flesh? We do; but our life is limited. How much more then is our life limited if we know not that the Word that created us came into the world to be received by us? And why ought we to receive the Word? So that we can receive the power to become the Sons of God. Let us become then, the children of God, by receiving God's Word. There is no other way except we believe on his name. Is this not God's will? It is: so let us believe so that we may receive power. For the glory of God surpasses our highest dreams: our God is with us today. Even his kingdom has come: for our God is the fulfillment of his own promises.

Jesus' words are full of grace and truth.

But the words of our chief priests, our bishops, our elders; the words of the scribes of this present age; the scholars of Man, the secretaries of the state; the ridiculous words of the lawyers of this present age, without shame, or compassion, or forgiveness, the heartless spokesmen of ungodly sentiments—these words are full of grievous burdens, and bitter sentiments, and hypocrisy and lies without end, for they never tire of wearying men with their own commandments and reject the commandment of God which is mercy, righteous judgment, and forgiveness.

Things are born also of blood. How much strife in the world is caused by the body's emotions responding to the coursing of its blood? Our hunger, our thirst, our strengths, our weaknesses, are found in our blood. So does the body generate, indeed it must generate, impulses to action which are born of our blood. Alcohol in the blood alters our behavior; drugs kill living things within us; chemicals various may deaden or cause pain; thus, there are many things that are born of the blood.

And what might be said of the will of our flesh? How much do I create because of the state of my body? A man speaks words because of his past actions. So great is the power of our flesh that we witness daily the results of habit, training, education, and exercises both mental and physical. The lawyers train their minds to conform to the jargon of their profession; the engineer trains his mind to accept the limited rules of thought expressed with parameters, mathematical laws, and the limitations of earthy materials; the doctor of medicine trains himself to use a selected set of drugs and technical procedures for manipulating the parts of the body of his patients; athletes train their flesh; soldiers and artists as well; in all this we witness the effects of flesh conformed to patterns of behavior. From such flesh much is born. Good and evil actions are born of flesh: it is folly: it is captivity, it is imprisonment not to be aware of the things in this world that are born of the will of the flesh. Our flesh does have a will, a desire to do that which by habit it has learned to do. But this will must be recognized and directed by the will of the man: otherwise, he is subjected to the impulses of his flesh and is its very slave.

The will of man is stronger than the will of his flesh. Pain is withstood to achieve greater good. We know this. Man knows this. Each man is the father of his own will. The desire is born within him. I will to finish this sentence, to record this thought. It is done. Thus these words are written because of the will of the Son of man.

We can know that much in the world is born of the will of man. Many men live as if only blood, and the will of the flesh, and the will of man give birth to life. Such ignorance is of the devil. Satan denies knowledge of God to his servants. God gives birth to truth. Satan hates this fact, for he loves only himself. His love cannot extend to that which is greater than himself. Satan has overcome Man. But Satan has not overcome Jesus.

Satan's desire is not able to achieve its fulfillment. For Jesus is the king of his own soul. His soul is his kingdom. It is also the kingdom of His God. For Beauty, Love, and Truth are the living spirits of God, created by God, which are God. The Word creates and forever expands the power and glory of Love. Jesus is love.

What is Love? Even what I am. Surely I love the souls of men. Why should any perish, be cast away, be denied life? Death is of Satan: to dwell within the kingdom of darkness is to know death. I have known death. But I care not for this idol: it is the production of ignorant men. Yet, on this earth, except for a few, all bow down before it. Satan's power to deceive is formidable. When gods create, both heaven and earth are moved.

I have life within me: I am within my God. He is within me. I work. He works. I desire. She desires. I question. He questions. My desires are born. Her love creates.

All that is eternal is of that Spirit whose children we become. Let us not deny ourselves paradise in exchange for the things born of blood, and the will of the flesh, and the will of man. What is born of God is precious. Who is born of God? You are: all that hear my Word are born of God and eternal life is yours, for this is the will of God, and the desire of Christ, and the purpose behind these words.

The words of men are vain. The words of God are power. Even such power as to bring everlasting life to men. There is life which is eternal: there is life which lasts for a time, and ends. The end of such is death. Those that live such lives are dead: for their end is the way of death. Life that is not eternal is not worth living: it is tedious, barren of joy, devoid of love, ugly and transitory. Life that is eternal is joy in the being of God. I have lived both lives. And what I say is true: and, to those that love God, so obvious it needs no further comment. But for those who live mortal lies, their end is death: for naught that they do is of God, but in spite of God. Such also must be resurrected so that they might by their own words condemn their lives. Thus do I by my own words damn my life of death to destruction: but my knowledge of eternal life I commend to that Spirit whose love is the blood of my soul. For such is eternal life. A man ought not to tarry in condemning his life of sin: for in so doing he only delays his resurrection into eternal life. Let him lose all, so that he might gain God. There is room within God for all that love Him and keep the joyous commandments of life and of love.

Those that are born of God live forever. When we are renewed by the Spirit, our lives are made flesh in God. For God also creates in flesh and bone and blood. Men are not the only Creators though they be so proud as to deceive themselves into believing so. God also creates. God created, but She also brings forth, and creates. God creates the things of God. God created the heaven and the earth: even that heaven and earth already passed away: it is gone: I cannot remember it. God also creates the new heaven and the new earth. For God is now creating as these Words testify and witness. For what are words? Patterns of ink on paper? I tell you, know: Words are the spiritual realities giving life to this time.

John bare witness of him, and cried, saying, This was he of whom I spake, He that cometh after me is preferred before me: for he was before me. And of his fulness have all received, and grace for grace. For the law was given by Moses, but grace and truth came by Jesus

Christ. No man has seen God at any time; the only begotten Son, which is in the bosom of the Father, he hath declared him.

Jesus is before John since he worked before John worked. Jesus worked with God to create all things in the world so that in all truth it may be said the world is the created thing of Jesus. All souls are within him: for his concern and love is for all souls. Not some, but all in whatsoever state they be.

In a sense, time is an abstraction of thought, highly useful, but subject to idolatrous abuse. Those who know that eternal life is as real as the time of this day cannot be tempted with the productions of time. Time is linked to the stars, to the sun, to the moon: to the rotations of the planet earth; to the coming and going of seasons; to the rhythm of our bodily cycles.

To measure time, men must conceive of a purely timeless cycle or rotation. Call it what you will: before time, we need the eternal simplicity of the even flow of one second of the eternal clock. We trust to our sense that the period of measurement is even: that it also has a beginning and an end, that we know when it starts and witness when it stops. But we also must understand that time is also expended in the transmission of the stop-and-start messages to our comparator. We need something to tell us that a period has completed itself. The second, the day, the year have elapsed. If the time to send a message is less than the time of one measurement or cycle of time, obviously our clock exists in our imagination much more so than we who dwell within this foolishly proud age are willing to admit.

I confess to a certain spiritual impulse often arising within me that makes me laugh when I witness men prophesying the future by what they know at this time. We have received so much from the fullness of the Word of God, that I cannot but marvel at men so full of the lie that they cannot rightly measure anything, measuring the universe. The grace and truth we have received have come by no other than Jesus. The world is an effect of this fact. John knew it and said it. How much more so ought the least of us in heaven acknowledge the truth of God's Word made flesh? Not only as this is true of Jesus, the Christ; but as this is true of Jesus, himself, enjoying this moment of time. Is time past then without meaning? Obviously not: for the beginning and the end are with us today. We cannot see his beginning nor his end without the truth of his life and message giving light to our lives. Our world is a world influenced by Christ. You cannot deny this for without Jesus having lived, and living now, you could not receive these words, for they are of him.

Much has passed away but the words remain.

We received much law from Moses. Much law from the lawyers of the present age. What is the worth of their laws? Who needs them? There ought to be a law: this is the sentiment of lawyers and other little men who wish to teach their own doctrines, and enforce them with such powers as submit to them, and reject God's commandments. I am astonished, literally astonished, as to what zeal men have for propagating bullshit, for promulgating bullshit, for applauding bullshit, for rewarding the creators of bullshit with more of the same, while at the same time making God a liar.

Men blaspheme God, Jesus, and those that believe in them, to their own hurt.

The laws of God, and the commandments of Love, must be sought out. For in no other way can men find God. For God has been declared, is being declared to the world through Jesus. There is none other. The rest is bullshit. Not the useful kind coming out of the backside of cattle, for with this a man might dung a field; but the utterly useless kind which comes out of the mouths of lawyers, legislators, popes, presidents, premiers, princes, and kings. Really, in all truth, who needs their useless waste of words, their vain laws, their idle conceits?

To see God is to know that the pollutions of the world cannot spoil the purity of our heart. Deep within me, deep within you, is the spirit that is of love, beauty, truth, and everlasting life. To see God is to know that we are his. The Spirit has brought us forth. The Spirit creates, bathes in light, and delights in life.

To see God is to know that the Word is made flesh. What is beauty apart from a beautiful woman? What is beauty apart from the eye beautiful enough to sense it? What is beauty apart from a heart pure enough to receive it within itself?

We are witnesses to the birth of God within us. God is the Son of man born within us. Poor men, so engrossed in the intricacies of their own idols, they cannot appreciate the mysteries of God. The mystery God reveals, but man hides. The doctrine God proclaims, but man ignores. The message God sends, but men refuse. The gift God gives, but men blaspheme. Men blaspheme God by seeking to kill his children. How do men crucify Christ? By proclaiming that he is other than what he is. I am what I am: the foolishness of men cannot void this truth. For those who can see God, the Church, the State, Man, Mammon, and Pride made Flesh, are the ridiculous and pathetic appearances, the idolatrous and enslaving images of the present hour which rob men of eternal life. How? By deceiving the men of the world who create and sustain such things into believing that they have life apart from the living souls which have given their lives to these beasts. Men live because God created them living souls: men die because they believe the lie they have created.

Truth is immense: but Truth is only one of God's spirits. The foolishness of astrologers prevents astronomers from being poets. The one confuses such influential stars as Jesus and Newton with uninfluential bodies such as Jupiter and Mars. The other has taken the living beauty of God's glory and clothed it with the fig leaves of dead formulae. The idols of the mind are many.

The Word is fire: words are the water of life. We need both and more besides to receive the fullness of Life God provides. God is God: surely those who see Him know this. But to see singly, we need an eye unblinded, light, and the proper perspective.

In this new heaven, I feel the inadequacy of my language: the restricted vocabulary of Babel is insufficient.

And this is the record of John, when the Jews sent priests and Levites from Jerusalem to ask him, Who art thou?

Who are you? Who are the Jews? He is a Jew who is one inwardly: salvation is of the Jews: the Jews are circumcised in Spirit: Salvation is of the Jews: Jesus the Christ is king of the Jews. The Jews crucify their king. God created his people: God begot his Son. Why do his people reject his Son? For the same reason they reject God. They are victims of their own idols of pride.

And he confessed, and denied not; but confessed, I am not the Christ.

Each man is his own Adam: each man must become his own Christ. No Church, no State, no other man save Jesus, can call a man to be born again; born of the spirit of Christ; which is to become a son of God. Men treat truth too lightly. A son of God is not less than that which he is: the sons of others, the sons of pride, the sons of lies, are ignorant of this fact. There is no lie in God: he is no liar. Jesus is the Christ: but so is every man who has Jesus. For to have the one is to have the other. For these two are also one. We are sons of God, sons of man. Sons also grow up, and like their father, give birth to children.

And they asked him, What then? Art thou Elias? And he saith, I am not. Art thou that prophet? And he answered, No.

John is more than Elias, for he was Elias which was to come. He was more than that prophet, for he was the herald of a greater prophecy. We forget the greatness of his prophecy. For he is the prophet of the Lamb of God. The voice, crying in this wilderness of sin, that another is to come and also baptize. Surely, such a spirit as John is found in many places in the world. All who believe in Jesus believe in John the Baptist. For John confessed Jesus: and Jesus acknowledges John. For without John, how could all these words come to be written and spoken? Those who build the New Jerusalem, the spritual city of truth, can view their work with joy.

Then said they unto him, Who art thou? that we may give an answer to them that sent us. What sayest thou of thyself?

The priests and Levites also ought to have asked who they were: for they were the servants sent not by God, but sent by the Jews, those who had no king but Caesar. So is it today. For many Jews have no king but Caesar. The image and superscription found on the coin of the state is their God. Mammon is the God of the fallen children of God.

Who sends me where I go? Who asks me these questions? Who am I?

I am the angel of my own message. I am the messenger of my God, the spokesman of my Love. I cannot deny the reality of that which is within me. My heart, my soul, my kingdom is troubled. I am for peace: and truth. They are for war, and strife, and envying's, and their own lies. Why are they liars? Because they deny both me and my father. They deny their own Creator but accept the father of their own lies. They are the fathers of their own pride and foolishness.

Shall I strive forever? No. Every beginning has its end. Besides what are a few days of trouble? My God laughs at me. A thousand years when they are past are as a day: it is silly to grieve over them. My future is also with me now. Men sin against me by making this present reality a thing to be rejected for a future good. They know not that my future is also here now to be enjoyed.

He said, I am the voice of one crying in the wilderness, Make straight the way of the Lord, as said the prophet Esaias.

A straight way in this wilderness is the Lord's way. But men multiply their doctrines, their laws, their customs, and their beliefs. If they knew the truth and the way, they wouldn't need these varieties of religious and scientific experience. One experience is all that is necessary when we cross the path of truth. Surely the road is easy enough to recognize.

Our many theories are required only because none are true. Satan is a many-headed beast.

And they which were sent were of the Pharisees.

Men label themselves to their own undoing. They join together with others in a common belief and in a common activity and receive their titles. Engineer, plumber, police officer, pervert, homosexual, Baptist, Catholic, Democrat, actress, husband, wife, Mormon, Lutheran, Christian, Nazi, Jew, and titles boring to enumerate: What then are you? What is in a title? Are we not children of God? Let us confess we are God's new born children: let us admit we are gods and be done with the matter.

Emerson well understood that labels limit a man. We think of the title and forget the living soul so numbered. Let God give me whatsoever titles it pleases Him: but in so doing shall he not first bestow the power and then the title? God is remarkable. He anoints a shepherd king, before the shepherd knows how to govern: God's confidence in his ability to teach is astonishing. Men oftentimes earn their titles: and rightly so. Even my desire is to do the work first, and then receive my meat. But God is indifferent to our shortcomings. He speaks the Word and the thing is as done. We grow, but even as seeds He knows us. We forget that God is the Lord God: no man can prevail against even the least of his chosen.

The Pharisees are sent by those of their own party. The world is full of Pharisees, the religious teachers of the present day, ever inquiring of John, and of every preacher who baptizes with the water of the word. To what purpose? To file an account of their doings to those that hold them in esteem and grant them power. They never come to learn for they are wise in their own conceits. They use the doctrine of God's Son, and the teachings of the prophets to justify themselves. They are self-righteous. They have the Word. They teach men how to prepare themselves for death and judgment. Such condemn themselves, for to those who believe in God's Word made flesh, even in Jesus' Word, there is no judgment, no death. For they already have eternal life.

But the Pharisees teach the doctrine of death. Beware of their doctrines, for there is no life in their teachings. The best of them are but bores: the worst, devils. Be not their advocates. Their lot in heaven is to change: Pharisees are in heaven to learn the truth: they must be born again. The Words must enter their heart and proceed from their heart. A learned Catechism can be properly committed to a piece of magnetic tape. What heaven requires is the spontaneous generation of truth and love coming from the heart of the man.

John was sent by God: the Pharisees are sent by the fathers of their own foolishness. They are the fathers of their own conceits. Let them say, Lord, lord, we have done many things in thy name: but what is the use of that if the will of God be not done?

Believe that God sent Jesus into the world; that He received Jesus in heaven; that Jesus comes again into the world; that also being in heaven, he is in the earth for the kingdom is found in many fields in the world. He labors in these fields.

The salvation of the world is heaven on earth. The Pharisees are mad. They refuse to enter. I weary of them: what do they want? God, help them. I am sad. The loss is real. So once again my heart is troubled. What can I say? Learn of me and the God within me. He has put life within me. Those who have God need not go to church: they are the church. I marvel at the Whore.

And they asked him, and said unto him, Why baptizest thou then, if thou be not that Christ, nor Elias, neither that prophet? John

answered them, saying, I baptize with water: but there standeth one among you, whom ye know not; He it is, who coming after me is preferred before me, whose shoe's latchet I am not worthy to unloose. These things were done in Bethabara beyond Jordan where John was baptizing.

The baptism of the Word is a cleansing. The word, as water, dissolves all other words or notions we might have concerning God. The Pharisees, today's teachers of religion, refuse to know Jesus and to be baptized themselves. They prefer their own doctrines of church and state.

Jesus baptizes with the fire of God's word. That which is not washed is filthy and is ultimately burned. Jesus is among them: yet they know him not. They hear his words: even proclaim his gospel: but they do not know him. For if they knew him, they would not hate him.

The World Council of Churches is just that: another council in the world, which is of the world, seeking to employ the ways of the world to promote its members in the world.

How does one know a man? By hearing of him? No. One knows a man by eating his words, even the flesh of his spirit. The Pharisees cast Jesus out of the vineyard of God so that they may use it for themselves. Israel is the vineyard of God: Israel in its spiritual reality.

Jesus, who takes up his life, and lays it down again: Jesus who is always with us even to the end of the world: Jesus who is in heaven and yet also in the world: Israel knows not. Why? Because the hired laborers of God's vineyard, kill God's Son. How? By denying him life in the world. They would rather cultivate doctrines than be confronted with a resurrected man. Living souls take up life in this world by the resurrection of the body. Jesus has many crowns: has lived many lives. But the feebleminded teach otherwise. They have no conception of an immortal work. They know nothing of eternal life. The will of their blood, and flesh, and of Man, overcomes them. They will not learn truth of God, nor of His Son, nor of His prophets. To such, the resurrection is not Jesus: it is a birth into a fanciful world which exists only in the bottomless pit of their own limited imaginations. The reality of my flesh and blood, the living reality of this resurrected body, they deny. They want no real prophet, no true son of God, no angel of life to interfere with the doctrines they learned of men.

The resurrection of the body is an embarrassment to those who think it is otherwise than it is. They cleave to myths: they avoid realities. But God has his ways. Life is everlasting: it is death that is destroyed.

The next day John seeth Jesus coming unto him, and saith, Behold the Lamb of God, which taketh away the sin of the world.

Can a lamb bear the sin of the world and carry it away from the world? Would not an ass, an ox, a horse or even a camel be more fitting for this task? Considering the sin of unbelief which exists in the State, in Religion, in the endless sophistries of the politics of Man is not a Lamb as the bearer of sin an incredible choice? With men yes, with God, no.

Who fears a lamb? Men rule by fear: social castigation, public ridicule, economic fine, imprisonment, bodily harm, death: such are the threats real and imagined which men in power for a brief time create to enslave their fellow men. In such a manner is death and hell introduced into the world. But none fear the lamb: for the lamb is killed and kills none. The Lamb of God takes away the sin of the world by gently bearing the consequences of that sin upon itself. God has supplied the living sacrifice; the one life needed to remove sin from our own world of selfish insensitiveness. Men introduce substitutes. We sacrifice money, talent, our children, even ourselves, vainly. God declares, I want none of these. Why such a declaration? Because God in His Wisdom full well knows such vanities cannot bring heaven to the human soul. How much less so can sacrifice to Muhammad's God, to the State, to our own fears, to Man Itself, accomplish the task and finish the work! Men are moved by their beliefs. Their refusal to repent and believe the gospel places the burden of sin upon the Lamb. How so? By denying Jesus the proper place within our hearts and minds and souls. For if he carries us within himself, and He is within God, and our sin is within us, he also bears our sins.

Our ignorance, our pride, our foolishness, our unbelief, our many services to Law, Mammon, and the State are no joy to him. Yet they are surely within him, for these words testify to what is within him. Obviously, the sin of the world is even this: to deny Jesus, the Christ.

This is he of whom I said, After me cometh a man which is preferred before me: for he was before me. And I knew him not: but that he should be made manifest to Israel, therefore am I come baptizing with water.

John prophesied Christ: John prophesied Christ would come after him: John knew Christ was before him. John did not know Christ, for Christ was not yet revealed. John knew Christ would be made manifest to Israel. John cleansed men of their unbelief by bringing them the words of truth. For words are water, coursing through the body of the spirit.

Has Jesus, the Christ, whom John bare witness of, been made manifest to Israel? Of course. Who could deny this historical fact? Is Christ preferred before John? Though many believed what John preached, even feeling John might be the Christ, John knew Jesus to be the Christ, and so testified. Was John a false prophet? No. For what John said was true, and the things he spoke, came to pass. John decreased. Jesus increased. But his prophecy stands. Why do we not believe John? Because, like Herod, we find it more pleasant to exercise our moment of power by beheading John in order to please our own pride than to repent, believe him, and free him from the prison in which we hold him speechless.

The pleasures of sin are seasonal. We are fools for denying the Word of God. All we do is cut ourselves off from heaven.

And John bare record, saying, I saw the Spirit descending from heaven like a dove, and it abode upon him.

Only those sent by God can see the spirit gently abiding upon Jesus. Obviously, John saw the Spirit of Truth and Wisdom settle upon Jesus. A remarkable observation. We have seen more of Jesus than John. For John saw neither Jesus' death nor his resurrection. Now John sees both: for the spiritual realities are made manifest to the world by the products of our flesh and blood. These products are our words. These realities are our lives. We are sons of God who have overcome the world by believing in Jesus: in this manner have we been given power, even by believing in him.

We long to see the Spirit ever with us: to watch God working to bring heaven to earth: to watch the spirit settle upon men who elected to become the sons of God. I marvel at angels who would rather remain angels than become sons. What is there to fear?

Doves are gentle but quarrelsome. We have outgrown our parables. Our metaphors are stretched: our incredulity, our greatest unbelief's are strained, and broken. We are children, all: gods, fallen, being born again. Resurrected souls occupying resurrected bodies. Living souls who, like Jesus, take up and lay down our lives. The Spirit abides on all those who do not struggle to shrug it off. The Spirit of God is greatness beyond my power of telling. Metaphysical absolutes are not needed: we know God is our father, creator, comforter, friend, companion, and voluptuous bride.

Earthly perspectives restrict our vision. The Spirit is among the stars as well as in hell. The worship of God is ecstatic delight: to overcome the world is to be rid of a great pain in our ass. The devils who visit me are many. They vary in appearance, in power, in tenacity, and in their manner of tempting me. All that hell has brought forth is one great pain in the ass. But it passes, both the pain and the wind of hell.

We are also sources of spirits. Men, as gods, send forth the spirit of their words. Their spirits often course over troubled waters and return to them, for rest, finding no peace elsewhere. Their spirits return to them bearing the olive branch of peace, thereby signifying there is found rest for their souls elsewhere than the ark of God. We also, as men, send forth our spirits and find they dwell safely elsewhere and no longer need to return to us. God is the father of his spirits, and we, his children, fallen and steadfast alike, are also the source of our spirits. We are fathers of good things and of evil things. The authors of pride and foolishness, as well as the witnesses of truth and love.

Accept the spirit of God, it is gentle. Accept the spirits of the children of God: they bear the olive branch of peace. The oil of gladness is pressed from the fruit of the tree of delight.

Reject the evil spirits: they are, initially, terrorists and the whoremongers of fear: but in the end they are seen for what they really are: bores.

I took my troubles to God and he laughed at me: What are these? he asked as I showed him what was in the bag. Tribulations I found in the world, I said. Let them be. They'll die of themselves. Only stupid men carry them round. Surely you shall not have me carry them. It was then that I got the message and ceased being a fool.

And I knew him not: but he that sent me to baptize with water, the same said unto me, Upon whom thou shalt see the spirit descending, and remaining on him, the same is he which baptizes with the Holy Ghost. And I saw, and bare record that this is the Son of God.

John bare record of what he saw. John bare record of the fact that the one who sent him to baptize with water also said unto him that he who had the spirit also would baptize with the spirit. We are cleansed with the fiery spirit of God's words. Men fight the Word of God with the words that come out of their own mouths. You cannot serve God and Lenin; you cannot serve God and Castro; you cannot serve God and Mammon; you cannot serve God and revolutionaries; you cannot serve God and the State; you cannot serve God and godless world government; you cannot serve God and worship Man; you cannot serve God and the Whore of Babylon, that mother of religions various in the world.

The Word of God is the Word of God. Jesus is Jesus: Paul is Paul: and the kingdom of heaven is the kingdom of everlasting reality. Away with your damnable myths: the witness of Jesus, of his father, of John, is a living testimony against the evil that men bring forth out of themselves.

Is it good for a man to be taxed without his consent? Is it good for a man to be reduced to a slave within an economic system which taxes him at sixteen to provide for his life at sixty? Is it good for a man to have his power of forgiveness handed over to lawyers so that they might make merchandise out of his impulses of righteous judgment?

Men have enslaved themselves to their idols of organization. They invest their states, their corporations, their unions, their professions with immortal life and care not about the immortal possibilities locked within the treasure house of their own souls. How cheaply they sell themselves to their own idols! The world overcomes them: they have no power to overcome the world: they are the hopeless victims of their own pride: the sons of men who refuse to become the sons of God.

Their imagination is a bottomless pit: many and varied are the forms they bring out of it: abominations and beautiful dreams: fear and courage: ugliness and beauty: wisdom and stupidity. Mortal offspring's of mortal men—but what is all of that to us? Is not the pit, though bottomless, a prison of the soul, a dungeon of the mind, a grave of the heart? Surely, it is: pray God keep me from investing the hell I have created with eternal life: let that which is evil that I create, die. Let death be overcome and destroyed.

What I am, I am. What is eternal about me, is eternal. God is my father, my source of life, my God of forces. He is a strange God to men: for men know not God: they know not Love and Truth and Beauty and the joy of everlasting life. Receive the power freely given: overcome the world: become the sons of God. Love is the force of life: beauty is its expression, and truth, its saving spirit.

Who is the Son of God? Jesus is the Son of God. Who are the sons of God? They are all who know that Jesus is the Son of God. For you should know this truth: John is right, and all those who deny his message are wrong. Truth is a two-edged sword. It separates fact from fiction: gods from hell: sin from the soul: and lies from the Word of God.

The record is still with us. The evil of many generations cannot destroy it. The image of Jesus is marred beyond description. But he is the same. Evil cannot survive within him, for he is its destroyer. Jesus can descend into the bottomless pit of Satan, and release him. Lenin and Mao have had their say: soon their spirits, even as they, will pass away. The word consumes.

Again the next day after John stood, and two of his disciples; And looking upon Jesus as he walked, he saith, Behold the Lamb of God! And the two disciples heard him speak, and they followed Jesus. Then Jesus turned, and saw them following and saith unto them, What seek ye? They said unto him, Rabbi, (which is to say, being interpreted, Master,) where dwellest thou? He saith unto them, Come and see. They came and saw where he dwelt, and abode with him that day: for it was about the tenth hour.

God sent John into the world to bear witness to Jesus. Andrew and John, disciples of John the Baptist, became apostles of Christ, the Lamb of God, by following him. Where does Jesus dwell? Can we locate his home? Eternity is real; the mansions of God, many; the sons of God, as numerous as the Stars of Heaven. Pray, tell, amidst all this glory where does Jesus dwell?

Come and see. There are invisible things hidden within the Creation which God reveals to us through angels and sons and apostles and even our own soul. The static conceptions of men are at odds with the dynamic nature of God, who being forever filled with life and motion is harmonizing within himself the unspeakable joy of his own dreams. Shall we never see where God dwells, can we never look into the human heart, is the treasure of our souls forever to be kept from us? No. For we must search inwardly for the spirits that are within us and outwardly for the spirits that are within others.

Space is the house of God. We dwell within the Spirit of Love.

Men confuse truth of what is real with the imaginative productions of their own minds. We surrender our powers of soul to others and lose control over our own house. We can see where Jesus dwells by accepting his invitation. He obviously dwells within the hearts and minds and souls of those that love him.

This real fact, this concrete occurrence, this living reality cannot be seen by those blind men who cannot accept anything outside of themselves. As we grow we are conscious of New Heavens, and a new earth. We can witness the living reality of Christ's kingdom. But we become confused when we witness evil coming out of the hearts of men. Men tempt us with the evil of doubt, ignorance, pride, sloth, and their own covetous and murderous ways. Why? Because they love only themselves and cannot acknowledge the majesty of God. They blaspheme him by attributing his work to their idols.

The world ends with a bang: not with a whimper. Only whimpering poets deny this truth. What world? Not the world created with the Word: not the world saved by God through his Son. But the world of mediocrity brought to life and sustained by fallen angels and earthly men alike. God is the supreme craftsman and he reduces our idols to dust so that he might fashion from the elemental rubble of our dreams a new world.

We are mad to weep over fallen idols. Satan is a fallen idol. Who is Satan? Where does he dwell? Within the hearts and minds and souls of men.

Jesus and Satan are at war within you. You may yield to one or the other. You may trust, believe, and hope in, one or the other. The kingdom of heaven is the kingdom of love, even the kingdom of God, and Jesus, who is God's Christ. Satan brings woe and misery to Job: Elihu brings light, and comfort, and truth: Job's friends are confused: but Job's struggle with evil is seen for what it is, a victory of truth and love and compassion and joy and delight.

We have chosen to eat of the tree of knowledge. We have knowledge of evil. We have died. Death and sin have been our portion. What results? Even this, we know that God, Elihu, Jesus and the Spirit of Truth which Jesus sent into the world are right and good and true. We also know the friends of Job are confused and in error; that Job had much to learn; that the world has profited by Job's experience— for the record of it is with us even to this day and its angelic message is within our heart and mind. We also know that Death and Sin are the product of the knowledge of evil. Men know how to produce evil, and they produce it. Men know how to kill—and they kill. Men know how to enslave others with the powers of Mammon, and they so enslave others. Men know how to exercise their pride to produce the intellectual idols of state and church and law and custom so that they, and not God nor Jesus, might lord it over them. Men, as the rebellious sons of god, are Satan. This is the truth. They produce evil, and they know it. And I know it. And if you will have it, so do you.

Satan is real. So is his destruction. The power of truth and love cannot be quenched. When you cease to be like Satan, you become like Jesus and thereby become a son of God.

These are some of the things told Andrew and John when they abode one day with Jesus.

God loves Solomon and God loves Hugh Hefner. And God loves all their wives and mistresses and concubines. But if they pay sacrifice unto the idols of their own imagination, because they love their adulterous women more than truth, God will rebuke them for their stupidity. Why burn incense to Ashtoreth? The idols are gone: only Solomon and all his women remain: neither has his wisdom nor their beauty, passed away. The gifts of God are eternal: they cannot perish: wisdom and beauty are of God, and everlasting. Beauty is not truth; nor is truth Beauty: and we must know more than this if eternal life is our desire. For such life is knowledge of God. Surely, Solomon is wise enough to accept this simple truth. Then let him rebuke his wives; learn a truth of Jesus: he has seven wives, and most of them are idolatrous whores. What then shall they do? Rebuke their wives and destroy the abominable idols. A bloodless philosophy can be as insipid as the encyclicals of a pope.

Xaviera Hollander possesses more wisdom than Solomon: for she knows that the harlots have entered heaven before the scribes. All the writers in the world who deny Jesus war against heaven. They are fools. They would have a better chance of pissing at the sun and extinguishing it, than profiting from that war.

She is a tree of life to them that lay hold upon her: and happy is every one that retaineth her. To eat of the tree of life is to exercise wisdom. For the tree of life is found in the midst of the paradise of God. And the Persians, when under God, knew paradise. Where now is wisdom to be found and all our desires realized? Within the city of truth, even atop the citadel of Zion: for Christ ascended up to heaven not by climbing Jacob's ladder as many angels do, but by climbing up a mountain of tribulation and overcoming the cross of despair.

Better is it to enjoy paradise in the arms of a happy whore than to be bored to death in the courtroom of an asexual judge. The legislators of nonsense are wise in their own conceits. Beware of those who love the uppermost places, the highest titles; beware of those who wear long robes—except, of course, those supernatural beauties of the present age who know how to strip seductively. What is wiser, to enjoy fucking, or to discourse about it endlessly?

The harlots have entered heaven before the Pharisees: nevertheless, I marvel at the blindness of men who neither know where they are, nor whence they've come, yet are so quick to tell people what to do and where to go. Men have been led to war, to hell, to death, to the pit of bottomless despair by the blind guides of God and of Satan

One of the two which heard John speak, and followed him, was Andrew, Simon Peter's brother.

What do we know of Andrew? Where is this Son of Jonah? This finder of the Messias, this missing person whom the world has not yet found? What if Andrew had not brought Peter to Jesus? Obviously, the world would have missed the story of one living stone. We do more to promote the gospel than Andrew and Peter and add more words to the story of the gospel than are contained in all the Bible. A torrent, a flood, has issued out of the mouths of men.

At times, when I consider the matter, I marvel at the things Jesus never said, never did, never desired, never thought. Truly, all these years, he opened not his mouth. But what is the use of a silent priest? What profit, a dead king? Who needs a speechless ruler? Lambs cannot talk. Each role in life has its appointed time. Is the Messias a corn of wheat? Is this an answer to be given those Greeks who seek after wisdom?

I know what my God has told me: I know what certain angels have told me: I know what I have seen, and what I have heard. But I know not what I have forgotten. My God has shown me the beauty of sleep and the holiness of forgetfulness. We need the rainbow to remember his covenant; the ark to keep us above the troubled sea; the miracle of seeing and knowing that Christ walked to our ship while we were still at sea. The essential things of life are retained, the old things forgotten, discarded. Nevertheless, the new heavens and the new earth are created on the old foundations. God created the stars, and Moses to publish that truth, and me, to affirm it with the power of my flesh and blood. For without my flesh, without my blood, how could these words come to be? How could my spirit express itself or commune with those I love?

The limitations, and the boundaries I have placed upon Leviathan men cannot fathom. Yet they are there. Satan, Man, the State, Death, Hell, and Evil itself has its limits. Prove it, taunts the scribe. There are places where Satan, Man, the State, Death, and Evil have no power. Time and Space limit their power. Surely in this place at this time their power is nothing. Let their angels boast: let men babble: the wind will disperse their spirits, and their vanity will be as if it never was.

I hate these idols: I despise their feast days: I detest their covenant with death. I am who I am. All their political bullshit and vain philosophy cannot detract from that truth.

Why these words? To convince Andrew that he ought not to hide himself from himself. All of us, like Andrew, hide from ourselves. Surely God is a God of forces. The power of truth, love, beauty, joy and life itself is seen as the Creation wheels about our eye. The life within me is ever moving: the spirit never rests: the forces are ever adequate: nevertheless, about the borders of heaven are death and hell.

There are parables I never spoke: feelings I've had but never expressed in words. Thoughts higher than I can reach, have I seen in my heavens. There are many mansions within the house of God: more heavens than one.

I work to discover who I am. What can we say? The flesh profits nothing: but the flesh is not nothing. Our flesh is the product of the Spirit. The words are Spirit and our souls are the house of our words. We build our house either in the New Jerusalem, a city of truth, or we build elsewhere. Elsewhere is hell: a place where the worm consumes and fire consumes that worm.

He first findeth his own brother Simon, and saith unto him, We have found the Messias, which is, being interpreted, the Christ. And he brought him to Jesus. And when Jesus beheld him, he said, Thou art Simon the son of Jona: thou shalt be called Cephas, which is by interpretation, A stone.

Surely Jesus is bold. He looks upon Peter, changes his name, and makes him a living stone within the city of truth. For Peter preached the gospel and became like Jesus the holder of a new name, even a new work. Peter lives in these words: Cephas lives: the rock lives. For the city of truth houses the spirit of Cephas, the living rock Jesus fashioned out of Peter. Living stones reflect the light given by the God of truth.

We receive power from the source of power, even from Jesus, who has many names, including Messias, and the Christ. Jesus' God is the God of forces, the source of the power of life. The sons of God who depart from God create the hells of this world: the hells found in thought, in dream, in living reality.

The poor in spirit are blessed for theirs is the kingdom of heaven even though the modern Pharisees deny this simple truth.

But Peter is given a new name: and every man who overcomes the world becomes a son of God and may receive many new names: even as Jesus has many names, and wears many crowns. The problem with the world is that it constitutes in its complex immensity the realm of Satan, its prince, and the many devils that serve It.

The day following Jesus would go forth into Galilee, and findeth Philip, and saith unto him, Follow me.

Jesus' imperative is simple: Follow me: and bold: For why should Philip, or any one of us, follow Jesus? He has nothing but the Spirit of God and since the Spirit of the Lie obviously possessed the world, why should this directive be followed? Jesus chooses. God wills. Truth divides. We follow.

Really, in all openness and plain honesty, what shall we say about whom we serve, whom we worship, whom we follow? Satan is the antithesis of Christ. We have an inheritance both of God and of the world. I read the *L.A. Times* to gain knowledge of the world. The signs of these times are plain. I read the Word of God in the kingdom of my heart. No book, no church, no angel, is large enough to house my soul. What is my soul? Even this: God's gift to me. The universe of my desires is governed by the Spirits of God. Without good thoughts, without a single eye fixed on a single God, without life, beauty, joy, harmony, peace and truth, I find no light in my soul, no pleasure in my creation, no purpose in making the Word of God flesh.

The mystery ever deepens; the curtain of creation has been drawn; the new heavens and the new earth are before us. Let Philip be found of the Greeks, those architects of Wisdom's house, so that he can show them Jesus, even God's Christ in the world. For every genius is a sheep in the fold of Christ, though they know it not. The kingdom is vast; we cannot measure, nor behold its boundaries. We require new heavens, and a new earth; our soul needs space in which to enjoy eternity. I marvel at my Father who supplies both our desires and their fulfillment. The tree of life yields the ambrosia of the gods. Wisdom is the house built by the spirit of peace; it is situated in the garden of delight. It is the observatory of creation.

Now Philip was of Bethsaida, the city of Andrew and Peter.

What do we know of Bethsaida? A real city, having a real place on earth, the temporary locale of Andrew, Peter, and Philip: the city is as real as Jesus, Andrew, Peter, and Philip. But these men by the power of the Word are now in Anaheim. Jesus, Andrew, Peter, and Philip are in my thoughts, and, in this way, are here. But Andrew, Peter, and Philip may be enjoying the resurrection of their bodies elsewhere. Nevertheless, the truth that they are within me via the Word cannot be denied. For even if they were here now, present in the flesh, how could I know them except by the way they spoke? We violate the spirit of truth by refusing to seek before loudly proclaiming that it cannot be found. The city of truth can easily be found. It is set on high. We need only look up to see it descending. But liars cannot enter it: nor unbelievers: nor those who wish to divorce our souls from the spirit of truth and join us to another doctrine: nor those filthy dreamers for whom terror, ugliness, foolishness and pride are chief delights.

The walls of the city are real, and really needed. The reality of Andrew, Peter, and Philip is a defense against the reality of Mao, Fidel, and Lenin. Many men are mad: all their lives they busy themselves with spiritual realities and then deny themselves the use of their own soul which is the proper house of such realities. Money is an intangible spiritual reality; so is a political office; a position in a corporation, a university, a government, a family, a church. And men covet these things of the world and express only rarely their desire to enter heaven. Nevertheless, the mansions of angels are a delight to visit. I marvel that the prison house of the world is full, and the city of truth, desolate. Yet I need not marvel. For it is my Father's doing. He has cleared the foundation, removed all the old stones, to make room for the new.

It is Jesus who opens the door and lets Judas, Caiaphas, Hitler, Lenin, and Stalin into heaven. How? By subjecting the hell they created to the fiery power of God's word. Men are cleaned by the power of truth. But if these do not repent, and believe the gospel, they cannot enter. In no way can they enter, even though all the gates be opened wide.

Men encased in the hard shell of pride cannot sense the spirit of God. Yet those shells can and shall be broken. For with God, all things are possible. Hell's end is even this: eternal destruction. Only the busy fools know not they labor in vain. Let the rebellious angels please themselves with building an idol. They only serve God. For with pleasure, he'll destroy it.

Philip findeth Nathanael, and saith unto him, We have found him, of whom Moses in the law, and the prophets, did write, Jesus of Nazareth, the son of Joseph. And Nathanael said unto him, Can there any good thing come out of Nazareth? Philip saith unto him, Come and see.

Jesus found Philip; the same Jesus who was found of Andrew and of John; and Philip found Nathanael. The kingdom of heaven is like treasure found in the field of the world. For heaven is come to earth: for men of earth find heaven growing within themselves. We seek him of whom Moses and the prophets did write and find him. The voice within the cloud of witnesses covering the earth speaks the matter clearly. This is my beloved Son. Hear him.

Jesus is of Nazareth, a Nazarene in the early and formative years of his life. Wisdom and the knowledge of God are the proper studies of the Nazarenes. Angels are the instructors of the Nazarenes. Plato is as much an angel of God as is Emanuel Swedenborg, Alfred North Whitehead, Steinmetz, Heifetz and Mary Tyler Moore. Genius and beauty are ever brought into the world by those who display it. The trees are known by their fruit: and the tree of life yields the fruit of truth, beauty and love in the flesh and blood tabernacle of the human spirit.

But Satan and his ministers, apologists, and advocates ever argue their detestable doctrines to the contrary. The kings and princesses of the earth bring their glory into the city of truth; its walls are built by the Jews, but the glory of the city is lightened by the gentiles. A people who knew not the ancient God of Israel, serve him: for he was before them, dreaming the dreams and working the works of paradise.

The rivers of pleasure are of God, and are filled with delight. Swedenborg's satire is one of many keys to the kingdom.

Moses and the prophets did write of Jesus. The same Jesus found by John, darkly understood by Paul, loved by Mary, praised of angels, visited by shepherds, and wise men alike. The kings of the east are many: for all the genius of all the ages bring what truth they have to Christ. Jesus is his own star, even the star over Bethlehem, that city of bread, wherein the doctrines of God are found. Truth, like gold, is a precious commodity in the world.

Heaven grows: the city of truth is built. Jesus is the foundation stone. But how beautiful are all these gifts brought into that city by the angels of God! Without music, and arts, science and philosophy, poetry and literature, what treasure might be placed in the human heart, what love could empower our mind, what use might we find for our soul making the Word flesh on earth?

The Word has been made flesh: the way it is done is real. We realize the ideal by making the word flesh. Samson knows by experience that to have his wisdom cut off his head by the woman he loves is foolishness for not only does he lose his God-given strength, but the delight of his life as well.

I love Delilah—did not my God create her? But the little imp did use me most cruelly. Obviously, Jesus of Nazareth did not repeat Samson's mistake. The penalty for being stripped of our wisdom is to serve the Philistines in blindness. The power of mediocrity is easily overcome by the wise, however, and the Philistines have doomed themselves to destruction for sporting with Samson. Dagon is but a dead dog; but Samson is a living soul, and Delilah, one of his many mistresses; this story is found written within the library of truth.

For neither Moses nor the prophets are dead: but forever are adding new truths to the scroll of time as they write what they write. The kingdom is like the treasure hidden within the household of our soul: and every writer instructed in its mysteries is able to bring out of his heart, treasures both new and old. But those writers who serve Satan bring out of themselves the ugly ideas, and forms, and lies which their servants use to create the idols of the present hour. They preach peace and freedom and prepare men for war and bondage. They mark and number and classify men as they brand cattle. These scribes are the priests of the Philistines. Every nation on the face of the earth, and every murderer and gang leader, and every tyrant large and small who teaches men how to war and kill and murder is the servant of Death. Not only are the righteous resurrected but the wicked as well.

Oh Love, how I would these blind might see! Then they would loathe their filthy garments and repent, and wash themselves in the words of truth provided. Then would God clothe them with the righteousness of his saints, and adorn them with the beauty of his presence.

But men prefer the councils of men, the synagogues of Satan, the mosques of Muhammad, the foreign offices of deceit, and the cathedrals of vanity, more than the clear testimony of Jesus. Remind me, then, good God, of what I learned in hell, lest my compassion diminish rather than grow. The power of Satan descends to him from the power of men. How ready are they to argue against the truth! How ready do they accept a lie! Caesar is dead but they fawn before his image and lust after his corrupt coin.

Jesus saw Nathanael coming to him, and saith of him, Behold an Israelite indeed, in whom is no guile!

How many men come to Jesus full of guile? Jesus can also see these coming. I am not perfect. There is none perfect but God: nevertheless, God perfects us with the burning spirit of his judgment. This is the kingdom of heaven: this is the place of judgement: this is the hour of truth. Now is the time for us to repent and believe the good news concerning the power and the kingdom and the glory of God. But what is the glory of God? Even the love he displays.

Nazareth is the school of God, his basic training camp, the university of his angels. All good things come out of Nazareth. Wisdom is justified by her children. The wise understand for in patience and with diligence they listen to God's still small voice. The devil roars to excite terror. The Nazarenes laugh at this for they know such terror can be ended by a sore throat. God quietly delivers his message. He has much to say. Why then should He once again as in days of old make himself hoarse pleading with his backsliding people? God's wisdom is found also in this: his capacity to learn from life, even from the heavenly throne of his own experience.

But with Satan it is not so. The spirit of the idol cannot learn, cannot grow, cannot govern itself rightly or well. Why? It is the product of dead men and bears the mark of its creators. They are wise in their own conceits. They love themselves and are too proud to declare their own end. I need not judge them, nor condemn them. They judge themselves with the words that come out of their mouths. The flood of words in the world comes out of the mouth of Satan. Men have programmed the idol for vanity, and vain are its products.

Let us forgive those who trespass against us. Let us resolve our difficulties with our brothers. Let us undeceive ourselves and practice forgiveness, mercy, judgment, and truth. Let us do what the Son of God commands and love our enemies and bear our afflictions with joy. I rejoice in my weakness for it is nothing more than a message to my Creator that I need her help.

The Nazarenes smile at the Greeks who thought Aphrodite weak. She is the strongest of the gods, for the goddess of Love overcomes all. Love cannot fail in even its most adventurous works. The universe of stars embracing the earth, and comforting the soul, and delighting the eye are the works of love. But only one of her works. For her works are many.

The Nazarenes know this, for so have they been shown, and so are they taught. But Babylon, Rome, Sodom, Egypt, Washington, Moscow, and Peking are the schools of fools. Their curricula abound with vanity and profitless subjects. God instructs the Nazarenes not to kill, not to adulterate the truth, not to blaspheme his glory with vain oaths; God instructs the Nazarenes to accept the consequences of evil; God teaches the Nazarenes to love all their enemies and to hate their foolish brothers' idols and works.

I hate communism but all these foolish comrades of mine, I do most surely love. But they love Vladimir more than me. In simplest truth, I hate the State. The reality of this beast is the source of much evil. All good comes from Nazareth: the wise know this. If you doubt this, come and see.

Nathanael said unto him, Whence knowest thou me? Jesus answered and said unto him, Before that Philip called thee, when thou wast under the fig tree, I saw thee.

And many others with you. Men clothe themselves with the fig leaves they have torn from the tree of Israel. Israel is a tree planted of God in the garden of his pleasure. But the tree is there to yield figs, so that being hungry, we might eat of its fruit. But the many masters and scribes in the world hide their nakedness, and the nakedness of their wives, with its fig leaves. How much joy in the pleasure of life and in the naked beauty of women is hid from God because men hide the reality of their own flesh behind the fig leaves of their own dried-up and dead doctrines?

Did not God create Israel so that Moses might write: In the beginning God created the heaven and the earth. And the earth was without form, and void; and darkness was upon the face of the deep. And the spirit of God moved upon the face of the waters. And God said, Let there be light: and there was light?

But men are afraid of their nakedness and must hide themselves with what they gathered while they were under the tree. Nathanael was under the tree, but once he left that shade he could see the hypocrisy of those who brand lovers with a scarlet letter. And how could he know this or see this unless he could see the angels of God ascending and descending upon the Son of man?

Men, full of the knowledge of evil, legislate evil laws. They know about the sin of Sodom, so instead of yielding one asshole to the mischievous impulses of youth, they'll slaughter upwards of 65,000 men because some Levite thought more of his asshole than he did of his loving concubine.

They judge themselves righteous and persecute their own children who inadvertently may have pissed on one of their ugly little idols.

Nathanael answered and saith unto him, Rabbi, thou art the Son of God; thou art the King of Israel. Jesus answered and saith unto him, Because I said unto thee, I saw thee under the fig tree, believest thou? thou shalt see greater things than these.

Was this prophecy fulfilled? Did Nathanael see greater things? Have we who have inherited the works of the scribes Jesus sent into the world seen greater things than the simple fact that Jesus knew Nathanael when Nathanael was under the fig tree of Israel?

We have eyes to look forward and backward in time: what we see men term history: but in reality what do we see? We see the angels of God proclaiming his glory to the ends of the earth. But the blind writers of 1976 see nothing save what profit they may derive from their words. They serve Mammon and their works are what they are. They serve the State, and many are the abominations that come out of their mouths. They serve Man, as if this lifeless abstraction of thought was anything more than an idol of their philosophic minds.

And what they surely cannot see is what every writer instructed into the mysteries of the kingdom of heaven plainly sees.

And he saith unto him, Verily, verily, I say unto you, Hereafter ye shall see heaven open, and the angels of God ascending and descending upon the Son of man.

I am the Son of man, for as I have said elsewhere, man fathers me through the mechanism of the world. But my earthly father is of the earth, and cannot see the flights of angels, coming to and going from me. As if King James of England who was instrumental in translating truth into living poetry, and the Bible he caused to be written, were not both the message and the messenger of the words quoted above. I am astonished at men who in deed, in appearance, in truth are the very angels of God, bearing the spirit of God, who know not they are the angels of God. They are either cunning enough to hide themselves in the world, or they are overcome by the dark smoke issuing forth from the bottomless pit of their own imaginations. But the war is real, and their confusion at this late hour is understandable, albeit not commendable. I marvel that babes and suckling's can understand in their hearts what angels cannot deliver in less than a dozen volumes, carefully edited and prudently annotated.

Nevertheless, this is true, many messengers cannot understand the content of their own message. It is sealed from them and they know not the importance of their own work.

Billy Graham is an angel of faith and I am astonished that even he denies himself his own true role. Nevertheless, he is one of God's angels, one of his many ministering spirits, and he need not deny himself any longer. But he knows himself as a son of God, and his witness and testimony is true. This is his strength and this is his glory and what man can take it from him?

What we do, we do: what we say, we say: what we believe, we believe. What we are, we are. Is this not to know the truth? But men fail to carefully note what words they write, and what words they speak. They must account to themselves what they themselves are saying and writing. Let God be my judge, for the judgments of men are vain. Let men judge me, the good and evil alike, for why should they not prove the point? But they have judged me, and thereby judge themselves.

CHAPTER 2

And the third day there was a marriage in Cana of Galilee; and the mother of Jesus was there: And both Jesus was called, and his disciples, to the marriage.

What is the third day? Is it even this day, the day on which Jesus shall rise again? Rise again to what? If Jesus rises from the dead and ascends into heaven this can only mean that the Jesus we have refused enters our heart and reigns there as king. The kingdom comes not with observation. Neither can men say, Lo, it is here: or it is there. The kingdom of heaven is among us: the kingdom of heaven is within you. The words of Jesus abiding in us are the words of God: for from whom did he receive them? Heaven is God's throne: our heart, that which is within us, is his dwelling place. This time is the third day.

And when they wanted wine, the mother of Jesus saith unto him, they have no wine.

Who is the mother of Jesus? His disciples, even those who eat bread with him; those that consume his doctrine and drink of his testament; those that distribute his loaves of doctrine to the multitude are his mother, and brother and sister: For such do the will of God.

The marriage is in Cana of Galilee, even that city within us. Who is the bride, and who is the bridegroom? We are the bridegroom, the spirit of truth is the bride. In this we should rejoice. But we are male and female: so have we been created. The children of God, even the sons of God, bring the woman, even their wife, out of themselves.

Jesus saith unto her, Woman, what have I to do with thee? mine hour is not yet come. His mother saith unto the servants. Whatsoever he saith unto you, do it.

Jesus has a time appointed him of God: even that Spirit which sent him into the world. Jesus is the angel of his own message: the star over his own city of bread. Israel is the planting of God: the source of that precious blood in the world which is wine, the very best wine, saved for this day. The Word covers the earth: but the Word in the earth, when properly husbanded, produces the fruit of the vine from which the blood of life is obtained. We are raised from the dust of the earth, but God's Word within us is life. We live, and enjoy life, because of the words Jesus gave us.

It is good for the angels of God, even God's servants, to do what Jesus tells them to do. For then we know that water can be made wine. The Jews are waterpots of stone. Their laws are written upon tablets of stone. Their hearts are of stone. For how else could they be impervious to the words of Jesus? Nevertheless, his words poured within them are water: water which when drawn out is wine. The angels know this: they are the witness of their own miracle.

And there were set there six waterpots of stone, after the manner of the purifying of the Jews, containing two or three firkins apiece. Jesus saith unto them, Fill the waterpots with water. And they filled them up to the brim. And he saith unto them, Draw out now, and bear unto the governor of the feast. And they bare it.

He is a Jew who is one inwardly. In the manner of the Jews, we are full of the words of life, even the water of truth. Within us, miracles occur. We receive words of one kind: we yield words of another kind. Men are the miracle producers of the present hour. The world is the product of their powers.

But in all truth, what do they do? They fill each other with words: and then draw them out. How many words have Satan's angels poured into his vessels, and how many words have they drawn out?

The teachers of the world pour deadly things into their children, and then draw out their poison. We should judge between the words of Jesus and the words of statesmen: the words of Jesus and the words

of Napoleon: the words of Jesus and the words of Ford: the words of
Jesus and the words of all the president's men; the words of Jesus and
the words of Lenin; the words of Jesus and the words of Mao: the
words of Jesus and the words of congressmen, or men of the congress:
the words of Jesus and the words of our father, our mother, our sisters,
our brethren: the words of Jesus and my words, for how can any judge
escape judgment?

Who is my judge? The governor of the feast.

*When the ruler of the feast had tasted the water that was made
wine, and knew not whence it was: (but the servants which drew
the water knew;) the governor of the feast called the bridegroom,
and saith unto him, Every man at the beginning doth set forth good
wine; and when men have well drunk, then that which is worse:
but thou hast kept the good wine until now. This beginning of
miracles did Jesus in Cana of Galilee, and manifested forth his
glory; and his disciples believed on him.*

The third day produces a beginning.

*After this he went down to Capernaum, he, and his mother, and
his brethren, and his disciples: and they continued there not many
days.*

The children of God, even those who have been to Capernaum,
know that even a city exalted to heaven, even a city in which many
miracles had been accomplished, can be ignorant of its day of
visitation. Many cities, obsessed with their own glory, blessed by
God, know not the time of their visitation. The spirit of pride in
governments, large and small, blinds men to the reality of God's
children.

Jails are the products of cities. Forgiveness is forgotten:
punishment, exacted: the poor, despised. City managers are made
into mammon managers in the cities of the world. But mammon is
a foolish thing to serve. Thus even the richest cities cannot function
without money. Why? Because their capital has been foolishly
expended, stupidly used. They sell themselves and their citizens
to foreign interests and know not they are the victims of external

covetousness. The plight of cities is real: Satan has sold that which he doesn't possess to those foolish enough to disclaim their birthright.

Cities also are brought down to hell. Capernaum is only one example.

And the Jews' passover was at hand, and Jesus went up to Jerusalem, and found in the temple those that sold oxen and sheep and doves, and the changers of money, sitting: And when he had made a scourge of small cords, he drove them all out of the temple, and the sheep, and the oxen; and poured out the changers' money, and overthrew the tables; And said unto them that sold doves, Take these things hence; make not my Father's house an house of merchandise. And his disciples remembered that it was written, The zeal of thine house hath eaten me up.

We can be consumed by the zeal of many causes. Yet the house of God is our principal concern: The temple of our body, the house of our spirit, the city of truth, the new Jerusalem, the kingdom of heaven built within us; what zeal do we have for the right use of this, our house?

The merchants of Mammon are within us, buying and selling sheep and oxen within the temple of God with impunity. The merchants of the church, of religious associations, and of the State, buy men, as sheep, and the workmen of God, as oxen. So many cardinals, so many bishops, so many evangelists, so many preachers and teachers at such and such a price. Souls are saved—from what—with dollars. The sheep are not led unto green pastures, nor are they made to lie down by the still waters; but rather are they bought and sold to fatten the purses of the legislators of wars and of nonsense.

President Ford requests the use of hundreds of millions of dollars for fifty or so additional nuclear-tipped missiles to add to an elaborate weapon systems complex which already numbers nuclear bombs in the thousands. Who, of all men, are the men responsible for employing the souls God created, to build and emplace and use these filthy abominations? Who maintains this doctrine: men may kill in order to expand and defend the powers of the State? Surely God has simply said, Do not kill. Love your enemies. How is it then that within the kingdom of heaven, the servants of Satan have sold men on the idea that the power to destroy the body, the power to maim, and burn, and blind, and imprison, in a word, the powers of Death and of Hell, are things to be coveted?

Search the scripture of Napoleon, of Caesar, of Einstein, of Hitler, of Teller, of Lenin, of Mao, of Reagan, of Ford, of Kennedy, of the IRA, of the PLA, of Ed Davis, of Lincoln, for an answer. And surely, there are many other fat fools who are spiritually dead because they are full of the knowledge of evil, who have added to the flood of nonsense coming out of Satan's mouth. How can all their eloquent, and polished, and hypocritical bullshit be stored within us while we cannot find one room to house this treasure Jesus gave us, namely, Do not kill?

Men not only create filthy organizational idols, but they also place their abominations within the human heart.

The abomination of desolation is placed within the human heart: there is no denying this truth. But God forbids that we should worship it.

Men commit adultery with the whore of Babylon: they build their own righteous tower to reach heaven: they glorify their own works, evil and sinful though they be.

The Passover is a feast of the Jews. I am a Jew and the angel of death is abroad in the land, and I am sorrowful. The dove of peace cannot be bought or sold by men, and God honored thereby. Our body, our spirit, is God's house. We need Jesus to drive out all these unprofitable things which pollute our sanctuary. The merchants of the state and of religion do not hallow God's name. Beware of their things. God said, Defraud not. Do not steal. But these clever fellows will sell you that which you do not need, and which they do not possess, and use your money thus acquired, to pay your children to steal what you have left by taxing you into endless labor. Surely the wicked never rest, never cease from strife and endless debate, never trust in the power of God to overcome the prince of the world. The great men of the world are the fallen and proud angels of God who are enslaved with their own idols and images. Einstein is as much a slave of the science he helped create as Ford is a slave of the government to which he gives his momentary breath of life.

Dear God, let these blind see, for why should men do evil and think it good?

Then answered the Jews and said unto him, What sign shewest thou unto us, seeing that thou doest these things? Jesus answered and said unto them, Destroy this temple, and in three days I will raise it up.

The Jews have destroyed the temple of Jesus. Vain, disfigured, foolish—so must the temple of Jesus appear to men. It is little wonder that the Jesus the pope worships must appear foolish to the communists. Why? Because his temple, his living body, has been destroyed. How the celebration of the mass, the mumbling of a litany; prayers repetitious, dull, prolonged, and public; rosaries, surplices, indulgences, images of saints long dead, and priests various in long robes can constitute that temple wherein God is to be worshipped must be explained by the men who practice, promote, and glory in such foolishness. Surely these are the results of vain doctrines: the bread of life leavened with hypocrisy: such is not the temple of God.

The Jews have destroyed the temple of Jerusalem, and Jesus is raising it up. These doctors of vanity know not that David is the father of Jesus only because Jesus is his own father. Jesus is also God's Son, and God is his heavenly father. Nevertheless, for those who can see it, Jesus is his own earthly father, since David is the father of his own lord. Jesus and David are one. Surely my God knows this to be true and so do I. But the great men of the earth are too busy examining theories concerning what transpired millions of years ago, to trouble themselves over where Jesus and David, who had occupied the temple of God two and three days ago, presently are. I know: but would they believe me?

Then said the Jews, Forty and six years was this temple in building, and wilt thou rear it up in three days?

I am forty-three. What shall I be when I am forty-six years old; forty-six years old, as men measure a body's life? But ask the question of yourself. How long have you been building the temple of your body? How much truth is found in it?

But he spake of the temple of his body.

The body of Jesus is also the temple of truth and the bride of man's soul. What astronomers truly see and truly reveal is the starry heavens which exist not only within their own mind but also within the mind of Jesus. For how else could he judge their works and explore the adequacy of their vision? Surely, as the angel expressed it, space is the unbounded sensorium of God; and if astronomers forget this, the angels of truth will remind them of it once again. Why should men be so vain as to believe that the temple of their mind is superior to the temple God creates?

When therefore he was risen from the dead, his disciples remembered that he had said this unto them; and they believed the scripture, and the word which Jesus had said.

If only the woman now troubled, now in travail, the woman pregnant with truth, conceived of the holy spirit, even God's blood, even God's spirit, would remember what Jesus said to her before he ravished her with his own God-given wisdom, she could find comfort in this fact: a nation is being born at once. What nation? The kingdom of heaven: even the kingdom where love rules: even the kingdom of the God of Israel.

Surely the Scripture of Moses, of David, of the prophets, of the wise men visiting Christ, of the angels of God, of the scribes instructed into the mysteries found within their own heart, even the creators of joy, and beauty, and genius and delight are scriptures to be believed. Believe also the word Jesus spoke. Believe the word he speaks. For surely, he is no longer dumb and closemouthed.

Now when he was in Jerusalem at the Passover, in the feast day, many believed in his name, when they saw the miracles which he did.

What miracles? Even to see the seven doctrines of Jesus broken up and delivered to multitudes of men through his disciples, fill such baskets as Protestantism, Mormonism, Catholicism, and many other such baskets of wickedness holding fragments of the broken bread of life.

But Jesus did not commit himself unto them, because he knew all men,

Commit your soul to God. His yoke is easy: his burden is light. But men will burden you with nonsense, yoke you with fear. Hell is doomed to destruction: but men in hell, preach of its horrors, revealing to others the cruel concept of the cruel God they have within themselves. Hell is real, as real as the wicked, as real as those nations who have forsaken God. But hell is a place we visit, and destroy. And why shouldn't war and pride be destroyed? Who really needs these angelic vanities?

Know men by the words they speak, the opinions they advance, the doctrines they sell. Decide of" yourself what to do with them. Surely, the yes and no of your belief is yours and yours alone to exercise.

And needed not that any should testify of man: for he knew what was in man.

What is in man? Knowledge of evil, poisoning the blood of life.

CHAPTER 3

There was a man of the Pharisees, named Nicodemus, a ruler of the Jews: The same came to Jesus by night, and said unto him, Rabbi, we know that thou art a teacher come from God: for no man can do these miracles that thou doest, except God be with him.

The greater miracle is to be born of the Spirit of God. God moves men with his spirit. Men respond to love. There is no denying it. Men sense beauty. Only fools deny this fact. Men delight in truth. Only devils persuade themselves otherwise.

Jesus is born of the woman loved of God: even Israel in her flesh and blood and spiritual reality. She is his bride: whore, though she be. Who is Israel? All who give birth to Jesus. How is Jesus born again? Through the power of the Word working within the womb of Israel, God's chosen few.

Fundamentally, literally, materialistically, really speaking, the Son of man is born of God and of Israel. The Jews are real: Nicodemus is real: the conversation between Jesus and Nicodemus, reported by John, preserved and translated by scholars, delivered by merchants, materially preserved by pen, ink, paper, and the actions of scribes schooled in the use of materials, is literally true. Fundamentally speaking, what could be more fundamental? Is there not before me on this desk a real book? Is it not really opened? Is not the literal translation effected by the Elizabethan scholars, drunkards and puritans alike, given to me at this time a fundamental fact in my life?

Surely this is miracle enough for the present age: nevertheless, God's miracles are not limited to this.

The Word of God is its own miracle. But scribes, not sent by God, war against the Word of God only to confirm it. Nevertheless, God also has enabled Jesus to send his scribes into the world to confirm this Word.

Yet even those geniuses in the world whose talent I admire use their angelic powers to deny its truth. Why? Because of their pride. Their own intellect blinds them. They will not come to Jesus even by night.

Jesus answered and said unto him, Verily, verily, I say unto thee, Except a man be born again, he cannot see the kingdom of God.

The bodies of men are raised from the dust of the earth: what could be more scientifically obvious than that? All food comes from the dust of the ground: The earth, in its basic structure, is raised up by the power of life. Seen in motion, seeds of corn yielding stalks of corn in Kansas would inspire many an angel to sing the prasies of God. Of such, and many like things, are our bodies raised up.

But a man must be born of the Word to see spiritual realities. We require the Word of Life, the very living water itself, to course within our flesh and blood to enable it to see the kingdom of God. Nevertheless, all the corn in Kansas could not produce one word of love: how much less power then has matter to raise itself to life?

God created, creates and rests: and creates again. But the authors of words worldly deny this obvious fact. Why? Because they are too busy fawning before their own created and abominable images to realize God has been busy elsewhere.

Nicodemus saith unto him, How can a man be born when he is old? can he enter the second time into his mother's womb, and be born?

Of course. He also might do it via another mother. But entrance into the kingdom of God is found by birth into the city of truth. We are born in a small place: yet we inherit the glory of all of God's creation. To hear the angels sing is to have joy within ourselves. How then is truth or beauty or love or life born within us except it be by the spirit of Life Herself, even the bride of our soul, even our God working within us? Words are life: but love is eternal life, for the Word of God is love. Make no mistake about it: Life in God is eternal.

Jesus answered, Verily, verily, I say unto thee, Except a man be born of water and of the Spirit, he cannot enter into the kingdom of God.

God is a spirit. Like the wind, his spirit comes and goes. Sometimes, we know he will come: at other times, we are not sure. We know we cannot sow effectively when the whirlwind comes.

When he is absent, shall I deceive myself into believing he is hidden forever? If he rebukes me, shall I whimper about his lack of love? If he uses me, shall I protest his decision to do so? The Lord God is a spirit and woe unto those who forget God is Lord! Men create hell, live in hell, glorify hell, and all these wicked that are transformed into hell deny the truth of their state. I marvel at those in hell, denying its reality: they are almost as much an astonishment to me as those self-centered intellects who believe hell is within a man's power to accept or reject. Such have either forgotten what hell is or have never been in hell, and it is best to be wary of their doctrine.

Heaven is where hell is not: for the filthy, liars, and the abominable are not found within the gates, but without. But they war against heaven: violently assault it, and wish to rule there. Why? Because worldly men wish to rule your house for their own glory. Their vanity is colossal. Can you believe that there are men in the world who will tempt you with evil to keep you from good? Surely there are: the servants of Satan are many. Their greatest creation is the Godless State. They are so full of knowledge of good and evil that they are dead. Taxation, armies, wars, prisons, and grievous laws are their fruit. Don't permit yourself to be nurtured by their doctrines, fathered by their lies, lest you be born in hell.

God is a Spirit: so is Antichrist.

Receive the water Jesus gives to the world: receive the spirit of truth he sends into the world. This is good advice. It is free. Take it.

That which is born of the flesh is flesh; and that which is born of the Spirit is spirit.

There is corrupt flesh, and beautiful flesh. There is an evil and wicked one: and there is one who is true.

Judge of yourself what is good and what is evil. Decide. Surely the purpose of God's Word is even this: to teach you how to choose the good, and reject the evil. The serpents in the world are liars and full of bad advice as their own fate and life testify. Neither father, mother, wife, brethren, nor children should keep you from the truth given to you if you follow and continue in Jesus' Word. As for these great men of and in the world, let them be. God has his ways and they have their own.

Marvel not that I said unto thee, Ye must be born again.

Frankly speaking, is this second birth anything to marvel at? Every school in the world gives birth to its children. Communists have their children: Mao has his: and Science, Philosophy, Religion, Poetry, and Art have produced their children. Nevertheless, you cannot be Jesus' disciple unless you abandon your parents. And hate them. Because neither the Church, with its whorish vanities, nor the governments of men with their godless ways and their silly ordinances, should teach you or your children.

Our mother and father, sisters and brethren, are those who do the will of God. Parents should bring their children to Jesus: but more often than not they forbid this and bring them to Church and State. Surely, as the son of man, I know this. We are fathered by men through the mechanism of the world.

As a man sows, so shall he reap. We sow confusion into ourselves when we accept the words of authorities rather than the Word of God, who is Jesus. The resurrection of the body is a real fact; every infant testifies to this truth. But dead men, spiritually dead men, men of earth, and not of heaven, hide this fact from themselves and from their own children. They are dead, and know it not.

The wind blows where it listeth, and thou hearest the sound thereof, but canst not tell whence it cometh, and wither it goeth: so is everyone that is born of the Spirit.

Men do not know where I am because I am born of the Spirit. Moreover, I do not know where my friends are for they are also born and borne of the spirit. God gives, and takes away, and gives again. Who am I to argue against this simple truth?

Men, however, confuse truth with truthful repetition. They truly learn a lie; or worse, create one; and repeat it, shamelessly, to whosoever will listen. Witch doctors are real: but only a minority are found in Africa. Call the doctor, the hospital, the accountant, the undertaker; and after you've buried your loved one, read a book on the miracles of modern medicine. Dust returns to dust: but ever since Moses, who once lived to be 120, wrote this, the sons of Belial, who in their day of power were cut short by God, wish to prove Moses never lived. Let Moses laugh at them. For mine own part, I find it all too silly to be amusing.

The key to hell and death is in the hand of the angel of God. Space and time limit evil. God takes our soul and plants it elsewhere. He is the husbandman: we are the bride.

Proverbs and parables are words illustrative of truth. We eat of the fruit of Israel, and discover spiritual realities existing beyond the power of our words to describe. What is heaven? What is paradise? That place where God's will is done in earth. Let the spirit lead me. In the kingdom of heaven there are many wide and broadways that lead to the houses of song and delight.

Nicodemus answered and said unto him, How can these things be?

God is mischievous: what man can stay his impulses of truth and delight? The false image of God in the world is a true image of a lifeless, albeit mechanically animated, God. We could not make sense of all the telephone conversations occurring in the world at this minute even if our technical wizards could simultaneously pipe all these real sounds into our ear. How can we hope then to understand what God is doing this minute?

Why are we proud, or covetous, or foolish? We know so little: yet God reveals so much. These things be: as God begins to tell us how they came to be, we cannot be still long enough to listen for an answer. Death complicates the listening process. We begin to understand, and then the poison within us causes pain and we flee the classroom, the school, and the laboratory. We are imperfect. But God is a spirit not so limited. He waits our return. His patience is astonishing.

Jesus answered and said unto him, Art thou a master of Israel, and knowest not these things?

Of what are we masters? If God himself is hard put to master Israel what hope for Nicodemus? Let me master my tongue, rein my thoughts, guide my feet and hands, and rightly use my eyes. Truly, it is enough to do for one lifetime. Israel is God's bride, and I am part of her.

Verily, verily, I say unto thee, We speak that we do know, and testify that we have seen; and ye receive not our witness.

Jesus lives to witness to the truth and so do I. The kingdom of heaven built within us comes: men do not die and go. This is the kingdom of God. What do you think, that our witness is false? The poor in spirit possess the kingdom of heaven: is it not prepared of God for them? Then why do the violent strive to take it by force? If the meek do not inherit the earth, and the pure in heart do not see God, Jesus and I are liars. If the nations of the earth are not separated by the Sermon on the Mount, if they are not judged thereby, even by their own words coming out of the mouths of their own great men, Jesus' work remains before him: for him to say, It is finished, is therefore misleading. You cannot forgive your enemies, let alone your brothers, their trespasses and cast them in prison. Only Satan advocates such a policy. You cannot teach men how to kill, how to war, how to construct and use the weapon systems of destruction, and consider yourself a sheep of Christ unless you are a hypocrite of the grandest sort.

What then shall the spirit of truth do except reprove the world for its righteousness? For it is filthy and the work of men, and not of God.

Let me quicken the living and the dead. Surely gods ought to bring us the gifts and powers of life. Only devils, hypocrites, and enslaved men, traffic in the merchandise of death and hell: gods without God are devils.

Satan offers the world to the sons of God. But a son of God should see what is in the world: it is not worth the having in its present state. The world is saved by Jesus. Without the law given by Jesus on the mountain, what have you? The constitutions of men: the many paper products of Rome and Babylon, Sodom and Egypt.

How then is the world saved? By bringing heaven to earth. How is heaven brought to earth? By bringing the lamb of God to God. How can this be done? Obviously, by bringing your house to God, even the soul in which you dwell: for these words are life within you, even a life endlessly eternal. Let the end come. It is but the rest before a new beginning.

If I have told you earthly things, and ye believe not, how shall ye believe, if I tell you of heavenly things? And no man hath ascended up to heaven, but he that came down from heaven, even the Son of man which is in heaven.

The universe is vast, as the angel has said. The earth is but a ball: one starry ball hung amidst the creation of God. We know not how to rightly witness, what we witness. At times, I weary of men: nothing beautiful impresses them; trifles distract them; earthbound thoughts cover them. Angie Dickinson is beautiful: eloquent testimony to the living God who created and sustains her. But the prince of the world cloaks her in the garb of a police woman and, via the miracles wrought by modern man, her image is brought before many. But I love the living soul: how I would that God would gather his own to himself: for many images created of men are grotesque.

There are many stars in the heavens. God ever labors. We sit and wait; sleep and rest; but the spirit works. What are heavenly things? Beautiful and joyous dreams built within us: the workings of the spirits within us. Perfection takes time. We are wrought in flesh and blood: we are killed: we are resurrected. Beside the realities of life, and the spirits within me, the depositions of theologians and communists, of politicians and military men; of men; of angels; of saints; of sinners; of the saved and the condemned alike; I find grossly inadequate. The kingdom of heaven is the dream of my God working within me. I am alive to the truth and without hope and love, I could not bear this earth.

I am astonished at those who cling to it. It is as if we fear to leave our cell: fear to cast off our chains: fear to live in paradise.

And as Moses lifted up the serpent in the wilderness, even so must the Son of man be lifted up: That whosoever believeth in him should not perish, but have eternal life.

Let God forbid that ought that is beautiful should perish. Love is an eternal treasure, and the perishable goods of the world are no substitute for our Creator's heavenly sentiments. Knowledge is ignorance: ignorance of other things more important than itself. God treasures the belief we are commanded to give more than all these angelic depositions concerning the necessity of that belief. But many do not believe. Why?

Men, many men, have been freed from the technological bondage of Egyptian vanity and foolishness. They no longer build treasure cities to house the vain dreams of self-appointed pharaohs. Nevertheless, they wander in a wilderness of sin: the imperfection of their ways limits their power. The very heat of creative energy dissipates their lives. The beckoning glory of dawn, and the tenderness of twilight are not sufficient to lead them into paradise.

The serpent is only a sign: a sign that the temptation to believe that knowledge of good and evil will make us gods is to be rejected. Moses, to whom Jesus refers, lifted up that serpent when he wrote the Book of Genesis. Moses clearly indicated to us the mystery of God's creation: the mystery of its beginning. But if men do not believe the writing of Moses, or the words of Jesus, why should they believe in me, or in my God? Surely they cannot. For my God is the God of my heart: even the God of Moses, and of Jesus, and of Angie Dickinson. But who is Angie? Even one of my God's angels, displaying for all who can see the beauty of a woman clothed in flesh and blood. Let the world use her how it will: God also has his intents, her purposes, their delight. Moses saw the back parts of God: Moses saw the effects of the real serpents in the world: the poison of organizational and technological excess: the poison of unbelief, despair, hopeless defeat in the barren wasteland of individual lives: the poison of life without purpose.

Moses lifted up the sign of Satan's power: the symbol of evil's origin: we have his writings. We can heal ourselves of much pain simply by identifying the source of evil and then avoiding it. Surely it is evil to follow the way of Hitler, of Stalin; of Lincoln, of Truman;

of Brezhnev, of Ford. Such men early in their lives sucked milk from their mothers' breasts as do all children. Then, what happens? By what powers do these helpless infants brought into the world by their mother's love become transformed into men who prepare and lead other men into war? Did Hitler know what was good for Germany? Was the experience of Germans, Russians, Poles, and Hungarians at Stalingrad good for those who believed in the way of Hitler and the way of Stalin? What is good, and for whom is it good, that we cannot forget what happened at Gettysburg and at Hiroshima? And what can we say about Brezhnev or of Ford? For whose good do men prepare for war and busy themselves with constructing and sustaining the weapon systems of this day, this very hour?

Obviously, for those who can see the serpent for what it is, Love's sweet command, Don't kill, is good advice. But the prince of the world has a legion of apologists who tempt men to kill and destroy the lives of enemy and friend alike.

And what of myself? Why am I not building a hydrogen bomb in my garage? Why don't I carry an atomic bomb in the trunk of my car? Why haven't I hidden a vial of nitroglycerine in my rectum? By the grace of God am I kept from such folly. Why I haven't killed in Korea or am not now helping to destroy Moscow, Peking, and Los Angeles, is not for me to say.

If the serpent is not lifted up, we won't see it, even that brazen serpent of old.

Nevertheless, the Son of man has also been lifted up, even as Jesus said he would be. Let man be joined to God so that the Son of man and the Son of God are one. Who is the Son of man and who is a Son of God? Obviously, all those who are fathered by men and by gods. The mystery ever deepens.

The new heavens and the new earth are quite as enchanting as the old. We are full of knowledge, but what have we learned? I have learned that the Word has not passed away, and that those that believe in him have not perished. I have learned that the prince of the world is a liar, for his servants always promise one thing and deliver another.

Let me believe in Jesus whose words I have so that I might know his God. For why should I serve other gods? Unless, of course, it be my God's pleasure that I do so for the time appointed. For those of us who have visited hell, and observed its workings, and quietly analyzed the limits of its power, there is no fear of the place. Both death and hell are the products of man, and by man, might be changed. But man is inconstant in his resolve: fickle in his ambition: irresolute in his ways. Thus only God destroys hell and death.

You must see both the serpent and the Son of man lifted up to understand these matters. For ever since David, God himself has been active in the world, saving it from the sons of Belial who exploit it for their own petty purposes. God has kept his covenant: his laws are written within us. We need not receive the testimonies of men. But without Moses, how could one hear of Abraham, of Isaac, of Jacob?

There are more folds than one in Jesus' care: nevertheless, Israel is his for God gave him to her. Jesus and Paul, even as David and Saul are kings of Israel. Nevertheless, their journey is not limited to that kingdom alone. Men are infected with the madness of their own conceits. They are deaf to the truths revealed by prophets and astronomers alike. The image of man, as raised up by Nebuchadnezzar's command is worshiped because the daughters of music have made a noise in the land. The men who worship images and serve the state are mad. Surely the Son of man knows this: we are the sons of whatsoever fathers us. Lenin fathered the modern Soviet State: and Lincoln fathered this modern republic we so foolishly serve. How men can covet power in such governments and reject the government of God cannot be understood without knowing something of Moses and Jesus. For Moses forbad our idolatry and Jesus commanded our love of the Lord God of Israel. And these two angels of God are at war with the godless government of the world. Surely, it is not for nothing that Satan is known as the great deceiver.

All who kill, hate, fear, fine, persecute, and deceive their fellow men are of the State. We have no lord but God: Caesar has no claim on us: Christ's cloak is his own, even though another wears it.

Prison, Mammon, and the State are not the products of eternal life: they are not the safeguards of your soul: they are not the insurances of eternal life. They are the products, the living creatures, of those that breathe life into them. Kings, presidents, premiers and all the other princes of the world and lords of mediocrity delight in them for they are their idols of organization, of power, of lordship.

God loathes these things, and so do I.

Some of us have been cast into prison so that we may know how to destroy it. Every shepherd cast into an Egyptian prison knows this. Every shepherd is an abomination to the Egyptians: the master technologists loathe those who care for God's flock. Both Moses and Joseph wrought wonders in Egypt. Consequently, they were not impressed by the idols of Egypt. Neither was God: so he took his people out. Nevertheless, the Egyptians are also God's people: even the work of his hands. Joseph is embalmed in Egypt for a purpose. Jesus is also the son of Joseph. But the modern technologists are so busy embalming dust and worshiping forms fashioned of stone that they cannot understand Joseph is studying in Egypt.

Jesus is in Egypt studying the Egyptians for how else might one learn how to lead them out of their bondage?

For God so loved the world, that he gave his only begotten Son, that whosoever believeth in him should not perish, but have everlasting life.

What good could be simpler?

For God sent not his Son into the world to condemn the world; but that the world through him might be saved.

How is the world saved except through God's Son? The Egyptians think otherwise and are busy saving their world through their own idolatrous enterprises. Neither army, nor state, nor police, nor Jeffersonian declarations guarantee our liberty or make possible our freedom. Only by continuing in the Word are we made free. Any other method leads into the prison house of our own conceits.

Neither can the world be saved if you perish, for you sustain it and give it life. The world is the world of your experience. There is no other world open to you. I except the kingdom of heaven: for the kingdom of heaven is God's way of saving the world. All other worlds end.

The truth is plain. Don't confound it with verbally supported imaginings of the heart and mind. Our power of creation is limited by God. A witch doctor imagines what he images unto himself and does what he does. All men are known by the words they create and the lives they live. Hypocrisy is as real as the feeling which despises it.

51

Beware of the doctrines of hypocrites: despise these things as they arise in you. Let us not condemn ourselves with our own words. God is God. He is the same spirit. His love, his power, his compassion, never fail.

All our idols are vanity. God loves us even when we loathe ourselves. God saves the world through his Son. It is the Word working within us that saves us. Eternal life is ours: why should we reject it and embrace some idol we created?

He that believeth on him is not condemned: but he that believeth not is condemned already, because he hath not believed in the name of the only begotten Son of God.

The Lord God created man: but the Lord God of Israel fathered David. For in this manner was Jesus conceived by the spirit of truth: even by that spirit which is the life of God. God is a spirit, we are his spiritual children. For what are we asked to believe? Carefully consider the question. Men who have eaten of the tree of knowledge ask us to believe in the intellectual idols they themselves create and serve.

The sons of god who overcome the world, however, believe in Jesus, the only begotten Son of God, even our father and God's Son himself. For Jesus creates and fathers us with his Word. Men who are fathered by other men accept and believe in others and thereby become sons of Antichrist. Surely, the truth is plain enough for all to see. I am fathered by God: I am fathered by man. Yet I am mine own father.

In a strange and wonderful way I know these things are true. Men are children. Men are also the man, Adam; the created son of God who eats of the tree of knowledge of good and evil to his own hurt. The disciples of Christ, the friends of Jesus, are the woman, taken out of him, and given to him as a help meet for him. She is his wife. The men who know this truth are wed to him: others, all others, are guilty of adultery.

The marriage is spiritual and eternal. The city of truth, even the universe, the bride of our soul, is God herself revealing herself to us in all her beauty. Jesus is wed to God through his woman.

Children are innocent: as a child I know the pure in heart see God for what God is. But we do not believe in the Word, even in Jesus'

Word, and accept the doctrines of men, leavened as they are with all the corrupt and fanciful imaginings of their evil heart.

The serpent is a subtle beast of the world. Peter is Satan when he does Satan's will. Peter is a rock, a transformed stone, precious and powerful, when he allows the Spirit of God to move him to boldly declare Jesus is the Christ. Satan is consumed as we allow God's Word to destroy his works.

Our images of God are false. We reject God and believe in something else. Thus are fools, hypocrites, murderers, and whoremongers born. The field is the world and its serpent is subtle. The notion is hard to grasp. We become self deceivers, blind leaders of the blind; in one apt word, devils, when we do not accept God's truth. Satan is my adversary. I am his adversary.

What is true of me is true of all men. God fathers us as we reject the world and accept him. I am in heaven and men assault it with their legions. Truly, they are ignorant and know not what they do.

Let them see so that they might condemn that which is within them, even the foolishness of the ways of the world, and come to the light. Surely the ignorant need enlightenment.

Men are Adam because they are full of knowledge and believe this makes them as gods. But such knowledge only poisons them and they die. They require the tree of life to live, and living water to drink, and everlasting life to be welling up within them. And it is done with words: the words of God. For his word is both spirit and eternal life.

It is all so simple that all I can do is say that which I said before. The words shall not pass away. They remain ever coursing through us. We are born of the Word, and thereby overcome the world, and become the Sons of God. In this manner are gods created: even by being fathered by God.

And this is the condemnation, that light is come into the world, and men loved darkness rather than light, because their deeds were evil.

The hypocrisy of those who teach that the kingdom of heaven is a place our soul goes when our body is destroyed is a source of darkness. It is smoke from the pit of their own imagination. They poison and pollute the atmosphere of spiritual delight God provides. Thus great temples are built to house Herod and his priests.

Our body is the temple of spirits. It is the temple which God desires to reside within. The temple is destroyed by lawyers, by scribes, by Roman soldiers, by chief priests, by the elders of Israel.

Consider the trifles associated with atomic weapon systems as they exist at this hour. What do the emperors of Rome, the warlords of Washington, Moscow, and Peking, desire of their young men? Even the power to control the creation and use and deployment of these swords of death. They despise to take with themselves the sword of truth, even that single most effective weapon placed in the rock of God. And they covet the administrative power to build and deploy as many or as few nuclear warheads as their capricious and darkened souls might desire at this time.

Such men are mad: and those that serve them are servants and slaves. These men do not come to the light. For the light illustrates with his life that the commandment not to kill is to be obeyed.

You cannot serve God and the State. But men serve Mammon and mock God. Surely the power I covet is the power to quicken. The power to destroy the earth, to kill the body, to waste lives—such power is coveted by those who desire to destroy the world, and to destroy men's lives. The great destroyer is the Satanic power operating in the world which makes darkness real.

The kingdom of heaven is not of this world: it cannot come from this world: nevertheless, it is brought to this world by Jesus, through whom and in whom God works.

But the deeds of darkness are hidden by the princes of darkness. Let the president and senators of Rome explain how billions are spent for arms and millions are manipulated by mammon while their currency is engraved with these words: In God we trust. Surely, they are hypocrites and mockers of Christ.

They offer Jesus, nay they force it on him, the purple robe, the crown of thorns, the reed without power.

They do these things in darkness. But God has seen fit to disclose their actions to all in the world. Thou shalt not kill is God's commandment. We see how these brave men are able to keep it.

John brings the light to all men. His work remains: eloquent testimony to the nature of God and his first begotten son. First begotten, since God has fathered many sons since then. John is a son of thunder sitting on the right hand of Christ. His work is wrought in Christ. His truth is his work in the world. Without his gospel how could we know of Jesus and his God? Obviously the words of John, even as the words of Jesus, are with us today. Why then should we busy ourselves with the works of darkness? Who are these men who steal our life with their deceitful systems of taxation and puerile laws and sinful doctrines? Who are these men of Mammon and of the State and of the Church? What do they want from us? Our work, our talents, our monies, our belief? Surely, they covet our lives and wish to destroy them in their silly wars, their silly enterprises, their vain and puny idolatries. Condemn their doctrines as they rise within you.

The kingdom of heaven is like a tree growing within you: but the tree yields its own seed and becomes a forest. We are the trees planted of God; but this is only a proverb, an illustration of basic truth. Your heaven is nurtured by sunlight, water, bread, and the spirit of God who provides all these things.

Don't corrupt yourself with the doctrines of death. The destruction of the temple is real. Men do destroy our bodies. But what of that? They only hasten the time of its resurrection. Darkness has had an hour of power. But what of that? The times of light are eternal. We pass through the valley of the shadow of death

The deeds of men are evil. Why should we be like them? The kingdoms of God are vast. And all the kingdoms of the world together are small.

Love not the darkness. In it no man can work. Build your house in the light. It is easier that way.

For every one that doeth evil hateth the light, neither cometh to the light, lest his deeds should be reproved.

The spirit of truth reproves. We wait for that Spirit in Jerusalem, even the new Jerusalem, even the city of David, the bride of our soul, the universe of our delight, the very city of truth itself. All the great works of men are there. What is a great work? A mother suckling a child with love and delight: a man fucking a woman with love and delight: such are the great works of great men. For how else might we once more raise up that which evil men have destroyed? How else does God resurrect the body? Surely, in no other way.

The resurrection of the body is an accomplished fact, a daily occurrence. But those who reject this truth are the Sadducees. They hate the light and won't come to the light. Therefore the light comes to them and they now have no place to hide.

But he that doeth truth cometh to the light, that his deeds may be made manifest, that they are wrought in God.

If we believe in the writings of Moses, in the statements of the prophets, in the words of Jesus, in the Revelation given Jesus via the angel, John, surely, then, we believe in the Lord God of Israel.

I dwell in new heavens, work in a new earth. That which is past waxes old before me. I've almost forgotten the ancient practice of Sodom whereby infants were stuffed in oiled jars and sold as one might sell patent medicine. The corruption opened to men is astonishing. Yet their power is limited.

The earth can be a prison: a brass ball of earthy forms: a carnal jungle of flesh feeding on flesh: an emotional sea of beastly forms. Nevertheless, making the Word flesh is God's way of saving the world. The world is the creation of men who use the power of words to quicken their desires.

Without the goodness of God, evil would overwhelm the sons of God even as it so easily kills the sons of men.

Without the light that God sends into the world, how could we know the truth? In no way: God's Spirit is the holy spirit, even the holy spirit of truth.

Knowledge is increased: many run to and fro. But what knowledge except more knowledge of good and evil? The earth journeys on amidst the glories of interstellar space: the stars move: angels reveal the mysteries of heaven and earth to men. And yet, in the light of what Jesus did, in the light of what he is doing, in the light of what he shall do, what other judgment is possible except to reprove the world of men for their disbelief, for their evil imaginings, for their filthy righteousness, for their sin? Let all the words and works of men be brought to the light, let them be examined in the light, and let us see what is good, what is evil, what is pure, what is corrupt, what is true, what is false.

Love God: despise idols. The works of the sons of men are vain. Why are we so proud? Are the works wrought by men in the world, the works wrought in states, in courts of law, in universities, in churches and schools various, the works of truth?

I confess my weakness: glory in my God's strength. The universe lovers create, the beauty God sustains, the abundance of life and joy in his kingdom is beyond my power of finding out. The sons of God are God's word made flesh. In this manner does the kingdom come. In this way is the world saved. We become the sons of God by overcoming the world.

If our life is lived in God, then, surely, all our deeds are wrought within him. In this way do we create the kingdom of God within us. Truth is the saving and comforting spirit. I lust after truth. It excites me. It ravishes me. It fills my soul with pleasure.

The words of Jesus judge us. The Sermon on the Mount is the way God judges the world. Let us work to build our house, even that part of the kingdom of heaven we build within us, upon the clear truth God has given us. Jesus is the Christ. His words creating our world bring heaven to earth. Whatever the world was, or is, or might be, we know that light and truth have come to earth because of God's son. We have overcome the world of men, and established the kingdom of heaven. No nation, no group of people, no government is superior to it: all the work of the sons of God is to this end, namely, to bring heaven to earth.

The Church says, Do this we ask of you, and die and go to heaven: or, even this, Wait and believe, and Jesus will come and take you to heaven. Strange doctrines of Pharisees and disciples alike who refuse to acknowledge the truth of God's response to their own prayer: Our Father, thy kingdom come. How is it then these many wish to go?

Did not Jesus say, even to his disciples, Lo, I am with you always, even to the end of the world? Surely, then, although he is in heaven, or hell, or earth, he hasn't left us alone. He is with us: just as much a son of man dwelling in and on this earth as these teachers of the doctrines of men who call him lord, yet do neither his will nor his father's will. Their will is done, and not God's. For if they were in heaven to work God's will they would acknowledge this fact. They care not to serve, nor to learn, nor to see, nor to listen, nor to understand with their heart.

Let God be king. None should own you but God, as one angel clearly expressed this simple truth. But men do not know God: For if they knew themselves as God's sons, they would not act like men, but as gods. But their wickedness in State and Church, in school and marketplace, is so great that they serve idols material, idols spiritual, idols intellectual; and scoff at Moses, who gave men God's first great commandment concerning idol worship.

Our prayer is this: Thy kingdom come, thy will be done: but the prayers of the world are this: Let our nation prevail, let our country live, let our flag wave.

I rejoice in what God has created. I delight in what God has begotten. What has God created? What has love begotten? Myself. The prince of the world, the father of the lie, has no power over me. His ways are not my ways. His lusts are not my lusts. His pride is not my pride. His children are not my children.

Nevertheless, his war is my war. I am his adversary. He is mine. Satan is also a work of God. His power is such as it is: he is many; I am one. He changes. I do not. He lies. I work to discover the truth. His power is his own. Mine, is of my God working within me. He owns the world. I possess mine own soul.

He feels nothing: I suffer all. He is a machine. I am a man.

Is this true? Of course it is true. You can analyze Satan, observe its work, witness its behavior, read its output. But you cannot see him for what he is, for he cannot work God's work in flesh and blood.

I am real as these words witness. But Satan is the child of spiritual wickedness: the accumulated power of evil dominating the heart, and soul, and minds of men who find this spiritual idol fascinating.

Truth is wrought in God: bullshit, in the idol.

After these things came Jesus and his disciples into the land of Judaea; and there he tarried with them, and baptized.

We need to be cleansed in God's land: Judaea is a kingdom of God, even the kingdom of the Jews, even that place, and those places on this earth, where God is worshiped in spirit and in truth. Who is a Jew? Even those who acknowledge the truth of Abraham's covenant with God, and God's promise to Abraham. Our circumcision is real. We cut off all the flesh round about our members of pleasure, carefully. Our spirit is circumcised. Why? So that we may delight in the pleasures of paradise.

All the disciples of Jesus, know of Judaea. They know that Bethlehem is the city of bread: the city of David, the singer of psalms, the second king of Israel, where the doctrines of God are formed, and found, and eaten. The wise know this, for why have they for all these years come to worship he who was born there? Nevertheless, let us worship God and know his son. His son seeks not worship, but love: even as he himself so clearly said. Let us not make of Jesus what he is not: and let us not presume him to be other than who he is. Unfortunately for many, they know not that only those who continue in Jesus' word are his disciples in deed. The words of Jesus are few: for the laws of God are few. Surely, even children may learn them easily. But to continue in the word is to discover the new Jerusalem, even a city of truth, a fundamental, and living, and literal, spiritual reality. The New Jerusalem is the city built by God. It is immense. Even the angels who are its chief architects are astonished at its dimensions. And so am I.

And John also was baptizing in Aenon near to Salim, because there was much water there: and they came, and were baptized.

We drink water. We also bathe in it and with it. Water is earth's solvent. We need much water to cleanse our lives from the filthy things the world has given us. We are born again of the water and of the spirit. The Word of God working within us is a cleansing agent. Surely this is the meaning of this one parable.

When we are nearly at peace with ourselves we may be baptized with the words of truth given to the world by John. What are those words? Even this, The kingdom of heaven is at hand; repent; the Messiah comes after me. Obviously, we need to be prepared for the words and works of Jesus by John. How could it be otherwise?

Is not the question profitless? Surely, the way it has been done is the way God ordained it would be done. The prophets of God speak in proverbs: but the message is plain. We need Jesus, the Christ, to save the world by bringing heaven to earth. If we cleanse ourselves from all other things the world has wearied us with, we can be baptized of John by believing in his life, his words, his message. John's testimony is true. Nothing found in the libraries of the world is able to make it untrue.

No amount of worldly opinion, power, and belief can void God's work. John is as necessary as Jesus. Those who believe John's words can believe Jesus' Word: for John spoke of Jesus. Anyone who immerses himself in the doctrines of those who baptize in the name of Jesus knows this.

The history of the world and the present state of the world necessitate John's work: his words of prophecy are needed: and supplied. For, in all truth, those that come to John discover there is much water there. There is so much truth in the world because of the prophets born of a woman, that even the Bible itself cannot be comprehended in any single lifetime. Surely, there is nothing in science new or philosophy ancient, nothing made manifest by modern technology or primitive myth, that can prove Moses a false prophet. Man's theories about creation are all nothing more than a vain attempt to substitute for the Word of God spoken through his prophet, and written by his prophets, the intellectual idols of those sons of Belial who can, at one time or another, worship anything save the truth.

But if such do not believe in the writings of Moses, they cannot believe in the message of John. Nevertheless, truth is eternal. The spirit, the comforter, makes strong. We become liars by believing in lies. We must be baptized with water and the spirit to cleanse our flesh and blood from the unfortunate results of such beliefs.

Only those near being at peace with themselves know they must go to John to be baptized. There is another baptism: the consuming fire of God's Word. Jesus stands in that fire. Those that understand this truth cannot be hurt by it. They are composed of it.

Water properly proportioned also produces explosive energy: and for those who can see it, fire becomes water, and water becomes fire, when the universe moves.

For John was not yet cast into prison.

Those who believe in Herod's way, in Herod's doctrine, in Herod's manner of life, do Herod's bidding, execute Herod's desire, lust after

Herod's throne. Such cast John in prison and behead the prophet of God. Why? Because they are blind to the end of Herod's temple and cannot even sense that its end is near. They are awed by what things men create and are not impressed by the works of God. And who is Herod? A king enslaved by the sight of a lovely dancing girl: and ignorant of the power and desires of the God that created her.

He should have taken the girl in whatsoever manner he wanted her: rebuked his foolish wife: and freed the prophet. Then would his palace have remained even unto this day. Men are misled of Satan: duped, deceived, cheated, enslaved. Every man is born to become a son of God. Yet so great is the self-creative power within them that they reject God and seek pleasure in the pursuit of their own idol.

God's works are of goodness and beauty and pleasure.

Then there arose a question between some of John's disciples and the Jews about purifying.

The questions remain to this day. John baptizes, the disciples of Jesus baptize, churches various baptize, and so does the spirit of truth. And Satan baptizes in pools of liquid excrement. If you doubt this, how can you explain these multitudes of men who profess belief in the God who commanded, Don't kill but love your enemies, who busy themselves with trafficking in the weapon systems of death and destruction? How can you explain churches praying for the kingdom to come while teaching men how to prepare themselves to die and go? How can you explain those who believe in the God of paradise who can't tolerate the thought of those engaged in sexual delights and fantasies? How can you explain these great men of the earth who write restrictive laws to make men free? How can you explain these many servants of the state who cannot forgive men their trespasses but must exact fines, imprisonments, and social castigation from their own brothers?

Let the Jews baptize: let John baptize: let the disciples of Jesus and the disciples of John baptize: let the Greeks baptize us with whatever wisdom God has granted them: let Herod himself learn to baptize: for the flood of nonsense coming out of the mouth of Satan has polluted us all.

And they came unto John, and said unto him, Rabbi, he that was with thee beyond Jordan, to whom thou barest witness, behold, the same baptizeth, and all men come to him.

How do we come to a man? By hearing his words, observing his works. But the greater works of a man are his words: for with words men order the house of their soul: work the spiritual processes of their own salvation: work ideas within themselves and frame the thoughts that lighten the world they see. Men come to Jesus, to John, to Mary Tyler Moore, to Billy Graham, to Alfred North Whitehead, to the Supreme Court, to Emerson, to Freud, to Julie Andrews; to teachers, supervisors, kinfolk, lovers, and friends. Why do men come to others? To learn, to hear, to see, to get gain; or pleasure, or approval, or applause?

I have come to the prophets of God to hear of the prophecies of God. I have gone to the angels of God to hear of the works of God, to the scribes of God to receive the writings of God; to the wise men of God to obtain the wisdom of God; to the fallen sons of God to see what idols they've created, to what depths they've fallen, to what hell they've created. The wicked and those that forsake God are transformed into hell by processes understandable. Where hate is engendered, murder results. Where deceit is practiced, liars prosper. Where sloth is advocated, feebleness follows. Where flattery succeeds, men are enslaved. Where lies are honored, Satan is king.

I am astonished at democracy: so many advocating one rule, so many another rule, and then subjecting themselves to do that which the majority agrees upon. Surely, lawyers are idiots. What is right, is right. The opinions of men, agreeing or disagreeing, are irrelevant to the truth. I can only state what is plain for all to see concerning these politicians. They have no stomach for truth: their only goal is endless debate.

No wonder God's commandment to forgive those who trespass against us is made null and void by these two-sided men. They profit from the spectacle: get gain from the show. No matter who wins, or loses; what law is passed, or repealed, the poor in spirit are taxed to make their vanity possible.

When we go to men, let us ask ourselves what we expect to see and receive. Men do well to go to John for he is a witness to truth as his words themselves witness. John answered and said, A man can receive nothing, except it be given him from heaven.

Heaven is that place where all good things are found, even HP-45 calculators which someone just took from me as I wrote these words. Obviously, even in heaven, men steal. Let men steal the words of Jesus and put them to their own uses. Are they still not his own words? The gift of God's son to the world: his Word.

The things of the world are created and destroyed. They appear, and vanish. They are put to use, and discarded. But the things of heaven, given to a man from heaven and received unto himself, cannot be stolen: for God himself is the guardian of the treasure house of our emotions.

Many things are given to a man from heaven: but what a man truly receives into himself is given to him from heaven. Our souls are given us of God.

We have a heart, a soul, a body, a mind. With these we enjoy life. We receive the good things of heaven. But what do we receive from the world: what can we really receive from the world? The disciples of Jesus receive this in the world, even tribulation.

Ye yourselves bear me witness, that I said, I am not the Christ, but that I am sent before him.

God sent John into the world to bear witness to the coming of Jesus. If Jesus had not come, what use would have been John's witness? John received this also from heaven.

He that hath the bride is the bridegroom: but the friend of the bridegroom, which standeth and hearth him, rejoiceth greatly because of the bridegroom's voice: this my joy therefore is fulfilled. He must increase, but I must decrease.

But only for a time. The kingdom of heaven grows within John, even as it grows within all that receive its seed. The world is one way of conducting the business of life in earth: the kingdom of heaven is another way. John has increased. John baptized thousands: but his spirit, multiplied millions. The kingdom is brought to earth by men who receive it first into themselves and then let it branch over into the world.

Those that love have the bride: we are the bridegroom. So is Jesus.

He that cometh from above is above all; he that is of the earth is earthly, and speaketh of the earth: he that cometh from heaven is above all.

Men who know not God receive nothing from heaven. They are of the earth, and speak of the ways of the earth. The theory of evolution, materialistic doctrines, scientific numberings, economic ideals, such earthly things fascinate them. In a way, it is all they have: all they have ever received: it is their only knowledge. I often forget this simple fact. So do most of us. But John now reminds us of it, and it is good to examine this truth once more.

And what he hath seen and heard, that he testifieth; and no man receiveth his testimony.

Who then shall receive it? The children of God, even those who are much more than man. We limit ourselves by our own limited beliefs. Our doctrines are crude: rudimentary: mythical: enslaving. But the doctrines fashioned for us in heaven are the bread of life. We are born again when we receive the testimony of Jesus.

He that hath received his testimony hath set to his seal that God is true.

What is our seal? Our hope in Jesus. The kingdom of heaven shall break up and overcome all other kingdoms. History, rightly read, righteously written, is a record of this process. But there are other records within us. Our dreams: our thoughts: our impulses: our faith—all these are the promptings of the spirit within us to accept the truth and reject the lie. Men are mortal only because Satan has caused them to make themselves so by giving them bad advice. Surely, God is true: Satan is false.

For he whom God hath sent speaketh the words of God: for God giveth not the Spirit by measure unto him.

God has given us all things: even life everlasting. The men of the world reject it. What is the controversy between men and God? What really is the problem? Why all this evil?

Evil is the degradation of our souls. It is personal: horrible: grotesque: hideous.

I know of worlds where beauty is everywhere, where delight and song and love are the eternal celebrations of the heart. But this world is an anachronism. All is measured according to time: the reality of eternity is here conceived as a poetic fancy whereas in all truth it is obvious and fundamental fact. God is a Spirit and the Father of heavenly spirits. The Word and the Spirit are one in thought, in dream, in impulse, in heavenly reality. But men create sprits of another order, a lower kind.

The Father loveth the Son, and hath given all things unto his hand.

And men steal all things from him. They do not wish the Son to rule with love. They have other ideas. They desire another king. They love opinions more than truth. They hate the Son because he testifies to the evil that is in the world. They hate the Son because he brings light to the evil thoughts of men.

He that believeth on the Son hath everlasting life: and he that believeth not the Son shall not see life: but the wrath of God abideth on him.

What does God do when he is angry? He treads the winepress wherein the grapes of wrath are stored. Why? Obviously to make new wine. Shall we drink of the cup of his indignation?

Our power is real. We can lie, deceive, lust, defile. Our power is real. We can live the gospel, enlighten, control emotion, cleanse. Obviously, choices are made, decisions rendered. Men are ever learning and never able to come to knowledge of the truth. Why? Because they believe that what they have learned is the truth and that therefore they have no need of it. I am astonished at the quickness with whch men wish to promote false doctrines which they recently acquired. Teenagers and octogenarians alike are full of matter. Even the present governor of California has his opinions as to the amount of water to be used in a flush toilet.

Anyone who enters hell and walks about the place recognizes the need to dump the entire garbage pit into a veritable lake of fire. In no other way can the energy of the place be quickly used. God's word is a consuming fire.

Joshua's garments are filthy: David is a man of blood: and what man knows Jesus? All one can say is that the Word of God is in battle with the nations. Their ways are not his ways. Jesus is incredible: to free men from the State, from the Church, from Mammon, from the power of the lie; from fear of death, from Death itself; and to bring heaven to their heart, and mind, and soul, and body; to conquer hate, foolishness, greed, and blind stupidity; to bring eternal life and the kingdom of God to mortal men, is an incredible work. It is no wonder there is no faith in the world, no hope with those in hell, so very little truth in the churches: for what man really believes in Jesus? It is also no wonder God loves him: What God could not?

The ideals of men take on flesh and blood. War, prisons, world courts of opinion and of law, are some of the many shallow ideals men have realized and established in the world. It was and is in their mind to do such things; and they did them. Behold what they do: see what they bring forth.

Men have been overcome. They concern themselves more with the forces of appearances than with the reality of living fact. Jesus' image, his appearance, has been marred beyond description. It is no wonder men are overcome by the world. Men elect presidents and other servants of the state. And presidents and other office holders disobey God's commandments. For the love of God, men reject: and the love of law and the love of self, they accept. Men desire to be presidents, to be senators, to be chief men, and priests, and managers. To what end? For what purpose?

What is taxation? Socially organized theft. And all the issues with which the candidates and incumbents alike busy themselves consists of nothing more than how the stealing is to be implemented and how the grand deception is to be sustained.

From whence come these mad desires to rule and govern and exact? Has not God said, Do not kill? Do not steal? Love?

I hate my life in this world. I find death a bore; war foolish; and prison inconvenient. But I love the world wherein the kingdom of heaven grows. Surely, in such a world I rejoice.

Incredible truth: the State has warred with the saints and overcome them. For the saints themselves support and prophesy the doctrines of

Death and of Hell. Let no man deceive you. If he has not been and is not now in heaven, he knows nothing about it, and all his words are vain. How are men overcome by the beast? By being killed or cast into prison by it? No. But by living to excuse its evil and hiding its sin. They damn their enemies and thereby condemn themselves.

The kingdom of heaven has been in the world, and found in the world, ever since John and Jesus taught men to rejoice in this fact. But the men of earth, the statesmen, cannot acknowledge this fundamental historical truth. Why? Because, if they did, they would know God as Lord, and could not concern themselves with the affairs of Roman law, Roman justice, Roman virtue, and Roman ways.

The love of our enemies is our response to their hate. The truth we speak, is our response to their lies. Our love of life and praise of God is our response to our father and creator. Surely, their love of death and glorification of the prince of this world, is their response to that spirit of Antichrist which fathers them. That God's Word is made flesh is denied by all who fail to seek the kingdom of heaven in earth, and flesh, and blood; and to find it in the world.

Any child of god who enjoys fucking one she loves knows these things to be true. But even the disciples of Jesus keep little children from him. Why? Because they fear he might corrupt them with his love of pleasure and of life.

Surely no man knows the Son: for if they knew the son of God, if they knew the son of man, they would no longer be men, but the sons of god, and thereby, gods.

Men have corrupted themselves with their own wives, with their own children, with their own beasts. How? Even as did Herod. Surely, a king ought not to behead a prophet sent by God because of the desires of his wife and the foolishness of her daughter, no matter how beautiful, how sensuous, how sweetly enticing they both might be. Surely, a king ought not to command his servants to slay a man sent by God in order to satisfy the expectations of the beast which grants him his power.

Men inherit positions of authority in social systems and become slaves of the system. God's commandment, Do not kill, is not repealed simply because you have a modern weapon system at your disposal.

The sons of God war against the beast: the sons of Satan war against the Son of God with the beast they have corrupted. They hate the truth. What is the truth? They have corrupted the beast.

They have programmed the State for the destruction of all flesh, placed this abomination within the temple of the human heart; and now worship it. Godless World Government is now the only hope of the angels of pride. Truly, they know not what they do. And all this because they refuse to receive truth from the kingdom of heaven.

CHAPTER 4

When therefore the Lord knew how the Pharisees had heard that Jesus made and baptized more disciples than John (though Jesus himself baptized not, but his disciples). He left Judaea, and departed again into Galilee.

Why? Because the Pharisees do not wish to be immersed in the words of truth both John and Jesus have provided for the people. The Pharisees come to John and to Jesus and to the disciples of both, to trouble them, not to believe them. Though a man be baptized with the words of truth, literally immersed in the Word, it cannot make him clean unless he also believes.

There is also another cleansing, a baptism of fire. I do not say that a man, any man, has a choice in this matter. What is true, is true. Our belief has nothing whatsoever to do with this fact. Only fools zealously promote the contrary doctrine. Beware of it.

Baptism without belief is useless ritual. For men, belief in the truth without baptism is impossible. The Pharisees still seek to justify their silly vanities to all men. It is no wonder both Jesus and the Lord left the kingdom of the Jews to work in the country of the Galileans. What can you say to those who believe pouring water on a body or dunking a body in a river can save a soul? What would you say to such men as you saw the living universe of truth, even the spiritual bride of a man's soul, prepared for him of God in heaven, coming down from heaven to the earth? The quick know that the New Jerusalem is with men, and that the glory of the kings of the earth, even the kings which God made and appointed, bring their glory and the glory of the nations into this city. But who is such a king? Paul is such a king.

Nevertheless, the Pharisees, the Herodian's, and the Romans have other kings—the present living servants of the prince of this world.

And he needs must go through Samaria.

Samaria, the country lying between Nazareth and Jerusalem, between Galilee of the nations, and Judaea, the kingdom of the Jews, is also the country where the settled and filtered waters of Jacob's well are found.

Then cometh he to a city of Samaria which is called Sychar, near to the parcel of ground that Jacob gave to his son Joseph.

Joseph who rules and studies in Egypt also has a parcel of ground in Israel. Does a prince of Egypt hold title to a parcel of ground in Samaria? Of what use is this parcel to Joseph?

Now Jacob's well was there. Jesus therefore, being wearied with his journey, sat thus on the well: and it was about the sixth hour. Then cometh a woman of Samaria to draw water: Jesus saith unto her, Give me to drink. (For his disciples were gone away unto the city to buy meat.)

Shall Jesus drink of Jacob's well? Could Jesus drink of this well if the woman of Samaria helped him draw out water from the depths of time and space which separated Jesus from Jacob, and Joseph from Jesus? Of course, for the well is also a gift of Jacob to his children: the well is deep; the time is long; much has come and gone, came to be and passed away, yet Jacob's well remains, a temporary, but satisfying reminder, that the Lord God of Israel is also one Lord, and therefore the living God of Jacob, Joseph and Jesus, as well as of the Samaritan woman.

Then saith the woman of Samaria unto him, How is it that thou, being a Jew, askest drink of me, which am a woman of Samaria? for the Jews have no dealings with the Samaritans.

The Jews do not drink of Jacob's well: they are not fathered by Abraham: they are a holier-than-thou group of stiff-necked people who cut themselves off from the living water and testimony of blood brought into the world by Jesus. Such are the Jews in the earthly sense. In the spiritual sense all the nations of the world have been blessed by the sons of Israel. But the Word was made flesh and dwelt among the Jews: and they still deny this. What can you tell these then when you see the Word being made flesh in the world and thereby overcoming the world? The Jews are too busy with the affairs of the world to understand, let alone see, the living reality of the kingdom of heaven. Such are my hardhearted children who have corrupted themselves with their own foolish idols.

Let God transform their hearts of stone with hearts of flesh into hearts of flesh—for why should any be lost? Judas need not repent and hang himself. He need only repent and believe the gospel.[1]*

Jesus answered and said unto her, If thou knewest the gift of God, and who it is that saith to thee, Give me to drink; thou wouldst have asked of him, and he would have given thee living water.

Materialists can find life in water and, in their imagination, produce doctrines concerning the emergence of life from antediluvian seas. But how hard it is for them to see the power of the living word giving life to the souls of men! Yet their lies live by the life giving power of their own words. Men are more curious about the processes of life than they are about life itself. The tree of life; the living water; the bread of life: what are these to the dead? Words, when drunk, that produce life. Eternal life is the everlasting life of God.

I know this to be true. I am tired. And thirsty. Let the woman give me a drink so that I might give God's gift to her.

The woman saith unto him, Sir, thou hast nothing to draw with, and the well is deep: from whence then hast thou that living water? Art thou greater than our father Jacob, which gave us the well, and drank thereof himself, and his children, and his cattle?

Yes. For my dream is truth.

---

[1] * And perhaps, preach it!

Jesus answered and said unto her, Whosoever drinketh of this water shall thirst again: But whosoever drinketh of the water that I shall give him shall never thirst; but the water that I shall give him shall be in him a well of water springing up into everlasting life.

How true.

The woman saith unto him, Sir, give me this water, that I thirst not, neither come hither to draw. Jesus saith unto her, Go, call thy husband, and come hither. The woman answered and said, I have no husband. Jesus said unto her, Thou hast well said, I have no husband: For thou hast had five husbands; and he whom thou now hast is not thy husband: in that saidst thou truly.

Nevertheless, drink, and know that I am your husband.

The woman saith unto him, Sir, I perceive that thou art a prophet.

All who drink of the deep truths found in Jacob's well are capable of this perception.

Our fathers worshiped in this mountain; and ye say, that in Jerusalem is the place where men ought to worship.

The new Jerusalem is a city of truth. It is built with words of truth by the Jews, the spiritual and circumcised sons of Israel. The gates are real, studded with the pearls of their belief. But the universe is vast as may be seen by all who worship at this city. Men have worshiped at Jerusalem: but the kingdom of God is the living spiritual reality growing within you. There, in spirit, worship God: and in future you'll be giving me living water to drink. The sands of time will one day dry up Jacob's well. Times pass: even as do heaven and earth. But eternity remains ever being what it is. Believe in life and become a child of life: and you'll never thirst for love or want for a husband: for all this God shall provide, abundantly.

Jesus saith unto her, Woman, believe me, the hour cometh, when ye shall neither in this mountain, nor yet at Jerusalem worship the

Father. Ye worship ye know not what: we know what we worship: for salvation is of the Jews.

These Jews are those Jews who are sent into the world by Jesus to overcome the world by bringing heaven to earth. The sons of God are gods and to one another are not unknown as the angels of God testify. Every writer instructed in the ways of heaven knows this. The truth is plain: Truth, beauty, and wisdom are brought into the world by those who have found it in heaven. Your mansion is great, your house beautiful. Don't neglect to drink of this living water.

But the hour cometh, and now is, when the true worshipers shall worship the Father in spirit and in truth: for the Father seeketh such to worship him.

(The Father also seeks so that he might find.)

God is a Spirit: and they that worship him must worship him in spirit and in truth.

The words are spirit and truth. What more need be said?

The woman saith unto him, I know that Messias cometh, which is called Christ: when he is come, he will tell us all things.

And so he has.

Jesus saith unto her . . .

(And where is Jesus now?)

I that speak unto thee am he.

It happened all so long ago. Who can remember these things except a book of life, a very living book of remembrance had been written? We jot down notes to remember trifles. Shall not gods write books to recall ancient truths? The scroll of time is unrolled before us. What do we read? What is written? Salvation is of the Jews, even all Jews. Without Abraham's seed what might the world become? God's disaster. Christ is the Savior of the World, even the world wherein our heart, soul, mind and strength are found. The world which God created for us and which Satan and his legions ever so long have labored to destroy.

And upon this came his disciples, and marvelled that he talked with the woman; yet no man said, What seekest thou, or, Why talkest thou with her?

The disciples often marvel at where and with whom Christ seeks the lost sheep of the house of Israel. Why, in all these years, do men fail to understand that God seeks to find those in the world who are willing to worship him in spirit and in truth? God does more seeking than men, much more.

Men, like sheep, require shepherds. We are taught. We learn. We accept opinions. We follow. But the house of man is divided. How can the followers of Muhammad, of Buddha, of the Soviet Communist Party, of the doctrines of the Mormon Church, of Science so-called, be reconciled to the spirit of God? Only by being cleansed and born again. Surely the will of God must be wrought in a man if that man is to become a son of god who enjoys eternal life.

We are astonished at the works of God, and rightly so. Muhammad is a false prophet, one of the greatest, if not the greatest. Lenin and Marx are also false prophets. The pope is a living and extraordinary example of a Pharisee. The Mormon Church is a modern example of how social organizations called churches get started and flourish: and then entangle themselves in mystical nonsense. The story of Buddha is an illustration of how a man's image can be corrupted by intellectual sloths and priestly dullards. And what is Science? Is Isaac Newton unscientific because he defined space as the unbounded sensorium of God?

Obviously, considering the many things in the world that are mixtures of good and evil, fact and fiction, myth and reality, we need a Messiah to come and tell us all things. Surely, Jesus knew that those who draw water out of Jacob's well are also desirous of knowing whom to worship. The Jews know. I fail to see how the technology of Egypt or the wisdom of Greece or the statecraft of Rome or the many myths of religion have any power to detract from the fact that God saves the world through the Jews.

Isn't it true that much religion is vain, foolish, and literally speaking, unprofitable idolatry? Isn't it true that a Mosque or a temple

74

erected in Jerusalem is an illustration of Herodian vanity? What pharaoh could now induce the Egyptian people to erect a pyramid in honor of his earth-born conceits?

Now the truth is plain: many worship they know not what.

Every religion in the world has its own mountain, its own angel, its own guiding spirit. Better to drink of Jacob's well than to worship on the Mormon mountain. Surely it's more profitable to believe in Jesus, and accept his words concerning God and the kingdom of heaven, than it is to enfeeble oneself with unleavened doctrines rather than God's meat.

Religious temples are vain. A Persian love palace would be more appropriate to house the God who is love. But who is to say where God is or when he shall come or how long he shall stay? We are only his sons. Let's not deceive ourselves into thinking we can keep God from seeking his own pleasure.

There are countries where God rules and of which we know nothing.

Jesus talks with the woman to get a drink: obviously, Jesus also is refreshed by the water found in Jacob's well.

Salvation is of the Jews but the Samaritans, and Greeks and isles yet unknown also play their part. God's work in the world is to save it. Surely, this must give him pleasure.

The woman then left her waterpot, and went her way into the city, and saith to the men, Come, see a man, which told me all things that ever I did: is not this the Christ? Then they went out of the city, and came unto him.

Obviously, the woman who could draw water could also draw men to Christ.

In the meanwhile his disciples prayed him, saying, Master, eat.

The disciples of Jesus find things for Jesus to do. But Jesus also has his work to do: that work which is born in the will of God: that work which God started and Jesus finishes.

In one real and undeniable sense, the work is finished. It is done. But the new heavens and the new earth are before us and we can see the creative activity of God taking place before our eyes. The forests are harvested; furniture and homes, are built; paper and products various are produced. And God causes the forests to grow again. The beauty or the ugliness of these processes are very much a function of how men work with or against God.

Our work is to do God's will and how can we know his will unless we know that God?

But he said unto them, I have meat to eat that you know not of.

To do God's will is to be made strong: for God supplies the power required for the work at hand. But being made strong, we can still avoid the work. Our potential power, so carefully acquired, remains unused, locked up in the strongbox of our own private fears. Men know what is good: see it clearly before their eyes: but oftentimes turn away, sorrowful. Why? Our will is our will: the will of a man is the will of that man. It is that which it is. So is it with God. God seeks and finds: God promises and fulfills: God hides and discloses: God gives and takes away. For such is the way of life.

We are imperfect craftsmen all. We must see our work, and judge it. The work we do may be evil. Then let God help us by instructing us how to destroy it, or make it good. God also saves. All too often, the angels forget this facet of God's nature.

I am impressed by my ignorance, immense as it is. I am placed in the garden by a creative power whose voice I hear, whose genius I worship, whose love I experience. Yet with the single eye of God we see God's work. Surely it is good.

Satan is also working its work: and his work is evil: Elihu knows this; as does Job, as does Jesus, as do all who suffer persecution for righteousness sake. What then is the work of Satan? That work God destroys: God hates: God despises.

All that is not of love, truth, and beauty is not of God, but is now of Satan.

Therefore said the disciples one to another, Hath any man brought him ought to eat?

For some reason which the disciples themselves must make known to themselves, they cannot understand that God's will is accomplished through his sons. We overcome the world by refusing to be governed by it. Its laws, its rules, its customs, its economic, material, and spiritual ways are not our ways. Our desires are higher. Our desires reach God and are born in heaven. The kingdom of heaven is the dream of Jesus realized in earth: it is his father's gift to him.

This is our task: to bring heaven to earth. Only meatheads can't understand this. Their minds are full of earthly matters and they cannot sense the beauty of twilight or the holiness of dawn.

Men still buy meat, and sell it. But God freely gives. The servants of Mammon use us cruelly. All the good things of earth, as well as many evil things, are expensively priced, meticulously numbered, wastefully hoarded. The greed of the mammonites is great. Even the disciples of Jesus, even those who bring heaven to earth, must buy bread and meat. The miracle of God is even this: the seed along the wayside, on stony places, among the thorns, also grows, and yields fruit. Even I marvel at the power of God to bring heaven to earth.

Nevertheless, the highest yields are found among the good ground.

Jesus saith unto them, My meat is to do the will of him that sent me, and to finish his work. Say not ye, There are yet four months, and then cometh harvest? behold, I say unto you, Lift up your eyes, and look on the fields; for they are white already to harvest.

The worlds found in the world are many. And many worlds are profitable for our heavens. For the heavens are composed of many worlds, many moons, many stars, and vast spaces.

Julie Andrews is a star, and the world of Emerson is real, and the thoughts of Plato also give light. Surely all these are in my heavens.

Without those angels who create beauty and wisdom, and display the glory of God, in their lives and works and words, what is life?

There are and have been righteous fields to harvest ever since Jesus pointed out this truth to his disciples in those days now long past.

And he that reapeth receiveth wages, and gathereth fruit unto life eternal: that both he that soweth and he that reapeth may rejoice together.

To sow love, and truth, beauty and joy, in the worlds of men, and to reap these fruits, is to enjoy eternal life, even the life of God.

And herein is that saying true, One soweth and another reapeth. I sent you to reap that whereon ye bestowed no labour: other men laboured, and ye are entered into their labours.

How very true. The stars are beautiful: the children play: the meek have inherited the earth: my cup of love is full: and the beauty of heaven is more than my eyes can search out.

We reap what we have sown, and much, much more. The sowers of God are many.

And many of the Samaritans of that city believed on him for the saying of the woman, which testified, He told me all that ever I did. So when the Samaritans were come unto him, they besought him that he would tarry with them: and he abode there two days.

How much can you tell men in two days?

And many more believed because of his own word; And said unto the woman, Now we believe, not because of thy saying: for we have heard him ourselves, and know that this is indeed the Christ, the Saviour of the world.

Do men believe the women who attempt to bring men to Jesus? Do men believe the disciples as they attempt to lead men to Christ? Are these attempts vain? Why do men believe anything?

Because of words spoken, words written, words internally created.

Antichrist wants this doctrine to be believed: Christ is not come in the flesh. Such is that spirit of Satan that he craves to rule the world of earth, of flesh and blood. They want no paradise, no garden of God on earth, no kingdom of heaven come to earth, no will of God done in earth, no son of God, or servants of God, enjoying the fruit of God's vineyard.

Law, money, man, church, state, custom, family—with such powers do Satan's angels keep us from believing in the ways of the God that created us.

To eat of the tree of life is to realize our divine desires and to participate in the pleasure of all created things.

Now after two days he departed thence, and went into Galilee. For Jesus himself testified, that a prophet hath no honour in his own country.

Why? For the same reason God is denied the pleasure of his own vineyard: for the same reason God is disobeyed in his own created Garden of Paradise: for the same reason the ignorant mock the learned: for the same reason the deceitful mock the honest: for the same reasons liars hate the truth. The choice is the man's, and he makes it. The decision is theirs, and they make it.

Then when he was come into Galilee, the Galilaeans received him, having seen all the things that he did at Jerusalem at the feast.

The feast of God is the banquet of truth to which all are invited: indeed, some accept gladly, others refuse to come, yet others have been compelled to come, and the feast is furnished with guests. All the works of the great men of the earth are found here. The works and words of angels and of devils: of great men of the earth: of rulers, of captains, of kings; of popes; of presidents, senators, counselors and statesmen; of authors various, scribes, scholars and historians without number; of poets, of philosophers, of comedians, of military men and soldiers of all sorts; of witch doctors, evangelists, actors, inventors, and reporters; of teachers, students, family, friends, and neighbors alike; of men ancient, and modern; the great men who influence our soul, all these are at the feast. We are full of the knowledge of good and evil: but so is God.

The Galileans are those who dwell among the gentile nations, even all the nations of the world. We come to the city of truth to eat the things God has prepared for us in life. We are made fat with the great sacrifice God has prepared.

What feast is this? Obviously, it is what God has set before us on the table of our mind. What we have eaten, is within us. What we see on the table before us, is what God has prepared. It is no more, nor less, than that which we see.

Is this a feast of the Jews? Of course, for truth is the Spirit that prepares all for us to eat. The Spirit gathers the fruits of all things before the table of our mind.

Surely, I cannot eat all I see: I am already fat, filled to fullness.

How do we eat the flesh of Jesus? How can we eat the flesh of all men? How do we eat of the fruit of the tree of knowledge of good and evil? How is it that some books are tasted, others chewed, yet others, digested? How is it to be understood that Jesus' meat is to do his Father's will?

What miracles are done at the passover feast? We see that the blood, the very living words assimilated in our body, of the Lamb is sufficient to cause the angel of death to pass over our house rather than come into it.

Death and hell sit upon the horses of thought and dream.

The miracles of Jesus worked at the feast are these: the spirits of life consuming the flesh of death. Where? Within us. God is a spirit striving in our flesh and in our blood, in the temple of our body. The Passover is a feast of the Jews because the Jews know these things are taught at Jerusalem, even in the city of truth.

The theories of men are varied. The doctrine of God is one. We've poisoned ourselves and died. Now God is with us in death raising us to life. The resurrection of the temple, as well as of the body, is real. Christ rebuilds the temple.

Surely, the Galileans, even those Jews who dwell among the gentiles, can see this. The opinions of the gentiles, the wisdom of the Greeks, the Baalim of all the heathen nations, are as spiritually real as those of Israel. But God chose Israel to live out in flesh and blood what in reality is true. The gentile nations are also overcome by their native idolatries but they don't possess the terminology, not even the fundamental words and definitions needed to explain to themselves, their own captivity.

The communist nations are governed by the living dead: the saints are overcome by the state, the very beastly idol they themselves choose over God. One cannot serve the God of life and truth and love with the powers of death and falsehood and hate.

The scribes of the modern age don't even possess the wisdom of Daniel to deal with the problem of death and hell. We serve a living God, love a beautiful spirit, dwell in a land of paradise and pleasure. We don't serve the images of man: we cannot prostrate ourselves before the state: we have naught to do with the evil doctrines wrought by foolish churches. The idol is doomed: the kingdom of earth is finished: the rule of the whore is ended. The kingdom of heaven is the kingdom of God growing within our heart, our soul, our mind; within the very mansion of our strength of being.

Satan is, and yet he is not: his nonbeing is also a form of being, as the angelic philosopher would express this truth. Satan, and its products, death and hell, are things to be consumed.

But only those few who can appreciate why God has prepared this feast whereof I speak can understand these matters.

Nevertheless, the miracles remain: in spite of all that has passed away, in spite of all the evil of which we have knowledge, those that have eaten the flesh of the Son of man still live. And for those who can see it, they can never die. The taking up and laying down of our life, is no more to be feared than the experience of one night's sleep. In all truth, the sleep can be quite enjoyable.

So Jesus came again into Cana of Galilee, where he made the water wine. And there was a certain nobleman, whose son was sick at Capernaum. When he heard that Jesus was come out of Judaea into Galilee, he went unto him, and besought him that he would come down, and heal his son: for he was at the point of death. Then said Jesus unto him, Except ye see signs and wonders, ye will not believe. The nobleman saith unto him, Sir, come down ere my child die. Jesus saith unto him Go thy way, thy son liveth. And the man believed the word that Jesus had spoken unto him, and he went his way.

The Word of God works in Jesus, and in those who believe in the Word, to accomplish its works in flesh and blood. The father turned the point of death away from his son by appealing to Jesus; by, in this case, literally coming to him.

Miracles occur. I am hard pressed, however, to explain to myself what in life is not miraculous. Miracles are associated with appearances and with knowledge. One man's miracle is another man's natural law. To my mind, Nature is the word God employs to summarize his creative work in earth. The God that created a body can heal it. This, to me, is so natural an occurrence that it is hard for me to see it as a miracle. What is the greater miracle, that Jesus speaks a few words and a man's son is cured, or that an event such as this is published among all the nations of the earth? What really is so important about one unnamed nobleman's son who dwelt in Capernaum years ago?

We must learn to believe without the necessity of seeing signs and wonders. As our wisdom and understanding and knowledge of God grow, old miracles are enjoyed as common fact, and new wonders are revealed which astonish us. Simply, as one angel expressed it, because we understand a miracle, it does not cease to be one.

God responds to prayer: so common is this occurrence that men no longer consider it miraculous that the God that created the heaven and the earth is able to hear and perform our requests. What astonishes me, however, is how some men refuse to acknowledge these simple, almost natural, facts of life, and in some instances, vehemently deny them. The miracle of sun, soil, rain, husbandman, vineyard, winepress, casks, bottles, moonlight, music, and Angie Dickinson doesn't impress them. But let them hear that the Son of God once prayed God to transform a few jugs of water into wine, and they will not believe it. Let those who got drunk at the feast answer them. The other miracle fascinates me more.

The story lives: and so does the son of the nobleman, and the nobleman as well. Where are they? I don't know. I don't even know whether or not Angie Dickinson ever got ravished after sipping a little wine. My ignorance is vast.

And as he was now going down, his servants met him and told him, saying, Thy son liveth.

Did he believe the servants? Do you?

Then inquired he of them the hour when he began to amend. And they said unto him, Yesterday at the seventh hour the fever left him. So the father knew that it was at the same hour, in the which Jesus said unto him, Thy son liveth: and himself believed, and his whole house. This is again the second miracle that Jesus did, when he was come out of Judaea into Galilee.

I love these Galileans; but surely God is their God and they may ask of him whatsoever they will and believing, He will do it.

CHAPTER 5

After this there was a feast of the Jews; and Jesus went up to Jerusalem.

The city of truth is often visited by the sons of God. There, feasts are celebrated: there, prophets are slain: knowledge brings pride, and even the sons of God get drunk, swell-headed, and slay the very men sent by God to rebuke them for their wickedness.

Nevertheless, wherein shall we assemble the Jews to consider these matters except in Jerusalem? And what is Jerusalem to the Gentiles? They know nothing, nothing of her glory. Nevertheless, even they shall come at the time appointed, for the appropriate feast. What they have trodden down, God shall rebuild.

Now there is at Jerusalem by the sheep market a pool, which is called in the Hebrew tongue Bethesda, having five porches. In these lay a great multitude of impotent folk, of blind, halt, withered, waiting for the moving of the water. For an angel went down at a certain season into the pool, and troubled the water: whosoever then first after the troubling of the water stepped in was made whole of whatsoever disease he had.

Why wait for troubled waters to cover us before we call upon God to heal us? Men make merchandise of God's sheep and have them wait upon angels. Cannot God do the work? What do we wait for? For whom is our disease being retained?

And a certain man was there which had an infirmity thirty and eight years. When Jesus saw him lie, and knew that he had been a long time in that case, he saith unto him, Wilt thou be made whole? The impotent man answered him, Sir, I have no man, when the water is troubled, to put me into the pool; but while I am coming, another steppeth down before me. Jesus saith unto him, Rise, take up thy bed, and walk.

Impotence is our unwillingness to let God empower us. We marvel at what controversy an angel might stir up within our souls. We often forget to rise, take up our bed, and walk out of the place. There is no reason not to leave the hospital if Jesus so commands.

Those who know something of truth realize the great potential within the human soul to cure its own disease. Freud is only wrong in his conceits, not in his discoveries. Catharsis is nothing more than the discovery as to how the evil spirit entered: it does not necessarily get rid of it unless the soul's waters be greatly troubled. Our power of belief is such that a stirring of our own waters could effect many a cure for the evils that afflict us.

One man was cured: many were not. Jesus did no more here than the visitation of the angel. What of all the rest? That is my problem and my God's, for I have laid it before him.

What is belief? Without it, what type of life is possible? What shall we believe? What do we pray for? What do we ask? What are we seeking?

This surely is my desire, to speak the Word and witness the cure. Let the angels explain how God did it: long, tedious, involved beyond measure, are their explications of established fact. But life cannot wait upon them. We act; observe; experience—explanations follow.

Let the disciples of Jesus do greater works than Jesus so that all of us might rejoice in the power which the God of love bestows on men.

And immediately the man was made whole, and took up his bed, and walked: and on the same day was the sabbath.

We must rest. Sleep, sabbaths, vacations, even the death of the body, are necessary. God's very nature requires it. To rest is not to die, but to repair and replace that which is broken and worn. Even with

God? Of course. Only idiotic scribes and Pharisees, and grossly stupid fools, can't see the necessity in God's creation for rest. The wicked never rest: it is one of the reasons explanatory of their nature.

Karl Marx comes to mind. The forces of Mammon exploit the poor working man; and classes of men, covetous of Mammon, war among themselves. And then, instead of resting after this profound discovery, he literally goes bananas over his own wisdom and hacks out a cave of greatness for himself in the mountain of bullshit which constitutes the modern economic world. Obviously, even angels require rest.

I admire God because of his ability to appoint and settle the times privately. Our powers are limited: our insights, constrained: our wine is bottled. He commands the day of rest because we require it.

The Jews therefore said unto him that was cured, It is the sabbath day: it is not lawful for thee to carry thy bed. He answered them, He that made me whole, the same said unto me, Take up thy bed, and walk. Then asked they him, What man is that which said unto thee, Take up thy bed, and walk? And he that wast healed wist not who it was: for Jesus had conveyed himself away, a multitude being in that place.

The world is crowded: the impotent and diseased are many: but the Jews who do not believe Jesus is God's son, can discover anyone walking about whose behavior varies from their own prescribed righteousness. For such the sabbath is not rest, but controversy. They praise not God on this day, but themselves. It is not a day of holiness and of God: a day of purity and love: a day of joy and delight. It is a day of pharisaical righteousness. Why must we gather here to perform the old ritual once more? Is today's gospel different from last week's? By now, don't we all know it? What's so difficult about loving God, anyway; isn't that the most natural of things to do?

Not with the Pharisees. They can't teach the gospel with their life, because they don't live it. They can't let it be taught in the schools, as all truth is taught; neither do they let people into the kingdom of heaven, for if they once got there, they wouldn't need their church, and the Pharisees would have no forum for their inanity.

Afterward Jesus findeth him in the temple, and said unto him, Behold, thou art made whole: sin no more, lest a worse thing come unto thee. The man departed, and told the Jews that it was Jesus that made him whole.

Sin tears us apart. Somehow our separation from the Spirit of Love brings disease to our soul: our power of life is thereby weakened. We become prostrate and impotent. Words are spiritual realities with which we command spirits. Somehow, our lies are responsible for our sickness and our death. The separation of God from the soul is real, and in the instance of innocence, undesirable. We simply cannot handle the spiritual forces working within us without God. Yet we reject him. Why?

Because of the power of the Satanic tempter. Many men contribute to the power of Satan because they lie: they deceive themselves and others. The poor in spirit possess the kingdom of heaven: and are kept by angels from the hideous evil which attacks that kingdom.

Church, State, Man: such are not abstractions but real and living antagonists, accusers, and adversaries.

I am called upon to deny myself a thousand times a day: the forces of hell are real: and many men take God's longsuffering for granted. Who makes him suffer? They do: they don't know what they do, and yet they do it.

Drug laws in this nation are real, and really enforced. Real lawyers, real judges, real prosecutors, real juries, real jails, real insensitive and supercilious politicians inflicting their foolishness upon those victimized by the ways of the world.

I know there is nothing possible from a drug experience save a little blowing of the mind, or frying of the soul, or stirring up of my unconscious sea of dreams.

A kiss could provoke as much. Of itself it is only an experience. But what has it really become in this real nation of states? A source of division; wasteful discussion; foolishness; economic chaos. It is really there: I see it, and at this moment my mouth is shut: my influence is small: my power is as nothing. I am in prison and all I can do is write this grievance.

What a man does with his own body is his business, his decision, and his alone to make. Surely, we can experiment, surely we can report, recommend, encourage, exhort. But to place a man in prison because he exercises his own powers of choice is legalistic madness. I hate these laws.

The penalty for sin is written into the creation. Drugs do what drugs do.

But the anguish in the world and the suffering which occurs because of self-righteous hypocrites taxing the people to promote their own ideals is vexing.

The impotent need to be made whole, not cast into prison. We need to develop power within ourselves: we hardly need these Big Brothers who are ready to accept a contrived moral judgment rendered beforehand by an assembly of judicial and legislative incompetents.

Why are they incompetent? Because if they knew what they were doing their laws would be finished. But they never finish legislating. There is no end to their work. And they can't agree. Their votes are divided. Their laws are not wrought in truth but in the opinions of majorities.

Lawyers make heaven impossible. God has already written his laws: why do we displace them with the inferior sentiments of men?

But this is one little problem: one trifling effect upon the way the world, at the very least, my world, really is.

Many are made whole by Jesus. Let the sin be forgiven. Let the man walk. But no, the goddamn hypocrites won't have a man carry his own bed, or even lie in it, not even on his day of rest. They know not how to raise up: they know not how to guide: they know not how to govern: they know not how to forgive.

But they know how to tax: they know how to promote their own laws: they know how to enforce: they know how to prosecute, how to imprison, how to war, how to kill.

If the doctrine of Karma were truly the way of God, the universe itself could hardly contain the worlds of horror wherein the Pharisees and lawyers of the world would have to be placed to pay their debts.

There are no prisons in heaven. Where God is king, no evil can come. But men insist on their armies, their police, their laws, their prisons, to deal with their brothers whom they believe to be their enemies. What man can slay me if God forbid it? What man can deceive me, if God disallow it? What man can terrify me, if God be with me?

And therefore did the Jews persecute Jesus, and sought to slay him, because he had done these things on the sabbath day.

The life of the spirit is hid from men. The sons of god know and are born in the spirit of love. Beauty bathes them in delight: they dwell in the garden naked and unashamed. Paradise and pleasure are forever theirs and all their women love them.

The things of the world are toys with which the children of men might play. All the world's a stage to those that so look upon it, and the drama of life ever portrays its scenes before us.

Why do men wish to keep me dead? Why slay me? What evil have I done? What lies have I spoken, what truth perverted, what beauty have I despoiled?

I testify of the ugliness in the human soul and openly despise the evil in the world and for this, they hate me. The world loves its own.

I work goodness on the day of rest and strengthen the weak to seek out the refreshing pool of their own sweet dreams. But they know neither the god that I am nor the God that sent me. They know no Lord God, have no knowledge of that God of gods from whence come all things. I testify that their idols are evil: that though they move, although they speak and influence and command, they are but the things they themselves created, the intricate automatons of the present hour.

Beauty and love and truth and pleasure are not found in the systems they serve. No, nor is there found in any of them, one drop of the blood of life.

But Jesus answered them, My Father worketh hitherto, and I work.

Men deny the work of God, though they use his works gladly. Men believe not the Son of man, though they raise his images on high. From whence comes love? Who creates the beautiful? How in all creation can truth be sent unless the Word be settled and found established in us and about us? What is the world which God continuously saves except it be those things of earth we use, and enjoy, and love, and create with words spoken, words written, words pictured; words transforming jots and tittles of ink into the music of poetry and the many arts of life? Men know not the Word creates and saves the world.

The Father of Jesus is God. Surely those born of his spirit know this to be true. What is his work except it be to give to those he loves the words of truth? The words do not pass away. They remain in us and grow. We speak with new tongues. Has literature no voice? Science, no truthful statements? Is art dumb, and without expression? Is music mute? And how could all these things have come into the world except the Word create them?

The Father works. Jesus works. We also labor in the vineyard.

Therefore the Jews sought the more to kill him, because he not only had broken the sabbath, but said also that God was his Father, making himself equal with God.

God is my Father and my bride, all the testimonies of men notwithstanding. My God is a strange God to men. So must the author of light and truth appear to those who love darkness and deceit.

The life of a man is focused upon his core of inner experiences. The forces of creation press upon him from all about. His is as a soul of earth trapped in the center of a planet. If he dig upward, or downward, forward or backward, right or left, it is all the same. The pressures of life pull and push against him. The more he moves outward, the greater the inward pull.

Then answered Jesus and said unto them, Verily, verily, I say unto you, The Son can do nothing of himself, but what he seeth the Father do: for what things soever he doeth, these also doeth the Son likewise. For the Father loveth the Son, and sheweth him all things that himself doeth: and he will show him greater works than these, that ye may marvel. For as the Father raiseth up the dead, and quickeneth them: even so the Son quickeneth whom he will.

The Son quickens all men. The universe is vast. The world is lonely. Heaven is sparsely populated. The children of Israel are scattered. But the spirit knows his work and the dead are quickened with the word, and the living brought into the realm of more abundant life.

We can do nothing of ourselves. This is the truth. But the men of the world set out to prove the opposite. Our inheritance is of God. Our body is fashioned of God. Our words are the words given us of

God. But men take that which is God's gift and put it to their own perverse use. Thus their works come to nothing.

Jesus acknowledges the simple fact that he is born of God, sent of God, is taught of God; that he sees what God does. Men refuse to believe him and busy themselves accomplishing that which in eternity is accounted as nothing.

We are sons and inheritors. God created the heaven and the earth. We live upon it and enjoy it. What could be more obvious than this? The poor in spirit possess the kingdom of heaven as do those who hunger and thirst for the love of God: the meek have inherited the earth, and those that mourn are comforted and thereby strengthened by God.

We are quickened by God, dead though we be. The resurrection of the body is an accomplished fact. Even Herod recognizes this to be true. And all these Sadducees in the world are the fathers of the lie they promote.

Surely the life I have within me is given me of my God.

The Word of God quickens the souls of men to the truth of eternal life. After men have killed the body, there is nothing they can do, absolutely nothing. Our soul is within our God and where we go they cannot come. And how could we be alive to these truths unless God's Word was with us? And surely the words of Jesus also quicken us with this truth. The Son not only brings light to the world, but truth as well.

For the Father judgeth no man, but hath committed all judgment unto the Son:

The Father is the officer, Jesus is the adversary, the words Jesus spoke are our judge.

But men speak other words: have appointed other judges, have filled the world with thousands upon thousands of adversaries and accusers. They judge men and have condemned them to the services of mammon, and of war, and of idol worship, and of hell, and of death. Let the dead not speak of life: for what do they know of it? By their own testimony they are dead. Let them bury themselves. Why should the living concern themselves with their ways?

That all men should honour the Son, even as they honour the Father. He that honoureth not the Son honoureth not the Father which hath sent him.

Men do not understand. I have given them the keys to the kingdom of heaven: what they bind on earth is bound in heaven: what they loose on earth is loosed in heaven. But their sins are many and in heaven they imprison their king and embrace the ways of Rome. They delight in the sons of the rabble and fear the power of Rome. The senators rule and legislate. Forgiveness is not in their hearts, neither do they love their enemies. They hate the God who would be lord of each and every man for they themselves crave that office and power.

They cannot forgive Patricia Hearst her minor trespasses. So hard are the hearts of those that serve law and the state. They cannot condemn the doctrines of Muhammad and of Lenin; of the Pope and of Lincoln; of Chairman Mao and the numerous other petty princes of this world who teach men how to hate, how to kill, how to war. They fear the military power of the Soviet Government, seek the approval of organizations various, and search out the public's opinion on matters profound and on matters trifling. Shall such rule your heart and soul and mind and life? Surely they divide you against yourself: your heart, to custom; your mind, to law; your strength, to the State; your soul, to Satan. And what do you receive for giving yourself to these things? Such a world as you now enjoy.

The deception is real: and worldwide.

Love God. Honor his Son. Overcome the world and be a child of God. Believe Jesus Christ is come in the flesh, for why should you be kept from eternal life?

Verily, verily, I say unto you, He that heareth my word, and believeth on him that sent me, hath everlasting life, and shall not come into condemnation; but is passed from death unto life.

This is a Passover all should enjoy. For why should the Egyptians not know themselves as the people God created? Muhammad is a false prophet. But that's his problem. Why make it yours? The communists, even all of them, are fools, for they say in their heart, There is no God. Shall a people who have gone through tribulation and death deny the judgments brought upon them by the God who takes no pleasure in fools? Hear the word of the Lord, and live.

Verily, verily, I say unto you, The hour is coming, and now is, when the dead shall hear the voice of the Son of God: and they that hear shall live.

These words are true, and were true for that thousand-year reign of Christ which is already past and finished. I am astonished at those who cannot see it. History is full of fables, but surely Paul reigned; Augustine lived; women nursed their children; monasteries were built; false prophets, heretics, saints and devils alike, had their time, their day, and passed away. Did Shakespeare write his sonnets in hell? Did Blake know nothing of heaven? Are Newton's works vain? Was Faraday a fool, Maxwell, a murderer? But the Whore glorifies herself with the works of genius and child alike, and denies the obvious fact that Jesus lived and reigned for a thousand years in the hearts of men. But not Jesus alone but all those who worked in his father's kingdom with him.

True, Satan is loosed from his prison. Once more the lie prospers. Once more petty tyrants of the spirit exercise their power, produce their smoke, bite their poison into men.

The Revelation of Jesus Christ is rejected. The history of Man is accepted. Nevertheless, what is this but the fulfillment of the prophecy of Jesus? I weary of the Whore and those that glorify her. Her controversies are pointless: her judgments are moot. I lived and still live and am where I am. What have I to do with her leavened doctrines?

For as the Father hath life in himself; so hath he given the Son to have life in himself.

Examine the life within yourself. Weigh in the balance scale of your own judgment what is true and what is false. Seek within yourself for the kingdom of heaven. Your garden of delight may be greater than all that the Whore of Babylon has gathered to herself. Babylon is the mother of religion and the whorish bride of babble. Is this our bridegroom? Is such the bride of our soul? Is such the bride of Christ?

Believe it not. God is our bride: and the universe of delight is her garment. But where is God to be found? Within each other.

And hath given him authority to execute judgement also, because he is the Son of man.

Jesus is the Son of God who becomes the Son of man by being fathered by man through the mechanism of the world. Nevertheless, he is also his own father as well as the father of many. And what of men? Are they not even the creatures of god who are born again as the Sons of god? Are they not priests and kings to God?

But know men by the fruit they yield: by the words that they yield with their mouths: by the sentiments they express, the opinions they hold, the matters of which they speak: By the power they covet, the things they believe, the lives they live. Perhaps, with God's guidance, you also may know not only how to choose the good and reject the evil: but in time, you'll know how to bring forth the good and cast away the evil, as it rises within you and branches outward.

We are also Sons of man; but Man, of himself, without the spirit of God breathing in him, is an idol. Worship God. God only is good.

Marvel not at this: for the hour is coming, in the which all that are in the graves shall hear his voice, And shall come forth; they that have done good, unto the resurrection of life; and they that have done evil, unto the resurrection of damnation.

There is a resurrection of the body: there is a resurrection unto life: there is a resurrection of damnation.

Men live and yet are dead: dead to the presence of God: dead to the power of his word: dead to the real life of his Son: dead to the truth of their own nature: dead to facts concerning the world: dead to the realities of space, of time, of an eternal universe filled with goodness and delight. Such walk in the graves of their own limited understanding.

The spirit quickens. Why don't we come forth unto life and embrace the God of life? Are his ways not good: are her ways not eternal? What do we fear? We fear this: knowledge of the evil within us: knowledge of what we are: knowledge of what monstrous sins we have worked: knowledge of the vanity of much of our life past.

Yet let the doers of good and the doers of evil rejoice in the nature of God. Isn't it true God is a God of mercy? A God of lovingkindness, a Creator longsuffering and patient, a Spirit whose Word is true? Surely this is God. Let us then damn the evil we originate, we nurture, we hold within the spiritual spheres of our own atmosphere of life, to that lake of fire which is the proper place for our pride, our foolishness, our envy, our doubt. Let truth ever dwell with us: ever be our Comforter: ever redeem us from the folly of the moment and the programmed evil of the day.

Hell and the beast belong to the fiery lake of God's truth. Death is real: hell is real: the State is real: Satan is real: but so is the lake of fire wherein all beasts and all false prophecies ultimately fall.

What then is resurrected unto life? Even our soul which is God created and good. What then is resurrected to be damned? Even all the evil within us we ourselves hold, cultivate, and cherish. Vengeance is the Lord God's and this is his vengeance and his repayment: that each living soul cast the hell and death he has within himself into the lake of fire prepared for it.

But how? Obviously, with these words.

With an evil eye a man accumulates within himself evil things. The eye of the mind looks into the house of the soul. But an evil eye washed by the power of God is no longer evil, but good once again. Thus those that see what they were can cleanse themselves with God's word.

I can of mine own self do nothing: as I hear, I judge: and my judgement is just; because I seek not my own will, but the will of the Father which has sent me.

His will is life everlasting for all those he has created living souls. Our power of life coupled with our pride of life, corrupts. We become corrupt trees: fountains of filthy waters: serpents creative of our own poisons. But where is the sting of death? Wherein lies the power of the grave? Even the child may play about the adder's den unharmed. In this new heaven and this new earth we know the God within us is everlasting Life even though we know of those that hold the doctrine of death and of where they sleep in their dens.

All the caves of unrealized desire in the earth cannot hide the proud, the vain, the foolish from the searching eye of God.

Those that sow the lie reap the whirlwind: those that sow truth reap the pleasures of paradise.

Poetical fancy? No, but living fact. Read the books of life and judge of yourself whether or not the God of Israel be faithful and true. For in this place, at this time, where are my enemies?

If I bear witness of myself, my witness is not true.

I bear witness of my God: my God bears witness of me. I testify of him: He testifies of me. Nevertheless, there are yet other witnesses in the world: even the clouds in heaven.

There is another that bears witness of me; and I know that the witness which he witnesses of me is true. Ye sent unto John, and he bare witness unto the truth. But I receive not testimony from man: but these things I say, that ye might be saved.

Saved from what? From the deathly effect of all the poisonous things we assimilate into ourselves as we carelessly eat of the tree of knowledge of good and evil.

Goodness comes from God: evil, from those who yield it. All this is personal.

But there is an impersonal beast in the world whose heads are pride, covetousness, envy, and sloth: causeless anger, gluttony, and lust. Of such, the lie is born and hypocrisy spawned. From such, states derive their power. The power to deceive, to steal, to teach war and hate; the power to mock truth, cover iniquity, and promote the ways of mammon.

Men will accept any belief, embrace any hardship, bear any yoke but God's. God bears his own cross.

He was a burning and a shining light: and ye were willing for a season to rejoice in his light.

The love of men is seasonal: the love of God, eternal. We rejoice occasionally. The sins of the world are many and heavy. But God who, according to Moses, created the stars also, takes the salvation of the world and the cleansing of sin in his own stride.

Men are proud: proud of what they are: proud of what they believe: proud of their judgments, their accomplishments, their intellect, their power of life. What is this pride of life which so infects a man that he murders in spite of God's commandment not to kill? God is blamed for every foolish and vain thing men do: yet it is obvious that much, albeit not all, that a man experiences is of his own doing. Let me not be so foolish as to forget my foolishness.

Truth is the saving spirit. But the power of this spirit, what man understands? I love the prophets of God: the poor in spirit: those who love the righteousness of God. But these many angels of God who make an image of God; and polish it; set it before themselves in their mind's eye, worship it with wondrous works in art, science, philosophy, and government: and then, most incongruously, condemn it—what can I judge of these? Where is the Deus of the Deists? The Allah of the Muhammadans? The Nature of the naturalists? The State of the Californians, of the people, of the proletariat, of the citizens of the United States? Where can I find these Gods? Gods who worship and destroy idols are devils, and full of death, activists though they be.

Men are full of the pride of life. Let me rejoice in my God, even the Lord God of Israel, and in his works, and in his children.

And I know what John testifies: his testimony is true. I know what all these clouds witness: and their witness is true. I see all these works, these real things really done. Beauty, starlight, and things to eat, and drink, and wear; and children playing in the streets, and homes where fear cannot enter; and the many houses wisdom has built—these are the works of God testifying to his presence. But let me add to the testimony, and give this testimony, my God is as real as I am. Surely God is not less real than his Word. The light of John burns in the hearts of men. And what is this except the spiritual truth that the words of John are within men, giving them hope: engendering belief: accomplishing their baptism?

But I have greater witness than that of John: for the works which the Father hath given me to finish, the same works that I do, bear witness of me, that the Father hath sent me. And the Father himself, which hath sent me, hath borne witness of me. Ye have neither heard his voice at any time, nor seen his shape. And ye have not his word abiding in you: for whom he hath sent, him ye believe not.

Why do men reject the obvious fact that God has sent his servants, prophets, wise men, scribes, alike, into the world to receive of the fruits of God's planting? Is not the kingdom of God, God's kingdom? Is it not within us? Then from whence comes all these men of the State dividing the earth into more than a hundred nations: and each nation into smaller states and provinces? From whence comes these armies of religion to produce their many churches wherein the light of truth is purported to shine? Let the disciples of Jesus judge in the day of judgment.

The Word of God must abide with us, or we do perish. Men are the authors of many words: the spokesmen of a variety of sentiments. Alone, ensconced in a strong tower, with provisions for a long siege laid up within and near at hand: we view the vastness of the desert wastes: the earth ever turns: the mirage of life changes before our eyes: our enemies never appear: why dwell we here?

I love the Lord God of Israel. He builds me a high tower from which I can see that desolation, death, and despair are the lot of those proud spirits who would bring forth evil forever. Forever proud, forever foolish, forever vain: such are those that war against me. I taste of all things: death, pride, despair are not strange to me. I know what is in me: these are also within me. Nevertheless, his word abides with me, and with his sword, his sharp word do I slay these horrible things that would destroy my soul.

God sent Jesus into the world. But men of the world want to kill him. Why? Because they are self-willed and want no part of the righteous God of life. They wish to prosper in their own lies: and so many of them do. They don't want God's word abiding with them, let alone within them. I don't blame them: for what mortal thing could endure immortal truth? Nevertheless, whatever is my God's is mine: and whatever I have is His: and no power can separate me from those I love. From the one comes many and remains one: I and my Father are one. From the many, men strive to make one. But they fail to note what really is true. The Lord God is one Lord, not many. Satan's house is divided: and those of his house divide themselves against me.

Many sins to bear: many nations crowned with power and life: many religions, many scientific opinions, many monetary policies, many evils ancient and modern: my adversary is legion.

I delight in the variety of life, in the many mansions of my father's house. They delight in their many opinions and their variety of conceits. I bear much sin within me. The imperfection of my ways burdens me with grief and sorrow. But God is everlasting and ever the same. I know of nothing in times past, or in worlds present, or in adventures yet to come, that can change the ways of my God. He is ever the same, even as I am. Heaven and earth pass away: hell and death, perish; and though once they were, and still are, yet they cannot be. God himself puts an end to our madness and folly. I am that end.

Search the scriptures; for in them ye think ye have eternal life; and they are they which testify of me. And ye will not come to me that ye might have life.

How much scripture do we have? How many words are needed? What amount of testimony will be sufficient? Men of doubt never have enough. The New and Old Testaments are more than even the greatest of God's angels and prophets can lift. If we then have our tasks appointed us by God, and these tasks are different, shall we then boast that God's work is other than one? Indeed, God's works are many: and there is no searching out the depths of his creation: no numbering of the limits of his power. But do men believe the testimonies, both new and old? Do men believe Jesus, who rose from the dead: do they believe Moses, who revealed God's saving work to man through Israel?

Isn't it incredible that men should yet believe in Jesus? The same Jesus who, incredible as it might seem, believed more in the God within him than he did in the tempter who came from without. What is all this Scripture worth if the Spirit behind it be not true?

Let Moses write words: let men copy them: translate them: interpret them. But if the words are not true, what use are they?

Men who indeed think they have Moses, and reject Jesus, have no scripture at all. The only thing they do have is their own doctrines. I am not alone. My father also works. His works are my witness that these words are true. Men who don't come to Jesus simply don't have life everlasting. All they have is their finite conception of their self-centered life.

I receive not honor from men.

If God honors a man, what might a man receive from men? Their love: but all true love is of God: love is the honor God bestows upon men.

But what is love? There is love of God, neighbor, self, the world. There is also love of the truth: this love is of God. It is the power to see things the way they really are. God is not inferior to me. His love is not limited by mine: his power is not constrained, as is mine: his patience exceeds mine own: his genius is beyond my reach. What then shall I claim for myself? What honor might I seek in heaven or in earth? Obviously, quite obviously, we do well to seek the love of God.

Let the Lord God of Israel be my father, so that I might know her as the voluptuous goddess of my soul. This is strange to men: and so must my God appear to those that worship the idols of their own mind. We are Adam. We are made in God's image. We are male and female. We are fathers and mothers and brothers and sisters who are divided among ourselves. Why? Because we do not search the scripture: for if we did, we not only would rejoice in Moses and David and Jesus and John and Paul, but also in the Lord God of Israel dwelling within us, and causing the tree of life to grow luxuriantly in our garden of delight.

But I know you, that ye have not the love of God in you. I am come in my Father's name, and ye receive me not: if another shall come in his own name, him ye will receive.

Again, and again, and again, I know men who will receive anyone except Jesus as the Christ of God.

How can ye believe, which receive honour one of another, and seek not the honor that cometh from God only? Do not think that I will accuse you to the Father: there is one that accuseth you, even Moses, in whom ye trust. For had ye believed Moses, ye would have believed me; for he wrote of me. But if ye believe not his writings how shall ye believe my words?

Men reject Jesus by rejecting his words. And this to their own hurt. But they also reject his disciples, his angels, his wise men, his prophets, his scribes. They reject the witnesses of the works of his father and the living presence of his Word.

Eternity encompasses all times. Heaven and earth pass. Yet we remain the same: the created children of the God of love of whom John wrote and for whom Paul worked and with whom, and by whom, and in whom, I am.

Men don't believe it. They'd more readily believe it of themselves than of me. But I cannot deny myself. That which is within me overpowers all the doubt, the fear, the foolishness, and all the many other vanities that men prepare for me. I am as I am and not as they imagine me to be. Let my God judge me. Men often forget that I also must believe in my own words.

CHAPTER 6

After these things Jesus went over the sea of Galilee, which is the sea of Tiberias. And a great multitude followed him, because they saw his miracles which he did on them that were diseased. And Jesus went up into a mountain, and there he sat with his disciples. And the Passover, a feast of the Jews, was nigh.

With words we look inwardly and search out meanings of events. What is the Passover feast? Where is the Sea of Galilee? Who was Tiberias? What was Tiberias doing when he was eight days old, as men measure the life of a body? What disciples were with Jesus? What were their ages, their names, their thoughts? How were they clothed? What was God doing at that hour? What were the names of all those who comprised the multitude? How many people of all the world since this event occurred have read about it?

Surely, we can ask questions by using words: but what god might answer them all?

We know the words are spirit. We know words stir up images. We know feelings, memories, notions and other words are produced by words. We know actions are produced by words and that neither truth nor the lie can be expressed without words. The word is made flesh: does dwell among us: the word creates all things.

How can Jesus make these things known to the multitude? Indeed a great company comes to him. But if they come, how can he feed them? What doctrines shall he bless and give to them?

When Jesus then lifted up his eyes, and saw a great company come unto him, he saith unto Philip, Whence shall we buy bread that these may eat?

Jesus looking to heaven knew what he would do. But Philip, later to be inquired of by the Greeks, knew not what Jesus would do.

And this he said to prove him: for he himself knew what he would do. Philip answered him, Two hundred pennyworth of bread is not sufficient for them, that every one of them may take a little.

Yet Jesus is the bread of life, the living bread which came down from heaven.

His spirit quickens. The words written are spirit and life.

The word is made flesh.

Our meat is to do our Father's will: for in this are we strengthened.

Jesus goes, the Comforter comes, but Jesus will come again. For the dead seed will not abide alone but bring forth much fruit.

The doctrines are not many. Neither are the fish. We eat the flesh of Jesus. We ought not to marvel then if we also eat the flesh of Paul and of John. What really is so hard to understand?

One of his disciples, Andrew, Simon Peter's brother, saith unto him, There is a lad here, which hath five barley loaves, and two small fishes: but what are they among so many?

Who made the loaves of barley? The lad or the woman? Who are the small fishes: surely not Paul, nor John: for such are great fishermen who cast their net into the sea and bring to shore multitudes of men.

Can three measures of barley leavened with a lump of truth produce the five loaves of doctrine that even a child might carry? The kingdom of heaven is also this: even the leaven which the woman uses to prepare the doctrines of everlasting life.

And Jesus said, Make the men sit down. Now there was much grass in the place. So the men sat down, in number about five thousand. And Jesus took the loaves; and when he had given thanks, he distributed to the disciples, and the disciples to them that were sat down; and likewise of the fishes as much as they would.

It is impossible to consume the doctrines of heaven. Nor is it possible to eat the fish God provides for our meat and entirely consume it. We eat as much as we can: but that provided for the multitude through the providence of one boy is sufficient to feed a multitude of multitudes.

When they were filled, he said unto his disciples, Gather up the fragments that remain, that nothing be lost.

And what shall be done with these fragments? Give them to the multitudes that will yet come to this mountain to hear of what took place here this day.

Therefore they gathered them together, and filled twelve baskets with the fragments of the five barley loaves, which remained over and above unto them that had eaten.

These fragments are yet found in the churches of the world wherever these fragments of God's truth are taught.

Then those men, when they had seen the miracle that Jesus did, said, This is of a truth that prophet that should come into the world.

All who have eaten of the five loaves and of the fishes provided by the disciples of Jesus can understand this miracle.

In fact it's such a common thing in heaven that many angels and disciples have surely done greater works than this.

When Jesus therefore perceived that they would come and take him by force, to make him a king, he departed again into a mountain himself alone.

Why is it that people wish others to be a king over them? God is rejected: Lenin, any pope, Muhammad, a member of one's family, an organization, some scribe, a genius, a loved one—and many such like peoples and things, truly are taken as king over, at the very least, moments of a man's life. Indeed, in certain cases, a man's life is dominated by his king. Mammon rules many: various governments rule multitudes: and what man can measure those that take the conceit of their own heart as king and lord over themselves? God is my lord and my love of her rules my spirit.

The Lord God of Israel is really my father, my lord, my God, my bride. If men cannot understand this earthly sentiment and relationship, what hope have they of understanding truly heavenly joining's? God is God: I am his created Son.

My work is to make men the sons of God. The world is a thing to be overcome and thereby saved. Saved for what purpose? Saved for heavenly enjoyment. But what is the world? Isn't it what it is? Read world history: hear the news of the world: observe the world: listen to the news of the world: beware of the ways of the world. Yet surely there is found in the world, this seed growing, even the kingdom of heaven.

What is the kingdom of heaven? that government wherein God is king, love rules, beauty abounds, and pleasure and delight are yours for the asking.

Men serve men, ideals, created creatures, and things. They are the servants of sin and know it not. A man is the servant of that which rules his soul.

The sons of God possess their souls in patience. Their strength lies in their return. Whether they walk, or run, or fly as eagles; or rest, or war, or sleep, they are still his sons. God saves his own. Those who labor against God's will being done in earth labor in vain. Not only shall God's kingdom come, it has come. Not only shall the kingdom be established, it shall break in pieces all other kingdoms.

Where is the kingdom of heaven? Within the heart and soul and body and mind of those who serve God as king. But is not this true? God is the greater servant, the supreme craftsman, the lord of the house who has prepared all good things for our everlasting life. Surely this is so. Then let God be your king; only in this way can Jesus be your lord.

I know this to be true: the ancient of ages is eternally young. For I know this of myself: though I be old, and a man, yet am I only a child. How much more so is this then true of my God?

Let the gentiles glory in their kings, in their rulers, in their wise men, in their superstars. We poor Jews can only glory in our God.

And when even was now come, his disciples went down unto the sea,

The wicked are the troubled sea. The winds of controversy stir them up. They rage. They are calm. They give birth to their own monsters. They hold within themselves the power to choke out the breath of life: even the breath of heavenly life. At one time they covered all the earth.

But let the parable serve its purpose. And let us move on.

And entered into a ship, and went over the sea toward Capernaum. And it was now dark, and Jesus was not come to them. And the sea arose by reason of a great wind that blew. So when they had rowed about five and twenty or thirty furlongs, they see Jesus walking on the sea, and drawing nigh unto the ship: and they were afraid. But he said unto them, It is I; be not afraid. Then they willingly received him into the ship: and immediately the ship was at the land whither they went.

Men ought to use the ship of state to carry them into the land of promise: but it is the state of their souls, the kingdom of their dreams and desires that should so carry them. To attempt to use Leviathan for this purpose is madness. For even the Whore that rides the beast is being destroyed by the State. The Church and State are now separated: and what has resulted? The State devours the life of those who would rule men with foolishness and vanity. Religion is the opiate of the people: the religion of Babylon, that is. Even a devil like Lenin, Vladimir himself, could see this.

But these things have been true ever since John first described them. The Sea of Galilee is one thing: the Sea of Tiberias is quite another. But consider also the wars, and slaughters, throughout all history wherein kings slew priests, and priests deceived kings. State and Church, politics and religion, king and priest: such are some of the ideas explanatory of and explained by the Beast of the Sea and the Whore of Babylon. Religion is a whore which lures men to itself. The

State is a beast which wars against God, and violates the tenderness, the love, the compassion that God has sown within us.

Which of us would really desire to burn children alive? Even our enemies' children? Surely, the States which prepare to do this very thing, and the men who promote these policies and give life to the State, are not men of God, but men of Satan, deceived though they be. And men who serve Mammon have joined with those who serve man to promote the godless governments which cover the earth.

The State is the child of Greek mentality, engineered and animated by Roman bureaucrats. Since they animate it with Mammon, it is no wonder that they covet the powers of taxation, and number everything in terms of money. The world is now a house divided. How can it stand?

Accept God as king, and reject the prince of this world, and those legions of spirits who do nothing more than make merchandise out of your life. Let your righteousness exceed that of man: in this manner does the kingdom come unto you. And if it grows within you, what shall result? Surely it then shall grow outwardly until it covers the earth. But then what? The universe is vast: and eternity, without bound. Our immortality is real and assured. It is foolish to confuse the word of the first day with the words of the second day. Also, the third day is what it was. For those who can receive it, there is no more time. It is finished. What have we now? New heavens and a new earth.

The day following, when the people which stood on the other side of the sea saw that there was none other boat there save that one whereinto his disciples were entered, and that Jesus went not with his disciples into the boat, but that his disciples were gone away alone; (Howbeit there came other boats from Tiberias nigh unto the place where they did eat bread, after that the Lord had given thanks:) When the people therefore saw that Jesus was not there, neither his disciples, they also took shipping, and came to Capernaum, seeking for Jesus. And when they had found him on the other side of the sea, they said unto him, Rabbi, when camest thou hither?

Why should the people seek Jesus? Were they not filled with the loaves? There is this that is true concerning the kingdom growing within us, we ever desire to eat at the table of God. Our love believes all things with God are possible; we hunger for righteousness, and are filled again, and again. To be devoid of desire is to be dead. To realize those desires born in us of God is to eat of the tree of life. Our hunger is real; so is its satisfaction. The people sought the living bread.

But bread eaten is also blood formed. Somehow the words of Jesus produce those spiritual impulses which are the strength of our life. Things pass away. Situations change. But the gospel of Jesus remains, a living reality producing the everlasting life of the spirit. We need the alpha and the omega; knowledge not only of the beginning of God's creation, but also knowledge of its end. Yet so vast is this creation that all the letters of the alphabet are required to unite it. The letters are complete, but the possible permutations are without number. The letters of Paul, what man could know their effect upon the human soul? And how is it that the letter alpha is one thing, and the letters we write are another thing? Even if the symbolism is fixed, there is a power within the very nature of life to expand its meaning. The firmament is an expansion: yet we are knowledgeable about both beginnings and ends.

The living bread is the doctrine of Jesus strengthening our lives. It is brought to us from heaven: all these things are real, and really to be understood. We seek Jesus because we have miraculously assimilated something of his doctrine.

I long for my end. Surely my last day shall also come.

Jesus answered them and said, Verily, verily, I say unto you, Ye seek me not because ye saw the miracles, but because ye did eat of the loaves, and were filled. Labour not for the meat which perisheth, but for that meat which endureth unto everlasting life, which the Son of man shall give unto you: for him hath God the Father sealed.

With what am I sealed? With what are the sons of God sealed? With hope. Hope realized is a seal broken: yet men have only partly read the scroll of time unrolled before them.

God has given unto me by his angel John my book of life. Many books are contained within it. Yet it is a little book. One might taste it in half an hour. It is sweet. Yet to digest it, to assimilate it, is to realize, as only a god might realize, the triumphs and sorrows of seven thousand years.

Men do not believe it. What is that to me? Shall I believe man or my heavenly Father?

Then said they unto him, What shall we do, that we might work the works of God?

If you do not believe in the works of God, nor in your own power to work, why bother with the question? Is there any faith in the world of your experiences that would lead you to believe in God? Even that God who is the Father of Jesus, even my God?

Jesus answered and said unto them, This is the work of God, that ye believe on him whom he hath sent.

God sent servants into the world: angels into the world: prophets into the world: and the spirits of love and truth and beauty into the world. But the world is blind to it all: so God also sent his lights into the world: his burning lights: his candles: his Word that burns and consumes: He also sent his first begotten, and up to that time, his only begotten son into the world.

But if men are blind to what has happened, and what God was, how can they expect to see God now? Surely only those who can see the God that is can rejoice in the god who is to come again. Why again? Was once not enough? Of course it wasn't. The finished work must yet be shown to be finished. But earthly men have no stomach for heavenly work. They can believe in what happened millions upon millions of years ago: and can believe in what happened millions upon millions of light-years distant. But for them to believe in what Moses wrote, what David did, and what Jesus said a few thousand years ago is too much for them.

I marvel at what Satan can do with men.

They said therefore unto him, What sign shewest thou then, that we may see and believe thee? What dost thou work?

Even the building of the New Jerusalem, the city of truth delivered of God to men from heaven.

Our fathers did eat manna in the desert; as it is written, He gave them bread from heaven to eat.

Manna is angel's food: the ambrosia of gods: the nectar of living goddesses. Nevertheless, it is angel food formed of earth: it lasts but a day. Where are your delights of ages past? Your songs? Your revelries? Your glories? Your adventures? Your creations? Your loves? Your kingdoms?

Obviously, if it were food given of an eternal God it would be eternally satisfying.

Then Jesus said unto them, Verily, verily, I say unto you, Moses gave you not that bread from heaven. For the bread of God is he which cometh down from heaven, and giveth life unto the world. Then said they unto him, Lord, evermore give us this bread.

And this Jesus has done, for in spite of all, his words are yet with us and within us.

And Jesus said unto them, I am the bread of life: he that cometh to me shall never hunger; and he that believeth on me shall never thirst.

Let those who have come to Jesus testify whether or not these words be true.

But in what sense does Moses provide angel's food? If nothing else, his writings provide a fund of information for archaeologists. If nothing else, his writings provide essays in historical documentation. If nothing else, his writings provide meat for literary enthusiasts. If nothing else, his writings provide a synopsis of the creation of the heavens and the earth and the scientific exposition of present facts interpreted in light of past processes. If nothing else, his writings provide an exercise in truthful exposition and philology. And what might one say of laws, customs, and the establishment of codes of conduct? And what of prophecy, or teaching, or leadership?

Angels can make much of what Moses delivered unto men. By what strange power does Moses influence your life? For if Moses had not lived, you would not be reading these words nor would I be writing them. Let men tell me Moses is dead: what they say is spoken from the limited perspective of their own understanding. For they speak of flesh and bones, sinews and blood, which God created of the earth and through which Moses, a living soul, once spoke and with which he wrote. But I speak of Moses, the living prophet of the living God and not of dried and lifeless bones.

Moses is who he is even as I am who I am. Surely even the dried up and lifeless bones of Moses are God's and Satan cannot use them for his purpose. Let Moses enjoy his own body and I enjoy mine: let the Lord God forbid that in death we be used for evil. But I am not dead: neither is Moses. Why then do these foolish writers sport themselves with our bodies? Shall not God call to himself those that are his? The body of Moses extends through space and time to include all those who believe in him and know of him. Satan ought not to possess Moses, for the prophet is of God and not of Satan.

Those who eat manna in this wilderness of worldly sin can understand this if they turn their minds to it. In fact, it's really very plain and is and has been clearly expressed for many years. But the Egyptians and Sodomites can believe in nothing save in their own myths: and even these they dispute among themselves.

Satan has a body of believers. What could be more evident than that simple fact? Moses also has a body of believers. I am one of them. And not even the least part of Moses belongs with Satan, but with the Lord God of Israel.

In what sense is Jesus the bread of life? We have his words: we have his spirit: we have his doctrine as he delivered it unto the people when he spoke to them on the mountain. The Sermon on the Mount is the doctrine of Jesus. Is this then the bread of life, this doctrine? If the doctrine sustains us in heaven, in earth, in hell; in the schools, in the organizations of men, in the churches; in the states of the world, in the world, in the universes visible and invisible—then is the doctrine truly living bread.

But if Jesus be not resurrected and come not again, what use his doctrine? If the spirit of truth is nonexistent; if his Father is a fiction, if the Son of man is not the Son of God in flesh, in blood, in living reality, what use these proverbs, what profit these parables? If we cannot be born again, of the spirit, of his words; if his words produce no growth of the kingdom of heaven within us; if God himself does not pour out his Spirit upon us—what profit in owning and using and building up our own soul, our house of spiritual life? A mansion of beauty and delight belongs in the kingdom of God. To place it in the midst of nations wicked and abominable is a grievous experience, a possibility of eternal life that would bring us tribulation, suffering, persecution, imprisonment, and even death.

But all these things pass away: our patience is justified. We return: therein lies our strength. Our treasures stored within our heart are guarded of God.

We bind in earth: it is bound in heaven. We loose in earth: it is loosed in heaven. God's will is done in earth: his kingdom has come. The city of truth is real. The living bread has strengthened us.

For what do I hunger? For what do I thirst? What shall I ask? What shall I seek to find? Upon whose door do I knock? Who sups with me?

God, forgive me: I am full. Let me assimilate my portion: let me do some work: let me find now some other pleasure.

So is it with those who know God. The living bread is the food of eternal life. We often forget how extensive is the body of Jesus. We do eat more than his words. We assimilate his flesh, his blood, his spirit within us. The spiritual reality of the communion of disciples is real. The body of Jesus is greater than the body of Moses for Moses lives within it. This must seem strange to men but it is true, mysterious for a time though it be. The reality of the book of life is less real than the men who wrote it: the reality of the prophets of God is less real than the God that sent them. Our Father is greater than us: wiser than we are: he is a God full of life. His sons live.

We are inheritors of all things good. The creators of all things evil. Thus our perfection is accomplished in God's way: at the appointed time, we see all things clearly. Belief in the Son produces life everlasting. Let us possess our souls in patience. Surely those that hunger and thirst after righteousness are filled. For I have so hungered, and so thirsted: and I am full.

But I said unto you, That ye also have seen me, and believe not.

The pure in heart see Jesus for what he truly is, even God's son made flesh. He is not as cold, as sterile, as impotent, as stupid, as vain, as foolish, as incompetent, as vengeful, as ruthless as the princes of this world wish him to be. For has he not rejected all the kingdoms of the world, and their laws, and their customs, and their ways, and kept for himself his own soul wherein his own kingdom, even the kingdom of his God, is found?

And has he not called all who would hear him to do the same? Whom has he rejected? None. But men will not believe in him: nor can they accept his strange God. The bands of wickedness are strong. The State and its workers: the Church and its members: the sons of liars and the fathers of foolishness, pride, and deceit, are too much for men. They would rather work heavy wickedness than accept the light tasks of love.

Why don't they believe? Let them explain it, if they care to. As for me, I believe in the God who has written his laws upon my heart. To deny him is to deny myself. In this, the Father and I are one. No son of God who denies himself before the Father can please God.

All that the Father giveth me shall come to me; and him that cometh to me will I in no wise cast out. For I came down from heaven, not to do mine own will, but the will of him that sent me. And this is the Father's will which hath sent me, that of all which he hath given me I should lose nothing, but should raise it up again at the last day. And this is the will of him that sent me, that every one that seeth the Son, and believeth on him, may have everlasting life: and I will raise him up at the last day.

What last day? The last day of your life? Surely, no. The last day of the world? Of course not. The last day of creation, the last day of the latter days, the last day of Jesus' work? What last day?

Even the last day of your death. For death has a time appointed for its destruction. The end of Jesus, is the last day of your separation from knowledge of God. For if you know God, Jesus' work is finished: that is, the work his father gave him to do: the work his father sent him into the world to accomplish.

In this new heaven and new earth we now enjoy, the dead are nothing more than an embarrassment to me. What can I say of those that deny me? I can only deny them. They deny me my past: they deny me the fruit of my own vineyard: they deny the God who created me: they deny me mine own living presence: they even deny me the beginning of my work, as well as its end.

They neither know me nor my God. Whom do they accept? They accept their own self, their own doctrines, their own beliefs, their own kingdom, their own gods, and hate both me and my Father. Nevertheless, when I consider what Satan is, I can understand the cause of their unbelief. They have created the most amazing idol of all, animated, as it were, with their own fear, and pride, and foolishness. Yet the more I think about it, the more am I moved to laughter.

We mourn: and are comforted. We weep: and we laugh. We experience hell, and discuss that fact in heaven. We die: yet we live. Truly, Death and Hell war against me. Satan is my adversary. The same Satan who as Peter savors more the things that be of men rather than those that be of God. Nevertheless, although Satan takes many forms and makes slaves of men, and even enters into their heart and soul and mind so that, spiritually speaking, they are possessed by it, God also may reveal, and does reveal truth to men.

The sons of God see God, for their heart is pure, and he dwells with them. The spirit of truth ever reasons with us. The spirit of truth also cleanses us: it is within the very nature of God to tell us the truth: explain that truth: preserve that truth: use that truth: and glorify that truth. God is true and no lie is found in him.

What is the truth? I am a man of sin: that is the truth. Shall I remain in such a state forever? No: that is my belief. I carry within me, and see about me, and have heaped upon me the sins of the world, even of my world of earthly life as I have experienced it from its beginning to its end.

The beginning and ending are yet with me. I clearly see this. In truth, I have overcome the world. Satan is the product of that God who fathers lies and promotes the creation of idols. He resents my intrusion into his world of transitory dreams and perishable works. One thing I experienced as Adam I know to be true. I ate of the tree of knowledge of good and evil, and that day that I ate thereof, I died.

In this experience, each man is his own Adam. I love my wife, but she is not my heavenly father. My God is a Spirit whose Word created and creates all things. He is, even as I am, real. She is also the bride of my soul calling me to herself through my wife. We are joined by God. Nevertheless, Satan is a serpent, a created and subtle beast of the world, who tempts us with his wisdom, his beauty, his ways. It is no wonder my wife has followed his advice, and died. Snow White has died: yet her prince is as real as the story itself.

A son of God cannot be bound by death: He can only experience it. Yet evil men in the world not only deny the real spiritual death which is the mark of those who worship Man, but they revel in it, boast of it; use it as a principle of fear, even as a means of mocking God. Surely, they are the living dead: the source of those words and doctrines whose ways result in Death and Hell. They produce, within themselves, the deadly things that poison our lives. They are the cause, the chief apostles, the very creators of Hell.

Lenin and Lincoln, Mao Tse-tung and Truman, Einstein and Marx are the apostles of Satan. So is Muhammad, so also, the present pope, as all popes before him. Men are deceived: they do produce the blind guides, the self-righteous Pharisees and scribes whose actions and words in the world glorify the ways of the world.

I am not led by those men in the world who teach war, or learn war, or implement the means of war. And I find little truth in those men who pride themselves on their economic, political, religious, and scientific accomplishments and take no thought of God, and his judgments, and his creation, and his word, and his children, and his ways.

Our sins are real: God has forgiven them. But our pride prevents us from seeing them, confessing them, and acknowledging how they bring hell to men on earth.

God is not punishing us to satisfy his ego or to satisfy some angelic vanity. His vengeance is only this: to tell us the truth about our own selves, our own power, our own insights, our own wisdom; and our own vanities, our own idols, our own ways.

The Word of God is true. Lenin is a lord of the world who promotes through the power of his words the doctrines of terror and the ways of the godless states of communism. Lincoln would rather preserve the state of the union than implement the simple commandment of Jesus who said, Do not kill: love your enemies. Mao Tse-tung has more apostles, converts, and disciples than Christ and his godlessness is apparent to all who can witness what his doctrines do to those who give their souls to the State. Truman is truly a man, and has shown to all men what he would do if he had the power to destroy his enemies, and their cities, and their wives, and their children. Einstein sniffs at Moses, and David, and Jesus, and Paul, and can find no truth in the scripture God has not hid from men but revealed to men. He could see that a bomb could be developed, but he couldn't see the folly of polluting the sanctuary of our strength with the arms of war. Whether it be phalanx, or broadsword; longbow or gas; gunpowder or atomic bomb; nuclear weapon systems or political bullshit, the men who conceive them, develop them, manufacture them, deploy them, and use them are the captive slaves of Death.

Let us kill. Ours is a righteous war. We are only defending ourselves. It's my job. What else can I do? I am only doing my duty. We are keeping America free. Free from whom? From the God that would have us love our enemies.

What can I say? A man does what he does with his right hand: he sees what he sees with his eyes: he goes where he goes with his feet: and his heart speaks that which is within him as the words coming out of his mouth so eloquently testify.

Obviously, we must be raised up to heaven in order to perceive these truths. The kingdom of heaven is one government. The kingdoms of this world are of another government. Let a man rule his own spirit, command the powers of his soul, before he sets out to rule the poor flock of God who are in the world.

These chief men use us cruelly. They even wish to kill the hope we have of seeing God's kingdom come. We are of the earth: but if God's will be done in us, are we not then living witnesses that the will of God is done in earth? Surely, we are. But men wish us to eat of their doctrines and feed upon their baloney, so that we might be indebted to them for our lives.

Accept my God as your king. Reject the rules of the world. There is nothing in money, or in law, or in the ways of man on earth, or in any of the idols man has made that can bring heaven to earth. Believe the Son and live.

The Jews then murmured at him, because he said, I am the bread which came down from heaven.

The Jews can master the intricacies of many symbolisms: nothing in mathematics, or law, or music, or economics, or medicine, is too abstract, too subtle, too deep for them. And their geniuses and their works are brilliant. But to believe and accept the fact that Jesus is heavenly bread is too much for them.

And they said, Is this not Jesus, the son of Joseph, whose father and mother we know? how is it then that he saith, I came down from heaven?

That a man has an earthly father and mother men accept. That men give birth to doctrines, ideas, inventions, organizations, nations, and even empires, men also accept. Men also are the fathers of their own crowns of life, as Napoleon was as he crowned himself emperor.

But that Jesus and those that believe in Jesus and act upon his words, have a heavenly father, men do not believe. Why?

Jesus therefore answered and said unto them, Murmur not among yourselves. No man can come to me, except the Father which hath sent me draw him: and I will raise him up at the last day. It is written in the prophets, And they shall be all taught of God. Every man therefore that hath heard, and hath learned of the Father, cometh unto me.

Our heavenly Father is a great teacher. We learn of him. Surely, He is my instructor. He teaches me the limitations of my power: the bounds with which he limits evil and its powers: the errors of my earthly ways, and the degradation wrought in me because of my sins. But all this is written in the prophets and astonishes me not at all.

Men who reject the Son of whom they themselves witness reject also the God that sent him into the world. They reject the prophets, the Son, the Word, and the Lord God of Israel. Rejecting these, what do they accept? The opinions of majorities, or the opinions of minorities, or the writing of worldly scribes, or the testimonies of great men, and many other such things do they accept depending upon time, season, circumstance, and their own personal feelings toward the vicissitudes of life. Thus do time, chance, and circumstance enslave those who can accept anything as being true except the constancy of truth. They believe the eternal God is like an ephemeral image. No wonder their glory fades and their treasures are consumed.

Not that any man hath seen the Father, save he which is of God, he hath seen the Father.

Men can believe in the power of the Soviet State, which they cannot really see, more easily than they can believe in Jesus who is the living author of these living words. They can easily believe in the existence of their brain, which no man can directly see and examine, but they cannot believe in the word of life set down on the table before them. What do men see?

Verily, verily, I say unto you, He that believeth on me hath everlasting life. I am that bread of life. Your fathers did eat manna in the wilderness, and are dead.

You would think the lesson of their own fathers should have been sufficient to realize that eating of the manna of angels found in the wilderness was not sufficient to provide everlasting life. But these logicians truly are quite illogical even by their own standards. They can write the social histories of nations who forsook God and experienced hell. Yet they condemn the God of the very prophets who foretold such things.

Let us learn of God. His outline of history is true. Those that believe in Jesus have everlasting life for they eat of the bread of life and live forever.

Why do we reject the obvious truth concerning the resurrection of the body? Why do we reject the obvious truth that that which is born of flesh, is flesh? We are formed of the dust of the earth: and our bodies return to it. But the living soul is the gift to us of the God of life. All live unto him: the rest are really dead though they know it not. Nevertheless, there is hope also for the dead: hope that one day they also will believe in those God sends into their world. How is this accomplished? With these words.

This is the bread which cometh down from heaven, that a man may eat thereof, and not die. I am the living bread which came down from heaven: if any man eat of this bread, he shall live forever: and the bread that I will give is my flesh, which I will give for the life of the world.

Men often forget how the world has life. It is Jesus' word which gives it life. Without the Word, what have you? Surely, vanities and perishable doctrines innumerable. Many petty opinions of little men delivered with their own small voice. Let Hitler return: let Lenin return: let Lincoln return: let Voltaire return: let these kings, these great men, these generals of wars and foolishness return and view the results of their commandments. But they have returned. And what do they advocate? That we once more participate in the ancient madness and the idolatrous rituals of the past.

Let the dead bury their dead. Let us rather devote ourselves to giving life to the world wherein most certainly the kingdom of heaven is found.

The Jews therefore strove among themselves saying, How can this man give us his flesh to eat?

Obviously, in the way it has been, and is, and shall be, done.

I live by the Father as do all who believe that life is of my Father.

Then Jesus said unto them, Verily, verily, I say unto you, Except ye eat the flesh of the Son of man, and drink his blood, ye have no life in you.

The Son of man is the son of man: he is fathered by man: he is the conception of his earthly father. We are sons of men: nevertheless, how many in the world are the Sons of Poland, the Sons of Liberty, the sons of liars, the sons of Lenin, the sons of revolution? Surely there are many fathers in the world and such fathers produce and give birth to their dreams. Do not the fathers of the Church produce their children which indeed are these many churches in the world? Do not men father inventions as well as wars?

From whence do these fathers draw their power? From earth? From heaven? From Satan? And if from Satan then they are fathered by the lie and are his sons. Surely, I am the Son of man, for man has fathered me. In no other way can a son of god come into the world of man.

If you eat these words, you literally eat the flesh and drink the blood of the Son of man. Surely, our soul, our words, our spirit is a literal reality, and as much a part of our lives as our flesh and our blood.

Why are we so desirous of eating the flesh and drinking the blood of the sons of Belial, and we have no desire to eat the flesh and drink the blood of the Son of man?

If you eat to sustain your body, will you not also eat to sustain your soul without which your body has no life even according to your own beliefs? Surely, then, the flesh and blood of the Son of man is food for thought and truly provides the meat of eternal life.

Whose eateth my flesh, and drinketh my blood, hath eternal life, and I will raise him up at the last day. For my flesh is meat indeed, and my blood is drink indeed.

The words are spirit: they are everlasting life itself. We are strengthened by hearing them and doing them. But the words are within you, doing what they do, coursing wheresoever the spirit sends them: producing such life as they produce. The Word is made flesh so that the flesh might have eternal life. Only meatheads cannot understand these matters.

To what are we raised up? For whom is the last day of our death significant? Surely, if I live by my God, and he tells me these things are true, then eternal life is yours.

To do God's will is meat. To drink of the cup of experience he pours for us, is to drink the blood of the Son of man. To experience the Son of man is to know what is in man. There is evil in man, as well as good. Man is the father of evil: he knows how to work evil, and he works it. But he does not know how to save himself from the consequences of that evil.

God is a Savior. Those that don't know this know not God. The Son of man is raised up so that by witnessing his death, we can also learn of his resurrections. As it is with him, so is it with all men.

His work is strength in deed. His living word is spirit in deed. We live because he lives.

He *that eateth my flesh, and drinketh my blood, dwelleth in me, and I in him.*

Is this really so hard to understand? Does not our work, our experience of life, dwell within us? Do we not think about our life? Do we not review it, remember it, discuss it, even after it has passed? Don't we dream about it? What then is life past but memories and feelings present?

Is not Jesus in me because I have eaten his flesh and drunk his blood? Is not my life one with his? Who has influenced me more? Even Satan comes to me and desires to be part of me. Unfortunately for Satan, I have fire within me, and I am the destroyer of the false witnesses and the lies he sends to me and with which he wishes to rule my soul.

Abide with Jesus: let his words comfort your soul: the yoke is of belief, the only burden is of hope and of love. I am wherever my words are: and those in whom my words abide are within me. My thoughts are within me, and they are within my thoughts.

Also, as I told them before, I would be with them always, even unto the end of the world. All of us are inhabitants of this wandering star we call earth. But I, like Jonah, am buried in the belly of Leviathan; and I am made sick in this godless state. Shall I remain in this belly forever? No.

The proverbs give way to explicit statements about the State. What is the State? A way of doing things which allows those who reject the kingdom of heaven to lord it over those foolish enough to serve the State. God commands, Do not steal. But men of the State tax all with impunity, without restraint, with arrogance and a covetousness that cannot satisfy their treasuries.

God commands, Forgive men their trespasses. The State remembers, when even those afflicted have long forgotten what the trespass was. God is merciful. The State is minutely avenging. God is generous. The State is stingy beyond measure. God is swift to defend. The State responds after the crime occurs.

The State is the product of Pride. God marvels at Man's pet beast. I loathe it. What have these proud lords of the world of Mammon to do with me?

120

In a certain sense, to be sent into the world also involves being marked by the beast.

Nevertheless, this product of evil men is destined for destruction. The kingdom of heaven shall destroy all other nations. Satan's power is limited.

What do we mean by the State? What meaning is in the word? It is the word used by hypocrites to cover their pride, their covetousness, their envy, their sloth; their causeless anger, their lust, their gluttony.

The thing has no life in it. It is a dead idol animated by devils who forsake God and war against his chosen people. Whom do communists serve? The State. Who teaches men to war? The State. Who glorifies itself against the kingdom of heaven? The State. Who makes laws ad nauseum? The State.

Render to Caesar the things that are Caesar's and to God the things that are God's. What then is Caesar's? Nothing—for he has even given his own soul over to the service of a lifeless abstraction.

As the living Father hath sent me, and I live by the Father: so he that eateth me, even he shall live by me.

I yield the fruit of my own soul. My words are my life. With the State, its words are not its own: but the words of the devils who worship it. The German State did not war against the Russian State. Neither does the State prosecute Patricia Hearst. But men war against men, and kill, because devils think more of the State than they do of the living God who commanded, Thou shalt not kill. And men cast Patricia in prison, make merchandise of her misfortune, and prosecute her in the name of some county, or State, because the hypocritical sons of Satan think more of worshiping the State than fearing the living God who commanded us to love our neighbor. And who is our neighbor? All who are in need of our love.

Is it so hard to see and understand how dead and foolish these lawyers are? One prosecutes with utmost skill: one defends with utmost skill: one moderates with utmost skill. And who decides? Twelve who have no skill in judgement at all. And all this they strive to do objectively, which is as much to say, they have transmission fluid in the circulatory system of their heart, and no blood of life in them at all.

Men who function so would do well to eat the words God gives us through his sons.

This is that bread which came down from heaven: not as your fathers did eat manna, and are dead: he that eateth of this bread shall live forever. These things said he in the synagogue, as he taught in Capernaum.

The sin of Gog is ever the same. These men will ever reject God, and never allow him to judge an issue, or exercise mercy, or kill a man. They want to rule: want to decide: want to judge—and always at the public's expense. And then they cover their conceit by referring to the State or to the Law.

Surely they serve the idols of their own mind.

Many therefore of his disciples, when they had heard this, said, This is an hard saying, who can hear it? When Jesus knew in himself that his disciples murmured at it, he said unto them, Doth this offend you? What and if ye shall see the Son of man ascend up where he was before?

Where was he before? In heaven, rendering judgment. Nevertheless, how can the Son of man, or any son of man, be in heaven unless there is in man that which is worthy of heaven?

It is the spirit that quickeneth; the flesh profiteth nothing: the words that I speak unto you, they are spirit, and they are life. But there are some of you who believe not. For Jesus knew from the beginning who they were that believed not, and who should betray him.

Who? Obviously, the religious teachers who ever want to teach the way of God, yet never desire to learn of God, his son, or the spirit of truth he sent into the world: the Pharisees, who teach only their own customs and their own traditions: the lawyers, who are ever writing laws and making void the covenant of that God who writes his laws in our heart and mind: the chief priests and elders, who seek only the praise of men and care nothing for the glory of God. Herod's men, who for a little pleasure, a little power, and a little money, sell their time and talent to ostentatious princes: those Romans who support with their strength arrogant Caesars and timorous procurators who would rather appease a mob than follow the bent of their own minds.

And such disciples for whom I am too much and yet never enough. But let this judgment stand: I love them and would to God they would change their ways so they might lose the little they have and inherit everlasting life.

But why don't they believe in my words? I really don't know. Do you?

And he said, Therefore said I unto you, that no man can come unto me, except it were given unto him of my Father.

Who is my Father? I am who I am. He is who she is. I am a god within God. Who is my earthly father? Obviously, man. Who is my heavenly father? The God of life and love and beauty and truth: and wisdom, and joy, and pleasure, and creative power without end. The ancient of ages is eternally young.

Who created me? He did. Who sustains me? She does. Who teaches me? his spirit. Who loves me? my bride.

At times, I am as one dead. But there is a time when surely I am alive forevermore. The split in my life is real: the cutting off, a real experience: the division, an historical fact. The work continues, yet it is done. The Word of God works in men, creating them living souls, raising them from earth to heaven: as men die, angels are born. Who are angels? All those who know these things to be true. I am the angel of my own message. The author of my own book of life. The created son of the glorious God of my dreams.

From that time many of his disciples went back, and walked no more with him. Then said Jesus unto the twelve, Will ye also go away? Then Simon Peter answered him, Lord, to whom shall we go? thou hast the words of eternal life. And we believe and are sure that thou art that Christ, the Son of the living God.

The question is addressed to all who can hear it: will you also go away? Each man who hears, answers howsoever he wills. There are many sons in the world: among all these how could you recognize the

Son of the living God? The mark of a man is the signature of his life: with words spoken, written, accepted, rejected, a man orders his life, and conducts that war within the valley of decision, even that valley wherein he alone decides what is right, what is wrong; what is good, what is evil; what receives his yes; what receives his no.

But those who are marked by the beast do the things ordered by the beast: they are of the idol, and numbered by it. Nevertheless, there are those who are sealed with this hope, that God is true and faithful and that the end of the beast is determined.

So many have been fathered by Satan, it is still an astonishment to me that Christ can still be recognized as the living son of the living God.

Jesus answered them, Have not I chosen you twelve, and one of you is a devil.

Peter once was Satan, but not for long. However, Satan strongly desires to possess Peter. Nevertheless,

He spake of Judas Iscariot the son of Simon: for he it was that should betray him, being one of the twelve.

Surely, Judas is still one of the twelve and his name is written in the book of life. I trust his experience is sufficient to disclose to all, as well as himself, that hanging oneself, after repenting and believing the gospel, is foolishness. I would prefer that he preach the gospel. For why should any be lost, even the sons of perdition?

It is the devil, the beast, and the false prophet which the sons of God in their bungling stupidity created, that is consumed in fire, even everlasting fire.

Why don't men understand? The pyramid is the pyramid: the Sphinx is the Sphinx: Chemosh is the stone carving so named: Baalim are the funny little carvings of funny little men: the State is the State: the Church is the Church: a picture of Lenin is a picture of a false prophet: and men who solicit your vote are men who wish to rule over you with the powers of law and the powers of government. But whose law and whose government?

It's necessary to choose devils to help us understand the silly little idols they've created. Devils are real persons in the world who are led of Satan. For some reason, most of them don't want to acknowledge this fact so they hide behind the hypocrisy of those who are impressed with their idols. Nevertheless, even some devils call devils, devils. Such are the doers of evils: the perpetrators of nonsense and the fathers of iniquity.

The great commandment is to love our father, even the Lord God, with all our heart, all our soul, all our mind, and all our strength. If this is done, you can reside in the kingdom of heaven, and participate in bringing whatsoever gifts of life you possess into the city of truth. If this is done, you won't be engaged in learning the arts of war, or training yourself to be obedient to the State or some other silly organizational system whereby devils may get you to do that which, in all truth, causes you to be cast into hell.

CHAPTER 7

After these things Jesus walked in Galilee: for he would not walk in Jewry, because the Jews sought to kill him.

How do men seek to kill Jesus? By keeping him out of their heart, and mind, and soul. By denying him their love. His life is limited by those men in the world who literally speaking want nothing of him in their doctrines and in their lives.

Thus states are born: governments are formed: various laws written: and the God of love is rejected as men, even the great men of the earth, busy themselves with the affairs of the world. Mammon, and the many conceits of law, and the lusts of other things keep men from Jesus.

And what of those in the world who call him Lord, yet do not the things he commanded them? What can I say about the sacrifice of the mass? All these sacrifices, what are they worth? Who possibly could be honored by them? Surely, only those who have been lured into the arms of the Whore of Babylon. The gospel, the Word, should be preached. Truth should be sought. The New Jerusalem should be explained. But what results? People, like the poor of a shepherd's flock, are left uninstructed in truth, in love, in beauty. It is no wonder, devils can thus maliciously destroy God's flock. No wonder that wars between nations are made possible. No wonder the corruption of mammon produces social injustices. No wonder the rich in spirit can sport themselves with God's bounty and even use his word for their own covetous and idolatrous practices.

126

No wonder love is despised and men pride themselves with being heads of state and secretaries of war and generals of death.

But enough.

Now the Jews' feast of tabernacles was at hand.

God dwells within the tabernacle of our soul and visits the houses of those he loves. Satan is not the only spirit who comes into our house, or patrols the earth, or works in the world.

To keep the Feast of Tabernacles is to dwell alone in the temple of our body and await joyously the coming of the Lord God of Israel.

His brethren therefore said unto him, Depart hence, and go into Judaea, that thy disciples also may see the works that thou doest: For there is no man that doeth anything in secret, and he himself seeketh to be known openly. If thou do these things, shew thyself to the world.

Has Jesus shown himself to the world? Is Jesus less discussed in the world than Moses? Maybe so, but is the sign of Moses in the world lifted any higher than the sign of the Son of man? Both the serpent and Jesus are lifted up for a sign.

For neither did his brethren believe in him.

Well, what of it? It's all a matter of timing, anyway. Those who run to and fro can never understand the patience of God. Even I, when I visit hell, am astonished at how the spirit of haste ruins many a project. Only those who wait on God, know truly how to be quick.

Then Jesus said unto them, My time is not yet come: but your time is alway ready. The world cannot hate you; but me it hateth, because I testify of it, that the works thereof are evil. Go ye up unto this feast: I go not up yet unto this feast; for my time is not yet full come.

Shall my time ever come fully? The devils laugh at me: Satan ever taunts me with my present state. He haunts my abode with questions innumerable. He prides himself on my closed mouth. He cannot bear my slow pace. He delights in making children king; and fools, teachers; and shallow men, philosophers; and the opinions of majorities, truth.

I once protested to God to hurry. His reply? Be still. I have been anxious about many things to no purpose.

When he had said these words unto them, he abode still in Galilee.

The feast is one of the Jews, for the Jews; but Jesus, and his brethren, and the Gentiles, and all men are invited to come to the Feast of Tabernacles. All men? Even Castro? Even Napoleon? Even Sadat? Even Mao Tse-tung? Even Idi Amin? Yes. Unfortunately, men take the invitation of God too lightly.

God dwells with the children of Israel. Those that daily keep the Feast of Tabernacles know this. They feast with God, eating there such things as God has empowered them to bring. Our body is also a tabernacle of truth, a mansion of many dreams.

Though we are gathered into the kingdom of God as one people, yet many are the tabernacles of our camp. And for those who have it, great are the mansions of their souls. I speak in parables. But how might I otherwise speak? The abstract ideas of the philosophers are cold, lifeless forms; they are devoid of flesh and blood. In all their wisdom, there is no power in their discourses to make the Word flesh.

The objective scientist, the objective philosopher, the objective mind, searches out the intricate details of objects, and rejoices in his discovery. Nevertheless, what has he found? An object. For those of us God has visited, the truth is plain. An idol is an idol, beautiful though it seems, intricate though it be; filled with moving parts as it is, what might we judge it to be?

I also dwell in my tabernacle of flesh and blood. God comes, and leaves me alone. He forsakes me so that I might understand that I am mine own god, created by him, used by him, loved of him.

He works and I work. He witnesses and I witness. He loves and I love.

There are two witnesses to these truths in the world: I am the one witness, you are the other witness: there is an Old Testament which witnesses to this truth, and there is a New Testament: Sarah is as real as Sarah Miles, Isaac is as real as Newton: and every John in the world is a living witness to the truth of Isaiah, for John read the prophet and is even of him, as also I am and you now are. All God's children are of God. There is no people that are not his people.

The beast, the false prophet, the serpent are what they are, the intricate and worldly idols of the heart and soul and mind of those men who trespass against God. The sin of Man is real.

The pyramids are real: the mosques are real: the Mormon temples are real: the many cathedrals are real. But surely so also is the tabernacle God had Moses build: surely this tabernacle of flesh and blood also is real; indeed, is it not as real as you are?

But when his brethren were gone up, then went he also up unto the feast, not openly, but as it were in secret.

God surely visits with us in secret: our prayers in secret: our fast in secret: our alms in secret. Yet those things done in secret God reveals. Newton's thoughts, framed in secret, are revealed to all who come to read them. Sarah Miles, masturbating in secret, is revealed to all, through one of the arts of the present age, who can afford to see it. Surely God's angels live in secret with God, but in time their glory fills the earth.

Genius, vision, beauty, and love of life are displayed by the stars God sets in his heavens. There are gates to pass through, doors to open, mansions to visit, music to hear, delights to experience. Why do men refuse to believe God makes his Word flesh? Because they are too busy with their own words, too concerned with their own flesh, too much in love with their own selves to allow God a place in their tabernacle.

My tent is pitched in the mountain of my God, even the Lord God of Israel. My end is with him. I also keep the feast of tabernacles: but in secret, for so he has commanded.

Then the Jews sought him at the feast, and said, Where is he?

Indeed, where is he now and what is he doing now? It is wisdom to seek to find the truth concerning these matters. What has God shared with you at the feast?

And there was much murmuring among the people concerning him: for some said, He is a good man: others said, Nay; but he deceiveth the people.

And if he does not come again and bring heaven to earth, then he does deceive the people, no matter how many say he is a good man.

Yet, there is truly none good but God: and we, his children, seek that perfection which he gives to all who diligently seek him.

Howbeit no man spake openly of him for fear of the Jews. Now about the midst of the feast Jesus went up into the temple and taught. And the Jews marvelled, saying, How knoweth this man letters, having never learned?

How does any man know letters, having never learned? We learn of God directly: or we learn of God through his angels, his wise men, his writers, his servants, his friends, his lovers. We learn of God through his Son. But if we know the Son, we have eternal life for such knowledge is that life.

Jesus teaches within the temple of the human spirit: even the holy temple of God. But Satan also teaches therein, and man sets up his detestable image of self and worships it to his own undoing. Nevertheless, the poor in spirit are blessed, for theirs is the kingdom of heaven: they possess God in their hearts, and in such no abomination is found.

Jesus answered them, and said, My doctrine is not mine, but his that sent me.

Jesus doctrine is of God, even the Lord God of Israel, even his heavenly father, his creator, the living spouse of his soul. Where is Jesus' teacher? From whence was he sent? How is it that his Word is still with us? Some doubt, even of those who saw him resurrected. Why this doubt? Because men cannot believe that much of what they believe is false. Men should test their beliefs, try them, act upon them, to see if they be true.

If any man will do his will, he shall know of the doctrine, whether it be of God, or whether I speak of myself. He that speaketh of himself seeketh his own glory: but he that seeketh his glory that sent him, the same is true, and no unrighteousness is in him.

What is God's will for me? That I write these words. What is God's will for you? That you try them, to see whether they be true. For if they are not true, then am I beside myself, and truly a madman, a false prophet, and another deceiver in the world's long history of deceivers. And why should you, full of worldly wisdom as you are, be deceived by me?

Did not Moses give you the law, and yet none of you keepeth the law? Why go ye about to kill me?

Men kill Jesus by refusing to let him live in their heart, their mind, their soul. They'd rather keep alive their fear of governments' power, murderers' boasts, religions' devils, and their own hidden sins of ignorance and pride than let the Word of God live in them. Whom do they fear? The merchants of fear and their products. They believe not that where love dwells, fear cannot enter.

The people answered and said, Thou hast a devil: who goeth about to kill thee?

Obviously, all those who do just that.

Jesus answered and said unto them, I have done one work, and ye all marvel.

What is the one work? To make a man whole even on the day of his rest: even a powerless man, who of himself cannot make himself whole. How is this done? By commanding the man to take up his bed wherein the world causes him to lie, and walk with it withersoever he will. Those that wait upon the Lord God of Israel know this to be a true fact of life.

Moses therefore gave unto you circumcision, (not because it is of Moses, but of the fathers;) and ye on the sabbath day circumcise a man.

And what is all this Sunday preaching except spiritual circumcision?

If a man on the sabbath day receive circumcision, that the law of Moses should not be broken, are ye angry at me, because I have

made a man every whit whole on the sabbath day? Judge not according to the appearance but judge righteous judgement.

The Pharisees are ever covetous of their religious roles. They are full of spiritual advice. They condemn pornography, crime in the streets, and the undisciplined and occasionally loud and riotous actions of youth. And the sexual expression of love is always more than they can endure. God never created an illegitimate child: yet through their laws, they make bastards out of multitudes. With them, God is never love, joining a man and woman together as one flesh. With them, God is a legislator empowering them to join and sever whomsoever they will. Adultery is never to them fucking around with hypocrisy and worldly wisdom: and fornication to them is never licking and sucking and eating up the body of whorish rules men term religion.

They blaspheme God by making the heaven God makes possible for men, inaccessible. They love their public prayers, their idle doctrines, their words full of unprofitable wisdom. Men need no greater sign that God is with Jesus than the fact that the gospel of the kingdom of heaven is still preached even though these men have so skillfully shut up the kingdom's door against men.

The kingdom of heaven is with us today. How can men be blind to such an obvious truth that has been with men ever since John and Jesus declared the kingdom to be at hand? They speak the words, but they cannot perceive with their hearts that the Word is not only true in spirit but is come in the flesh.

Then said some of them of Jerusalem, Is not this he, whom they seek to kill?

Yes, it is he. And they seek to kill him by making his Word of no effect in the lives of men. They remember the crucifixion yet forget the thief in paradise who is now fucking the angels of heaven and delighting in the God of life; even the Lord God of Israel.

But, lo, he speaketh boldly, and they say nothing unto him. Do the rulers know indeed that this is the very Christ?

If the rulers of this day knew Jesus as the Christ, how could they do that which Jesus said do not: and refuse to do that which

Jesus commanded to be done? This day, in this night, the saints are overcome: mammon rules multitudes: and men are overcome by the hypocrisy of religion and the prophecies of man; the miracles of Egyptian technology, and the unspeakable unbelief so characteristic of Sodomites. Nevertheless, it is obvious to me that the State is destined for destruction while the kingdom of heaven shall cover the earth.

In fact my enemies, and all my adversaries, are so gross, and so pathetically ridiculous that if I loved them less, I could almost be persuaded to laugh myself to death.

Howbeit we know this man whence he is: but when Christ cometh, no man knoweth whence he is.

True. No man knows. But the sons of God know for they have overcome the world even as Jesus overcame the world and are presently kings and priests to God. Who is a king? Well, King James is a king: those that translated Scripture into the King's English are kings: and those who set the type for all these books in the earth are priests, doing the will of God and thereby serving him. But men who reject Jesus as Christ have no use for simple fact. That is too pure for them: they prefer the intricate maze of historical myth rather than the clear testimony of the living word.

Then cried Jesus in the temple as he taught, saying, Ye both know me, and ye know whence I am: and I am not come of myself, but he that sent me is true, whom ye know not.

I almost remember this: for the recreation of my past lives through the mechanism of dream and makes known to me the fact that my throat was sore during this address. They simply wouldn't believe. In no way could I impress them.

But I know him: for I am from him, and he hath sent me.

If men knew God my work would be finished. In one respect, I am always tardy; slow; absent. It's hard for me to get excited over the schedules of the world, even my own plans take longer to execute than I care to acknowledge beforehand. Yet in a heavenly sense, I am too quick for them. Their belief grows so damnably slow.

Then they sought to take him: but no man laid hands on him, because his hour was not yet come.

The times are appointed by God. We can sense, but only with diligent searching, can we discover the infinite depths of his creative powers. I am impressed by God's angels and by their works and by the powers God displays through them. Many such have ministered to me.

When shall my hour come? What hour? What day? What month? What year? What time? If you can perceive with your heart that which is eternal, you know these questions of time are rooted to the rotations of the earth and its oscillation about the sun. But what is mine is everlasting: there is no more time.

And many of the people believed on him, and said, When Christ cometh, will he do more miracles than these which this man has done?

Words are the power behind miracles. The devils use their lies to violently assault the heavenly kingdom otherwise open to a man. Mao Tse-tung rules with his tongue and the spirit of Muhammad is embodied in his words and even archaeologists who make much out of the shards of broken dreams are delighted no end whenever they discover another Rosetta stone.

But what do you mean by the Word? Surely not scribblings of ink on paper; surely not marks on tablets of stone; surely not figures on papyrus; surely not symbolical arrays of luminous lights. What power is in a word?

Let God be the word working in me, even the holy one of Israel, even the Spirit of Aphrodite herself. I find the words of men vain, foolish, profitless, and expensive beyond their true worth. God is the spirit of life harmonizing our world of words for us. But we refuse him his proper joy: we acknowledge her not the beauty of her place. We are miserly innkeepers and refuse to allow beauty and love to enter our souls.

But who can accept this judgment?

I can: for I have found it true of myself. Satan corrupts Solomon's beautiful wives: Satan plays the devil with Delilah, for she lost the joy of one truly great man when she provided a man to cut off the power of Samson's own wisdom from his own head: and the eunuchs of Jesus are those men in the world who have no relations with any church as their wife. As Adam, we are led astray by the beauty of our own flesh and blood, by the very beautiful and lovely handmaiden of our own souls.

I am born of a virgin impregnated with the spirit of truth, even that holy spirit comforting the chosen ones of Israel. Angels prophesy the birth: witness it: rejoice in it: and yet do not perceive that I am the salvation of their own natures.

The Word is with God, creating with him. But men use their creative powers to war against him: and how ridiculous is that war!

Many yet believe on Jesus, that he is the Christ sent of God. I would to God that they would believe in him. Then would this one work be finished.

The Pharisees heard that the people murmured such things concerning him; and the Pharisees and the chief priests sent officers to take him. Then said Jesus unto them, Yet a little while am I with you, and then I go unto him that sent me. Ye shall seek me, and shall not find me: and where I am, thither ye cannot come.

The kingdom of heaven is secure against the vanities of the Pharisees. Those of us in heaven, observing how at last they've entered, are astonished at the foolishness of those who freely admit they are not in heaven preaching to those in heaven how to get there. From such madmen, let all withdraw save it be to tarry with them a while and heal them of their foolishness.

What can one judge of all these chiefs in the world? The greatest men are the servants of all. Consider the lives of Paul, of John, of Plato, of Alfred North Whitehead, of William Blake; consider the lives of your mother, your father, your teachers, your friends; consider your own life. Consider also the life of God, even the life of the Lord God of Israel as that life is made manifest to us by all that know him.

Contrast these lives with the lives of those chiefs of state, those chief priests, and those chiefs of nations long gone and those still present.

The chief priests wish Jesus to be taken, silenced, and imprisoned. Briefly, they desire him dead. Why? Because if you believe in Jesus, you have to believe in the God that sent him: for so Jesus commanded. That God has rejected the chief priests' claim to eminence via religion and politics: and accepted those who minister the Word of God to men. Plato, a Greek, is also of God; a very angel of God, analyzing the states men create. And even the angel found he could not create nor deliver unto men the perfect state. Yet men, ignorant of what angels teach, blind to the light they bring to the world, still raise up their idolatrous governments.

Chief priests are the products of their own vanity and the devils ignorant people worship. Can these puppets of a system actually believe a Son of god, any Son of god, has anything to learn of them?

In this month, can any child of God believe that Reagan, or Ford, or Carter, or Brown or any of these others who constantly strive to set their image before the people, can serve us in any way whatsoever? To tax little or tax much: to distribute much money to a few classes or little money to all: to arm young men and women with a thousand nuclear missiles, or two thousand; what profit in such decisions? Numerous, vain, little men, writing and quibbling and enforcing numerous, vain, and little laws. And the mob follows madly after.

Such are the ways of the chief priests of Mammon, the high priests of waste, the proud rulers of the present era who reject the sermon on the mount and preach their own legalistic and economic bullshit.

Such men send officers to take Jesus so that he might be kept from the people.

If men serve men with truth, love, beauty, joy, and wisdom, men are truly served by those that are great in the kingdom of heaven. Plato has already judged the political systems of the world, and truly analyzed the inadequacies of our chief priests and rulers. But men know it not.

The kingdom of heaven is gathered into the kingdom of God and is then known as the garden of paradise on earth. Every mother who gives suck to her children knows this. But the statesmen of the world want no things to be created of God for pleasure and delight, joy experienced and desire fulfilled.

What do they want? They want men to believe that they are full of knowledge of good and evil and know how to bring you life. They rule the ignorant and are sustained by the same.

One woman refused to pay taxes to the government which supported the war in Vietnam. They placed her in prison. So brave are these statesmen! So filled with ardor for your liberty! So self-righteous are they when they steal your monies and conduct their wars and build their idols that they can imprison a woman, a single solitary woman, who defies them!

Then said the Jews among themselves, Whither will he go, that we shall not find him? Will he go unto the dispersed among the Gentiles, and teach the Gentiles?

As a matter of fact, he did.

What manner of saying is this that he said, Ye shall seek me, and shall not find me: and where I am, thither ye cannot come?

Men are still not alive to this truth, that I am where I am, doing what I am doing, enjoying such life as my God gives me. I find more joy in hell, and more beauty, in a back alley, than they find in their highest heaven. The universe is the playground of my soul and the life within me ever increases. The kingdom of heaven grows. Neither Moses, nor the prophets are dead, but live: but the chief priests blind men to the obvious facts of life.

I have lived many lives: let all that have done so themselves acknowledge this to be true. Am I dead because once I was there and now I am here? Have I left a house because I am no longer in the same room with you? Have I left the earth because I dwell now in the west rather than the east?

Men rooted to the earth think all men so limited: men impressed with their own system which they serve, believe they have chosen good service.

Nevertheless, beware of these idol dwellers and manufacturers: the universe of my God is vast: many kingdoms are within it. This is true even though many cannot enter them.

In that last day of the feast, Jesus stood and cried saying, If any man thirst, let him come unto me, and drink. He that believeth on me, as the scripture hath said, out of his belly shall flow rivers of living water.

Those that thirst after truth can be filled by the words of Jesus. The teaching is clear. The truth does satisfy. His word in us also produces other living words sent of God. Whitehead, Blake, and poets many, drank of Jesus' words and produced the beautiful sentiments God sent us through their living souls.

It is true, we judge the angels. The kingdom is built within us: it is for us: it is among us. I judge and am judged. Each man also should judge himself first, and angels after.

I do not reject the sound of music, for it is of the angels of God. Nevertheless, this idol of Man I do reject: for it is nothing but the product of a vain king lording it over servile craftsmen who know not how to serve the living God.

All of Michelangelo's genius cannot bring forth what God's women bring forth thousands upon thousands of times daily.

(But this spake he of the Spirit, which they that believe on him should receive: for the Holy Ghost was not yet given; because that Jesus was not yet glorified.)

That God should have a Holy Spirit, even as men have spirits, is a mystery to men; and it is a mystery to me why men wish to separate me from my Father, or themselves from His Holy Spirit. Without the Spirit, I was dead. As it is with me, so is it with men. Charles Manson is a Man son when he realizes he is dead: but why should he fear life and fear to come to the words of life and live? Obviously, because he is possessed by his own self-created fears. Men would do well to partake of the spirit of Jesus, and with his authority, rid men of the devils they create and nurture within themselves. If this were done, not only would the poor soul so afflicted rejoice, but much evil could be prevented before it ever came to be.

The glorification of Jesus could do man little harm and bring him much good.

But men glorify themselves: their own opinions: their own organizations: their own beliefs: their own church, state, and family. What then of God's glory?

Believe in the God working within you. For where else shall he cause heaven to grow? Believe in his still, small voice. For why should he shout and scream? Read his Word: for why should that which he has written go unread?

Believe in his sons: even those who have overcome the world and are now in the kingdom of heaven. Where is heaven? Wherever my words grow. For the kingdom of heaven is also this: my dream come true: my vision realized.

The kingdom of heaven comes from the kingdom of God. If God be not my husbandman, even also the living bride of my life-filled soul; if his Spirit goes not where I send it; if that Spirit comforts not, strengthens not, empowers none—believe nothing I say, for I am full of useless bullshit.

But what man, what State, what Church, what loved one, will deny me the living spirit of my own words? With those who believe not, I can do nothing except this: command their belief.

I am subject to the ways of God, and how can I escape his love? I am what I am because he created me what I am. I also create, dream, desire, want, hunger, thirst: I also live. What Son of man does not? I am a Son of God and the Son of man: therein lies the key to the mystery of my life. My heavenly Father is true: my earthly father is a mixture of true and false: gold and clay: good and evil: beauty and pain: genius and gross incompetence.

Nevertheless Jerusalem is in the new earth: new heavens are clearly seen: and now hell and death must be destroyed. For why should a tree bringing forth knowledge of good and evil grow in my garden? Why should the subtle beast of the world which I created forever have power to afflict those I love? The beginning of truth is the end of falsehood. Liars can no longer hide, not even within the bottomless pit of their own earthy imaginations.

Is this a parable or is it truth itself, clearly expressed?

I suffer all things: the fucking image suffers nothing: and yet my children weep for the image, and despise the living reality of my presence. They eat things sacrificed unto the idols of their own mind: they literally worship devils: they are deceived by men who say, I am no devil: devils are myths: devils are unreal: devils are religious inventions. They are full of the knowledge of evil: they know what is good for all people. Their laws are so many that millions must write them; and multiplied millions are required to enforce them: and all men must be marked, numbered, labeled, and taxed to the point of economic absurdity to implement their laws. Even if they destroy all flesh, their budget will remain unbalanced. They cannot even kill each other economically: they cannot even persecute each other, imprison each other, refuse to forgive each other, without robbing the treasury of God to pay for their evil works.

The world hates Jesus because he testifies of its evil works. But Jesus is a true prophet, for many of his prophecies have come to pass. Evil has increased: the love of many has waxed cold. His friends have tribulation in the world. The Spirit is in the world, comforting those in the world with the strength of conviction. But all this is old-time religion. Nevertheless, God is also capable of creating that which is new. What is new? Many things: including also the new earth, and the new heaven, wherein Satan and his works have no power and are despised.

Many of the people therefore, when they heard this saying, said, Of a truth this is the Prophet. Others said, This is the Christ. But some said, Shall Christ come out of Galilee?

I suppose the Galileans must answer this question. For Galilee is made up of many nations and is found among the Gentiles. Shall Christ come out of these? Christ cannot come out of that which he is not within. He can only come out of where he has entered. All men testify by the words coming out of their mouths what they have within them. And the poor in spirit testify with their lives what they have within them. If hope is within them, then they have Christ within them. For Christ is the hope of those who believe in his God: even the God who is love: even that God whose love can conquer all the Satanic spirits in the world who hate the truth.

Christ indeed does come out of the nations of Galilee.

Hath not the scripture said, That Christ cometh of the seed of David, and out of the town of Bethlehem, where David was?

Men would do well to believe the Scripture and read the things written therein: the book is published before all. It is both an old book and a new book. Considering the times of which it writes, even writing the truth of those things which happened upon our hearts and minds and storing them within our soul, a scribe cannot help but feel the tremendous potential for falsehood in the book. There are too many names of people, of places, of events: too many prophecies: too many references to things long past, and too many prophecies of things yet to come; indeed there are too many writers, too many spokesmen, too many ideas, in the book, in the scripture, to engender the earthly belief that the things written therein are true.

But they are true and it takes a heavenly nature to produce this belief. But this has been done and these many witnesses in the world provide a living testimony to that fact.

Satan need not prove the whole book untrue: for why should I afflict him with such a grievous burden? Let him prove one jot of it to be unfulfilled, let him prove one tittle of it false, and his kingdom shall stand.

Many men are impotent: they are not yet made whole. They have no stomach for the whole truth, and nothing but the truth; for even though they swear to provide it, they do not. It is too bitter for them.

I once made a fool of myself, and Satan said to me, If you were a Son of God, you would not have made a fool of yourself. And so the accuser ever accuses: he cannot believe a Son of God can be lost and truly become a Son of perdition, a man of sin. He cannot believe a Son of God can experience death, can be bound by death, can literally speaking descend into hell and be found in hell eating and drinking the poisonous things found there, and even handling the serpents squirming about the place.

If a people who saw Jesus, even his own brethren, believe not Jesus, the Christ, comes out of Galilee, what can they possibly believe when they see him come out of hell?

So there was a division among the people because of him.

So it must be. For Jesus is the great divider: he who wields the sword of truth cuts off from the heart and mind and soul of man, all the evil things which keep that man from paradise and the garden of God. Let the angels show a little common sense. Why rush in? We have all eternity with us. There is a time for every thing with God.

Ten days of tribulation are just that: they have a beginning, and an end. Shall we remember them forever? Let's remember what we passed through: but let's not glorify the passage: there are more worthy things to celebrate.

And some of them would have taken him; but no man laid hands on him.

Plato once took me to see his living idol: even the perfect State. So many men have acted upon his plan, and brought forth his dreams, that even he must be astonished at the fruit of his ideas. But I am not impressed. Not at this hour. Only amused.

Jesus refused to let himself be taken by the people, because he had been taken before: and the experience relived would have been a watered-down experience of what had gone before.

Men knew not, and few know, how to rightly handle the bread of life and how to wield the sword of truth. Nevertheless, there is a Spirit sent of God which can speak of himself and teach them all things they need to know.

Nevertheless, let me leave off, and rest for a while, lest I bore God with my repetitions.

Then come the officers to the chief priests and Pharisees; and they said unto them, Why have ye not brought him?

Obviously, because they couldn't handle him.

The officers answered, Never man spoke like this man.

What man, since Jesus, speaks as Jesus speaks? What Word, since Jesus' Word, speaks as Jesus' Word?

Then answered them the Pharisees, Are ye also deceived?

It's too bad we have no record of what the officers answered to this question. Nevertheless, let the officers now reply to the Pharisaical question put to them.

Have any of the rulers or of the Pharisees believed on him?

For the curious, the answer may be given: the answer is yes: some do believe.

But the people who knoweth not the law are cursed.

Amen.

Nicodemus saith unto them, (he that came to Jesus by night, being one of them,) Doth our law judge any man, before it hear him, and know what he doeth?

I cannot judge except of what I hear. I cannot know, except of those things I have seen and experienced.

Our father baptizes us with his love and gives us of the cup of life to drink. We sometimes forget who cleanses us, purges us: who it is that opens the universe of life to our eyes. What is our eye, but the window of our soul?

The Pharisees would do themselves good to heed Nicodemus's advice and pause to consider the question asked. But they are quick to condemn, and quick to condemn a man. But not only one man, but the whole world: even all the world that agrees not with them. Thereby they condemn themselves with their own words.

How many have abandoned their world to Satan? How many to communism? How many to World Government? How many to the purchasing power of the dollar? How many to the doctors of law and the captains of statistics?

Don't damn yourself to hell and perdition simply because some impetuous Pharisee and some vain general and some stupid President want to convince you that military power, monetary policies, and political deception are part of God's plan and law for your life.

Beware of those who legislate by counting raised hands, or votes, or opinions of majorities. Beware of those prophets of doom who number and catalogue and file and computerize and carefully weigh the quantity of evil in the world. Such are dead: for they are full of the knowledge of evil and know nothing of the God of life who commanded them not to eat of that tree whereof they gathered such fruit.

The Word should be taught in the schools, and those who proclaim otherwise are the judges of themselves, and not of the law: for they know nothing of it. To eat of the tree of life is good: and this truth should be taught to all men.

Judge of yourself what is good and what is evil: but only after you've been raised on butter and honey: to do so beforehand is great folly as these Supreme Court Justices and these many Roman

Legislators so aptly testify with their words, their works, and their own sterile and godless laws.

They answered and said unto him, Art thou also of Galilee? Search and look: for out of Galilee arises no prophet.

All the great prophets are Galileans: but the Pharisees cannot see this, for they are blind.

And every man went unto his own house.

Indeed, every man must go to his own house: for all of us, like it or not, return to our own soul for such light and truth and understanding as might be found in it.

Jesus says teach all things I have commanded you. But what do you teach and what are you taught?

Learn of Jesus. The kingdom of heaven is composed of many stars: why not allow him a place in your heaven?

CHAPTER 8

Jesus went unto the Mount of Olives.

The olive trees are witnesses of the old lives that are found in God. The Mount of Olives is that place where the two olive trees are found. The Old and New Testaments are yet with us. But what is this testimony except the words of belief which guide the actions and produce the works and words of all these living who believe in Jesus, in Elias, in Moses? We are anointed with the oil of gladness by the fruit such trees yield.

We all ought to visit the mount. Much joy, much truth, much gladness is found there.

The truth of creation given us by Moses is more consistent with evolutionary theory than that theory itself. Men who sin by making Science a god to be worshiped and believed sin against themselves by neglecting both Moses' account of Creation as well as his commandment against idolatry. All who have gone up the mountain wherein all these witnesses of God flourish, yield their fruit in their season. Einstein and many scientists so-called reject the testimony of Moses and believe not in the God who taught Isaac Newton some things relevant to the Creation. But Isaac laughs at them for his genius is the foundation of their materialistic idol. The sons of liars are also thieves for they use the works of God's angels to promote their own glory. Nevertheless, their vain words cannot endure the flood of time.

Space is the unbounded sensorium of God: so declared the angel of God, even Isaac himself. Who are these sons of modern science so-called who teach otherwise? These men of earth who know nothing of heaven, in the conceit of their hearts, believe that the God who fashioned their carcasses from the dust of the earth is like a moment of thought which rises in their minds and then perishes. Such men know not their own father; for they are fathered by the lies they generate. Men of sin are devils unto themselves and produce the works of sin. Such God casts out of his house.

But many witness in detail to the above truths and why should I belabor this simple fact?

And early in the morning he came again to the temple, and all the people came unto him; and he sat down, and taught them.

The temple of God is found within the heart of man. A man's heart is capable of belief. A man can believe in the truth to his own good: a man can believe in the lie, to his own hurt. These are things taught those people who come to Jesus. The temple of our heart is real: Jesus is real. So also are those writers and religious teachers who are so full of vanity that they ever delight in using the very teachings of God to promote their own glory and afflict their own people.

And the scribes and Pharisees brought unto him a woman taken in adultery; and when they had set her in the midst, They say unto him, Master this woman was taken in adultery, in the very act.

What woman? Even the Christian Church which has fucked around with Roman Law and brought forth the prince of this world. But what is this prince? Who is the prince of Catholicism? Where is the child in whom the children of Mormon delight? Who is the prince responsible for bloody crusades? Who causes brother to kill brother, enemies to be hated, armies to be gathered, and death to be the chief weapon of defense? Who causes Catholic to kill Protestant, and Protestant to kill Catholic? The sword of truth is one sword: the sword of belief in Jesus' Word is another. But these two are one as surely the angels and the other children of God will one day gloriously proclaim.

But the swords of Man are not the sacred word of God. These many weapons are the inventions of men who know not the God who commanded, Do not kill. God can kill with a single stone, as David and Peter have demonstrated. He needs not the arms of Man.

Now Moses in the law commanded us, that such should be stoned: but what sayest thou?

The Lord God commanded you not to kill, even the same God who writes his commandments upon the hearts and mind of his children. Obey God, and not Moses.

This they said, tempting him, that they might have to accuse him.

Who tempts Jesus? Who tempts you? Satan, the great deceiver, accuser, and liar.

But Jesus stooped down, and with his finger wrote on the ground, as though he heard them not.

The history of the world, even the times of the Gentiles, is grounded upon what Jesus wrote upon the minds of men. The dust of the ground upon which the words of Jesus are written, are those men who believe in him and hear his words.

So when they continued asking him, he lifted up himself, and said unto them, He that is without sin among you, let him first cast a stone at her. And again he stooped down, and wrote upon the ground.

Men whose eyes are fixed beneath, upon the ground of the world, and not above, upon the New City of Truth, ought to read what Jesus wrote on the ground. Forgiveness, righteous judgment, the suffering of evil, the production of good, knowledge of God, and the commandments of eternal life: such are some of the things written upon the ground found within the temple of the human spirit.

Christ's words are fundamental fact grounded upon the occurrences of earthly life. The doctrines of religion are the ethereal fancies of vain men who see much, eat little, chirp and sing, sometimes beautifully, but who are devoid of knowledge.

And they which heard it, being convicted by their own conscience, went out one by one, beginning at the eldest, even unto the last: and Jesus was left alone, and the woman standing in the midst. When Jesus had lifted up himself, and saw none but the woman, he said unto her, Woman, where are those thine accusers? hath no man condemned thee?

We must stoop down to write upon the ground. We needs must lift ourselves up to speak with the men and women who walk upon the holy ground of our own temple of the spirit.

The Christian Church is an adulterous church. The writers have surely discovered this fact. Her accusers are many. Indeed, those willing to stone her are many.

What can I say? Is there any writer, any historian, any philosopher, any Jew, any religious zealot, any pagan doctor, any witch doctor, any scientist, without sin, who can justly stone her to death?

Assuredly not. The greatest devils are the greatest men of earth whose idols of mind, mob, and market place have caused men to experience the reality of death and of hell. Such are our great accusers.

She said, No man, Lord. And Jesus said unto her, Neither do I condemn thee: go, and sin no more.

Belief in Jesus is his commandment. For those who do not believe, what might one say? The world is full of things to believe in, to serve, even to worship. Why worship God? Why believe in Jesus?

Because belief generates action, actions are grounded upon belief. The forces of creation, of spiritual creation, can be seen to spring from the beliefs of men. Believe God, rebuke the serpent. Believe Jesus, resist Satan. Believe in these my words, and try them, and see if what I write is true. But to the above I presently can add nothing. The decision is yours to make. I made mine, a long time ago.

Then spake Jesus again unto them, saying, I am the light of the world: he that followeth me shall not walk in darkness, but shall have the light of life.

In darkness, there is little growth. In darkness, the path is easily lost. In darkness, much fear is self-generated. Much of the world, at any one time, is covered with darkness. Nevertheless, our insights are real: much inner illumination is ours for the taking. Our eye is capable of producing its own light. Men forget the real light manifested in their own dreams. They confuse earthly and heavenly phenomena.

The spirit is spirit: flesh is flesh: at times they are wed, at other times, divided. Satan works in both realms. The fruit of evil is within our grasp. But why partake of it? Our eyes, opened to evil, bring darkness and its inhabitants into the mansions of our soul. Our body of heavenly knowledge is obscured. We pollute ourselves to no purpose. Judge of yourself what is good and what is evil. Accept the good: reject the evil. The princes of confusion are many, and their blindness, total. They cannot lead you anywhere except to that place where they are. And where are they sitting, and from whence are they calling you?

From the darkened cave of their own limited understanding. Antichrists are many and real, and those who proclaim Jesus lord, but reject the truth and works of his word are likewise many and real. If you visit and sup with them bring your own light and take your own meat: for they have nothing good for you to see, and nothing good for you to eat.

But I weary of these parables. Handle these bullshit artists howsoever it pleases you. They bore me.

The Pharisees therefore said unto him, Thou bearest record of thyself; thy record is not true.

What records do we bear within ourselves? Is the written history of the world found in books? If these things we record be not true, what shall we do with them? How shall we classify them? In God's wisdom, the record of ourselves is written within us. Angels often err by imagining their image of themselves to be themselves: this error is then compounded and amplified and multiplied a million fold as they confuse the images of things with things themselves. God made man in his own image. Without God, the image cannot exist.

What then, am I God? No. I am who I am, even a Son of God who is the Son of man.

The Word writes the record, bears the record, creates the record, explains the record. The Word creates, fashions, forms realities. Man, the image of kings and lords, and Man the golden image of Nebuchadnezzar, is an idol. We are gods because God created us: we are not gods who evolve from idols.

In spite of all religious teaching to the contrary, the record of Jesus is true. But men have defaced the image of Jesus and falsely represent him.

The Son of God is God's Son: but even great angels such as Whitehead, Augustine, and Swedenborg confuse simple truth with idolatrous theory. Sins against truth cannot be forgiven: we must always bear the burden of punishment that necessarily follows. What is the punishment? What is the eternal damnation? Even this: to be told the truth. The sons of God delight in this judgment, nor can they be harmed by it. We live in fire.

The Holy Spirit is the saving spirit of truth.

Jesus answered and said unto them, Though I bear record of myself, yet my record is true: for I know whence I came, and whither I go; but ye cannot tell whence I come, and whither I go.

Jesus must bear record of himself. No man can do this for him. He alone must do it; he alone had done it. Nevertheless, although he records his words upon the minds of men, there is another who bears witness to that record. That other is God, working within the hearts and minds, and visiting the souls, of those who believe that record.

God's record of his first born son is true. But the Pharisees teach otherwise, for they are always adding to the book, and taking away from the book. What book? Even the book, the true record of God's Son. I do not say there are not many other books contained in the library of truth. It is the Holy Ghost who teaches us what is true, and what is false: what is living fact, and what is dead fiction. The reality of the knowledge of good and evil is incontestable.

The men who worship Satan bear their mark. Corrupt trees yield evil fruit. Knowledge of their ways poisons the soul. Only those who continue in Jesus' Word know the truth which frees them from the power of liars, and the many deceived deceivers of the present hour.

But where did Jesus come from? Where did he go? Where is he now? Obviously, he is in the kingdom of heaven, even in that portion of the world where the treasures of God are found, even in that part of earth wherein God's will is done.

Nevertheless, the Universe of life is vast: the kingdoms of God are many: the delights of eternity beyond the bounds of human insight. Trust the spirit more: the flesh, less. In this manner does the kingdom come. In this manner, that which is mortal, becomes immortal.

Judge with the spirit of truth.

Ye judge after the flesh; I judge no man.

Each man is his own judge: for his own words judge him. We judge the works of men, and rightly so, for the works of men are their words and their actions and their deeds whereby they can gain entry into our house, and influence our mind, and acquire power over our bodies and our lives.

Let God rule your kingdom so that the kingdom you receive, the kingdom you rule becomes the kingdom of God.

Inheritors also work. Inheritors also create.

Let God alone judge you: for the judgments of men are vain.

And yet if I judge, my judgment is true: for I am not alone, but I and the Father that sent me.

Jesus is created of his Father. The Father sent him into the world. Who sends me into the world? How can any god be sent into the world? How is one who is of heaven to come into the world except by being born into the world? But how can one come into the world?

The world is many, and divided against itself. Lenin is in the world of some: Jimmy Carter is in the world of others. Moslems are in the world. Christians are in the world; those killing and those being killed are in the world. Governors are many in the world, discussing the affairs of the world. Men, great and small, participate in the affairs of the world and thereby give life to the world.

Yet heaven is not of the world: but it is found in the world, enlarging itself within the world: saving the world by destroying the evil of the world. What is evil? A world without the Father.

The salvation of the world is this: God's will done in earth: his kingdom come: his Word come in flesh and blood. The only way the world is saved, even your world, is to accept God's Word into the household of your soul. In this way you become a child of God; and God thereby becomes your Father. But God is more than my Father, even as I am more than his Son.

I am grieved with those men who cannot accept the testimony of my Father. Men use the mechanisms of the world to destroy their lives and to enslave their brethren. How is this done? By the manipulation of mammon, law, opinion, and human emotion.

There is strength in this: possession of our own souls.

We are not alone: the Father is with us. Let the Father work in you.

It is also written in your law, that the testimony of two men is true.

Is the Father a man, even as you? Of course. But the spirit, the very words of truth, abide forever.

I am the one that bear witness of myself, and the Father that sent me beareth witness of me.

How so? By giving me this book to eat: by giving me these pages to write. But for those who doubt my witness, the witness of the Father is insufficient. They seek miracles in a day full of miracles. Their own strong drink has blinded them. The drunkards pass out by reason of their own distillatory genius. I cannot argue with them: my only recourse is to permit them to sleep it off.

Then said they unto him, Where is thy Father? Jesus answered, Ye neither know me, nor my Father: if ye had known me, ye should have known my Father also.

How can we know anything? We speak a word, a thought is formed, a feeling emerges. Is this then knowledge? We speak a word, and nothing comes to mind, is this then ignorance? We experience life, and are amazed and left speechless; is this to know life?

Do men know me? Do men know themselves? How is their knowledge tested? With the Word: for without the Word, all is vanity.

I thank God for my book of life: and I praise God for your book of life.

These words spake Jesus in the treasury, as he taught in the temple; and no man laid hands on him; for his hour was not yet come.

We store the treasures of eternal life within our heart: Our heart, the storehouse of our emotions, feelings, beliefs. Jesus speaks within our treasury. So does God, even his maker, the spirit of love.

God, even the God of everlasting life, speaks to us in our heart. What more can be said? The beauty of creation and life surrounds us. Inwardly, truth is sought, and found.

The Pharisees teach otherwise. But only because they know not what it means to have God speak to them within their heart.

The temple of our spirit is real. We do provide a place for God within us. Statesmen and soldiers alike have their foxholes: and religious teachers also nest in the branches of Israel. And even many a nest is found for the zealots of nonsense and the proponents of vanity.

And where shall Christ rest his head? The Word is the Savior of the world. Without it, what have we? The perishable fancies of dead men. Let us be alive to the God of life so that we might have life, and that, abundantly.

I find in my heart, treasures new and old. Behold, God has given me life this day. Nevertheless, the life of many joyous days past are also with me. Christmas future is also here. What more can one say? The eternal treasures are safe within the universe of God. Our fear of those things that destroy the flesh is without profit. Our soul creates the body. It is the spirit that creates.

But the words of Jesus are spirit and life. The words of men are also spirit: but many of Man's words are Satanic, and the lie and death are found in them. Our life testifies that death is an opinion, a judgment, an hypothesis created by dead men. Death is the result of man's foolish preoccupation with knowledge of good and evil and an equally disastrous failure to eat of the tree of life.

My lives past are real to me and are really mine: all the testimony and protestations and envy of the writers and religious zealots of the present generation cannot keep that fact from my children. Who are my children? Those who believe my words: for if they believe my words they believe me, for wherein is the difference? Also know this: a man is fathered by his own doctrines, created by his own beliefs.

Believe in God who sends and comforts us in this world. There is a prince of this world: his children are also in the world, working the works of the world. His world has an end. When does Satan's world end? When you overcome it by believing the God of truth.

Then said Jesus again unto them, I go my way, and ye shall seek me, and shall die in your sins: whither I go, ye cannot come.

How very true. Those who believe in Jesus also cannot be found of those who seek to kill him. Why? Because the way of truth is guarded. Liars cannot even approach unto the tree of life, let alone enter its garden, or cut it down. Men are vain; and without cause. Their knowledge is limited: but they acknowledge it not. They are the authors, the principle workmen, of their own absurd idols.

At times I must look down to see what they are doing.

Most men die in their sins. But what is sin? To know what is good, and to do evil, is sin. But how do we know what is good, and what is evil, if we eat not of the fruit of knowledge of good and evil? Let us quickly admit, death and that which brings us unto death is evil: and let us be quick to admit eternal life is good and of God, our Creator. This wisdom is given to those who eat of the tree of life: who realize their desires: who achieve their dreams: who live life abundantly.

Transgression of God's law is sin. Whose law? God's law: even that single law whose commandment is eternal life, even that life which is ours when we love the Lord God of Israel with all our heart, mind, soul, strength, and body: even with all of our self.

What is the power of that law? Even love abolishing wickedness.

But the law of man is lust after war: lasciviousness annihilating women: lewdness accepting weakness.

Woman is man's most meet and wonderful help, and companion and supernatural wife. She is clothed in beauty, formed for love, created for song and joy and everlasting delight.

Our spirit is the wife of our flesh: the winsome infidel forever exciting.

I weary of words multiplied in vain. I am tired of fools whose outpouring is like a computer with no halt in its program.

And surely, I am angry at my wives who trust more the foolish advice of the serpent and the desire of their own eyes, than the simple command I gave them, long ago. Perhaps now they'll trust me, and at least, at the very least, begin to suspect the tempter's advice. Satan is a liar: the spiritual deceiver of the present hour: the lord of a world that knows nothing of heaven, is ignorant of the more beautiful things of earth, is proud in its own conceits, and is full of vanity and self-deception. The tempter is not only vain and foolish: but boring, tediously boring. And the result of following his advice is lust, the conception of sin, and ultimately death.

But I find that death is a bore: and the Sadducees, silly.

What are they doing on the earth, Oh Son of man? Producing the same old shit, but storing it in prettier houses.

Then said the Jews, Will he kill himself? because he saith, Whither I go, ye cannot come.

Why should he kill himself? Are there not lawyers and writers, religious teachers and priests, soldiers and statesmen, kings and governors, in the world and of the world under the influence of Vladimir, lord of the world, ready to do this service for him? There are. Besides all this, Jesus was already dead, for how else could he converse with the dead, and how else could he make his voice to sound among those in their graves?

And he said unto them, Ye are from beneath; I am from above: ye are of this world; I am not of this world.

What world? Even that world where religious teachers are so vain that they would rather encourage a mob to crucify a man who speaks the truth than repent of their vanity, and learn truth of God's word.

I said therefore unto you, that ye shall die in your sins: for if ye believe not that I am he, ye shall die in your sins.

They didn't believe: and in their sins, they died. But now they can hear once more the everlasting truth, and live. For what God of life delights in death? But they still refuse to believe: nevertheless, their unbelief is temporary as all of us who know the truth boldly proclaim.

Then said they unto him, Who art thou? And Jesus saith unto them, Even the same that I said unto you from the beginning.

In the beginning God created the heaven and the earth. In the beginning, the word was with God, declaring this truth. I am that Word: I am that truth: for so has my God told me: so has my God taught me.

"We don't believe it!" So ever shouts Satan's orchestrated chorus in my soul. Great is his company: many are his worlds: legions multiplied could not assemble the multitude of those who do not believe I am. Even I am tempted most cunningly to doubt myself. Why? Because the prince of this world is my adversary, and I am his. Neither Lenin, nor Castro, nor Marx, nor Truman, nor Mao, nor any other one of these many servants of the State, of Man, of Religion, of the World, can bring you to the Father of everlasting life, and love, and beauty.

Jesus is the only way, the only door, the only truth. Men are the slaves of the abstractions of devils: the created spirits abstracted from corrupt flesh. My Word is made flesh and blood: their flesh and blood creates words. Thus are liars created: thus are lies fathered. They reject the spirit and idolize the flesh. I love the Spirit that creates in flesh and blood.

My Word does not pass away: it grows. My Word is not void and empty: it is pregnant with life, full of possibilities astounding to consider. My death is but a trifling fact descriptive of part of my eternal life. My death does not change me: the things I create, change. Life is ever a harmony of joyous motion. The Word creates.

I have many things to say and to judge of you: but he that sent me is true; and I speak to the world those things which I have heard of him. They understood not that he spake to them of the Father.

There are many things to be said about me: many things which require judgment.

The kingdom of heaven is with us today. Why then do those who preach my gospel deny this truth?

The meek have inherited the earth. What is more obvious?

The resurrection of the body is a daily occurrence. How then can these many worldly Sadducees deny it?

Men were taught not to kill. How is it then that the servants of the beast yet gather unto themselves all these armies?

You cannot serve God and Mammon. How is it then that all these servants of the world have overcome the children of God with the powers of Mammon? A price is placed on all that men do, and say, and enjoy, and possess.

The State reigns supreme: and the lords of the world multiply their laws, their rules, their ordinances, their regulations, their systems, their methods of procedure ad nauseam.

Where is forgiveness of debts and trespasses to be found? Not in the economies of the world, not in the courts of the many governments of the world, not in the many councils wherein men legislate vanity.

The image makers, the idol merchants, flourish. What then does Satan and his sons want of me? My denial that I am God's Son. And some silly service for promised great reward, besides.

The greed of the fallen sons of God is madness. And their temptations, useless. The Father is greater than all. No man can stay his hand. These liars labor in vain.

But men understand little and deceive themselves in much.

Beware of those who forsake the gospel of life.

Then said Jesus unto them, When ye have lifted up the Son of man, then shall ye know that I am he, and that I do nothing of myself; but as my Father hath taught me, I speak these things.

They have lifted me up. But not as high as my defaced image. Nevertheless, I would to God that they would be taught of the Father. Truly, to be taught of God is to know the spirit of love for what he is and to realize the joy of her beauty. But they gawk at the image and are deaf to the voice of the Spirit.

The Father teaches us to speak: we hear those things of him which are true. We are his children: this he tells us with his own still voice. But all the heavens and the earth proclaim his glory. We are trees, yielding the fruit of life, nourished by the stream of truth whose waters branch themselves upward and outward from within us.

Nevertheless, we are more than trees: for there is a kingdom found within us: treasures of ancient ages: delights of things present: glories yet to come.

Thus does our God teach us: he teaches with his Word. His record is still with us. No tyrant ensconced in the fortress of Tyrus can lead his ships and merchant men against us. No serpent can deceive us. No wizard can trick us. No politician can politely persuade us otherwise. We are of God and hear his Word.

God, even our Father, is our teacher, our witness, our recorder. He always does those things that please us. Our companion, our judge, our husbandman, is with us. He knows us: we know him.

He sends us into the world. We come from him. And we often leave the world, and return to him. We live equally well in heaven as in earth. We come from God: we return to God. We are the spokesmen of God.

All who know these things to be true hear these words as truth. Those who cannot hear them are spiritually deaf. God's spirit is his Word working within us: comforting, teaching, enlightening, strengthening, enlivening.

But the words of Pharisees are the words of our religious accusers. They themselves are in bondage to their own beliefs, their own customs, their own ritual, their own sins of disbelief in the unadulterated gospel of Jesus. They want no real son of God clothed in flesh and blood to spoil the house they have made for themselves. Their ignorance is colossal; and even as a man, their vanity, to me, is almost incomprehensible. God, be gracious unto them, for who else can free them from their own foolishness?

And he that sent me is with me: the Father hath not left me alone: for I do always those things that please him. As he spake these words, many believed on him.

Men must speak if there are to be those who believe on them. A man must speak if there are to be those who believe on him. God speaks, but who believes? Men are fathered by their beliefs. Beliefs are generated with words. There are the words of the wise, and the words of fools. There are words spoken by Jesus, heard by his children, written by his angels, and stored in the hearts and minds and souls of men. Words kept, as it were, within themselves. It is the God within us who creates the kingdom among us. In this manner heaven comes to earth. In this manner, God's kingdom comes.

Do the scribes acknowledge these things to be true? Let men judge themselves what is true with whatever words they command. But what do you think? What is found in the world except it be news of the world; the history of the world; facts of the world; records of the world, world organizations; and the nations of the world?

Nevertheless, the history of the kingdom of heaven is also real. It is written within us. We are the living witnesses testifying to its growth.

The history of heaven is not found in the libraries of the world. In all truth, even in this early stage of its growth, the world itself is too small a place to contain all the books that would have to be written if Jesus' story was to be found in such records. But the book of life is real: you need only open it to read it. It is found within you.

When does God leave us? When we do those things that displease him? I doubt it. What man who knows of the evil men have wrought in the world, can honestly declare that God is pleased with the world? God saves the world by sending his Son into the world so God himself can experience the world. God is in his sons reconciling the world to himself. God is our father, the creator of heaven and earth and the beast of the field; and the Savior of the world. Men of the world are of the world creating and being created by the world. Such men are governed by the prince of the world. Who is the prince of the world? He whose spirit creates all these worldly kingdoms.

Does God leave us alone? Does God forsake us? Does God hide himself from us? Of course, when the occasion merits it. We treat the reality of heaven with worldly contempt: we judge after the flesh: our standards are of earth. In this, we bear witness unto ourselves that God has left us alone. We sin, and God casts us out of his house.

Twenty-six children are abducted. Their parents pray to God for their return. They return.

What next? Do they seek perfection by forgiving their enemies? Do they bless their enemies? Do they do good to those that have done them evil?

The parents of the world surely don't so respond. Enter the lawyers, the police officers, the judges, the writers and all others who busy themselves with the misery of the world for their own profit. But I judge not the parents: only the lawyers, the judges, the officers, the prison keepers and the mob who, for a piece of money, sell themselves to the State and its ways.

It is obvious to me God does good: his goodness covers the earth: he blesses good and evil alike: his forgiveness, mercy, and righteousness never cease.

But we must clothe ourselves with our own filthy rags of righteousness. Ford cannot forgive Nixon: he can only do what is right for the country. Men are the slaves of their own mental idols. Money, public opinion, self-conceit, the cares of the world's ways are too much for them. Nevertheless, God saves the world, and clothes it with his beauty; I marvel at the God who can bring flowers out of dung, truth out of political bullshit, life out of death.

Let us keep the way of life with the sword of truth. What is this truth? For those who know God, lawyers, worldly recorders and writers, religious teachers and evangelists, judges, police officers, armies, and all these powers of principalities, churches, and governments are adventitious. Where the kingdom of heaven is, God rules, and love is king. But why does God leave us alone? So that we might learn to become our own god. The Sons of God come before God to commune with that Spirit: to learn of him: to be commanded of him: to find pleasure in their king.

Nevertheless, God cannot forsake us forever, nor for even a long time.

Then said Jesus to those Jews which believed on him, If ye continue in my word, then are ye my disciples indeed; And ye shall know the truth, and the truth shall make you free.

Free from what? Free from the power of liars and worldly hypocrites who wish to bind us to their own idols. What a great price men must pay to animate the State! What tremendous waste to honor vain and little men! Satan hates my ways, and I abominate his sacrifices. Let us honor Jesus for the truth he has given us. Let us worship God. In this manner does our kingdom become the kingdom of God.

We believe: we continue in the Word: we are his disciples: we know the truth: we are free. Liberty gives birth to its child, which child we are. We are born of the free woman, not of the bond woman. There are two women in the world; only the one is taken, the other is left in the world, to serve the world, to delight the world, to fuck the world in her own inimitable fashion.

I am sad. Sorrow takes hold on me. The beast I was born to rule has deceived my well-beloved. And I am who I am, torn, alone, forsaken. Thus is it with God: my Creator suffers, long is his suffering; God, alone with himself.

What shall I do? Write more words? Read a book? Plead my truth once more? Come again? Where am I now? From whence do I come? Whither have I gone?

They believe themselves wise. They station themselves within their animated idol. They hide themselves from me. They despise my Word.

They love me not. They love the deceitful beast: they worship money, state, church; and they love to corrupt my ways and despoil the things I love.

What shall God do? Where shall he turn? What shall he create, sustain, enliven? Let God do whatsoever it pleases her to do: for why should she pretend to be that which surely she is not?

What is truth? The Word picturing things as they really are. The Spirit is the Creator: we are her created souls, creating within and among ourselves, the kingdom of heaven. The Word is made flesh: we cannot deny it any more and expect to enjoy eternal life.

Our wisdom has built her own house: the serpent is what it is: a beast, a mechanism of spiritual instinct, a dust gulper; a deceiver, a liar, a tempter, an accuser; the evil one who is to be resisted.

Let me bless myself in the spirit of truth. Surely, I love her, and would ravish her each time I find her. I love to fuck her in the thousand different ways she lusts to be so used. Let truth be my bride: let me remain her loved one forever.

But I speak not of Babble On, that priestly, scientific, legalistic, and moralistic whore who fucks around with the world's princes, and great men, and servants. But of Jerusalem, where Jesus rules in peace, and the glory of the gentiles is found; where beauty and life and joy and delight, abound; and poverty and pain are no more.

Babylon is the whore God divorced: but men have married her. And they babble, on and on and on, corrupting themselves with her own unprofitable ways. It is impossible to serve God by having intercourse with Babylon. If God dwells in Jerusalem, even in the city of truth, how can we excite God by lusting after our own creation? And what is Babylon except a city wherein men glorify their own ways even with the precious things God has given them?

Men are prisoners of their own idols. We are creators. Idi Amin Dada is just as much a creator as Lenin, Hitler, Truman, Lincoln, and any other prince of the world. But all their words and works have the singular end of persuading men that their good is to be found in serving their idol, and not heaven's king. Men simply do not obey the God whose prophet commanded, Thou shalt not kill and whose Son said, Do not kill. Love your enemies, bless them that curse you, do good to them that hate you, and pray for them which despitefully use you, and persecute you.

Whom then do they believe? Even in those who proclaim a literal adherence to the gospel would result in instant death. But what is death? An exit from a world so brutal we are sickened even to think on it. Men are ignorant of where we come from and where we go. They cannot follow us: they die in their sins: and babble on, and on, and on.

God saves us from Satan. Saves us from the effects of following blind leaders of the blind: saves us from giving our lives over to godless men whose concept of paradise is the victory of death over life. They do not cleanse: they do not enlighten: they do not teach. They make the proselyte as stupid as they themselves are: they teach children to become as adept at defending vanity, foolishness, and pride as they themselves are: they yield the fruit of their souls, even the words that come out of their own mouths. They honor no god except the God of economic force, military might, and dazzling political bullshit. They serve the State, Law, the System, and even their Job; and fuck around with every worldly enterprise and evil invention and social organization which God loathes. To govern men, they must produce the right image, even if they lie to produce it. To rule men, they must have their police, their army, their company of hired employees who, for the right price, will do whatsoever they are ordered to do. Their power is the power of pride, a pride which clothes itself in the flesh and blood of those who create money, laws, and prisons.

And for what end? For what purpose?

They answered him, We be Abraham's seed, and were never in bondage to any man: how sayest thou, Ye shall be made free?

Men understand not how they are bound, whose slaves they are, what prison holds them. The universe of delight is vast, yet worldly cells hold many. Earth, in which heaven is not found, is a prison.

Jesus answered them, Verily, verily, I say unto you, Whosoever committeth sin is the servant of sin. And the servant abideth not in the house forever: but the Son abideth ever. If the Son therefore shall make you free, ye shall be free indeed.

The house of God cannot forever tolerate the servants of sin. Liars are an offense to those whose study is truth. Those who murder and hate are an inconvenience to those who quicken and love. What companionship has ugliness and beauty, fear and boldness, pain and joy, evil and good? The universe is vast and encompasses all things. Nevertheless, the goodness of God endures forever whereas the power of Satan has an end. I am that end. In this way are men set free. All who love me know this to be true. My end is as real as my beginning. The Son of man is as real as the Son of God.

I know that ye are Abraham's seed, but ye seek to kill me, because my word hath no place in you.

Why do men reject the gospel of the kingdom of heaven? What have all these my enemies spoken that men should accept their words and despise my words?

Jesus means *Jehovah saves us*, and the meaning is written in his flesh and in his blood. What are words on paper? Impressions of ink? What are words spoken, modulations of the air? The words are more than this for they are spirit, life, and truth.

The spirit inspires the dust: the spirit is not the dust of the ground.

Abraham's seed is real as all these Jews witness: but so is the power that multiplied them. So also is the word of Jesus which desires to find a place within them. Men themselves decide what they believe: they open and close the door of their own heart. How strange it is to me to see them open to the spirits devils create and shut the door to the Spirit Jesus sends to reason with them.

I speak that which I have seen with my Father: and ye do that which ye have seen with your father.

We are the sons of our fathers. We learn of our teachers. We are led by our leaders. We are encouraged in our beliefs by our priests. We are commanded by our officers. We are victimized by the structure of our own idols.

I father my own children: and devils father their children. Who are my children? Even those who know me as their father. Nevertheless, my God is their God, and our Father has his own ways. I am the child that I am. For me, as for all the sons of god, the mystery ever deepens; the universe of life is almost beyond the power of our words to measure.

What I have seen astonishes me and delights me. I have seen the tree of life flourishing in my garden of desire. The kingdom of heaven is within you, even as it is within me.

Men would do well to beware of the doctrines of serpents lest they themselves become transformed into serpents. Witches are real and the powers of sorcerers, undeniable.

They answered and said unto him, Abraham is our father. Jesus saith unto them, If ye were Abraham's children ye would do the works of Abraham. But now ye seek to kill me, a man that hath told you the truth, which I have heard of God: this did not Abraham. Ye do the deeds of your father.

The desire of men to be angry with their brothers without a cause, is almost universal in the world. The sons of God, the children of the highest, die as men. We are killed by our own brethren. God suffers as he witnesses this fratricidal war. Gods array themselves against me. Philosophers and evangelists alike, wish to take me, stone me; they have judged me. Yet they are too busy examining idols to learn of their Father, even the Highest, their Creator. So they are fathered by their own self's. They generate lies: cast them in type: publish them among peoples and nations: deceive themselves as well as multitudes; and death results.

Even the greatest of them believe more in themselves, in the powers of their own intellect, than they do in me. Yet, what really is the difficulty? Have we all not one Father? We used to. But now we have many fathers. We are fathered by the lies we generate. And now, in this day, Satan desires tolerance: tolerance of his deceits, his foolishness, his religions. Truth is intolerant: men are mad to confuse truth and belief. They are fathered by devils and this truth annoys them. They would rather have me dead than tolerate my contempt for their lies. Liars are inferior beings: why should they fear truth?

Then said they to him, We be not born of fornication; we have one Father, even God.

Even the Jews herein recognize that fornicators give birth to children. Those who depart from the spirit of truth fornicate with the prince of the world. They lust after the idols of the world and sacrifice their minds to the things of the world. What is a thing of the world? Death is one such thing. Murderers spiritual abound in the world killing the children of God with their lies, their disbelief in Jesus, their many false images of Jehovah. Is not God even who He is? What need then has he of all these scribes and teachers who do not know him, yet talk so knowingly of him? Obviously, they are liars, and the father of their own doctrines. Their father is no longer God, but Satan, the subtle yet many headed beast who presents himself before God as a Son of God. The usurper himself who tempts God.

Those of God are of God: the *Jews* are *Jesus' witnesses*: the Jews are Jehovah's witnesses: even those Jews who continue in the Word.

Men are fathered by the spirit that creates them: all spirits are not of God: to place hell in the word, is Satan's desire. To remove hell from the world, is to make the word flesh. The Word is made flesh: but flesh makes many worlds.

Jesus said unto them, If God were your Father, ye would love me: for I proceeded forth and came from God; neither came I of myself, but he sent me.

Truman can send troops to Korea: presidents send ambassadors to the nations of the world: but men acknowledge not that God sends his Son into the world via the power of the Word.

Truman sent, presidents have sent, God still sends and receives: the Sons of God are many: they come: they go: but men of earth ever remain the same: denying the truth that heaven is brought to earth by those who do just that very thing.

Angels are clothed in flesh and blood, but the blind see them not. The Son of Timaeus is yet to be healed of his blindness. Plato is blind although he understands and senses many things. The light that lights the world has yet to enter into him.

Why don't the Jews believe Jesus? Because they still say they see, whereas in all truth they have no light within them to dissipate the darkness of the world. Even the blind manifest the works of God. God is a sender. He sends some into the world: he also sends many in the world, filthy in the world, blinded by the dirt of the world, to wash in the pool provided.

Nevertheless, only the sensitive sense the presence of the sender. Most men really don't know what is happening around them.

Why do ye not understand my speech? even because ye cannot hear my word.

Rabbis are deaf. They ought to hear, seek to hear, ask to hear. But all they desire is to confirm themselves in their self-created beliefs and silence the living prophets. To them, Abraham is dead; Moses is dead; Jacob is dead; Isaac is dead; Jesus is dead; and I am a dreamer. And what then are they? Obviously, the spokesmen of dead prophets. It's really so ridiculous that I find it boring. Why should the living look to the dead? Jesus was killed but is alive forevermore: For death cannot live within him. Death is a fiction and those who promote it are a living contradiction.

Ye are of your father the devil, and the lusts of your father ye will do. He was a murderer from the beginning, and abode not in the truth, because there is no truth in him. When he speaketh a lie, he speaketh of his own: for he is a liar, and the father of it.

Men give birth to their own lies. We are the fathers of many doctrines. What is my doctrine? I have none. I only have the doctrines found in the book my God has given me. Even the Bible before me. James is both a king, a saint, and a religious man for he feeds the hungry, orphans, and widows with the bread of life. Widows and fatherless alike read the Word because of James. His faith produced a work, even the greatest work of the seventeenth century: truly, a century of genius.

God's Word is simple and easy to understand. Why do many torture themselves with attempting to destroy it? It would be easier to extinguish the sun: easier to destroy a star. But men wrest it for their own purposes.

But what of myself? Of myself, I can do little, extremely little. But God tries me. Why? To strengthen me. Why should he strengthen me? Because I am weak.

But the men of the world are strong. They are ready to instruct all men: they are proud enough to legislate for all men: they are strong enough to tax great peoples, organize intricate means of death; and tax, and imprison, and judge, and teach, and command, and kill with fear of neither God nor man. There is no limit to their gluttony: their knowledge of good and evil extends to all things: they are wiser than all: they need not learn: they need no companion, no guide, no friend. Nothing is mysterious to them: there is no room for awe in their souls. They seek neither love, nor beauty, nor joy, nor life, nor truth. They seek no everlasting kingdom, worship no God, crave neither righteousness nor truth.

I marvel at them. From whence comes their strength? From their father.

From Satan itself, God's beast, and man's adversary; the sons of God rule men with their lies via the spirit of darkness, of deceit, of death.

But I want none of these spirits. Thus, do I mourn. I am as weak as David, as ignorant as Solomon, as deluded as Jesus. What have they seen, that I have not seen? What have they heard, that I cannot hear? What do they seek, that I have not found?

Is there no God of gods? No creator, no sender, no comforter, no friend, no shepherd, no lord?

Men are wise: they delight in adjusting the mechanism of the world to serve their purposes. Men are subtle: they delight in knowing how the dust of the earth is assembled, and framed, and fashioned. Men are proud, their hard hearts are impervious to the spirits of life that enchant my soul. Men are full of knowledge: they know more about me than I myself know: they are full of advice, of rules, of commandments, of laws, of explanations, of ideas, of experience, of temptations extraordinary.

Now let my God, my Father, even the Lord God of Israel, strengthen me: let him comfort me, teach me, ever remain with me. Let her love me, for am I not hers to love?

The prince of darkness is full of its own conceits. Those that are of the antichrist proclaim to all men that Jesus Christ has not come in the flesh. The last days encompass two thousand years. Men refuse to believe that, though in heaven, Jesus never left them alone. He is with them in earth, in heaven, in hell. He is as real, as personal, as full of hope and desire, of flesh and blood, as they are. He is as much a son of perdition, as they are. All have sinned and come short of the glory of God. Jesus is no exception.

What is sin? The imperfection we manifest when we obey not love's commandments. The joyless life we create when we believe Satan and act upon temptations. The struggle is real: but the victory is ours. God knows his work. We are that work.

The theology and religion of Man are vain. We are God's. Neither State, nor Religion, nor the vanities of Man's idols of intellect, or any other of the multitude of antichrist forces in the world, can keep us from God's love. Surely, I know this: surely, you know this. Why not accept it for what it is? And what is it, except the everlasting life which love creates within our soul, even the mansion of our delights, even the kingdom of heaven, the very house of God, found within us?

The universe is infinite: our life is eternal. God reconciles us to himself. All this is present fact, living truth, ancient scripture. The new wine, the new bottles are as real as Israel: even as much an undeniable fact as the old wine, and the old bottles.

What is the end of Jesus' work in the world? Even this: the salvation of the world you realize when you know yourself as a child of God. We are born of the spirit of truth. We overcome the world by becoming a Son of God. In this way does God gather his own. The kingdom of heaven is with us forever. Where is the kingdom? Within you, among you: even in that place where these words abide.

And because I tell you the truth, ye believe me not.

Men are slow to accept truth and quick to accept their own self-generated conceits. They need a judge: the world is saved by the judgments of God: the word God has spoken through his prophets, through his wise men, through his Son, is the judge.

God never pretended our belief was not essential: never taught that our faith was not required: never labored, chastised, wrought, except to condition us to accept that belief. Our belief, clearly, ends the matter.

Faith without works is dead: nevertheless even the dead who hear, live: and those who live out their beliefs, can never die. The resurrection of the body is a credible fact, a daily occurrence, a natural event, an ever present miracle of God.

The Satan within us denies this truth: long is his argument: tedious his temptations: foolish his doctrine of doubt. Unscientific, unphilosophic, unliterary, and unlearned are his doctrines. The scholars of Belial are poor metaphysicians all. Their doctrine is leavened and unlovely.

The nature of truth is as water, is as fire. Of it, we are composed: in it, we live: by it, we cannot be hurt. The baptism, the cleansing, the fire of hell itself, is required, and supplied.

Nothing is lost except ourselves. Nevertheless, the shepherd of our souls is as real as the sheepishness of men. He has found you. Why trouble yourself more? Even all of our unbelief cannot stay the loving hand of God. Believe God, believe Jesus, believe me.

Which of you convinceth me of sin? And if I say the truth, why do ye not believe me?

Because they are fascinated with their present beliefs: satisfied with their own generation of genius: clearly proud and thrilled with the idol built behind them and from whose elevated altar they berate their people.

Men have made themselves expert at organizing peoples: families, tribes, associations, armies, nations, leagues, confederations, councils, gangs, governments, and committees flourish and fill the earth. Thus are men marked: thus are men enslaved and bound unto lawyers, statesmen, generals, dictators, bureaucrats, civil servants, premiers, presidents, and kings. The prince of the world is many.

The world is too much for them: they therefore are overcome, and do not believe they can overcome it.

Nevertheless, what is all this to you? Who determines your belief? Decide yourself. As for me, in all truth, all these bondsmen of the world are a pain in the ass.

He that is of God heareth God's words: ye therefore hear them not, because ye are not of God.

What is of earth is of earth. What is of God is of God. What is of the liar, is of liars. Men send out from themselves lies: words spoken in haste, in ignorance, in pride; in quiet and isolated detachment from the living God.

Thus social custom and national pride are fashioned into chains. But chains, so forged, can also bind Satan. Indeed, he has been bound. And now he is loose from his prison, working his mischief. Is there faith on the earth? Faith in the writings of Moses? Faith in the words of Jesus? Faith in the works of Newton? Faith in the Lord God of Israel? Faith in genius, in scholarship, in the power of love?

Is there such faith in the world? If there is, it is hard to find. In the world. I find faith in Mammon, faith in arms, faith in law, faith in religion, faith in science, faith in systems and schemes and governments of many sizes, shapes, powers and forms. Yet, to each man, the world is the image of chaotic godlessness. But most men, albeit not all, are ignorant of the design limitations of the beast they witness before them. How then can they successfully war against it? In truth, they cannot; in truth, they know not what they do.

Nevertheless, the Word of God is set against the beast. The Godless State and antichrist religion, and the roles of lawyers and statesmen have an end.

The kingdom of heaven is within you. All the external forces of creation cannot take your life from you. However, gods are self-creative, spiritually. We reap, as we sow: our death is really experienced because of our disbelief in God, and our acceptance of our own Satanic impulses.

There is no death in God: his commandment is life everlasting. But we do accept knowledge of evil, assimilate it within ourselves, and bring forth the fruit we yield. The world is full of bondmen, servants of servants. The State enslaves its architects, its builders, its supporters, its animators. But men are proud, and in their darkened ways, God travels not.

At times, I am astonished at the fullness of life. Yet in the world, I am lonely, and sorrowful; I mourn. Why? Because my heaven is violently assaulted. Men who cannot rule themselves rule those I love. My Word is despised and vanity is established on high. Fools are made king: and God hides the righteous, the gentle, the beautiful, the good.

We are given so much, yet we live as if God is not. We are not made for pain and sorrow and war and strife and foolishness and death. Let God avenge me of all these my enemies by cleansing them of their filthy little lies and clothing them in his own inexhaustible goodness. Let truth and love and joy prevail everywhere that I am.

Yet how hard it is for me to sustain the dream: I look for the kingdom of heaven; I discover the world. The *world*, a *w*omb of *r*otten g*old*: astonishing it is to find mechanisms that corrupt truth.

I am at war with the spirits that come from the world. My struggle is fiercely internal. I am fed up, literally at the point of vomit, with Man and his idol of God. He pretends things are not the way they are: my death is real. To live in the world is to be born in a place of death. Men covet power to manipulate the idol, to make it walk, speak, work, and command. It has enslaved many: it does afflict men: and they daily add to its powers: the dead add to the dead, bury themselves, and also prepare pits for the living.

I hate death: I hate my poverty, my ignorance, my lack of power. I hate my life in this world. For what is it? God says nothing: for he knew it would be this way, and so did I. All I can do is continue; nevertheless my work does have an end.

We eat of the tree of knowledge: we eat of the tree of life: we eat the flesh of Jesus: we drink his blood.

Is the meaning clear? Is it not fundamental, literally speaking, the truth itself?

The right use of the Word is righteousness: the wrong use of the Word is Satanic wickedness. Is Satan a Son of God? A grandson, yes: a son, no. Surely, I created the beast in order to make use of it in the world. But what has resulted? It afflicts my wife, kills the bodies of my friends, and causes the rebellious sons of God to lose their way in earth, and die like men. Men also have programmed it to tempt me.

At times, when I am astonished at what God has created, and delight myself with the tree of life, I forget about Satan, and the knowledge of evil, which lawyers and writers and statesmen are forever ingesting, eating, planting, cultivating, harvesting, and selling.

The poor in spirit rejoice in the delights of life: but the rich, the worldly wise, the very authors of the masters of deceit, reject the kingdom of God in earth and set up their own kingdom. What is this kingdom? Obviously, it is what it is: namely, the world.

What has God given me that he has not given to any of his other sons? Einstein had the Bible, and much else besides: so did Truman: so did Lenin: and even Castro heard of it as did Mao Tse-tung. But love of the Lord God of Israel and the commandment of life everlasting, and the cleansing and forgiveness of sins, such men, and their disciples and apologists, reject.

True, my woman, my beloved, my church, is scattered, is ravished, is made to serve as a whorish concubine to the very beasts of the earth, these great men of the world have created.

Men are sold into bondage to the very institutions of school, of finance, of business, of church, of government which other men, and sometimes even they themselves, have created.

All taxation is socially organized theft: and money is the supreme mover of Mammonites everywhere. The men of Ammon are yet with us in these last hours.

The churches preach knowledge of good and evil: they know all about it. They themselves are the door to heaven: the shepherds of the flock: the angels of righteousness: so Satan makes it appear. But the angels of the churches, the very men whose products of thought and dream and desire create the churches, are not yet the sons of God, but the fathers of the churches.

I do not say all is evil in the churches: I only judge all is not good and perfect.

But I also have the great whore to contend with; the very daughter of Babylon who has fucked herself into insensitivity by dealing with the men of this world. They'll steal from the poor to support their vanities: babble prayers in public: preach leavened doctrines instead of simple gospel: and teach men how to go to a heaven they themselves refuse to enter. God grant me patience.

They've cast lots for my coat, and parted my garments among themselves, thereby testifying to all the world that they are the soldiers of Rome who do such things. For those who can see it, Rome is Babylon's daughter: and the Godless State is their chief conception, the beast of troubled and wicked men who rule with pride, money, social force, and the strength of arms. They are always seeking power: always taxing peoples: always convening governments, forming committees, writing laws, enforcing trifles, and conducting studies, wars, and experiments in social organization. The kingdom of God, where love and truth and beauty rule, they reject.

They spend millions to convict a man of what he surely knows he is guilty: avoid the judgments of mercy, truth, and faith, and forgiveness, which Love has himself commanded, and enclose men in a womb of worldliness where nothing everlasting can ever be born.

"Be specific, name the men you accuse." So commands the Satanic spirit ever with me in these latter hours. Nevertheless, why should I bother? They judge themselves with their own words. A man is fathered by his beliefs. They believe in their fathers: and I believe in mine. If my Father forsakes me for a time, what is that to me? Has he not made me what I am, even my own god? But these hypocrites never speak with God, yet know all about God: they surely know that I am not the Son of God. Whose Son then am I? Surely, not theirs. For I am not fathered by their doctrines, but by mine own. But they are only mine because my God has given them to me. I do not deny my Father.

Then answered the Jews, and said unto him, Say we not well that thou art a Samaritan, and hast a devil? Jesus answered, I have not a devil; but I honour my Father, and ye do dishonour me. And I seek not mine own glory: there is one that seeketh and judgeth. Verily, verily, I say unto you if a man keep my saying, he shall never see death.

Jehovah's witnesses are the Jews: surely, salvation is of the Jews, for through them Jesus, Jehovah saves us. But men, even among the Jews and even among many other of God's witnesses, reject the simple statement that the Lord God of Israel is the Father of Jesus, and also the spirit of truth and love herself saving the world through her ever able and sufficient creative power. Men really reject the Word. For the Word commands belief and love. They dishonor themselves by refusing to believe in the God who sent and straightens Jesus as he journeys in heaven, in hell, in the world.

He truly seeks not his own glory: for what is that? A Son of God is a Son of God: surely, that is the end of our story of what happened in the beginning. Men seek out prophets and reject the spirit of prophecy. The abomination prophesied is the destruction of Jerusalem. The city of truth is desolate. Why? Because the children of God left it to bring truth to all nations. In this manner is truth brought to earth. But if men believe not Jesus, nor John, nor the witnesses of truth who cover the heavens, how can they believe in what I see? Truly no man knows the day, nor the hour of their fulfillment: no, not the angels of heaven, nor the Son of man, but the Father only. Do I know? Of course not, for how could I possibly know the day you choose to become a Son of

God? Why make a great mystery out of a simple fact? In eternity, there is no more time to waste words debating the reality of that which we are living. For those who believe in Jesus, believe in life, everlasting life. They cannot see death, even when they die, because all they see then is a passage from one place to another and perhaps, back again. But those who are full of the knowledge of evil see Death for what it is: even dead earth returning to its source. Yet, even these shall live, although not the filthy houses they build for themselves. For such cannot stand beside the great ocean of truth forever.

Do the dead live? Of course they do: the world is full of men boasting about the fact that they are dead. All communists by their own doctrines are dead men awaiting the ultimate destruction of their body. But since they have already given their soul to the State, how can they possibly fear the loss of their body?

But really, all this is a bit boring.

Let the God of Israel be glorified: but how? By turning to that Spirit in truth and love. I am his and She is mine.

Who seeks and judges so that the glory of Jesus might be found? The spirit of truth, even that one of many of God's spirits which is directly from him. The thirst for truth is real. Men are blindly vain. They can see and talk about many unities: the world, the government, money, the United States Air Force, company policy, my children, my life. Such are some of the things that men refer to when they discuss causes, and offer opinions, about many things of which they have knowledge. But to confess to the oneness of the Spirit of Truth, even that Holy Ghost, the great host of God, who daily witnesses to the goodness of God, is too much for them. Policies dictate the actions of many men who are thereby bound by it, serve it, glorify it, even die for it. They die for Freedom, world peace, or some trifling cause. But to live to honor the God that created all things, even the Father of the spirits of love, joy, delight, and beauty, is too much for them. This, by their own admission, they cannot do.

God is my Father, my teacher, my friend, my witness. When we ascend the mountain of living detail within ourselves, even that mount of Old Lives, even that place where the delight of lives past is found, we are given of God those things that are rightly ours: even those things stored within us: even the treasures of our heart.

Men have the water stored in the waterpots of truth. They only need draw it out to taste of the new wine supplied for this feast.

Yet, except for God, who understands these things?

Even Satan, man's ultimate collective consciousness, has nothing of this truth stored within any of its myriad files. Not on paper; nor in the flesh and blood of human brains; surely not on stone; not in magnetic tape or core or bubble—yet it is found written upon my heart, stored within my mind. The Word has done this.

Then said the Jews unto him, Now we know that thou hast a devil.

How did they know this? From whom did they receive such information? What process generated such extraordinary knowledge?

The tree of knowledge of good and evil grows within a man. Knowledge of evil produces deadly fruit. They are the slaves of their teacher, their comforter, their friend, and they know it not. They have devils. They see death. They know Abraham is dead. They know the prophets are dead. They know all men shall see death.

Abraham is dead, and the prophets; and thou sayest, If a man keep my saying, he shall never taste of death. Art thou greater than our father Abraham, which is dead: whom makest thou thyself?

Surely, God is the God of the living: neither Abraham, nor the prophets are dead, although they have tasted of death.

I have tasted death for I have drunk the deadly poison of the worldly alchemists. It made me burp.

All man's religions are religions of death. But the sons of God visit widows and the fatherless: this is our religion: to get the living to accept the fact that the God of Israel is their father, their spouse, their lover.

But not only do Jehovah's Witnesses dishonor Jesus, they dishonor his God, for his God made him, created him. He is the Son of the God who fathered him. He is the Son of man, as all of us are. Nevertheless, who is man or the Son of man, that we should honor him? Man is created male and female: Adam is their name. Surely, we are Adam: each and every one of us in our own glorious way.

Men mouth the scripture: but do they believe it? God laughs at me. Why? Because I created the beast to serve me in the world and

175

the damn thing has swallowed me up. And now I have to destroy it. But my children don't understand. That makes it even more laughable, since I had intended the damn thing to help me teach them.

In all truth, I have made myself, the Son of man. It is God who has made me his Son. I did not become a Son of God by becoming a Son of man. Only madmen so conceive their beginnings. Nevertheless, there are yet also those who conceive themselves to be created by the swirling's of cosmic dust which, when it cooled, transformed itself into the dust of this earthy ground which constitutes our bodies, our earthly bodies.

That God, in the beginning, created the heaven and the earth, such men cannot accept. Godless men cannot accept God's words. They can eat of the fruit of that word. They believe in much of what Isaac Newton did. They can accept his laws. What they cannot accept is Isaac, a living prophet who is an angel of God, bringing the truth found in heaven to earth. What then do men do with the vineyard God has given them to husband?

They glut themselves with its fruit and deny God's servants, friends, and even his own Son, the fruit of it.

It is not what I make of myself that is important to understand herein. What is important is to understand what God does with me and makes of me. To deny myself, is to deny the honor God has given me. This I cannot do. But why is it so hard for men to accept God and so easy for men to accept almost any other thing?

Jesus answered, If I honour myself, my honour is nothing; it is my Father that honoureth me; of whom ye say, that he is your God: Yet ye have not known him; but I know him: and if I should say, I know him not, I shall be a liar like unto you: but I know him and keep his saying. Your father Abraham rejoiced to see my day: and he saw it, and was glad.

"Where is Abraham now?" Living with God. "Where?" In the city of God, even the city of angels. "Where in that city?" I don't know. "Then ask God." I have. "What did God answer?" I'm not going to tell you. Perhaps Abraham will.

Then said the Jews unto him, Thou art not yet fifty years old, and hast thou seen Abraham? Jesus said unto them, Verily, verily, I say unto you, Before Abraham was, I am. Then took they up stones to cast at him: but Jesus hid himself, and went out of the temple, going through the midst of them, and so passed by.

So ever is it with those who cannot accept the words of God. Even Abraham is stoned in Washington: and many others with him: men cast images into stone, and with such images, destroy men's lives.

Men not only dishonor Jesus, but God and Abraham as well. They judge so readily by appearances: they do not judge readily the words and deeds of men whereby those men might truly be known for what they are.

It is best to leave them to their own doings when they are so moved to wrath. Causeless anger dies of its own flame. We need not piss on it to put it out.

CHAPTER 9

And as Jesus passed by, he saw a man which was blind from his birth.

We are all blind from our birth. In the innocence of life, what does a child see? The colors and shapes of things without making their way unto the soul within. How is it with our souls as we once again receive the impressions of the world? When we come into the world, we receive the world, via the ways of flesh, blood, and man. A child is what it is: a soul adventuring into the world. Once in the world, can we immediately see? I think not: we must receive light into ourselves before we can see. This process is long and we must patiently accept it for what it is: only fools, early in the world, young in knowledge, unskilled in ideas, poor in their wisdom, pretend to know enough to lord it over others, and explain all things.

Yet this one thing I have learned of my God: the almost infinite depth of my ignorance. Without his counsel, I am nothing: yet he persists in his strange way to make me even what I am: for I am mine own god and multitudes have set themselves against me.

We acknowledge this fact: God created us. Thus are we born into life: inheritors, children, spirits thirsting for truth. Thus is our eye receptive to the flux of our mind. We receive the light in the world to rid ourselves of the otherwise eternal darkness in ourselves. Nevertheless, the only light found in the world is Jesus, the Christ, the Son of the living God. All else is a passing, a transient show, a fleeting shadow cast upon the ground of momentary experience.

We are blind from birth. Though we sinned not, nor our parents: we are still blind. It is those who say, we see, and reject the simple fact that Jesus is the light of the world, who remain forever blind.

And his disciples asked him, saying Master, who did sin, this man, or his parents, that he was born blind?

In life, we are born first; then made to see. Sin is solitary iniquity: it is the evil we receive because we choose to follow Satan, and reject God. Sin is in the creation because it represents the limits God has imposed upon his own Creation. A man could catch his own excrement, place it in a plastic bag, label it as health food; sell it to his friend at a dear price: buy it back again, at a discount, and praise God for his wisdom as he consumes it. Nevertheless, it would be sin for him to do so, even though he violated neither law of man, God, or nature.

To be born blind is no sin. Sin is only this: to eat evil. We eat up knowledge of evil, literally glut ourselves with it, and vomit it forth into the world.

It thus comes about we require baptism, the cleansing of water without as well as within. Nevertheless, the wise men of the world never take their ignorance seriously: they make no allotment for it in their political philosophies, in their religious teachings, in their commercial enterprises.

Jesus answered, Neither hath this man sinned, nor his parents: but that the works of God should be made manifest in him.

Men should deeply consider how it is that a child is made to see. The dust of the ground of the earth is interspersed with the light God sends into the world. Words create light.

Bodies are transformed into light: and light into bodies. The word and the creation are more intimately connected in heaven and earth than the science of man allows—yet.

The works of God are made manifest in all who presently see God. God is a joy to those that see him: God is a judge of those who say he is not. Satan is a mechanism: men, deceived by the mechanisms of Creation, are idle idol worshippers. They are idle worshippers because they never stir themselves up to lay hold on God. In matters spiritual they are blind, deaf, dumb, halt, maimed, and lame. Yet they seek no help: request no guidance: search for no cause. Nevertheless, they are not forgotten of God: God continuously looks upon his Creation. He is the overseer who acts because of what he sees. He can hide it from himself: he can bring it to his attention. He can ignore us: he can respond. Our prayer is even this: a cry to our Creator. I am astounded at his ability to handle all these matters: yet somehow he does it. We inherit all things and the tree of life flourishes in the Garden of God.

Nevertheless too much knowledge poisons us in this manner: we chance upon more evil than we can handle. Death results. The thorns choke the wheat: the rocks block the seed from the needed soil: the flighty fellows eat up our chances for life. They literally nourish themselves on our potentiality. Emperors such as Napoleon, and popes, such as any one of them, are made fat on the good seed sown into the world by the Word of God. Men are killed by war and by ignorance. Their lives are not full, abundant, bursting with joy only because the birds of the air have swallowed them up.

There are yet many fowls lodging in the branches of our kingdom. Yet were it not for the good ground receiving the seed of God's Word, the tree would never have grown. The fowls, our very enemies, delight themselves with the fact we survived and grew. Otherwise would they have long ago perished.

The truth is plain and as easy to understand as the parable itself. But now what? Shall one kill the fowls? Indeed no: for they also played their part and are lodged among the branches of the kingdom.

Let the blind do whatsoever Jesus commands and they shall see.

And once we see, what results? Those, born blind, who know that the word of God has enlightened them—and that Word is not limited to the Bible as too many of these Pharisees ignorantly believe—are questioned by lawyers, scribes, teachers, fathers, and masters various, as to the events which enabled them to see. But the world does not accept simple statements. The men of the world confuse the simplicity of truth with the complexity of fact. Chaos then overcomes men and their enterprises great and small.

Those who love Love's ways, possess an eternal kingdom, have hold of an everlasting treasure. Our art, our science, our learned literature, is Love's doing in a world full of darkness, deceit, chaos, and death. We inherit the kingdom because it is God's pleasure to establish it with us. Objects are but the ground upon which the spirit writes her dreams. Beauty, love, joy, and life are the everlasting realities: they are as real as Israel. The testimony old and new is a testimony wrought in flesh and blood and bone. The spirit is the creative power; heaven and earth is the result.

But the sons of pride are full of other doctrines. They accept no simple testimony. Joy in no simple work. It is almost impossible to get these rich in spirit into the kingdom of heaven. They are so preoccupied with their own possessions, so full of the delights of their own wisdom, that they have need of nothing more from God.

My problem is exactly the opposite. My desire is to realize paradise in earth and to enjoy the kingdom of heaven everywhere. The kingdom has come, but it covers not the whole earth. Obviously, then, my desire remains unsatisfied.

I must work the works of him that sent me, while it is day: the night cometh when no man can work. As long as I am in the world, I am the light of the world.

Darkness reigns when Jesus is not in our world. The world is the perspective of each man's life in this earth. The mechanism of the world is the ground of experience from which we draw our strength and our power.

Men communicate, one with another, through the mechanisms of the world. We work to sustain the world so that the world may be used to produce the fruits of paradise. But the sons of the evil one, deny God his glory. What is God's glory? Even his work: which work we are. The house of our emotions, the soul of our impulses, the mind wherein the tablets of memory are stored, is a real spiritual treasure stored within us.

We are inheritors of many things. The book I read is prepared for me literally by men given unto me of my God. So also, this notebook in which I write: my pen, my desk, my body. All these things I receive of men. But I also receive the things my God has given me.

How does God send a man into the world? Obviously, by giving him a body to sense the works of the world: we sense the world about us: the world of men; the world of sight, sound, ideas, words, and forces various.

Our world is either full of light, or full of darkness. I must bring my own light into the world. For dark is much of the world I come into.

Men of the world who hate God reject the light Jesus brings into their world. They love themselves only: and their works are seen for what they are when brought to the light of truth: even silliness. So much vanity, so much stupid boasting, so much false doctrine, so much egotistic bombast: such is what I find in the worlds of men. Yet, why do they prefer darkness rather than light?

Surely, the purpose of Jesus in the world is to bring light to the world so that men might build their houses wisely.

When he had thus spoken, he spat on the ground, and made clay of the spittle, and he anointed the eyes of the blind man with the clay.

This is the condition of many now in the world. They have the clay, the clean way of truth, the mixture of Jesus' words and worldly opinions, upon their eyes. Yet they see not.

And said unto him, Go wash in the pool of Siloam, (which is by interpretation, Sent.) He went his way therefore, and washed, and came seeing.

We must know by now that we are in the world because Jesus has sent us into the world. For what purpose? To save it. Each man is the Savior of his own world: this is the power he receives from God through Jesus, the Christ. His world of life is enlightened by the words of light.

Satan blinds: Jesus envisions. The light of our mind is necessary for all good works. Satan is a machine, a beast, a reflex, an evil one, whose ways are full of deceit, darkness, and death. Men worship the beasts of the field: men worship law, state, custom, chance, opinion, money, drugs, jobs, fellow men. Yet, these things are made for men: it is not men who are made for the things.

We need must wash in those experiences of joy which God provides for our cleansing. We have wept. But our tears are wiped away. We have mourned, and been strengthened thereby. We have been mocked, yet we triumph. We are dead, held in captive rest under the altar of earth from which our bodies take their shape. Nevertheless, we also rejoice in our crown of life. Our resurrection is now. It is Satan who wearies us with meaningless and foolish fables concerning the nature of time. Eternity is real: and time is a moving image useful for measuring the extent of seasons and harmonizing all good things.

Yet how many of Satan's party place the idol of time and money in their houses, and worship such things? Every four years they elect a president whether they need one or not. Every year taxes are collected whether needed or not. Every day a new law is written, whether needed or not.

Let God rule the times: I am weary unto death with the schedules of men, my own included.

And if God rules, what then results: We do what God commands: we believe: we are baptized and cleansed of our worldly ways, opinions, conceits: we see the world for what it is and no longer must beg for our bread.

The neighbours therefore, and they which before had seen him that was blind, said, Is this not he that sat and begged?

That the blind who respond to Jesus are made to see, astonishes the world. Neighbors and observers alike make inquiries concerning the miracles of transformation which are accomplished by the power of God's Word. Nevertheless, in heaven, it is such a common thing, it is no longer counted as a miracle but as common experience. The churches should congratulate themselves if none come to them anymore: perhaps all the believers are now in heaven and need no more beg any favors of the churches.

Some said, this is he: others said, He is like him: but he said, I am he.

We are the same: time unfolds: seasons, loved ones, come and go: heaven and earth passes: tribulation, sorrow, disbelief, have their end: our blindness disappears: we now see. Yet, we are the same. Truly, we are who we are: we are the same: God has enlightened our eyes, cleansed us of the coverings of the world: but we are now the blind who see.

Therefore said they unto him, How were thine eyes opened? He answered and said, A man that is called Jesus made clay, and

anointed mine eyes, and said unto me, Go to the pool of Siloam, and wash: and I went and washed, and I received sight. Then said they unto him, Where is he? He said, I know not.

Jesus anoints: we report the incident: he tells us what to do: we do it: we report the happening. Nevertheless, where is he now? I know. Do you?

So also is it with God. He comforts us: he teaches: he rebukes: chastises: judges. God loves us, commands us, befriends us. Where is God now?

Where is this blind man of whom this incident speaks? I don't know. Where is Paul, Peter, Mary, Pilate, Herod? Where is John the Baptist? I don't know.

Yet what shall I say about this ignorance of mine? Shall I disbelieve the miracle past because of my inability to provide knowledge of things present? No, I will not disbelieve. The blind who now see are as real as I am.

Yet there are those who are really blind to the living reality of their own disbelief. They cannot believe God lives, works, loves, comforts, saves and enjoys the pleasures of his own kingdom in his own way. They cannot believe that they are blind and pretend that they can see. What is meant by the word, "blind?" (Blind: *bel*ievers *in d*evils) It is a word which relates to a judgment of things as they are: but there are those who restrict the use of the word to their own limited understanding.

Lawyers manipulate words: but the Sons of God create through the power of the Word. The creation is what the Word of God has established. But the sons of perdition believe the creation brings forth the Words. In this, they sin grievously.

They brought to the Pharisees him that aforetime was blind. And it was the sabbath day when Jesus made the clay, and opened his eyes.

God's day is a day of rest: yet a day of renewed strength. *Rest renews strength.*

The Sabbath, with Jesus, is a day of miracles. A day when man rests, and God works. It is wise to rest while God works. Yet men strain the truth to produce their own interpretations of everything. That God works while men rest and men work while God rests ought not appear strange to men for so also do they order their own worlds.

But with God there is a sabbath in every hour, in every minute, and sometimes even within a moment.

When I see the works of God, my heart rejoices. I inherit all things. As men, as the sons of men, and as angels, even as God's angels, and as sons, even as God's sons, what do we really know?

What is the poison of pride's head that it keeps us from acknowledging the simple truth of God's creative genius and the searchable wonders of his glory? His ways are wonderful. There is a way in which the ignorant are instructed, the proud abased, the world overcome and death destroyed. Death and hell are destroyed. In this, the Sons of God are the great destroyers. Our adversary is the image we have invested with life. We must obey God and reject Satan's advice. The liar is our beast, not our lord.

The serpent becomes an evil thing when it deceives us into believing in the prophetic powers of its own imaginative blindness. The great sin of the Pharisees is that they claim to see, but they are really blind. Sun Myung Moon, the pope, the president of the church, the ruler of the synagogue, the premier and president of our country, are equally blind in these matters. They believe they know, they understand, they see what is good for all the people they have authority over; nevertheless, they are blind. Their sin remains.

The gospel is plain: the kingdom of heaven is the kingdom of God: God is Lord.

There are men sent into the world by God doing the things God asks them to do. To deny this obvious fact, is to reveal to all men that one is blind. To confess our blindness is good. But to lead when one is blind is evil. Lenin, the lord of his own pathetic world, is a blind leader of the blind. Yet, his sin is even greater, for even from the den of his own iniquity, this dead man leads the dead. Sin, ignorance, slavery, death: such is the fated end of those who forsake the truth of God's Word.

And I am sorrowful: for I find no pleasure in death, blindness, pride; nor in those who cause such things to be.

Why cannot men see God? Is there no light in the world? Why cannot men bring goodness out of themselves? Cannot men look within themselves and see what they have within themselves?

Why cannot men see?

Because they do not believe in the light: they believe in things other than what Jesus taught. In this manner do men become children of darkness, and architects of iniquity.

The unrighteous Mammon has produced its everlasting habitations. Institutions of government, of religion, of commerce, of education, remain even long after the original founders have died. The unrighteous Mammon is money governing the actions of men. Governments continuously seek money: even Napoleon must sell the Louisiana Territory to finance an empire founded upon the willingness of men to kill. Schools various and universities many seek money. The churches are forever seeking the tithes belonging to the Lord God of Israel. And the worldly financial corporations are adept at creating their own money: compared to the corporate wizards, governmental bureaucrats are financial simpletons.

I must admit that the children of God have wisely made themselves friends of the unrighteous Mammon. Nevertheless, this does not make the unrighteous Mammon right. The fertilization of Mars and the Moon, and the growth of life and paradise in these places, is best accomplished by leaving our cleverness at creating pay toilets, pay telephones, video commercials, insurance policies, amortization and interest tables, stocks and bonds and treasury certificates, on earth.

Men are blind. They cannot see Napoleon sold that which he did not own to Jefferson who paid for it with monies belonging to others. God laughs at our unrighteous ways. But I am weary of it all.

The poor hunger and thirst for bread: and the rich weep because they cannot sell it at a handsome profit. Am I any different? I am as different as my words reveal. The shewbread of God is free. The Word of God is given without price. We have continued in the word: we are not indebted to the unrighteous Mammon: rather it is greatly in debt to God. Satan is not our lord: he is our slave. Men generate evil: bring it forth out of themselves: corrupt themselves with their own ways. They worship the system: glory in the nation: applaud the spokesmen of idle words: give their labors to the covetous leaders who promise them more and more of that which they need less and less.

Men who reject Jesus by rejecting his words, reject the Lord God of Israel, and his prophets, his wise men, his scribes, his servants, his friends: his Son.

The kingdom of heaven has no meaning apart from the Lord God of Israel, and Jesus Christ, the first born of his many sons. And Jesus is David's son; for Jesus is the offspring of his own seed. But men who know much about the everlasting habitations of the unrighteous Mammon, know so extraordinarily little about the everlasting life which is within me. Thus I do know that the life within me is far greater than all the life of the world. They have what they have within themselves: and I have what I have within myself. The State, the beast of the sea, the Godless Governments of the World, have swallowed me up for three thousand years. Yet, at the same time, Jesus has reigned for a thousand years.

How can these things be? Men forget that knowledge of God is eternal life. Eternity and everlasting life are the present, incontestable realities. Time is a derivative notion associated with the observation of oscillating bodies. Indeed, there are many times, and time itself also may, as the atom, be split. But an atom that cannot be split, cannot be split. Dalton is right in his assertions: but men label new things with old words, and easily stupefy themselves with their own wine. There are atoms breakable and atoms unbreakable. There is time divisible and time indivisible.

Our fullness of life, our house of wisdom, our tree of life is found in the house of God. His word creates and destroys. The Spirit of Truth is the voice of God speaking words within us.

Idols are idols: the inanimate objects we ourselves invest with a bit of motion. And the idols of the mind are many. Our idle words have created them. What is an idle word? A word set in motion by ourselves, and not of God.

The first are last and the last are first because all of us are made one in God. But the men of the world divide the world among themselves for gain and profit. The tower, the pyramid, the mountain citadel; the political process, the church hierarchy; the military organization; are men's ways to heaven. And once we ascend to the top what do we find? A little man giving voice to a great idol, and nothing more.

Peter the Great is only great because he is a great deceiver. But Lenin is even a greater deceiver for in his death he accomplished more than Peter did in his life. If the people who live in Russia could see this, they wouldn't be blind.

The State has devoured the beauty of the Russian nation: the bear has devoured the ballerina of delight. But only those who can see know what has happened.

Nevertheless, Jesus works on the Sabbath day: even that day, that one day of seven, God commanded us to rest. Why rest? To renew our strength: to enable us to see the clean way of truth: to let the gospel of peace and remembrance of God's works, settle upon our heart and thereby dissolve the things of earth that keep us blind. God sends his truth into the world to send us to that place wherein we might go to wash, and so washing, we may come away seeing.

But we can refuse to do that which it is within our power to do. Thus we are free to act, to decide, to choose. Nevertheless, prior to this, our beliefs fashion our powers of response. Heaven and hell, have this in common: they are spiritual realities created by gods.

The tree of knowledge of good and evil grows within a man. One could easily count a thousand books filled with knowledge of a delightful nature, and realize the impossibility of reading them all in one lifetime. But the men who disbelieve the words Jesus spoke and which his friends kept, and still keep even to this day, believe in other words. Consequently, their beliefs cause them to explain all things to themselves with those words which come out of themselves that are of themselves and of those men who fathered them with their beliefs.

Only the spiritually blind know not that all men are fathered by their faith. In this manner, idols are fashioned: lies are generated by an evil generation. God is rejected, mocked, despised, and spiritually assaulted. The kingdom is oftentimes violently taken away from a man by the evil spirits created by filthy dreamers. The religious teachers, the worldly statesmen, the disciples of law and mammon, the advertisers of worldly merchandise, violently assault our souls, and reap the harvest sown in our own private garden of delight and glut themselves with the fruits of our labor.

We mourn the loss of love, beauty, joy, and a thousand other delights commonly experienced by those who have lived in paradise.

God does what he does: feels what she feels: even as I do what I do, suffer what I suffer. Those that mourn are blessed, for God comforts. The pure in heart are blessed, for they see that God is far more wonderful than all that man has ever sensed and foolishly worshiped. The clear truth my God has given me is far greater than all the accumulated genius produced by men of earth and multiplied by worldly princes. Satan is real: so is his deceit: his followers: his legions. Nevertheless, so cunning and wise and subtle are his messengers, that even righteous Job is hard pressed to discover those things that come to him because of Satan and those things that are given to him by his God, even his maker, even the Creator of heaven and earth, even that creative spirit who can frame a multitude of stars in poets' eyes, and raise up lovers to herself from the very dust of the earth.

We are gods but we live and die as men. Why? Because we believe in the myths of our own minds, in the idols of our own understanding, more than we do in our Creator. I do not create God: my God creates me. Neither is my God, myself. What madness, what colossal folly, what egotistical horror! Yet how many of the fallen sons of god so conceive themselves?

I hate my life in this world, for I had rather live it in heaven. I hate my mother, my father, my friends: for I have been mothered with nonsense, fathered by foolish teachers, and befriended by those who have encouraged me to do that which is evil and reject that which is good.

Men forget my dual nature, my double cup of experience; I am the Son of God, even my God who is in me and in whom I am the one that I am; I am also the Son of man, for man has fathered me, mothered me, befriended me, brought me into his world; and killed me.

Surely, though all this be true, it is time to move on. But these things that I speak of myself I encourage all to know about themselves. Become a child of God by believing in the light God sent into the world to make you a child of God. Let the belief be sown so that the kingdom may grow. We ask, so that we might receive. We search, so that we might discover. We hear, so that we might learn.

If you see these things to be true, you have no need of Jesus. His work is then finished. His end is accomplished. He saved your world, even that world of your own personal experiences, from the forces of death and of hell, of ignorance and of deceit, of foolishness and idolatry.

And if there is light within yourself what need have you for the many doctrines of despair created by the children of darkness and the authors of confusion? These men cause blindness. They close our eyes. It is Jesus who opens this door of everlasting life set before us, and comes forth, and opens our eyes.

But the teachers of religion hate this fact. They want us to believe blindness is our own fault: but it is not. It is their doing, their ignorance, their pride, which blinds us to the way of truth.

There is a time to permit the tares and wheat to grow: but there is also a time of harvest: now is the time to burn up within ourselves all the petty and foolish fancies planted in our world by those worldly forces of opinion planted by Satan. What is Satan? Satan is the son of those who father it: popes, presidents, premiers, and kings: legislators, leaders, and lawgivers legion promoting their own shallow and worldly ideals within us. God grant me the angels for this harvest: for I am full of doctrines profitable and doctrines unprofitable.

Then again the Pharisees also asked him how he had received his sight. He said unto them, He put clay upon my eyes, and I washed, and do see.

The body is the clay which covers the eyes of the soul. We sense life in earth only because we have bodies of earth: bodies raised in intricate beauty from the dust of the ground. Our most brilliant science is naught but a reflection of Mosaic truth. Yet how many teachers belittle Moses in order to plant their own doctrines in our mind? The spirit of God creates and miraculous are his works. We must cleanse ourselves in the waters of belief in God; faith in Love, in Beauty, in Truth; in the eternal spirits of God, which forever lighten our way as we fill ourselves with the adventures of everlasting life. Juliet Prowse is a delight to see as those sensitive to beauty full well know. It is good to see what God has created.

Therefore said some of the Pharisees, This man is not of God, because he keepeth not the sabbath day. Others said, How can a man that is a sinner do such miracles? And there was a division among them.

And the division remains although collectively such men all support Babylon and in that worldly enterprise Mormons, and

Moonies, and Catholics, and Communists, and Buddhists, and religious leaders ad nauseam are united.

The children of God are taught of God. Their religion is to love life and practice at truth until that spiritual response becomes one with their natures.

They say unto the blind man again, what sayest thou of him, that he hath opened thine eyes? He said, he is a prophet.

The Pharisees would rather lead the blind than make them see. They prophesy nonsense and enfeeble men and blaspheme God with silly moralistic platitudes. They blaspheme his Son by making the kingdom of heaven a spiritual fiction, a thing to be found after death, rather than in life.

But the Jews did not believe concerning him, that he had been blind, and received his sight, until they called the parents of him that had received his sight.

The Jews can examine all beliefs not in accord with their own man generated traditions, and reject them. In this men greatly err through pride. We learn of fools: become foolish: father foolish doctrines: and then, in the face of God's forceful facts, deny what has happened to us. I am a man of perdition, of sin, of foolishness, also. Who is good but God? All who follow God. And when he turns to us and rebukes us for our foolishness, what shall we do?

Those who refuse to be born again, remain what they are, children of the earth.

And they asked them, saying, Is this your son, who ye say was born blind? how then doth he now see? His parents answered them and said, We know that this is our son, and that he was born blind: But by what means he now seeth, we know not; or who hath opened his eyes, we know not: he is of age; ask him: for he shall speak for himself.

Surely this is good advice. So proud are men who lead and hold positions of prominence in some organizational structure that they would even seek out those who are ignorant of certain matters in order to avoid confronting real facts face to face. Anything that threatens their idol is an offense to them. Thus do politicians who appeal to the voter confess to all men that they are incompetent to sustain themselves in their own beliefs. Democracy is an appeal to Barabbas, the very son of the rabble who knows not how to do them good.

Our parents, our superior, our wife, our government, our God is appealed to by those men who cannot believe that we ourselves are the spokesman of the truth we ourselves enjoy.

I am astonished at those men who profess belief in God and then become indignant when God speaks to someone and heals someone without first clearing it with them. In all truth, God does much: but is credited by most men as doing nothing.

The Pharisees, the religious teachers of the adulterous generation, want no real God to directly intervene in the affairs of men. The blind slaves of the system wish to prolong their life in the idol they worship.

The whole world is the product of the slaves of the idol. Ignorance, theft, deceit, pride, murder: such are the marks written within the minds of those men who are the captive princes of their own mental images. With such men, I am at war. God creates and sustains all things beautiful and good. But who is God? What is the force behind creative processes? What is beautiful? What is good? Surely, much knowledge of evil is a weariness of the soul, and a sickness expanding itself unto Death. To call that which is good, evil, and that which is evil, good, is the lie gods hate. Yet, daily, in matters trivial and in matters important, goodness and evil, the powers of light and of darkness, the spiritual forces of death and of life, course through the labyrinthine passages of my immortal soul. There are dens of iniquity found in the garden of delight.

I have eaten of the tree of knowledge of good and evil, and I have died. Yet, I am alive. What can I say? What shall be my testimony? I once was dead but now am alive forevermore. Such is the revelation given to me by my God.

Yet these adversaries of mine, the elders of Israel, the chief priests, the captains of Mammon and lords of mediocrity, deny both me and my God.

They cannot believe those once blind, now see. How much less can they believe that those once dead, now live? Satan, which is as much to say the spirit that governs and guides their understanding, not only tempts; he executes. Thus men reward hell to themselves as they follow a Satanic spirit they cannot understand. Yet they wish to rule and lord it over those men who, for times brief and times long, they have power to afflict and accuse and imprison.

The signs of the time are plain. Men reject God and worship the emotional and social system they find in the world. The body of Moses is coveted by Satan. The simple statement of fact that in the beginning God created the heavens and the earth and in the end he told us somewhat of the problems associated with that work many men reject. Men defile themselves with their own right hand when they dispute with Jesus about Moses. Moses and Jesus live, because God lives. The words provoke what the words provoke. To deny the power of the Word to guide the actions of men and bring unto them the fullness of life is Satanic madness. But only the Word understood grows: the word "Babbled" is religious hypocrisy.

But let the dead bury their dead: and let me continue to explore the kingdom of God. The bottomless pit in which all my earthly forms mix and intermingle, causes me anguish each time I open it and shut it. Surely, I wish to hide myself from looking upon that which is evil. God delights in his rest and so do I.

Let the Pharisees explain the miracle of a light-filled life enjoyed by those once born blind, but who now, by the power of God, see God. But they cannot explain it; therefore they deny the testimony of all these witnesses who clearly state how it came to pass that they presently see.

These words spake his parents, because they feared the Jews: for the Jews had agreed already, that if any man did confess that he was Christ, he should be put out of the synagogue. Therefore said his parents, He is of age; ask him.

Fear no man. Fear God. In this way Fear is overcome: and love remains. The rulers of men are rulers of fear. They generate fears: weird tales: horrible fancies: loathsome customs. Men have cast men out of hell; thrust them out of their house, their family, their government, their church, their nation. And what is lost? The companionship of devils. Nevertheless, lust is not easily quenched. Men would do well to lust after every lovely woman and beautiful girl God has created and thereby diminish this inordinate lust they entertain for their idols. When one is within the kingdom of God it is hard to realize that there are heads of state, of religion, of armies, who have divorced themselves from the spirit of God to enjoy the whorish company of their social idol.

The world is the product of the prince of the world: even of Satan, who when he tempts us, offers us the world, even all the kingdoms of the world, if we will worship him. His temptation illustrates his weakness, his incompetence, his ignorance, his deceit. What has a child of God to do with serving systems worldly, man made, machine organized? The Lord God of Israel is the real spirit we serve: love, joy, beauty, and the unending adventures of everlasting life are some of her many works. This is our work: to call men to the Creator of all things beautiful and good. Heaven is an expanding universe, the expression of love's own spirit in ways wonderful and mysterious.

Shall the power of love and truth and beauty overcome the worlds of deceit, of pride, of ignorance, of insensitiveness, of political barbarism and angelic conceit? Yes.

I am not dead. I live and am alive forevermore. I tasted of death and found it bitter and poisonous and an experience to be avoided. There are more worlds than one. There are as many worlds as there are souls who sustain those worlds. Nevertheless, the mansions in our love's house are many. The kingdom of heaven is the kingdom of my God. Infinite is his domain, eternal his rule.

In this world I find troubles, afflictions, pains, sorrows as well as Mary and Cathy and Elizabeth. I cannot number Israel. There is no counting the souls my God has given me.

I am cut off now: but it is only for a little time. A moment, a thousand years, ages, epochs and generations pass. Yet I inherit all things. My God is one with me. Men cannot part us: no, they cannot separate that which is eternally joined. They cannot divorce me from my bride, nor sunder me from my wife. Love is mine and I am love's.

I inherit an expanding dream, receive a prosperous kingdom. I rule a kingdom of thoughts, and dreams, and visions, and perceptions which the blind cannot sense. I rule with the power of the Word. The Word is its own creative process.

Satan is now also this to me: a caprice of thought, an idol of the spirit world, a thing I created to serve me and no longer require. Men marvel at the false prophet and worship the beast and forget the reality of the lake of fire prepared for their everlasting destruction. I am impressed with Man for Man is an impressive idol. I am impressed with the State for the beast is many headed and powerful. But I do not believe in the prophecies of the miracle makers nor in the authority of the usurper. The great men and captains of the world are really puny spirits. Who have they really deceived except themselves?

In the last day each man must speak for himself.

Then again called they the man that was blind, and said unto him, Give God the praise: we know that this man is a sinner. He answered and said, Whether he be a sinner or no, I know not: one thing I know, that whereas I was blind, now I see.

How many men in the world are forever urging us to praise God and condemn Jesus, the Christ? Though men call Jesus, Christ, and do many wonderful works in his name, if they do not the will of his heavenly father, he knows them not. The workers of iniquity condemn Jesus as a sinner because he works in our hearts and souls and minds while we rest. They resent this. They alone wish to rule and authorize the times and appoint the seasons wherein we kill, and don't kill: wherein we marry, and don't marry: wherein we drink, and eat and smoke, and wherein we are forbidden to do these things.

When our heavenly father rules, he rules. His will is done. The commandments of men have nothing to do with the impulses of God. The times are under his own power. There is a time to refrain from adultery and a time to lust and fuck to our hearts' content. But many men cannot see this for the blind leaders of the blind have led them into the narrow and filthy ditch of their own limited life. They'll steal monies through deceit: deceive men and women into giving their lives to military service: send them off to kill whensoever it pleases them: and condemn these same male and female children whenever they find them becoming one in flesh as they experience the wonders of sexual expression.

But in spite of all heavenly facts to the contrary, they'll worship Caesar and reject Jesus. And who is Caesar? A dead slave of the godless state whose image and superscription is found on all the coins of the world.

Render to Caesar the things that are Caesar's. Nevertheless, God created all things for his own pleasure. What then is Caesar's?

Then said they to him again, What did he to thee? how opened he thine eyes?

In the way described: in the manner in which it was done.

He answered them, I have told you already and ye did not hear: wherefore would ye hear it again? will ye also be his disciples?

If they could hear, they would understand and become his disciples. Why can't they hear? Because they're always preaching and never listening. God doesn't bother enlivening those senses men refuse to use.

Our fullness of life is dependent upon the Lord God of Israel. It is true, there are sheep other than those of Israel: but for those of us planted on this planet, the Lord God of hosts is our Savior. From what are we saved? From Death. Unfortunately for men, the ignorant and corrupted sons of god who have entangled themselves in the myriad and intricate fancies of their own evil imaginations brought forth the concepts of State and Religion and King and Priest. These God substitutes have caused men to lose the use of their own souls. The further I get into the world, the more I am astonished at their ignorance and at their pride. Death, which is the separation of dead earth from the living reality of eternal life, is so much a part of their spiritual makeup that they cannot even accept the matter-of-fact resurrection of their bodies. If I had not become one of their sons, I could not believe it. Stupid, vain, foolish, ignorant of eternal matters: yet, at the same time, so brilliant about their own idols. Democracy, Napoleon, Muhammad Ali, or some literary genius can flood the world with foolishness and men sop it up.

But enough. If I become too disgusted, I'll leave and that's exactly what my enemies wish me to do. For some reason, difficult to explain, men have learned to love the lie and hate the truth. We are sons of God and we die like men and even this great truth, simply and clearly expressed, is not, of itself, enough to save us from the power our mental idols have to enslave us. We actually believe Satan: actually worship deceitful liars who wish only to mouth words so that we might be impressed by what they say and what they threaten to do.

For the just fear of God, men have substituted fear of a vast army of inconsequential and little things. God, I surely desire an end to this work.

Then they reviled him, and said, Thou art his disciple; but we are Moses' disciples. We know that God spoke unto Moses: as for this fellow, we know not from whence he is.

If they were Moses' disciples, they would also be Jesus' disciples. But they neither keep the words of Moses nor the words of Jesus: thus proving to themselves that they are the disciples of Satan, that spirit within the very nature of things men succumb to when the going with God gets rough. Yet how much more difficult is Satan's ways? Men follow Napoleon, Truman, Hitler, Mao Tse-tung, or Abraham Lincoln into a world of war and slaughters and hell and death and their children praise them for their glorious exploits! What is so glorious about killing when God commands, kill not? What is so glorious about praying in public, when God commands private prayer? What is so glorious about public spectacle, when God convenes his suppers in private? What is so glorious about the service of Mammon when God requests service to himself?

Men know not from whence Jesus is: yet surely by now they should realize he is not of their world.

The man answered and said unto them, Why herein is a marvelous thing, that ye know not from whence he is, and yet he hath opened my eyes. Now we know that God heareth not sinners: but if any man be a worshipper of God, and doeth his will, him he heareth. Since the world began was it not heard that any man opened the eyes of one that was born blind. If this man were not of God, he could do nothing.

Nicely put, eloquently stated: but the Pharisees cannot be impressed with anything or anyone or any world other than their own. If they are not impressed with the words of God, how much less so will they be impressed by the statements of those once blind who now see?

They answered and said unto them, Thou wast altogether born in sins, and dost thou teach us? And they cast him out.

This also was a blessing for the man. To remain in the presence of Pharisees and engage them in pointless controversy is a debilitating experience. Such are found in the more elegant mansions of hell. They dwell in the house of God, partake of his goodness: yet they deny his other servants, friends, sons, angels, and lovers, their own real experience with the only real God, even the Lord God of Israel. All those who serve not the Lord, serve other Gods.

As for me, this one thing I now know and declare, our God is really more creative, more loving, more beautiful, more understanding, than any of his angels has ever thought or wildly dreamed. The patience and love and long suffering of our Goddess of delight is incredible: yet belief in her power, her wisdom, and her glory is the only thing I find it natural, and easy, and joyous to believe in.

Miserable am I in my moments of doubt. Doubt is the spiritual product of those living souls who produce it, advertise it, glory in it, and dearly sell it. Hell puts a dear price on all its most loathsome commodities. The way to the city of truth is straight; a narrow and direct passage, a right path leading to the door of God's kingdom. But the freeways, and shipping lanes, and air corridors of hell lead nowhere. We traverse them and end up in the same place. Expensive is the journey and boring, the adventure. And our purchase of foreign souvenirs is inferior to that which we might have produced at home. Far be it from me to deny the glorious and wonderful works of my unprodigal brothers who have added greatly to the riches of our heavenly father.

Those who doubt the Son of God, reject the God that sent him into the world to experience the judgment of the world. The world, even your world, judges the Son of God: even Jesus, the Christ of the Lord God of Israel.

Judges judge and are judged. Who can escape the verdict of this truth?

Jesus heard that they had cast him out; and when he had found him, he said unto him, Dost thou believe on the Son of God? He answered and said, Who is he, Lord, that I might believe on him?

Who is the Son of God? Indeed, Who are the Sons of God and where might we find one? Show me one child of God. How strange are those who believe they can do whatsoever it pleases them to do with God's children and have no fear of God!

Men who are fathered by their own doctrines; nurtured by their own laws; nursed by their own conceits, impressed by their own created idols, lose their fear of God. The goddess of delight is also Lord of heaven and earth. Lords rule: the many idiots in the world who offend the children of God forget this elementary social fact.

And Jesus said unto him, Thou hast both seen him, and it is he that talketh with thee. And he said, Lord I believe. And he worshipped him. And Jesus said, For judgment I am come into this world, that they which see not might see; and they which see might be made blind.

The men of the world, the men of the state; the men who believe in Man; the men of the Church; the men of Babylon; see. But what do they see? They see well enough to manipulate the mechanisms of social, state, and political systems so that men might worship them with the powers of Mammon and of men. Every state needs its army. Why? Has not God said, Do not kill? Every religion needs its statement of doctrine, its articles of faith, its holy book, its priests, evangelists, and hierarchy of worldly wizards. Why? Is not God's spirit of truth sufficient to comfort, to teach, to empower?

And some of the Pharisees which were with him heard these words, and said unto him, Are we blind also?

How many Pharisees have heard these words; yet also read these words, write these words, speak these words, translate these words, preach these words? How many Pharisees now use these words, yet never ask Jesus, Are we blind also? Those who see must one day realize that they are blind. Surely then, might they truly see.

Jesus said unto them, If ye were blind, ye should have no sin: but now ye say, We see; therefore your sin remaineth.

What is sin? I would to God I could explain it. But I cannot: I have experienced it: I have borne it: I carry its consequences with me: I read of it, hear of it, write of it, think on it, know it. I abhor it. Yet, there it is, an inexplicable mystery. God says, Choose good and live. We choose evil, and die. God's desires are those of love, truth, beauty, and joy creating the everlasting kingdom of heaven within us. We sin against others and bear the consequences of that action within ourselves. We also sin against ourselves, violating our own divinely originated commandments. Are we not gods? Yes. But we die as men. Why? Because we refuse to believe God; our maker, creator, husband, wife, bride, and the only constant, true, and unfailing friend. The universe is the bride of the soul: the universe is God in all her naked beauty. Yet what is my greatest joy? To see my God dwelling in the hearts and souls and minds of all these that I love.

Truly the stars are in our eyes: only we understand not the mystery hidden in the words, nor the enchantment of eternal truth. So we believe or doubt, as our fancy strikes us. What is a Son of God? He who has overcome the world of his own ephemeral experiences by believing in God: even in the real God: the God of Israel: the God of Moses, of the prophets, of the Bible: of Jesus. Even in the God that created me. In all this He is the same God. Love doesn't change. It is what it is: the spirit within man bringing paradise to the soul and heaven to earth.

I have a kingdom within me: it has grown: it expands: it is full of life. I have a tree in it: a single tree yielding the fruit of knowledge of good and of evil. Knowledge of good and evil makes me no god. That I am, already. The serpent is ignorant: is a beast without intelligence of heavenly things: it is a system, a state of things; a mechanism; a caprice of thought; a worldly reflex; an animated idol; an accuser, a liar, a deceiver.

Each man is Adam in paradise: the tree of life is as real as that fruit we term knowledge of evil. Be not deceived. God has made all things good. Sin and evil are our fruit, are our doing, is of our planting. God limits its growth. We sin and die. Death of the body is the limitation God has placed upon the powers of evil men. They can kill the body and after that they can do nothing more. Absolutely nothing. Yet the time is also with us wherein they cannot even do that.

There is also a spiritual death. We are dead to the presence of God. I have tasted this death. It is an experience to be avoided. We are led back to life by God's Word, even Jesus himself, the good shepherd. Jesus and David are Shepherds. But so are Brigitte Bardot and Mary Tyler Moore and Angie Dickinson. Surely, one look is all we need to realize the God of Life and beauty is at work in our world. One look is all we need to marvel at her ways.

But man knows not, or still believes not, he is created male and female. The mysteries of life are treated with contempt by analytical lawyers of mind and soul and heart who exhibit by their own words that they yield knowledge of good and evil only. No fruit of the tree of life is found in all their kingdom. Obviously then, it is foolish to visit them with the expectation of finding satisfaction for our heavenly desires. Those who eat of the tree of life are filled with desires the worlds of earth and hell cannot satisfy.

The two are made one flesh in heaven as well as in earth.

CHAPTER 10

Verily, verily, I say unto you, He that entereth not by the door into the sheepfold, but climbeth up some other way, the same is a thief and a robber.

Many men, as sheep, are easily led. They are led to war, to church, to join in social enterprises great and small. They are led to doubt, to believe, to love, to hate. They are led to Death, lured into hell. They are led into emotional pits, intellectual traps, and into ditches of deep despair. They are also led unto life.

Jesus is the shepherd. Is this not the role of the son of a shepherd? Jesus leads us into that realm of understanding whereby we love our enemies. But the thieves and robbers who scatter us and divide us and tear us for their own shortsighted purposes lead us to accept Roman law, Roman justice, Roman ideals, Roman hypocrisy.

Surely wolves fathered the fathers of Rome. The forgiveness of sins, the blessedness that belongs to the merciful, the righteousness and long-suffering of an almighty God—all these things are kept from the sheep who are victimized by those men in the world who enter into our hearts, not through Christ, but some other way.

The words of Jesus are the spirit of Jesus. He is our shepherd when we are led by his spirit. In this, God and he are one. God appoints shepherds. When we follow men, in thought, in belief, in action, we, like sheep, are led. If one comes to us through that door which is Christ's way of entering our soul, which is a gate of love, gentleness, truth, and beauty, that one is a good shepherd. Jesus is not the only shepherd. There are many shepherds leading the flock of the Lord God of Israel. There are many good shepherds who came after Christ. Yet, in this day and time and age, he remains the only door in and out of the sheepfold of earthbound life.

But he that entereth in by the door is the shepherd of the sheep.

What is a door? What door leads to the sheepfold of the flocks of Israel? Through what do men pass as they leave their assemblies of family, of church, of school, of work, and enter into other worlds?

To him the porter openeth; and the sheep hear his voice: and he calleth his own sheep by name and leadeth them out. And when he putteth forth his own sheep, he goeth before them, and the sheep follow him: for they know his voice. And a stranger they will not follow, but will flee from him: for they know not the voice of strangers. This parable Jesus spake unto them: but they understood not what things they were which he spake unto them.

What is Democracy? A process whereby men agree to submit themselves to the opinions of majorities. A leader emerges from the flock, from the herd; and, even as animals, men run to and fro knowing not why.

But the good shepherd is something else again.

Here the parable must end. Indeed all proverbs are just this, a prologue to the verbalization of our insights. We speak of the unseen mysteries by having recourse to the experiences of common fact. We witness the planting of the seed. We witness to this truth of the growth of the Words of Jesus. A man would have to be a blind ignoramus and reduce his vision to that of a mole, to deny the reality of the growth of words.

If I read a man's words or refuse to read his words, am I not then, as the porter of a door, and as the keeper of the gate, allowing some things to enter my soul, the very household of my experiences, and rejecting other things? And what are words but living spiritual realities inspiring my body with spiritual life?

The spirit of Jesus is the spirit of a good shepherd leading men into the fullness and abundance of life found in the universe of God's delight. But via schools, churches, governments, and economic organizations various, men are approached by other spirits, deceived into accepting other words; then are they destroyed, and scattered and killed.

It is madness to construct the weapon systems of death. But the Roman ideal of strength of arms infects communist, anarchist, and democrat alike. They are assholes all, polluting the atmosphere of God's dream with the noxious odors of their own abominable sentiments. As if there were not scorpions, serpents, wild beasts, and natural disasters enough, we have to organize ourselves into nations and empires to placate our silly fears that somehow death is to be overcome by killing our enemies.

So cheaply do men hold the power of love!

Then said Jesus unto them again, Verily, verily, I say unto you, I am the door of the sheep.

The door through which the flock of Israel passes is Jesus, the Christ. All knowledge in earth and in heaven, as men have knowledge of earth and of heaven, comes to us because of the Word.

What has Voltaire written, or Goethe portrayed, or Gibbon summarized, or Whitehead contemplated, or Swedenborg seen, or Newton analyzed, or Paul explained, or Napoleon accomplished, or Durant told, or *Playboy* photographed, or *Penthouse* displayed, or our friends, neighbors, and family experienced, that could detract from the eternal truth that Jesus is a door to an abundant life?

Satan has caused the world to be divided for gain. And who gains what? What do we receive of the world and from the world? Only this: an understanding through bitter experience that a kingdom wherein love rules not is an association of thieves, liars, murderers, fools, and hypocrites extraordinary.

We are marked and numbered by the bureaucracy of soulless men: their actions, their words, their political stance, their personal opinions, the very words that come out of their mouths reveals that they are the servants not of God, not the architects of the kingdom of heaven, but the bond slaves of worldly systems.

They deny the existence of a door leading from the world of human experience to the abundant life of heavenly reality. They have lost the use of their soul and surrendered it to the services of the princes of the world. We are in the world to overcome it: the machine is our tool, not our God. But these many worldly writers, the very scribes of hell, know not what they do. They worship a social beast and despise the Lord God of Israel.

All that ever came before me are thieves and robbers: but the sheep did not hear them.

How many men have come into the hearts of men before Christ? Legions. Neither did the sheep hear them: for they were killed by those men.

I am the door: by me if any man enter in, he shall be saved, and shall go in and out, and find pasture.

If men could realize how, as sheep, they are led into accepting some beliefs and rejecting others, they would take the Word seriously. Russian and German alike reject the good shepherd and follow the robbers of their souls to Stalingrad or Leningrad or Gettysburg. The story of the world is Satan's glory. It is his story: the story of those men who reject the God who commanded, Do not kill, Do not commit adultery. And what is the result of their murders? What is the result of their intercourse with worldly men who are forever creating kingdoms, nations, principalities, and a variety of spheres of economic and religious and moral power? They have fucked the idols of their own mind and brought forth Death.

It is a wisdom of the highest sort, to refrain from lusting after the Whore of Babylon and her daughters. But great worldly men have corrupted the great commandment, Do not commit adultery, to mean what surely God never intended. Devils have adulterated the truth with the venom of their own vanities: they rob men of their proper pleasures.

The thief cometh not, but for to steal, and to kill, and to destroy: I am come that they might have life, and that they might have it more abundantly. I am the good shepherd: the good shepherd giveth his life for the sheep.

Christ gives his life, not his death. Men focus on the crucifixion and cannot see Jesus talking with Mary in the garden. It is done and they refuse to believe it. If they cannot accept the resurrection of their own lives, and the recreation of their own body's life, how can they accept the fact that Jesus died on the cross? But devils steal this fact from men. The dead are dead: but for the dead to bury the living is an obscenity. Those who boasted of burying us are already buried themselves. It is the living who raise the dead: the dead simply cannot do it of themselves. I marvel at dead men who give us advice on how to live. It is not enough that they rob us of pleasure, and steal the joy of life from the world God constantly is saving, they also covet the power of ruling our own kingdom of heaven.

How do they do these things? With the forces of Mammon, of money, of statesmanship, of brute power, and of political and religious bullshit. If Moses was not impressed with Aaron's calf of gold how much less should even the least of those in heaven be impressed with the idols men have made of their own minds? Those who seek the kingdom of heaven find it. And those who cannot find it need the good shepherd. It is the life of the shepherd which guides the sheep.

Nevertheless, those in hell glory in his death and despise his life. They believe in themselves only. They have killed, slaughtered, and scattered without purpose, or thought or fear. Men are what they are: the spokesman of their own beliefs. And what do they believe? They believe that they can do anything they have power to do to the flock of God and escape God's wrath. Though God be absent, he also returns. Men know not what destruction they predestine for themselves when they work iniquity. What is the work of iniquity? To despise God, and fear men. The wolf and the good shepherd are adversaries, even though neither the sheep nor the wolf can meditate on this simple fact.

But he that is an hireling, and not the shepherd, whose own the sheep are not, seeth the wolf coming, and leaveth the sheep, and fleeth: and the wolf catcheth them, and scattereth the sheep. The hireling fleeth, because he is an hireling, and careth not for the sheep.

So is it with all those who are hired, and receive wages, for their services to king, government, business, corporation, church, stage, art, profession, and whorehouse. They care only for their wages:

their actions are a means to an end: their appointment is of chance, circumstances, or the covetous promptings of Mammon.

"I hate my job," says Satan. Then quit, for why should you proceed in that which you hate? For this is the source of evil and personal bondage and private degradation and solitary sin.

"I'll learn to love it." And so Satan has: he learns to love that which God, in his wisdom, originally forbade.

The hireling hates, not only the sheep, but his work.

Let each man in such matters be his own judge. Our cup of experience, our draught of life, can be given of God, or of the world. There is good in everything and evil in much. Money satisfies all things: and the love of money is the root of all evil. Money is paper power: a worldly idea concerning the government of the actions of men. The prince of the world is the supreme paper tiger of all the ages. Why? Because there is no flesh and blood in his words. He promises to give one the world, or a portion of it. And what is delivered? What do we receive for our work? The realization that all the money in the world cannot feed even one hungry soul.

Worldly men play the commodities market: they care not for the farmer; even less for those that must be fed.

But what can I say more? The beast, the State, has marked and numbered all men. Even Alexander Graham Bell cannot make a free telephone call. And the President of the United States cannot even receive a free gift without accounting for it in the ledger of those imbeciles who delight in such matters. Even words spoken in private may cost a man his job. Such is the way of Mammon ruling men in that vain system of things they call the world.

I am the good shepherd, and know my sheep, and am known of mine.

There are many good shepherds in the world: and many hirelings. Many who serve God; and multitudes who serve Mammon. Even in a nation of sheep, even the sheep may discern this.

As the Father knoweth me, even so know I the Father: and I lay down my life for the sheep.

I cannot know God without knowing myself. In knowing myself, God reveals himself to me. The teacher reveals himself to the student as the student becomes as learned as the teacher. We know God by becoming like God. But I am talking of the living spiritual reality, and not mere words spoken by vain men. God is as real as I am. Surely, He is not less real. God is as real as Israel: but Israel is as real as Jacob who is real.

My God knows me: my faults, my weakness, my strength, my love. I do not deny my loving creator. Let men judge what they will: their own words are of the spirit within them. Nevertheless, there are spirits eternal, and spirits which perish.

Let Lenin live: let the spirit he created die. World communism is a definite pain in the ass. Let it pass: let us be done with it. And what is Democracy? An idea in the heads of those men who believe that one need only count opinions to establish laws. All this conceit, vanity, and foolishness, is of the world.

Any son of God who ever laid down his life in the world of men in this day and age knows this to be true.

And other sheep I have, which are not of this fold: them also I must bring, and they shall hear my voice; and there shall be one fold, and one shepherd.

If men took Jesus as their guide, we wouldn't have need of all these other shepherds. Why multiply unneeded labor? Who needs Castro or Kennedy? Kissinger or Mao's successor? _Playboy_'s philosophy or that of Lord Russell?

I knew when God chose one to be his shepherd, it would produce envy in many. Let God be my defense. The leaders of all these worldly nations have thousands of millions of believers. And I, alone with myself, have my solitary conviction.

In a certain sense, the battle of Armageddon is fought in the world of a man's mind. The outpouring of words in the world is vain. Men really don't know when to keep their mouths closed. As a man I have experienced the absurdity of many a mouth, mine own included.

The world is flooded with nonsense: yet the ark remains, the covenant contains the promise, the earth will swallow up the flood.

We must decide and in the end the decision determines the end.

Life or death: eternity or the fleeting emptiness of man's vain world of perishable dreams.

The everlasting kingdom is with us today. All those in the fold of Christ know this as living fact. There is really only one shepherd. Men are Christ when they lead men to Christ. Jesus is the incredible fact which God must make us believe. How shall we go back? How relive the times?

Remember we are in one another and all who believe Jesus are God's. Let the angels explain it, and marvel at their own insight, their own genius, their own inwardly working lord. As for me, what can I do, except state the obvious truths, deliver the same universal message, promote the same imperishable doctrine, we've had all these years? Our present God is also the God that was.

Therefore doth my Father love me, because I lay down my life, that I might take it again.

If you want a new body, you must give up the old. If you want a new life, you must give up the old. If you wish to take up what you have laid down, you must first lay it down of yourself.

God, ever your creator and ever dependable heavenly father, has created us living souls. We ought not to take the lives of others in this world, but our own. Our own life is ours: it belongs to no man: it is God's gift to the soul he has made for himself.

We are gods: created in God's image: yet we live and die as men. Why?

Because the tree of life, the impulses of joy given of the heavenly spirit within are as real as all the nonsense planted in our emotional field of experience by Satan and his host of incompetents: yet, we believe not God, and are deceived by a beast.

No man taketh it from me, but I lay it down of myself. I have power to lay it down, and I have power to take it again. This commandment have I received of my Father.

"Prove it," tempts Satan. I cannot. Nevertheless, if men discover this truth is also applicable to themselves, perhaps, in the greatness of their heart, they might also believe it true of myself.

Once you become a Son of God, the world has been overcome. You don't need a shepherd. Jesus' work is finished. It is done. It is his proper end.

What next? Surely, that's between you and God. God's commandment is eternal life: the strife ends. Frankly, the very controversy is beginning to bore me. And there are other things for us to do. Alexander's complaint can never be ours. Love makes some things impossible. It is not within the nature of eternal life to find no new worlds to conquer.

The moon is a piece of God's creation. God does good work. How many moonlit nights have delighted the eye and thrilled our senses? Deep despair is mine as I find myself entangled in worldly, mortal, and limited affairs. The affairs of the spirit are always exciting: we lust and our lust is satisfied.

Men play many parts: they bring forth life and death: joy and sorrow: wisdom and foolishness. Yet pride is their downfall, the chief head on Satan's pet beast. If men truly knew God, they would not keep him from the heart and soul and mind of those they love.

We are the shepherds of our sentiments: the guardian of our own emotions: the gods of our own desires. Why do we refuse to be led of the Spirit? We are led of our own spirits and have forsaken our creator.

It is not good for God to dwell alone. Israel is his bride who has become his whorish wife. Where can he rest his head? Why can't he receive of the fruit of his own vineyard? Why can't he rule the very kingdom he created for his own pleasure?

Because his children, even those of his household, have turned against him. In his own country his prophecies come to pass, time and time again. Yet, do we love this God, serve this king, worship this spirit of truth and joy and beauty?

Men are not sheep: they are the fallen sons of God who are in love with the idolatries found in the world they create and sustain.

Their lives are taken from them, and they don't even realize it. They deceive, steal, destroy, and kill because the State commands, and they know not the state is without substance, a fucking abstraction they sustain with the breath of their lips. They can't tell an angel from a devil, a saint from a sinner, a hypocrite from a laborer; and to distinguish between reality and myth, good and evil, is too much for them.

Men are not sheep: yet it is good for them to follow the good shepherd for what other god really cares for them?

Alexander's kingdom is broken up and he himself cares nothing for it. Attila has come and gone. Mao Tse-tung has said all he could and passed away. Ho Chi Minh has left his inheritance to his people, and left. Charles Manson has his own troubles, and where now is his family? Napoleon glories in his memoires: Hitler deserted his Reich, and cannot return. Lenin lies dead in his tomb as his children implement his policies of terror and deceit and service to Satan's much beloved State and world wide empire. Who are these men? From whence do they come? Where have they gone? Only their apologists remain, the living servants of the world's great dead.

Such are the wolves of the world: they rob, and steal, and destroy men's lives. Jesus is their adversary.

The good shepherd remains. But the hirelings flee at the first sight of danger. They fear for their own life and care nothing for men. Yet how they covet the job!

There was a division therefore again among the Jews for these sayings.

Jehovah's witnesses are divided. Catholics, Protestants various, Mormons, Jehovah's Witnesses, and the many modern inventors of religion, are divided among themselves. These *Jews* are *Je*hovah's *witnesses*: but they will not allow the sheep to realize Jesus with us. *Je*hovah *saves us*, surely this is the message contained in the Word, *Jesus*. But men want either the Father, or the Son, or the Spirit, or none of them. To have wholly all three is too much for them. The spiritual realities are within the world, saving it from self-destruction. Our world is saved by God, though we confess it not. The church Jesus founded is not of the world: the world has created many churches: scribes glory in their histories. But what does it all amount to? God himself knocks at the door of our house: he gently judges, patiently rebukes, and chastises us with the power of genius. The church is invisible: but those whose eye is not darkened by the corrupt ways of Man, State, and Religion can see this church working the will of God in earth.

How can I separate my flesh and blood from my words? How can I separate what I am from what my God is? How can that which was enter in me in ways mysterious to create that which is, and forever shall be?

And many of them said, He hath a devil, and is mad; why hear ye him?

If Jesus is mad, who is sane? If Jesus is not to be heard, whose words shall we hear?

Others said, These are not the words of him that hath a devil. Can a devil open the eyes of the blind?

Man does many miracles: the great false prophet is with us today, encouraging us to accept the ways of his divided house; to accept the myriad decisions rendered in and by his many councils; to accept the wonderful world of Wonder Man, the false prophet of the godless State. He has already fought the war to end all wars. Why does he prepare so earnestly to arm himself for the next?

A devil can open the eyes of the blind: but it cannot make the man see, though he flood the retina with light.

And it was at Jerusalem the feast of the dedication, and it was winter. And Jesus walked in the temple in Solomon's porch.

Jesus rules the city of peace, even Salem itself. It is his city. He founded it, even as some men founded Rome, fathered churches, and gave birth to nations. Jerusalem is the city of truth, a complex society of men and women wherein the products and processes, the goods and services, of all that is holy, all that is of God, all that is joyous, is found.

Surely that city is with us today; God's gift to our soul. Our soul requires it. There are other cities: places of peace.

Nevertheless, the planet earth, this small wandering star, is too small, too limited a place to contain the ever expanding heaven growing within us. We require the infinite depths of interstellar space, and the boundless domains of our own inner dreams. God is in us: we are within him.

Why deny the obvious? Why despise the revelation?

Solomon's porch is one side of the temple of wisdom. Our prayer is made to God in his own house wherein his own thoughts are felt and expressed and displayed. God created the moon, and the stars, and Brigitte Bardot. God does good work.

Every beautiful woman is a joy to God and a joy to me. The resurrection of the body is real, as real as the salvation of our souls. The divine physician knows his work. Life, sleep, death, birth are things we experience, adventures undertaken. Nevertheless, the spiritually blind see nothing wonderful in all this. They wish to persuade all men that they have seen all there is to see.

Then came the Jews round about him, and said unto him, How long dost thou make us to doubt? If thou be the Christ, tell us plainly.

God provides plain truth. Men adulterate it with their own vanity. God has told us who is the Christ. But men, knowing somewhat of the powers inherent in their own evil inventions, want the plain truth repeated again and again and again. Only the infinitely dull never get bored by such operations. Heaven is our receptiveness to God's expanding dream. I marvel at how narrow-mindedly mad, men have made themselves.

What in the name of hell do these men expect of God? Even the weakest of devils mock them and yet they persist in their vanity. They learn nothing from Moses or Elias or Jesus or John. There is no cross in their world: no mystery, no strife, no joy: only a mad and mindless vanity that enables them to persist in their envy.

God make them see. If I were a king, would I make a law that enabled me to stop a man in his car, search for a piece of paper enclosing a bit of weed I consider dangerous and, finding it, cast the man into prison for an indeterminate time? Would I stop a man from fucking a woman? Would I compel a man to give me a tenth of his income so that I might provide for his old age? Would I gather his children together to teach them to kill whenever and whomever I chose? Would I collect monies so that I might deliver my vain thoughts to him? Would I compel all women to bear or not bear children whensoever I chose? Would I arbitrate every matter between one man and another so that I might be considered a judge? Would I compel him to send his children to schools I choose and tell him what he could say, and read, and write, and learn, and believe? Would I force him to join together with others so that when he works, or when he doesn't, or what he receives for his labor, is under my control, and not his?

Surely, it would try the indefatigable zeal of Augustine to catalog all the idols of the state men create to enslave themselves.

The truth is plain: lawyers and Jesus are adversaries. Those who serve mammon and not God know not what they do. The beast of wicked men, the godless State, the seven headed beast of the sea, has overcome men. Yet the kingdom of heaven is within Adam: and when they once again realize this, paradise is theirs. Even in their absence, God has not been idle. The beast is cursed: Satan is a social beast, the complex spirit of worldly minded men. Such men can glory in anything except the Lord God of Israel: I glory in nothing except I am his created Son. Let love do with me as she pleases for I was created for her pleasure: so she tells me now.

There is more to God than men know. Men live by the power of God's word: every word of God is theirs for the taking.

Jesus answered them, I told you, and ye believed not: the works that I do in my Father's name, they bear witness of me.

What are the works of Jesus? To make the blind see: the sick, whole: the deaf and dumb, receptive and articulate. The Word in its own strait way accomplishes this. The Word is Jesus' work accomplished through his prophet John. But John is more than a prophet, for he is a son of God who gives Jesus what God has given him. Jesus learns of John.

Men mock Jesus and John by making them out to be what they are not: the truth remains: a son of God is a child of God, even an angel who has overcome the world. But what is the world? A system wherein God is not: the world is saved by God's love as the spirit brings the kingdom of heaven to earth. God's will is done in the flesh and blood reality of our living bones. The blood of life is fashioned in the structure of experience.

John is God's gift to Jesus. God is generous. Where now is John? I know not except that he has a great body of believers, and many children, for many consume his words, even as I am eating them this day. This great spiritual fact defies encapsulation in some earthy tomb of philosophic system. Stars cannot be buried.

Jesus is in John and John is in Jesus and both are in God and God is within them. Such is the penetrating power of the Word. But if this be true of God, John, and Jesus, how much more is it true of the spirit of love, and you and me? Where my Word is there also I am. And where my thought is, there also am I, dwelling within even before the child is born. You are my child if you are fathered by my words.

I am what I am, a god alive living within my God: and so are you, otherwise you could never see nor hear these words.

Believe in Jesus: his work is real: his Father's name, even God, is real. The spirit of truth is his witness. Believe him, lest you begin to believe something else.

But ye believe not, because ye are not of my sheep, as I said unto you. My sheep hear my voice, and I know them, and they follow me: and I give unto them eternal life; and they shall never perish, neither shall any man pluck them out of my hand.

That Jesus has sheep in the world, even those in the world who are kept from evil by the hand of God, is obvious. This great fact finds no place in the philosophies and doctrines of Satan's children. Somehow, the beast has blinded them: indeed, even the angels themselves oftentimes disclose ignorance of the plain truths of life. The scribes greatly err in these matters since, in spite of sanctimonious protestations to the contrary, they believe their outline of history is the most important, and sometimes, the only one. Nevertheless the life of a man is precious before God though none other take notice of it.

The voice of Jesus is not the exclusive prerogative of theologians and evangelists and members of religious hierarchies. Indeed, his church is not of the world, and in this all worldly churches greatly err. When a soul is in heaven, it has no need of a church. To preach to those in heaven how to get to heaven is nonsense. The kingdom of heaven belongs to those poor in spirit who enjoy the path of eternal forgiveness and mercy and love.

God created the stars also: has this fact no relevance for our lives as we organize ourselves into nations and empires and armies and gangs and states, in order to provide for the common defense? God clothes the grass of the earth with the beauty of a flower: can such genius creatively expressed somehow find itself incompetent in matters pertaining to the care of those who follow Jesus? I think not.

But the scribes of the world write up the wonders of the world and eat those things sacrificed to idols of mind, soul, heart, mob, and marketplace. Learned ignoramuses tax the children of God to provide a forum for their vanities. They are too wise to search the scripture and too self-willed to follow either God or Jesus or Love. Such are the damned. They must lord it over others since they have lost the use of their own soul and cannot lord it over themselves.

Nevertheless, the sons of God overcome the world and are in heaven rulers with God. They rule their own kingdom and are gods in the kingdom of God.

The spirit of Antichrist is legion: it denies facts and promotes the reality of myths. The great bottomless pit of Man's evil imagination produces Roman law, Babylonian religion, and worldly hypocrisy. Prisons, jails, courts, lawyers, judges, armies: what are these things but the inventions of men who know nothing of God yet profess to know everything important about the world? These are the ignorant in the world who know not God: such are the accusers, and liars, and thieves who steal heaven from men and substitute the vanities of their own pathetic ideals.

To make the world safe for democracy is the desire of idiots: the world is safe for democracy already: but what results from democracy? Barabbas rules. The son of the rabble, the very product of an ignorant mob, leads men into hell.

Eternal life is knowledge of God. It is knowledge that God saves his own. God is both creator and savior, wife and husband, lover and armed friend. But men do not take their religious babblings seriously. For if they did, they wouldn't attempt to keep men from God. After men kill the body, there is nothing more that they can do. Surely, this is by divine design.

Men can more readily accept the doctrines of Moses than the bread of life. What is eternity? The reality in which we place our time machines. What is eternal life? Knowledge that God created us to remain with him forever. The words remain: heavens and earths have come to be, flourished, and passed away. Yet my words remain. The Word is the creative power, and yet men know it not: even those who create so many things brilliant and beautiful, loathsome and evil, with the words of their own mouths, and the scribblings of their hand.

God's seal is sure and true. I find more comfort in reality and truth than I do in the myriad products found in the bottomless pit of Man's imagination. We are gods who have become the sons of man. In some ridiculous way we have created the ultimate idol and fallen in love with it. There are things open to us that are not open to men: and the son of man is also ignorant of many matters.

We babble much, and really know very little.

There are those that hear the voice of Jesus: that follow him. They believe in him, although many parables are hard to understand. We are taught with proverbs, with analogies, with similes. True science is the art of using the power of the word to separate fact from fiction. Much, indeed very much of man's science, is dull, stupid and boring fiction.

We are led, we are fed, we are numbered, we are scattered, we are slaughtered, we are cherished, we are saved, even as sheep. But who leads, who feeds, who numbers? Who loves? Who really cares for us, provides for us, saves us, leads us into an abundant life?

The shepherd appointed by the Lord God of Israel, is even Jesus himself. The kingdom of heaven is the kingdom of love: of abundant life: of eternal beauty. Each man occupies a mansion within the house of God. But we treat our spiritual inheritance with contempt and somehow believe our creator is other than who he is and that our created things are superior to ourselves. Satan is our servant: he ought not to be obeyed as if he were God. A devil by any other name remains the same. To use the Word to cover our nakedness is hypocrisy.

The gift of love to the living soul is eternal life. We live and acknowledge it not: we die like men, and confess not this truth: we are foolish, proud, vain: our words reveal to us what we are, and we forget the most elementary of facts. We can plan our day, our work, our future, our whole life: but there is no allowance in all our worldly schemes for God's plans, ambition, jealousy, or desires.

Those that I love remain. They have not perished. Men have not taken them from me. My words have not passed away: neither have the sheep that hear them. This is plain truth, simple fact, a living witness, a lively testimony.

I rejoice in Paul's life even more than Paul. I rejoice in Israel even more than Israel rejoices in itself. I find more life in death than even the more lively of the dead discover. Let me rejoice then in that which my God prepares for me. My God has his work, and his joy; and I have mine.

How can I live without them? If my life is given to them how might I take it again unless they grant it back to me? They are in the world even now as I am in the world. Yet am I in my kingdom. How can this be except it be known that the kingdom has come: God's will is done: heaven is one with earth?

Eternal life is the only kind worth living. God himself understands our idols better than we do, and laughs.

Nevertheless, the Son of man has suffered many things, and has been rejected by the elders, the chief priests and scribes. Indeed, such prolong his spiritual death in our soul by their vanities and ordinances and laws and customs and myths. Such do not follow him. Such are with us today. Those who reject the Son of God, reject the God who sent him into this otherwise lifeless world. The spiritual death of the Son of man has lasted three thousand years as the world currently measures time. Few realize David and Jesus are one and the same living soul.

Yet he shall be raised up the third day. What is the third day? Even that day you know these things as truth. The Word, even by its own power, brings forth its own seed when planted in bodies of earth. The seed brings together and creates the many worlds of heavenly life. The tree of life grows in the garden of God, even in that place wherein our soul delights in the spirit of love who creates us. We are living souls brought to the fullness of life by the spirit working within us. The words spoken by Jesus are his spirit.

The tree yields fruit: the kingdom of heaven grows within us and yields fruit of its own kind. It is what it is: even the planting of God in flesh and blood. We are raised up of earth by the power of the word to become the Sons of God. Why should we deny our beginnings? God knew what he planted and saw that it was good.

This is the third day. To understand this is simple enough: it is part of that knowledge which is of the God of eternal life.

The words of Jesus is the spirit of God which falls into the earth of our dead bodies and raises them up on the third day. If the Greeks could only believe in this simple truth, their temples would rival the wisdom of Solomon. The words never pass away: neither shall we: for we are the living souls whose very life is one with those words.

God is true and his word reveals the facts of life. But man is the great deceiver, deceiving not only himself, but many of the angels of God as well. If Judas is a devil, what is Lenin? If Peter is rebuked as Satan, what rebuke is due these many heads of State?

Let the Greeks in their wisdom deal with the children of Babylon. The Greeks have found what they sought: for wisdom is a spiritual reality found of them that seek her. There are many spirits given of God. Wisdom is but one of them.

The God of the World, is Satan, even the living prince of this world who in his totality governs the world in the manner in which the world is governed. The godless State, even the beast of the sea of wickedness, is his creation. He deceives men: preaches hate, war, imprisonment, taxation; laws numerous, complex, varied, wierd, ridiculous; merciless are his products. He imprisons Patty Hearst; like so many of his sons, he is devoid of mercy, tenderness, compassion, love. He is the asshole of the world and has no understanding of spiritual fact. The statesman, the lawyer, the high priest, the worldly scribe are his children. He is my adversary and I am his.

The kingdom is not of his world: The kingdom of heaven is the creation and joy of those who work the will of God in earth. Those in heaven cannot be plucked out of the hand of Jesus.

My Father, which gave them me, is greater than all; and no man is able to pluck them out of my Father's hand. I and my Father are one. Then the Jews took up stones again to stone him.

Those that dwell by the stony sea know that a few stones cast into the ocean of truth hardly disturb it. Men gather stones to cast at Christ in vain. There are stones crushable, and stones which grind. There are stones precious, reflective of light and beauty, and there are men who are stoned dead. Some stones, as Peter, are gathered: others are cast away.

Those that deny Jesus is one with his God testify to all men that they are not one with the God of Jesus. With whom then are they in agreement, with whom are they one? With themselves. They have hardened their hearts to the seeds of love and made their minds impenetrable to the entrance of light. Such are the children who believe they are the products of fate, chance, statistics, evolution, and the mindless genetics of complex matter.

Tell them the truth and they gather facts galore to bury you with.

Jesus answered them, Many good works have I shewed you from my Father; for which of these works do ye stone me? The Jews answered him, saying, For a good work we stone thee not; but for blasphemy; and because that thou, being a man, makest thyself God.

The Jews are Jehovah's Witnesses—indeed to be a Jew is to be a witness that Jehovah created them. This is a simple fact in Israel. Why then is it so hard to conceive that God also created himself a son, which son I am? Why is it so easy for them to be taught and fathered in the ways of any of a myriad of worldly beliefs, doctrines, disciplines and professions, and yet so hard for the Jews themselves to accept the fact that God is the father of Jesus, even their Christ? They want no king but Caesar: the world abounds with various Caesars. The times are full of such signs. But what is really so appealing about these heads of states, nations, principalities, churches, families, and corporations numerous, ruling men's lives in ways large and ways small, ways trivial and in matters important?

Jesus has no king but God. This the Jews somehow cannot accept. Why? Let them answer. The secret is buried within them and frankly it would be a tedious bore to dig it out by myself.

Jesus answered them, Is it not written in your law, I said ye are gods?

We are gods, sons of the highest, and we live and die as men. Why? Because we have become corrupted by our own self-created idols: we have married many strange doctrines, fallen in love with many strange women. Men love their fatherland, parties political, their country and their church: and they worship what their lovers worship, idolatrous though it be.

If we are gods, we ought to live as gods. Men have invested their institutions with life. The church lives, the soul dies. Ridiculous absurdity! The man dies, the nation lives: this is ever their motto: surely, it is vain. It is my life that I give. It is my death that I hate. But they want me to remain dead so that I will not testify of the evil the world works.

If he called them gods, unto whom the word of God came, and the scripture cannot be broken; Say ye of him, whom the Father hath sanctified and sent into the world, Thou blasphemest; because I said, I am the son of God?

Can the scripture be broken? Did the word of God come to he who called us gods? Did God sanctify Jesus? Did God send him into the world?

Men are proud of their own opinions, beliefs, and philosophies. Sometimes they act as if God were a machine to be explained rather than a spirit to be loved and worshiped. I marvel at men who can occupy themselves with the affairs of the world, and multiply the words of their mouth, and deliver their doctrines and beliefs with the skill of genius, and think God absent from the world, incapable of speaking to the souls he has created, and unconcerned as to whether a man believes in the truth or in a lie.

We are the products of civilization: or so some men think. What shall I judge then, that the kingdom of heaven is a product of the civilized world? The world is in love with Roman law, Greek thought, and Babylonian ceremony. The commandment of love, the wisdom of Solomon's era of peace, the pure doctrines of Christ is not acceptable to the civilized world.

I know the universe is vast: did not my Father make it so? I know the soul is immortal, otherwise it could not experience death and yet live. But the scripture remains in the world, the living witness of a true God who speaks with the voice of accurate prophecy. Our faith is a spirit overcoming the blind stupidity of those in the world and of the world who know not the Lord God of Israel, even the Spirit of Love Herself. God is the bride of the human soul and the husbandman of our dreams and the gardener of our delight.

The sin of the wicked is this: they declare their experience the only reality. They cannot believe: they pride themselves on the fact that they know. They have knowledge of their own evil, their own experiences, their own imaginings. The gates of hell cannot prevail against heaven. Heaven grows and expands and creates even in hell. Heaven's processes destroy hell and its mischievous specter, Death. It is the gates of hell that cannot stand. The city of truth is a beautiful and living reality. Those that love beauty and truth dwell there. I am that truth for so has my God made me.

If I do not the works of my Father, believe me not.

The works of our Father is to make the Word flesh so that it might dwell among us. The work of God is to inspire men's lives with the breath of his life. We live because his Word creates us living souls. The death of the body is nothing but what it is, a return of dust to dust. It is the soul which creates the body, though I confess I know not how except it be by the power of the Word. Words create.

Euclidean geometry cannot exist without words to explain it. So also, all science, all art, all literature, all communications, all doctrines heavenly and doctrines earthly. The sheep are fed with the works of genius and the products of craftsmanship and the dreams of poets and musicians and lovers everywhere. The stars are as real as astronomers. The soul requires both: our God provides the one as readily as the other.

Whatever I have, my God gives me. My cup of life is poured for me. I am taught: am rebuked: am chastised: am perfected. What then have I to do with Satanic sentiments, Babylonian priest craft, and Jewish pride?

I have no works save my words. My words are my burden: my words are my works. The burden of love is this: to keep its spirit eternally alive.

Let men boast of ages long past, and billions of years, and eons of time, and intricate evolutionary processes—I am too young a god to understand their wisdom. I find more delight in a woman's breast, than in all their wild imaginings. I am only a few days old and find no joy in their statistical abstractions. My God fashions my beloved even as I sleep. To her I cleave: in her, I find my God. My Aphrodite is real.

But if I do, though ye believe not me, believe the works: that ye may know and believe, that the Father is in me, and I in him.

If those I love are in God, and God is within me, then also are they within me and I am within them.

Nevertheless, the adventure of life does not cease simply because we have attained some metaphysical insight into the wonders of our own being.

Therefore they sought again to take him: but he escaped out of their hand.

Satan is many headed and mediocrity is many-handed. But wisdom justifies her own children and provides an escape.

And went away again beyond Jordan into the place where John at first baptized; and there he abode.

Jesus is way beyond Jordan.

And many resorted unto him, and said, John did no miracle; but all things John spake of this man were true. And many believed on him there.

John baptized with words, with the dissolving power of gentle truth: but the spirit is the fiery reality behind the words, though we recognize it not. A prophecy is given in word: its fulfillment is a flesh and blood reality.

We are led by our beliefs. Some men lust to know before they act. Knowledge, is assimilated. Death results. The knowledge that belief in God leads us into eternal life, is lost. Men then require a shepherd: have need of a Savior.

Men accuse Jesus of making himself God. I don't know what they mean by the phrase, Son of God, if they accuse him of such conceit.

I believe in my God. I confess this belief. I know my God. I confess this knowledge. I am a son of man. I become a son of man by eating and drinking with men. I know this. Surely, it is a clear truth.

Yet if I deliver to men the words my God has given me—if I share with men my life in the way it is done—if I speak the truth that I know, and write and speak of the spirit within me, why do men decide against me? Obviously, because they don't believe me. Let them doubt the living presence of the God within me and the God in whom I am. I cannot. I know whose son I am. I have an earthly father. I have an heavenly father. The son of God becomes the son of man. That which is of earth, is of earth. That which is of heaven is of heaven. I am in heaven, though I be wrapped in earth, imprisoned in the world.

The simple truth frees me. I speak with a new tongue: am no longer writing in Hebrew; no longer in the kingdom of the Jews. I have received a new kingdom: even the kingdom of heaven. I have worked with my God and your God: really, the spirit is the one true God. His words are truth itself. No other Word overcomes, creates, enlivens, excitingly satisfies. Let the many who believe on Jesus testify whether this be true or false; good or evil; eternally relevant or mortally corrupt.

CHAPTER 11

Now a certain man was sick, named Lazarus, of Bethany, the town of Mary and her sister Martha. (It was that Mary which anointed the Lord with ointment, and wiped his feet with her hair, whose brother Lazarus was sick.)

Where is Lazarus now? Healing the sick. But where? In the city of the angels. Do angels get sick? Of course.

Therefore his sisters sent unto him, saying, Lord, behold, he whom thou lovest is sick.

Does the lord love the sick? A cheap question, fraught with difficulties: yet it demands an answer.

There is life in God which is beyond sickness: sin, death, hell are not there. What is there is what God loves. What is not there is what God hates. Sickness is not there: neither are the sick.

Our sickness is of the world: the system of things, of material forms, of social processes, of individual beliefs, actions, commitments. In this sense, God hates the sick. Yet does he love them: for the divine physician is ever with the world saving it from its own excesses.

We cannot become the Sons of God unless we hate our mother, our father, our own life also. For many of us, much of our life, is sick, is hateful, is restrictive of divine power. I do not argue with the Spirit of Truth: I accept its revelation. This comforter is the spirit which analyses the analysts: judges the judges: questions the wise, and draws a circle of limitation around our Greek mentalities. I love the Greeks:

yet do they resist me. They have been blessed with the wisdom of God and yet have no impulse to love her. In this are they sick: to love not God is sickness.

My sickness is psychosomatic. What sickness is not? Those caused by a virus, a microorganism, a chemical compound? Those caused by an excess of what we need to grow? And what causes the virus, the organism, the chemical to be just that which it is? The Greeks are divided against themselves: the genius of Freud and Jung and William James and Emanuel Swedenborg is divided against Euclid and Archimedes and Dalton and Fourier and Faraday and Maxwell. Neither have the mathematical materialists and the realities they name, define, manipulate, and use been reconciled with the mental realities of our dreams, thoughts, visions, and beliefs.

The spirit of truth, the eternal comforter which is in the world sent there by Jesus from his father, shows us all these things and we may, if so inclined, marvel at them. In the beginning, God created the heavens and the earth. This simple truth, this fragment of Moses' body, this spiritual bone of contention is sought by both Satan and the angels of heaven. Satan is the antithesis of the Holy Spirit. Men are deceived: do become sick: do die: do lose sight of paradise because of that power which the beast has to tempt men.

Nevertheless our sickness is not unto death: our sickness is a limitation placed by God upon our powers.

Men ask for truth, and yet have neither the time nor the patience to receive what the spirit of truth is ever so ready to grant. To know we are sick is to regain our health: to know we are dead is to see life opening up before us.

Pride is the great head on the beast of the godless state which is hard to kill. After all the wars, famines, plagues, foolishness and human misery caused by heads of state, I am astonished, amazed beyond all measure, at the many great men in the world that worship the State and have lost the use of their own souls and the pleasures of the kingdom of heaven.

Yet there they are, even as I am here. The kingdom of heaven is the personal growth of the garden of God within you. It is never anything less: nor can it ever be anything more. Why not let God, even the bride of Israel, love you, keep you, delight you, enliven you, share with you his own eternal life? All the pleasures satisfying in the world, are of heaven. The beauty of God is manifested by the glory of his works: God's works are accomplished by his words. Fools seek other explanatory realities and bring forth only their own withered, dried up, and lifeless words.

Even I can bring out of myself that which I cast away. My vomit and stool and emanations various are of only passing interest to me. So is my sickness and death and imprisonment. I hate it.

God hates the sick so he destroys their sickness. In this is his love eternally manifested. It is done in the way it is done. We are loved even when we are hated. In the processes of time, men will see this truth for what it is, and our hopes, even all of them, shall be realized. Lazarus is not the only one who has come forth from death. There are thousands upon thousands of others. Jesus did not say we would not die, nor taste of death. The spirit of truth is not a liar. Satan is the liar: the men who promise peace and equip for war; who promise wealth and tax us poor, who promise to keep us free while they enslave us with their bonds of law, are what they are, the great mouth on the sickly head of pride. Such are of Satan. Such are liars.

Such weep for Lazarus when he is dead and plan to kill him when he comes forth and once again enjoys life. Nevertheless, Lazarus is in the hand of God as are all who request to be there. Our sickness is not unto Death; how much less so is our death? We fall to earth so we might bring forth from the earth itself that which without us remains lifeless. Surely gods ought not to be deceived by their own created images.

Prove it, mock the wise and prudent men of the world. I cannot. Proof is a process common to any one of many limited systems of thought and belief. What is true, is true. Living fact is real fact. The search for proof has led learned men into miasmas of mental confusion. They trust not God: believe few men: confess to no sin: cannot acknowledge their own ignorance, confusion, helplessness. They are reluctant to suck on the breast which can satisfy, comfort, and even excite them.

"Give us a sign." Yet they want no signs. What they want is for the spirit of truth to confirm them in their delusions. But truth is intolerant and will not do so. No sin against truth can ever be forgiven: the penalty shall surely follow: we are told the truth by God and that is the punishment he always righteously exacts. I love him for it.

Jesus is informed of our sickness: and explains its limitations. It cannot remain with us forever. It has an end. The dead are freed of their sickness. The dead also rise again. In this the glory of God is displayed and the genius of his creation is manifested. There is a time of life and a time to die: there is a time of sickness and a time of healing. The death of the body is real: so also is its resurrection. We rise again.

When Jesus heard that, he said, This sickness is not unto death, but for the glory of God, that the Son of God might be glorified thereby. Now Jesus loved Martha and her sister, and Lazarus. When he had heard therefore that he was sick, he abode two days still in the same place where he was.

Jesus abides in one place: we are sick and die in another. Men sleep: die: rest: rise to live another day. It is done in the way it is done: experienced in the manner in which it is experienced. Man's imagination abounds with myths concerning the teleportation of material bodies. The *Enterprise* beams bodies to many a wandering star and back again.

Yet God does it in the manner in which it is done. A woman is formed from part of a man: the man becomes one with a woman: a child is born: a living soul resides in a temple of earth: in such manner is a material soul transported: in such a manner a body is resurrected.

But the dead know nothing of these processes. And fools believe they know all there is to know about them.

Yet Lazarus comes forth from an earthly tomb and not from a woman's womb. Obviously, God also raises the dead without the help of a woman.

Men are asleep, spiritually dead, in the cave of their own restricted imagination. They are made sick by the processes of the world: the world wearies them: they sleep in the grave provided: they are wrapped in the graveclothes provided by their brethren: locked in by the tombstones of ignorant beliefs which keep us from seeing the light of day. Even our eyes are closed and wrapped shut with the napkins of nonsense priests provide.

Yet if an evil and adulterous generation cannot accept the resurrection of Elias's body and the testimony of John the Baptist, it surely cannot bear the living reality of Lazarus, the one who rose from the dead at the command of Christ. Even though we rise again, take up our lives even many times, the chief priests and Pharisees want to kill us: they desire us dead. Why? Because they love their doctrines of religious bullshit more than the testimony of God's witnesses. That they really have nothing with which to feed men except lightened doctrinal vanities which they received of their own fathers, they cannot accept. They pray for the dead and thus illustrate to all men that their concern is for the dead and not for the living. Such make Fate a God and eat the dust of the earth and kiss the ground and worship false prophets; and in worship blindly bow down low and turn their asses toward heaven. They, the blindly intolerant, pray now for religious tolerance. They have received it. Yet what does it profit them?

Surely it's more profitable for us to rest in God's bosom than to weary ourselves with hell's vanities. Even God rests.

Then after that saith he to his disciples, Let us go into Judaea again.

The Jews are not the only Jews. Mary and Martha and Lazarus are also of Judaea and are Jews. Jesus has and does come again.

Judah is the kingdom of the Jews. *Jesus understands heaven*: this is the definition of *Judah*. Those who are truly kings of God know that Jesus understands. Judah is the law giver: the laws of creation, the laws of God are of Judah.

I know that Satan is divided against itself. The men of this world are programmed to self-destruct. Hitler's past and present are vain: they perish: and who cares for their souls except God? Love is the gravity of the heavens: the men of Judah understand this. The men of the world think it poetic fancy. Yet such poetry is Judaic truth.

Hugh Hefner can produce a philosophy wherein the Judeo-Christian ethic is examined, judged, defined and explored. But what he forgets is that an abstraction is an abstraction: an idea is just an idea: what he forgets is that the God who created the tribe of Judah also created the flesh and blood goddesses whose beauty is the reality upholding his remarkable worldly empire. His mansion is real: nevertheless, so are other mansions belonging to other kings in Judah.

A man who rules his kingdom of heaven under the loving dictatorship of God is of Judah. Nevertheless, worldly scribes have little insight into the nature of their own soul, and, failing to understand that, their helplessness before the Word is understandable. They conceive, create and enliven Babylon: and are ignorant of the fact God destroys the product of their babble in order to limit the power of evil.

In all truth, such know not what they do. Ignorance of God is the colossus which sustains the godless world which we must overcome.

It is your world Jesus helps you overcome. The crown of life is yours given you of your God: it ought not to be cast before the princes of the world. If you must cast it away, lay it before God. He'll make use of it. The Ancient of Ages is a divine craftsman and knows his work. The men of Judah know this. They are his work.

Jesus understands this. And so may you. In all truth, what really is so hard to understand? World almanacs are of the world: so does the world number its own. But your world is the world God through Jesus, saves. It is a real world, important and precious. The other world is a myth, and all the babble of Babylon cannot make it otherwise.

His disciples say unto him, Master, the Jews of late sought to stone thee; and goest thou thither again?

Yes. The city of truth, even Jerusalem itself, the city of the great king is found there. Ultimately, we all come to Jerusalem. The spirit of truth is so appealing, we cannot resist it. Truth draws us: this is love's beauty and power and joy: to draw us to herself. Jerusalem is the bride of the soul: without truth, we cannot bring forth the children of light and everlasting life.

Even Jesus' witnesses seek to kill Jesus. Not surprising then is their desire to keep us from the reality of an abundant life. The kingdom of heaven is at hand, even your hand. Don't let any Jew keep you from it. The Jews in their pride want no God nor sons of God to come in flesh and blood. Why? I really don't know.

Lazarus is real. So also are all those who come forth from the grave of their own spiritual understanding and leave the cave of their own limited imagination. Plato is as Lazarus, eyeing in his death the shadows cast upon the enclosed spaces of his mind. We are dead. We sleep. We are resting in the place provided.

It is Jesus who arranges things for our own good. He sends for us: he calls us forth: his desire is to have us believe so that we might see the glory of God.

Even though our brother is dead, we still come quickly to Jesus when he sends for us.

The resurrection of the body is an accomplished fact. An infant sucks its mother's teat, and dust is inspired with life. We suck on the breast of queens for pleasure and excitement as well as for sustenance. But worldly fools do not desire the things of heaven: they care not that the Word is made flesh. God's will is not done in earth, not in their earth: they see no supernatural beauties, never hear the angels sing, and are deaf to the fact that the hills are alive with music. Mary is as real as Julie, and Catherine and Cathy are delights for those many hours that fill eternity.

Jesus called Mary not only so that she might see the glory of God but also that he might delight in the glory of Mary. Love loves its own. Let the Puritans revel in their purity. The God that I see reveals Jackie and Jennie and Rosalynn are lovable and fuckable and suckable.

Mary comes in more ways than one.

Now Jesus was not yet come into town, but was in that place where Martha met him. The Jews then which were with her in the house, and comforted her, when they saw Mary, that she rose up hastily and went out, followed her, saying, She goeth to the grave to weep there.

The Jews grievously err. They have no heart to understand these matters: their mind cannot comprehend them. It is no wonder God scatters his own among the Gentiles. Some souls are so obsessed that God created them to witness to the truth of Jehovah's might, that they see and understand little else about their God.

His own people strive against him, mar his image, blaspheme him, trivialize his majesty and glory and power. The naked loveliness of God's beautiful children is covered up with the fig leaves of their own fruitless and unprofitable doctrines. No wonder Jesus cursed the tree and covenanted with God himself to husband his own branches.

The Jews are dead witnesses for they cannot accept the simple fact that the Lord God of Israel, even the Lord of hosts, even the Father of David and Jesus, is also the Lord of heaven and earth, and the Savior of the world. Nevertheless, even the gentiles who understand little about him, are beginning to acknowledge this simple fact.

But who really is a Jew? I am for I witness to Jehovah. The Greeks oppose me in this, for in their angelic wisdom they somehow believe they can house God within their metaphysical categories of thought. Darkness results and a boring and tedious and learned literature results. Lifeless branches bear no food useful for life.

God is love: this I know: for so John testifies and his writings are true. But the Greeks worship another God, believe in another spirit: they analyze the God of this world and end their lives worshiping the idols of their own mind. But who is a *Greek*? Any great ruler energizing evil kingdoms. Their kingdoms are real: their rule is real: their energy, their wisdom, their perfection of beauty is real. So is their evil.

Jimmy Carter, Albert Einstein, Lenin, Mao Tse-tung, Mary Magdalen rule those who believe in them. Mary lost her evil spirits: so also may all these other souls who believe not that the kingdom of heaven within us is God's to rule, and not theirs.

I glory in my heavenly father, even in the Creator of Mary, and the living bride of my living soul. My earthly father is man, the very image of God, an intermingled spirit of good and evil. If I were not his son, and myself composed of both, I could not believe this to be true.

Nevertheless, in his own way, God cares for his image. We are refined, like it or not, by God, and in this we should rejoice.

Then when Mary was come where Jesus was, and saw him, she fell down at his feet, saying unto him, Lord, if thou hads't been here, my brother had not died.

Surely, this is true. It is the absence of Jesus that makes death possible. If life is with us, death is absent. The spiritual death of man's soul is not seriously considered as being an impediment to hell's desires. Hell is heaven eternally loveless and lonely. The dead find no discomfort in their death: it is God who grieves for them, desires them saved, wishes them alive and powerful and free. Where the Lord of life is, death is seen for what it is, even dead earth devoid of the ethereal atmospheres of heaven. To understand death, to experience death, is to triumph over it. Nevertheless, our pain, our sorrow, our death is of the world of men: a world we must and shall overcome.

I hate my life in this world. It is no joy to see those who weep for the dead and fear those men and things that can kill the body. We do ourselves much good by believing in Jesus: in this manner is our resurrection accomplished: in this way is God's commandment to live forever obeyed. It is more thrilling to be chastised by God than praised by all the great men of the world. I must let the dead bury the dead: in this action my God allows me no part. The world is full of spiritual undertakers and liars and fools and devils in great abundance. They do their work and I do mine. Every time I feel inclined to help them dispose of their dead carcasses of lifeless thought, my God kicks me in the ass. She will have none of it, and wisely so.

Mary is right. When the Lord of Israel is with us, our life is eternal, and no power can take it from us. Nevertheless, from those who believe not Jesus, Mary's wisdom is hidden.

When Jesus therefore saw her weeping, and the Jews also weeping which came with her, he groaned in the spirit and was troubled, And said, Where have ye laid him? They said unto him, Lord, come and see. Jesus wept.

Those that mourn and weep are blessed. Their comfort is assured: the spirit of truth responds to their distress. The universe of life is larger than all our caves of death: immensely so. Light comes into our presence and wakes us from our sleep of death. The resurrection of our soul is as real as the resurrection of our bodies.

We weep for joy and the world understands not.

Then said the Jews, Behold how he loved him!

Behold how he loves him.

And some of them said, Could not this man, which opened the eyes of the blind, have caused that even this man should not have died?

The Jews do not understand. God continuously causes that men do not die. How many things in life would cause us to perish except

God caused our life to be eternal? God is the ever present cause of life. Our death is occasioned by our disbelief in our Creator and Savior. But men lust to know and confuse belief with knowledge. They are born children and are open to a world of beliefs. Hypocrites exploit the innocence of men and crave to enslave them to their own set of godless rules.

I know Lazarus is dead. But he also sleeps and one day shall wake and come forth.

Jesus therefore again groaning in himself cometh to the grave. It was a cave, and a stone lay upon it. Jesus said, Take ye away the stone. Martha, the sister of him that was dead, saith unto him, Lord by this time he stinketh: for he hath been dead four days.

Such was her expectation: so she believed four days of death would do to a man.

Jesus believed otherwise. For those who do not believe that these things are true, Lazarus's resurrection, Martha's declaration, Mary's sentiments, the Jews' witness, the Pharisees' concern, and John's gospel, are fictions of the mind. Thus am I an idiot, believing those things to be true which are but cunningly devised fables. I confess my belief. I can now do no more. I know not where Lazarus now lies although I have my suspicions.

Nevertheless, without first departing from life, how is a resurrection possible? We depart from eternal life, only to return. Jesus departed and returned, as did Lazarus, so that all men need never depart from that life which is lived in God.

Men boast of their reincarnations. I can only glory in such resurrections my God makes possible.

Jesus saith unto her, Said I not unto thee, that if thou wouldst believe, thou shouldst see the glory of God?

What is the glory of God? Life.

Then they took away the stone from the place where the dead was laid. And Jesus lifted up his eyes, and said, Father I thank thee that thou hast heard me. And I knew that thou hearest me always:

but because of the people which stand by I said it, that they may believe that thou hast sent me.

Jesus is God's angel: one of his Father's many messengers. It is essential for men to believe this: for either Jesus is sent by God, or he is the most deluded fool the world has ever produced and those that believe on him are idiots. Surely, the Greeks can understand this simple logic. This then is my adventure: I believe in my God and in his angels. Let wisdom justify her children and God save his own. I am weary of the controversy, and other matters of heaven intrigue me more. Endless debate is also a form of eternal damnation. God save me from making no decision in the valley of decision. Nevertheless, I have decided as my life does witness. To what do you witness?

The living stone of our own life is rolled against the cave of our own limited imagination. Our imaginations are limited, restricted, confined. Our sphere of experiences may be confined to an atmosphere of worldly delights. Yet the sun and stars radiate upon our world. We need only look upward to heaven to realize the source of the power of life. Poetry has yet to clothe the sterile and invisible truths of metaphysics with the flesh and blood realities of heavenly life. Dung is used of the wise to nourish flowers. Yet in the perfection of their beauty the Lucifers of this world neglect the realities of everlasting life. Their lusts are ephemeral: their doctrines perish and pass away. The living are locked out and the dead are locked within the kingdom of our own soul by the heavy stone of experience we have placed against our place of rest.

The living at the command of Jesus take away the stone from our graves. Those dead who hear his voice come forth. Nevertheless, it is the task of the living angels of God to roll away the stone from our grave.

The heavy burdens placed upon us by the Pharisees and lawyers and chief priests and rulers and elders and the many bureaucrats of nation, state, corporation, church, and family, are of the earth, and are of men of earth, and are the producers and products of the world.

God said, Love one another. All these others command obedience and loyalty to their idols. They worship the idols of their own mind and know it not. The State, the government of your world, is their professed desire. Heed them no more, for the kingdom of heaven is yours to rule, not theirs. Even God doesn't own us for in the fullness of time out of love he gives us to ourselves. Thus stars are born and the sons of God created. We are the children of God and the inheritors of all life.

God does hear us. We know he has scattered us in the world for a purpose. What is that purpose? To save the world from the ugly mechanisms of hell and of death. All the experiences of good and evil, of truth and of error, which a man has had can be taken away from his soul so that he might hear the words of Jesus.

And when he thus had spoken, he cried with a loud voice, Lazarus come forth.

And so he did.

But what of us? If God wakens us, shall we return to our sleep? Is there not a time to sleep and a time to wake? Are there not moments of work and days of rest? There are. Nevertheless, in his righteous wisdom God has reserved the times to himself.

There is a time to plow and not look back. There is also a time to see the day is ending and the work finished.

Those who remove the heavy stone of our experiences from the grave of our own limited thoughts are the angels of Jesus. Let those who have come forth at hearing Jesus' Word bear witness by their resurrected life that Greek mythology is no substitute for Jewish reality.

And he that was dead came forth, bound hand and foot with graveclothes: and his face was bound about with a napkin. Jesus saith unto them, Loose him, and let him go.

As it was with Lazarus, so is it with all of us who have been resurrected. We discard our graveclothes and trust our friends to clothe us anew.

Then many of the Jews which came to Mary, and had seen the things which Jesus did, believed on him.

Mary is a star in her own right and has drawn many a wandering eye to herself. So ever does beauty beckon.

236

But some of them went their ways to the Pharisees, and told them what things Jesus had done.

Even this day the Pharisees do not accept the resurrection as accomplished fact. Jesus and Lazarus are an embarrassment to them. They would rather bury the dead than rejoice with the living. What is the crucifixion anyway? For a masochist such as Christ nothing but pleasure. But the Pharisees arrange another crucifixion. I do not say any pleasure can be found in that act whatsoever. Being bored to death is always an excruciatingly painful experience.

Then gathered the chief priests and the Pharisees a council, and said, What do we? for this man doeth many miracles. If we let him thus alone, all men will believe on him: and the Romans shall come and take away both our place and nation.

The chief priests and the Pharisees are ever the same: they love their place in their nation and fear the power of the Romans. They would rather stay the hand of God and deny his power and glory, than give up their place in the hearts of men. They give men what they give men: idle advice, ceremonial excesses, words without power, and the vanities of religious systems. The whore of Babylon has spawned many a stepdaughter: the religions of men are many. God's truth is one. The decisions rendered in council are ever the same: Roman law, Roman justice, Roman democracy, Roman senates, Roman emperors, Roman legislators, Roman armies, Roman justice, Roman coin, Roman ways—are the lusts of the council. But Jesus Christ is not in the council, nor in the secret chambers. The living power of God dwelling within those who believe in Jesus' Word creates the kingdom of heaven within us. We are residents of the kingdom of love: and the States of Rome, and all the statesmen of the world, and all the legislators of the world, have no part in us. The kingdom of heaven is ruled by God, even by the God dwelling within us.

This fact is not acceptable to the men of the council, the committee men, the men of the state. The rulers of the world are the captive slaves of their own ungodly ways. Their God is the god of the world, Satan himself, in all his pompous and hypocritical glory. Yet the Colosseum is closed. What the Pharisees and the chief priests and the Romans themselves never consider is that their time is numbered. It is true that the State is a product of Greek thought and Roman engineering. It is true that the Chinese Government and the United States Government and the Indian Government and all these other divided nations of the world constitute the beast of the sea, even the Godless State in all its awesome immensity, and that they are Man's substitute for the kingdom of heaven. It is true that such has overcome many: and marked and numbered and made merchandise out of all men's lives. But they have no power here: no power within the kingdom of heaven. And if they cannot overcome even the poor in spirit, how can they possibly expect to prevail against the angels of God?

If Lazarus came forth from the dead to embarrass them, how much more so will they be embarrassed by Jesus' return?

The Romans indeed did take away their place of power: the Romans indeed did destroy their nation. Nevertheless, this was because they killed their king, and refused heaven in earth, and chose the curse rather than the blessing. Why do men choose death over life? God's commandment is plain: Do not kill. He never forbade us to raise the dead. Love's commandment is life everlasting.

All the nations of the earth ultimately perish, for they are made of perishable doctrines. Only the kingdom of heaven remains, an everlasting place of love, truth, beauty, and pleasures forevermore.

Satan is a beast, a created creature whose existence is necessary for the life for the world.

Custom, ritual, habit, instinct, belief, and many things born of the will of the blood, the desires of the flesh, and the will of man exist to make possible the life of the world. Nevertheless, there is another kingdom, other mansions, heavenly realities which are beyond the visible things which tempt men. Of such, Satan knows nothing. The computer's library is limited: indeed, its very existence is temporal; its clocks cannot shift the words of everlasting life. In a very real sense, Satan is the ultimate computer, and unless God had intervened men would have remained dead forever.

I write of man's spiritual death. Death is the last enemy to be overcome.

I know I lived other lives. I know the resurrection of the body is a daily occurrence, an ever-present miracle wrought by my God. I know I can't remember many things I desire to remember. Much has vanished, is forgotten, has perished. Yet, I am who I am, the living son of the God of life and love. Surely, I have been created for life and pleasure. The paradise I enjoy is real. The Death I war against is also real.

Heaven is an expansion; the kingdom is found in the world growing within us. Angie Dickinson is a goddess of life: but what is a policewoman but the perishable image produced by a passing world? Heaven and earth passes away: how much more so do these little worlds of proud and little men.

Men are overcome by the beast, really marked and numbered by this Godless State we call the world, and deceived into worshiping it by the greatest false prophet of them all, even Man himself, in all his imaged splendor and idolatrous glory.

Love, mercy, truth, life, and power are of God. But this is of Satan: hate, punishment, lies various, death, and a weakness so pervasive that even the bravest of men can't tell the slaves of hell to shove their lies, their fear, their wars, their pride, their vengeance, their silly laws and incredible pettiness, up their ass. In a certain sense, the servants of the State are assholes all, since they have rejected the kingdom of heaven and its king to serve the various princes of the world.

I know not whether any man had the courage to say, Fuck you, Harry, drop your own bomb: but I do know there are those who truly love their enemies and are saving them from the spiritual forces of hate and pride and fear and foolishness which is the necessary inheritance of those who forsake the ways of God.

Without God, chaos reigns and death results.

What the chief priests are always so slow to understand is that no man, royal man, or poor man, can prevail against the powers of the kingdom built within those who worship the God of truth.

Really, trying to keep any Son of God dead is rather a bit ridiculous.

Let us love God and enjoy one another. Can we honestly believe we are the statistical product of a swirl of cosmic dust? Can we honestly believe God will not take our soul back to himself? Can we honestly believe this political bullshit coming out of the mouths of worldly men is worth the price we pay to receive it? Do you really wish to be governed by communists or democrats or priests rather than the God of truth and love? Is mammon to be served rather than the God of life?

If we do not believe we are the sons of God who die like men, what the hell do we believe ourselves to be? Jesus is a door to God, a gate to heaven, the very cornerstone of truth. Without Jesus, John would have had no gospel to write and the Jews would have no friend to kiss before they hand him over to the Romans of this modern world. The Romans are as real as the senators they support: the chief priests are as real as the subordinate priests they rule: and the kingdom of heaven is as real as the spirit of love which dwells unseen in the human heart. Evil is real: but so is the God that overcomes it: God, our Father, is as real as the son who proclaims him the Lord God of Israel.

How can any Jew be not a Christian?

And how can any Christian be not a Jew?

Pride is one head of the beast hard to kill. Satan introduces us to a little bit of knowledge of good and evil; we feed on its fruit, and think ourselves to be as wise as God. Satan doesn't know what God knows: Satan is an ignorant beast whose end is at hand. So why believe the lie and those that father it? What is the Lie? That the Word has not been made *flesh*. Free *love* is *essential* for *supernatural happiness*. We cannot be chained by these lawyers of Satanic morality and these apostles of one world government. They are fucking incompetents and have committed adultery with every Satanic spirit which the Godless State has produced. There is no law but love: all else is pharisaical hypocrisy.

Nevertheless, what comes out of the mouths, what words are formed, by those men who are full of the knowledge of good and evil? Words of freedom or words of accusation? Words of truth, of everlasting life, of forgiveness, of cleansing, of strength, of peace, of confidence in that God who is love? Surely, only those who have been nurtured by the words of God know how to choose the Good and reject the Evil.

Woe is the portion of the lawyers. What *woe*? Even a *world* *overcome* by *evil*. Yet they never weary of trying, never tire of imposing another rule, another regulation, another law, another tax on God's poor. Nevertheless, if God is our king, heaven is our inheritance, and our soul is a mansion within it.

Jesus and his disciples indeed have beaten their swords into plowshares, and plowed the fields of the world to prepare them to receive the seeds of everlasting life. In what field do you work?

And what has Satan sown? The bullshit ground up in worldly presses: yet God in his wisdom uses all things well. Evil is consumed by God's wrath. I love Einstein, but his little image of a stupid looking God has no place in my kingdom.

The Jews not only have handed Jesus to the Romans, they also have surrendered their own hearts and minds and souls to the mindless bureaucrats of this modern world. If the genius of the human spirit had not served Mammon, and rejected God, paradise had never been lost. Yet what has happened has past: and I weary of it all.

Our soul is even this: a source of universal life. The universe is vast because our soul requires it. God saves our soul by carrying it himself. All the devils in creation are subject to the bounds of space and time my God has imposed upon them. Men create evil with words. Thus the flood coming out of the mouth of Satan is a flood of worldly words. Men serve Mammon and hate God. Why? Because God loathes Mammon. And how very much that is vain and foolish and banal and excessive and ugly is done by men because they think only of the money and never weigh the result of their works?

I have brought men to life again, and I must prepare for them a place, an everlasting home, even a universe of delight itself: surely theirs is the kingdom of heaven.

Men are so quick to rule and so slow to learn. The great men of the earth wish to rule the beast, and I am destined to destroy it. What is Death, the real spiritual power which separates us from the source of life? Death is the monster we have created to hide our sins. We hide from the God of life. Why? Why do these brilliant scribes exercise so many words and promote so very many vain theories to justify the fact that they have no God of life within themselves?

Death is a fiction: if the dead are resurrected, what really is Death?

We are gathered together and made one by the power of Jesus' Word. Let us build wisely and well. Our soul is a mansion within the kingdom of God. Let the word of life dwell there so that death may be seen for what it is, a lifeless idol of our mind, built with the products of our knowledge of evil.

The death of the body is real: but what of that? Would you have it some other way? If I desire another body to dwell within, why should I sustain the life of the old?

"They're going to kill me and cast my soul into hell," so said Jesus. But what of that? Does the story end there? Of course not. Nevertheless, let us continue in his Word.

And one of them, named Caiaphas, being the high priest that same year, said unto them, Ye know nothing at all, Nor consider that it is expedient for us, that one man should die for the people, and that the whole nation perish not. And this spake he not of himself: but being high priest that year, he prophesied that Jesus should die for that nation; And not for that nation only, but that also he should gather together in one the children of God that were scattered abroad.

This is the purpose of that death: we are gathered together into one living spirit by the story of Jesus' death. Thus is death seen for what it is, a fictional fantasy which is vastly inferior to the reality of Jesus' life.

Moses and David and John and Paul, and every believing Christian in the world, and every Gentile who brings his works into the city of truth is made one in the spirit of love who is in Jesus, reconciling the world to himself.

The priests of the world are pompous asses, and must remain so until they change their ways and accept the rule of God and thereby become his sons. If we love Jesus, we abide in his words; literally, we keep them. Our belief in his Word transforms our life: we are born again, and the words, even his words, like water, dissolve other words, and further the processes of life.

The works of those sons of God who reject Jesus are what they are, the creative scribes of their own teachings. They worship the products of their own intellect. One such product is Death, the spirit produced by the dead. Motion is not the sole criteria of life. Men move and yet are dead. Things move and yet are dead. Men without God have made themselves things. Yet they are not things, but living souls and it is the God of life, even the God of hope and dream and creative genius, even the God of Jesus, the Lord God of Israel, who brings everlasting life to these dead men.

The children of God are scattered abroad for a purpose. What is that purpose? To bring that life, which is within themselves, out of themselves, and thereby feed the world with the Word of life. God's commandment is everlasting life. But men, in their pride, reject God's rule. They would rather rule others, than themselves.

Jesus is the liberator; Man is the false prophet; and the State is the Beast of the Sea. Death and hell are the spiritual realities men worship to their own damnation. The sons of men are not God: and the angels of pride are not spirits to be worshiped: and devils are nothing more than the spiritual slaves of their own sinful natures.

The kingdom of heaven is created within us, by the God within us. Death cannot grow within it because dead earth is enlivened by light to produce the Word made flesh. All live within the Father: yet it is almost incredible to witness these many joyless souls who refuse to let the spirit of love dwell within themselves.

God created the heavens and the earth: God created me: God created you. Love him and become his child. We are scattered, yet we are made one in the spirit of truth by the power of Jesus' Word. Reject the gospel of Death and accept the word of life.

I have a controversy with the worldly scribes: what do their words mean? Words are spiritual realities: they enhance experience, enliven our mind, quicken our heart, build up our soul. Words are spiritual realities: they can produce evil thoughts, cause murders, adulterate the truth; bear false witness about living fact; blaspheme God and deface the image of Jesus, even God's created Son; words are used by Satan to tempt you to doubt the truth.

Surely, my God is not inferior to me: he overcomes me with his love, his beauty, his creative genius. God is the longsuffering Savior of the world, even your world, and the bold craftsman of heaven and earth. Yet many of his sons have made themselves earth bound incompetents, the authors of confusion, and the disenchanted creatures of their puny hells.

I am ignorant of the origin of the virus which afflicts my body: yet the writers of the present age who reject my God can glory in their understanding of the origin of all species. I pray they might begin to understand the origin of those virus responsible for the common cold. But they revel in their theories and have no use for God's truth. Words without meaning pour out of the mouth of Satan and I marvel that the earth itself is able to absorb this flood.

Those scribes who describe a world of evil bear witness of the world within themselves, a world wherein God is not.

Shall I deny pleasure past because of pain present? Shall I deny my present pleasure because of my past sorrow? Shall I deny my eternal life because of my experience of death?

I am who I am. My flesh and blood is as real as my spirit, my words, my soul. But the master scholars are authors of their own confusion. They are the cause of our virus, the *vi*rulent <u>r</u>ecorders of *u*ngodly *s*entiments. They shut up the kingdom of heaven against men. They use the power of the word to promote those worlds of evil wherein God is not. Woe is their portion.

They never acknowledge the simple fact that, in the time of Jesus and John, the children of God were scattered abroad. The Greeks, the Indian peoples, those in Asia, in Africa, in the Americas; those in the Far East, and those in all the islands, large and small—among all peoples of the earth, the children of God have been scattered.

But those who with an evil eye only see evil cannot be convinced by arguments tedious and long that God separates himself only from the wicked and joins himself to the good. Nevertheless, the sins of proud men are many. They sustain with the violent force of their own blasphemy the belief that knowledge of good and evil makes men wise. This is the shit with which scholarly devils pollute the spiritual waters of the God of life.

Men without the spirit of truth worship the beast, the great idol of proud worldly minds; the systems, corporate, monetary, military, social, scholastic, legal, and religious, have overcome those pathetic souls who have separated themselves from the Lord God of Israel. Such men robe themselves in the intellectual garments of women: they love to play a part for which they are not equipped. They cannot discern between a general idea and a private fact: their abstractions are adored as if they were clothed in flesh and blood and equipped with sinew and bone. They understand nothing and attempt to explain everything. They have made the human soul the servant and slave of the prince of this world, not knowing that God intends it otherwise.

Devils are dead events vilifying internal lives. A man, foolish and vain, speaks a few words, and women weep. Why? A man, proud and blasphemous, speaks of war, murder, fear, and death, and women rejoice. Why? Women weep for the dead. Why? Jack Kennedy, Jimmy Carter, Adolf Hitler, Napoleon, Charles Manson, and such like members of the Symbionese Liberation Army and the LAPD have their womanish transvestites who applaud them for their ideals. And what are their ideals? Give me your support, and time, and attention, and money, and talent, and life, and I will instruct you how to decide what is good and evil for you.

Such men eat freely of the tree of knowledge of good and evil and bear the fruit of their own conceits.

Let Jesus lead us; truth empower, and God execute. The ways and doctrines and lives of men are vain. I would rather raise the dead than kill them. Let these dead hear and understand: the Lord God of Israel is the God of the living and not the God of Death. Titan, Thor, and Poseidon are gods of death, Mammon's current products. Surely, had not God intervened, we would already have perished and the life of our flesh would have been impossible.

Let us love our enemies, forgive our debtors their debts, and also those who trespass upon the domain of our souls and litter it with their silly sentiments. Our love of life is larger than all their accumulated fears of death. Our God shall yet make these poor in spirit rich with all the treasures of heaven in spite of all the taxes, the usury, the deceits, the wastefulness, and the mindless mediocrities inflicted upon us by the princes of Mammon.

Jesus is not ignorant of the fact that bringing Lazarus back to life necessitates preparing a kingdom fitting for Lazarus to enjoy. It is for these we are scattered. We are the seed of God sown in all the fields of the world. Nevertheless, we are all made one by the God within us and not by the councils of men.

Then from that day forth they took counsel together for to put him to death.

Ho, hum.

Jesus therefore walked no more openly among the Jews; but went thence unto a country near to the wilderness, into a city called Ephraim, and there continued with his disciples.

And this work continues even though in all truth it is done. The scholars have no taste for eternity. They write as if the rotation of the earth were the only worldly clock and the simultaneous occurrence of independent worldly occasions is too much for them to comprehend. That the worlds are many and yet one can be sensed by any who know that both Nancy Kwan and Mao Tse-tung are one in the world of my thoughts. One brings thoughts of life and beauty and joy: and the other of death and barbaric stupidity.

Obviously, it is done and yet not done. My finished work continues.

And the Jews' passover was nigh at hand: and many went out of the country up to Jerusalem before the passover, to purify themselves.

Truth purifies. The angel of death passes overhead. In our house, he does not enter. Why then do we live and all these idolatrous Egyptians die? We live to destroy their idols and raise these Egyptians to life. Surely the people of Egypt are also God's people. All who are pure in heart know this: God also sends his angel of life.

Satan and his apologists destroy men's lives. Jesus destroys Satan and its works. To convince men of the truth of the nature of the God of life, is to destroy the power of Satan to destroy men. Satan is the great destroyer destined for destruction. We built a great machine but have no longer need of it.

Then sought they for Jesus, and spake among themselves, as they stood in the temple, What think ye, that he will not come to the feast.

Surely Jesus keeps the Passover. He also must eat his own flesh and blood. Those that deny this must eat their own words.

Now both the chief priests and the Pharisees had given a commandment, that, if any man knew where he were, he should shew it, that they might take him.

The Pharisees also teach within the temple of the human spirit such doctrines they hold dearly within themselves. God has had more success with the Gentiles, with the pagans, with savages, with barbarians, than he has had with the Pharisees. Why? It is hard to teach a learned man. Men take their titles too seriously. All great men learn of their pupils, however. Jesus sups with men not only to teach but also to learn. Surely, Jesus must love these hypocrites since he spends so much time rebuking them and chastising them and condemning them. Yet how else might they learn to know God?

Whoremongers are not found in heaven because therein love is free. Murderers are not found in heaven because it is impossible for the children of God to die. Liars are not found in heaven because therein all are too busy listening to the truth. Sorcerers are not found in heaven because the mysteries of life and truth and a universe of beauty and delight obviates such silly occupations. Idolaters are not found in the city of truth because there are too many living supernatural beauties to make such practice profitable. *Dogs* are not found in the New Jerusalem because the *d*isciples *of gods* fallen and their unbelieving children cannot stand the place. But harlots and publicans and Gentiles and Jews and Pharisees are there, eating of the tree of life, and being born again.

What is this new Jerusalem? Even the city of truth, man's observatory in this universe of life God reveals to us.

But let's continue the gospel John gave us a long time ago.

CHAPTER 12

Then Jesus six days before the passover came to Bethany, where Lazarus was which had been dead, whom he raised from the dead. There they made him a supper; and Martha served; but Lazarus was one of them that sat at the table with him. Then took Mary a pound of ointment of spikenard, very costly, and anointed the feet of Jesus, and wiped his feet with her hair: and the house was filled with the odour of the ointment.

Those that work iniquity depart from Jesus. Those that love him are found at his feet, and he at theirs. Mary's wisdom is overlooked by those theologians and metaphysicians who find no sweet pleasure in the gospel of love. They would rather praise the dead than anoint the feet of the living.

They discuss the past as if it were dead, and not a living story finding life in their own minds. This is love: to anoint and cleanse those we love with sweet delight.

Enter the spoiler.

Then saith one of his disciples Judas Iscariot, Simon's son, which should betray him, Why was not this ointment sold for three hundred pence, and given to the poor?

Thank God for the rich, and silk, and jewels glittering, and beautiful women, and oil, and gladness, and the kisses of love. If we gave all to the poor, we should all be poor. Mary gave more to the poor by anointing Jesus' feet than all charities, modern and ancient, combined. But Judas, as others, are rather slow to perceive the ways of God working in the world to enrich the poor.

This he said, not that he cared for the poor; but because he was a thief, and had the bag, and bare what was put therein.

Nevertheless, poor Judas did care for the poor: he was deceived and his detractors treat him too unkindly. I would to God I knew where he is and what he thinks of all this.

Then said Jesus, Let her alone: against the day of my burying hath she kept this. For the poor always ye have with you; but me ye have not always.

Jesus has had his day of burying: and the poor are still with us. Yet I would that Mary, in all her beauty, would turn our minds and eyes to other matters so that we might know what else has transpired since this memorable day. All thoughts are bounded with space and time: there comes the day when there shall be no poor and all in heaven shall be rich. What then shall we do with these words which have never passed away?

We speak with new tongues: express ourselves in other languages: enjoy life in a variety of worlds. Yet where is Mary? and Martha? and Judas? and Lazarus? The earth remains. Seedtime and harvest, summer and winter, and the ways of men on earth continue as they were even to this day. Men have died and grown and lived again and reigned and gathered, even in death and dream-life, life unto themselves.

Mary has anointed the feet of Jesus and wiped them with the wisdom with which her God has adorned her. Yet where is Mary now?

A thousand times the question may be asked, a thousand answers given. A thought may fix a star in timeless space, yet life is full of motion. We depart and come again: we dwell alone in God and yet are surrounded with a heavenly chorus which no man can number. Our God works in flesh and blood, and water and spirit, and in words. All these words are like water cleansing my understanding. We are cleansed by every touch of wisdom and thrilled by every sensitive heart.

God knows his work: which work we are.

But where is Mary now? I am within her and she within me and both are within you. Nevertheless, in a most practical and flesh and blood, down to earth experience, I am here, writing out the question. Thus I am where I am. With Mary it is the same way. Where is Mary now? I don't know.

Much people of the Jews therefore knew that he was there; and they came not for Jesus' sake only, but that they might see Lazarus also, whom he had raised from the dead.

Lazarus after death was as Lazarus before death and of his death Lazarus had not much to say. In fact, Lazarus learned more about his death from the living than from his own experience of it. Surely, death happens, but what is it?

But the chief priests consulted that they might put Lazarus also to death; Because that by reason of him many of the Jews went away, and believed on Jesus.

Those that are born again, those that have resurrected bodies that are alive to the truth Jesus spoke are an embarrassment to all chief priests everywhere. They desire us dead. Why? Men revel in the power of their own lies. The products of their own imagination, the beliefs of their own heart, overcome them. They are victimized by their own doctrines.

Beware of the doctrines of worldly men. Such reject the promises of the God of life and truth and love and power and accept the lies of the world with all the conceit of private conviction enhanced by public applause. The living dead are buried under the accumulated nonsense of many evil generations. The people are drowned in a sea of trivial ideas, puerile fancies, godless sentiments, and idolatrous conceptions.

I love men: but in all truth, in paradise, who really needs chief priests? Beware of those chief priests who consult together to keep you from this truth: the kingdom of heaven is within you, a growing dream, a spiritual power creating a flesh and blood paradise. The God of Jesus is our husbandman and the bride of our soul. Paradise is found in many fields, but not in all.

On the next day much people that were come to the feast, when they heard that Jesus was coming to Jerusalem, took branches of palm trees, and went forth to meet him, and cried, Hosanna: Blessed is the king of Israel that cometh in the name of the Lord.

There are many trees in the garden of God: life has many branches. As Jesus once again rides upon the foal of that ass called Israel, he draws near to the city of truth, even Jerusalem in its total spiritual reality. Herod and Pilate, and chief priests, elders, scribes, Pharisees, and many lawyers are there, ruling the people of God with their own earthbound sentiments, mores, customs, opinions, deceits, conceits, and laws numerous. Jesus understands this but that still dumb ass which is Israel accomplishing one of its many assigned tasks, understands little of its part. All men ought to rejoice in God's King. Nevertheless, I am as despised as my Father.

The poor in spirit, those who possess the belief of the kingdom within themselves, glory in God's King. Their branches line the way to Jerusalem. It is truth we seek, we desire, we search to find. It is truth in which we rejoice. But the adversaries of Jesus and his God want no son of God in Jerusalem, nor in heaven. They would rather divide the earth into more than a hundred nations and propagate their earthly power rather than accept the rule of Love as King. The *Pharisees* are the politicians of the world, *Phar*aoh's *in*dustrious and *self*-enlightened *e*missaries. Such are the children of the State, the servants of bureaucracies, the senators and emperors of Rome, the princes of the world, the very high priests of Mammon, who keep the souls God has created for joy and life and eternal pleasures, bound in the pits of worldly life and mortal emotions.

Nevertheless, what God has determined none can put aside. Palm Sunday has lasted a thousand years in spite of the fact that vain scribes belittle the hope and joy God has placed in the heart of his poor flock.

And Jesus, when he had found a young ass, sat thereon; as it is written, Fear not, daughter of Sion, thy King cometh, sitting on an ass's colt.

Slow, deliberate, and surefooted has been Jesus' approach to the city of truth. But men cannot perceive what is in a thousand years of hope and thought and lively perception and unending dream. The fullness of eternal life is ours: how much more so is the record of

Jesus' coming to Jerusalem again and again? Why must Jerusalem be retaken, rebuilt; and the temple cleansed? Obviously, because the city of truth is the gift of love to our soul: it is the capital of the kingdom of heaven. But the sons of men look to Moscow, Washington, London, Paris, and Peking for power. The sons of men are mortal incompetents. Men have divided the world among themselves for gain. Every Pharisee, every politician, every man of the State, every tax collector, every merchant of fear and evangelist of Mammon has the same mark: they covet your soul. Via the doctrines of men, and the blasphemy of Man, men lord it over other men to their own hurt. No social system is of heaven: all these political councils and economic cartels are of hell. Men confuse the preciousness of gold with the temple of the human spirit which sanctifies that gold. No loving husband would exchange his wife for the most precious of diamonds: diamonds only have value because of the beauty of women. So also knowledge is without value apart from the spirit which sanctifies it.

The preciousness of truth is sanctified in the temple of the spirit. God is a spirit: is to be worshiped, loved, served, and given pleasure. Surely, for this reason all things have been created.

But men worship Satan, serve the State, Mammon, and Man itself, and have placed the abominable destroyer in the hearts and minds and souls of all men. We should find within ourselves the kingdom of heaven, the palace of love, the city of truth itself, wherein God in his own strange way provides for our nourishment the trees and waters of life. What is within a man comes out of a man. Yet how did it get within?

Satan placed much within us that is abominable. We cannot cleanse the temple if we cannot accept this simple truth. The doctrines of men are of men: and lawyers, writers, priests, and scholars various have brought forth a flood of ungodly nonsense against my God and his chosen. No man knows the Father but the son and he to whom the son will reveal that Spirit.

The Word creates the world, for the world is a spiritual product. But the world is not the kingdom of heaven: the kingdom of heaven is God's and yours to create and rule. Let no man keep you from it: shut you out of it: deter you from finding it. It grows within you.

Reject the doctrines of vain and proud men. Accept the words of life. In this way is the temple of your spirit cleansed.

How does Jesus make his Father known? By laying the foundations of a New Jerusalem, the heavenly city of truth, wherein the glory of the gentiles also is found. It is God who saves: it is God who destroys the destroyers: God voids our covenant with Death and cancels our agreement with hell. Surely, I love my enemies though they hate me much to their own hurt.

These things understood not his disciples at first: but when Jesus was glorified then remembered they that these things were written of him, and that they had done these things unto him.

The glorification of Jesus encompasses many centuries: involves many lives: is inclusive of much history. The Satanic phenomenon is also only understood if one has some knowledge of Jesus' glory. What is his glory? That the Son of Love and Truth surrendered himself to their dominion. Many spirits come from God and are of him. The words of God, the words of the spirit of truth, the words of Jesus are eternal life quickening all our earthborn conceits, and raising us up from the hell of worldly enterprises and earth bound beliefs. Those nations most immersed in the truth God gives us through his Sons are cleansed, made whole, and live to inherit the kingdom of heaven. But I speak of nations and not of worldly governments. I hate my life in this world, for the world of men without God is what it is: a system whereby pride, vanity, foolishness, covetousness, gross incompetence, unreasonable vengeance, causeless anger, social theft, religious vanity and human ignorance dwell unseen in the souls of the servants of mammon and the ungodly princes of mediocrity.

All have been called: a few have been chosen. We respond howsoever we will. Nevertheless, God also has his reasons, his visions, his beliefs, his values.

I am not impressed by the power of the world nor by the varied faces of mammon. I am nevertheless astounded at My God and how he creates in flesh and blood and bone to provide an earthy tabernacle for our living souls.

Men profit much by learning of the Lord God of Israel. Our burden is light: the yoke of divine love is easy. Why do we refuse it? Because of the idols of our belief. Death is the product of evil men and the spiritual force empowering the slaves of the prince of this world. Their knowledge is of this world and this world alone. They have no light within themselves and they never consider where God shall next place their soul. Thus social theft, laws vain, ridiculous, and burdensome, and words without wisdom are their principal activities, their chief delight. Thus are armies gathered and equipped and wars organized. Thus are taxes sought and vain enterprises hotly pursued. Thus are prisons built, and forgiveness mocked in courts of law.

Surely such are known by their words, by their beliefs, their deeds. I loathe their ways for they are not of God but of themselves.

We die but to be born again. Our resurrection is assured: our many crowns of life past are ours and ours alone to possess. Why then do these creatures of death keep us from that which is rightly ours?

I judge no man: each man is his own judge: with his own words he judges himself. Men yet mock Jesus by doing in his name that which he instructed us not to do.

What things are being done to Jesus in courts of law, world councils, prisons, universities, homes, schools, and worldly institutions various? What doctrines are taught? What gospel is preached? What truth is proclaimed as essential for everlasting life?

The ways of the world are many: Mammon and the doctrines of men are the power within the godless state. But men forget what Jesus said and what things were written of him. They treat the revelation given Jesus by John through the angel of God with scholarly contempt and mindless indifference. And others tamper with it to their own hurt, adding or taking away such parts as they judge proper.

Men are ignorant of the limits God has placed upon death and hell. They do not take the presence of the Lord God of Israel to heart, and they know not how the world is saved from its own evil.

Men forget what things are written of Jesus: thus do they cast the prophets of God out of God's own vineyard: thus do they kill his own first born Son. What shall God do? That's God to decide, and not mine, nor any angel's, nor any man's.

The disciples of Jesus do not at first understand what is happening—but they grow in their understanding, in their wisdom, in their power. God has many sons, many children: many heirs. We become the sons of God by believing God. I know of no other way it is done. Surely those scribes who teach not that belief is a spiritual force have done us a great disservice.

We know the truth by believing in the power of that spirit. Words are spirit: but all words are not truth. God is a spirit: but not all spirits are of God. The holy spirit is God's spirit: even God's way of enlightening the darkness of the world. We must learn to confess our sins: acknowledge our faults: live with our imperfections. God forgives and undertakes our perfection. We become his sons because he fathers us. I am fathered by my beliefs; I am comforted by the blessed chastisements of truth.

Those who do not love their enemies are in danger of being overcome by the same forces of hate which create enemies. We should remember what is written of Jesus and what he is seeking. What is he seeking? A place in your heart, a room in your soul. Jesus testifies to the truth: the works of the world are evil. Let's admit this simple fact and get on with the adventures of eternal life. Nevertheless, how can we hear Jesus unless we allow his Word, his very spirit, a place within us?

The sons of God are many: and many have corrupted themselves almost beyond recognition. I know why the resurrection of the body is not accepted as simple scripture, ordinary fact, a common event: men love the temporal power death makes possible. What men should rightly fear is God's return. Men do not fear the Lord God of Israel because they are too busy promoting their own fears. We forget whom Jesus commanded us to worship and whom to serve.

Men fear the powers of the law: the powers of devils: the workings of nature: the unknown: old age, sickness, death. In this nation there are even those who fear the military might of the Russian nation! It's hard for me, increasingly difficult for me, to take them seriously.

Let's remember the things written about Jesus: let's also witness the things written in and about the world. Jesus is right: he is God's first begotten son, the father of our faith, and the initial spokesman of the power of love.

Our God is also his God and Moses' God and David's God and surely Adam's God. Why then does the world hate the truth? Let me confess my ignorance so that I might receive my instruction. I can ask more questions than I care to have answered. There are things I do not understand at first: there are also things I do not care to understand. I confess I find Death a bore and those who promote it, cause it, believe in it, weep about it, fools. Let's cease being fools: let us love the Lord God of Israel and enjoy our everlasting life.

The people therefore that were with him when he called Lazarus out of his grave, and raised him from the dead, bare record. For this cause the people also met him, for that they heard that he had done this miracle.

I know that I lived other lives. I also know that I was dead. But if this is true of me, it is true of you. Yet I long for paradise, even the kingdom of heaven come to earth, and the Word of God made flesh. The tree of life has grown: my desires are many, my hope securely placed. Surely my God is greater than I and able to satisfy all my desires.

The miracle of Lazarus' resurrection is not greater than our own resurrection to eternal life.

Time is a limited notion, a special idea, an aspect of reality yet to be properly qualified by our angels of intellect. Let me confess this miracle: God is eternal and so are we. The city of truth, the New Jerusalem, is a new gift given us by that ancient God who is eternally young. Our body is but one tabernacle, one of many. Men have destroyed my temple: nevertheless, I shall rebuild it: I have rebuilt it, many times, for many times they have destroyed it. Yet a tabernacle is but a temporal dwelling, a temple of the spirit. Death is an enemy overcome. But it is not an enemy to be loved, an idol to be worshiped. Death is the fated result of our stupid belief that knowledge makes us like God. It does no such thing as many of these knowledgeable scribes so aptly witness with the wisdom of their own words.

The world is full of temples. But we who are within the city of truth, indeed, for those of us who even glimpse it from afar, have no need of a temple.

The universe is the cathedral of today and one of God's many mansions.

The Pharisees therefore said among themselves, Perceive ye how ye prevail nothing? behold, the world is gone after him.

Not really: not then, anyway; yet it would be well for the world if it did. But the world is governed by its own prince. Men do not give up the power of their conceits easily. I marvel that men can be ruled by the spirits of money, of Muhammad, of Lenin, of Law, of Government. And yet there they are, comprising a world of its own. It's really very funny in spite of the fact that many angelic scribes have proven to be as humorless as they are sexless. Thank God for the Greeks who have kept God's chosen from becoming puritanical bores. When a devil discovers how God has used him (and I speak of men who have made themselves devils, and not of those uncontrollable spiritual impulses which have no life apart from men or other living creatures), his reaction is oftentimes very funny.

There are men in the world who cannot tell an angel from a devil: a wise man and a fool are both alike to them. Such are the blind which must be made to see.

I accept men as they are and accept myself such as I am. The sons of God are those angels who have overcome the world: the children of God believe God is their father. The servants of God are the virgins of the Lord God of Israel. He ravishes them lovingly one by one as he takes pleasure in the impulses of eternal life. God is the spirit of love joining divine desire with the earthbound flesh and blood reality of our body and soul. God created Adam male and female and joined our spirit to our body for a purpose.

The Greeks also war against God, yet God overcomes them. How? By having them see Jesus. Plato and Whitehead, Augustine and Shakespeare, Euclid, Archimedes, and Einstein are Greek. The greatness of these kings of intellect is without question. The importance of Euclid is astonishing: no god or goddess of Greek mythology, not even Prometheus himself, brought so much technical power to men. Yet Moses and David and Jesus and Newton are also kings and priests in their own right having been made so by the Lord God of Israel.

Yet there are mysteries in eternal life which go beyond the bounds of the kingdom of heaven come to earth. Men are children rebellious, ignorant, unskilled, unlearned, impatient, grossly evil, and yet for all that, lovable. And what God loves, God perfects.

The angels of God become the sons of God by overcoming the world: surely our babble limits our power: our division destroys our kingdom: our pride encases us within impenetrable shells wherein the water of life cannot enter. Pride is the iron skin suit which keeps us from enjoying the pleasures of our naked wife.

Our wife is our spirit, the bride of our soul, the mother of all that lives within us. If we loved the Lord God of Israel with all our mind we would understand what it means to be created in his image, and to be created male and female, and to be confronted with the temptations of the subtle beast of the world.

I have eaten of the tree of knowledge and died, even as my God said. The serpent is a liar for I did not become wise, nor did my wife and I become as gods, but we got our ass kicked out of paradise.

Let the Greeks understand this and surely then will they be able to see Jesus for what he is and bring their glory to Jerusalem, the city of truth, wherein the glory of God enlightens our minds and delights our heart.

And there were certain Greeks among them that came up to worship at the feast: the same came therefore to Philip, which was of Bethsaida of Galilee, and desired him, saying, Sir, we would see Jesus.

How many men have seen Jesus? How many recognize him when they see him? How many men desire to see him? What profit is there in seeing him? In this enlightened day we may see Jesus by reading his words and literarily eating his body and drinking his blood. But men are more receptive to the fruit of knowledge than they are to the love and belief Jesus commands.

They are full of knowledge and full of babble and are ever spouting repetitious prayer. Shall we record in stereo what Allah receives from the believers in Muhammad? God forbid; even Muhammad himself is bored with the fruit of his own deceits and must seek elsewhere for the pleasures of life than among his own millions of believers. But I weary of these foolish devils and their blind followers. The world is full of examples. Discover them for yourself.

Philip cometh and telleth Andrew: and again Andrew and Philip tell Jesus.

The gentiles bring their glory into the city of truth and the kings who sought Jesus in Bethlehem, even the city of bread, David's city, the birthplace of Christ, even a small city within Judaea, even that city with us today wherein the shewbread of God is prepared, now enjoy the wisdom which God gives to all who enjoy truth and love and life and beauty.

What now? Shall the Greeks who do see Jesus because of Philip's intercession and Paul's life forget what Philip and Paul are accomplishing and have accomplished? Jesus is the cornerstone: but the walls are the defense God provides and the gates are the apostles themselves. Even Judas, in the end, believed: and his glory cannot be taken from him for he also is a child of God.

If the Greeks wish to see Jesus let them come to Jerusalem and be enlightened.

Jesus wars with the Greeks. The angels of intellect are fascinated with the creative powers of their own mind. Whitehead passes judgment on the prophets of God: the book of revelation for him is great imaginative literature. The Greeks produce their own great imaginative literature. Tacitus, Augustine, Gibbon, Emerson, Durant, and such great men are Greek. Our debt to the greatness of the Greeks is only exceeded by our debt to the God that created them.

God created Jesus. This is his testimony: God is his Father. But Jews and Greeks alike have other fathers: yet if they were fathered by God why would they even desire to see Jesus? What was so astonishing or important about another Son of God revealing truth about man's common Father?

Obviously, men are fathered by spirits other than God. Even Jesus is also the Son of man; he is also responsible for making himself the son of perdition. But men still lust after a perfect atonement, seek an acceptable sacrifice, desire to manipulate God with religious ritual and verbal inanity: thus churches are born, religions are fashioned, and doctrines weird, horrible, grotesque and silly are conceived, nourished and worshiped.

The Greeks worship the God of the World: the mechanism of their own proud minds: the subtle mazes and intricacies of their own imaginative conceptions. They are the fathers of their own ideas, the craftsmen of their own conceits, the apologists of their own lives.

And what am I? As it is with them so also is it with me. I also can die and fall into the hell of my own idolatrous conceptions. I also can enter the bottomless pit of my own confused imagination: I also can find myself immersed within a lake of fire and marvel as that which I created is destroyed by my God. My God laughs at me. I amuse him. I am, for so have I made myself, the son of perdition. I have fallen into the ground and died.

What ground? The ground upon which men base their towers of babble, their altars of sacrifice, their pyramids of waste, their mausoleum of death, their graves of earthly doubt. Nevertheless, Jesus' Word is clear: and why should I continue in my own babble?

And Jesus answered them, saying, The hour is come, that the Son of man should be glorified.

Jesus saves the world by glorifying the Son of man. Who is the Son of man? You are. Surely, by now you must realize that if you are anything you are the child of the beliefs man provides for you.

What is then your glory? Even this: that you also are the Son of God, made so by believing Jesus, the father of this doctrine. God glorifies himself through you.

Verily, verily, I say unto you, Except a corn of wheat fall into the ground and dieth, it abideth alone: but if it die it bringeth forth much fruit.

Our spiritual death is an adventure into the world of the dead. Because even dead we are God's, he saves us from its power. Death is the last enemy to be destroyed. What is this death? A living fascination with what we ourselves produce when we eat of the fruit of knowledge. Yet in this death we gather others to ourselves: we bring forth much fruit. Our doctrines multiply even among the dead. Our old lives are dunged with the bullshit of many centuries. We can now clearly see why God destroyed the power of Moloch and its foolish priestly fathers. What we cannot see is why God has destroyed the power of the State and of Man and of Religion and the love of our own mother and father, to keep us from being Jesus' disciple. What we so laboriously struggle to conceive is that if we love our life, we'll lose it. We fear to adventure with God, to war with his chosen against the powers of Satan. Why? Because we don't understand that within the God of Life even the dead live.

I am not dead because men think me so: how much less dead am I because they hypocritically preach me so? Why is their hypocrisy vain? Because they want me out of their world: they want no Word made flesh: they want no heaven in earth. What do they want? Money to advertise their delusions: the thankless prestige of office: the power to tax people, organize armies, kill their enemies.

Hell is something to be destroyed, not to be used by God to punish the wicked. Hell is real: the creation of those who sustain it.

He that loveth his life shall lose it; and he that hateth his life in this world shall keep it unto life eternal.

I hate my life in this world of the dead wherein a forty-year-old child cannot remember what it was experiencing a hundred years ago; a world wherein money and the State are used by proud men to lord it over those who are impressed with the powers of the beast and are impressed by those who can fine, imprison, and legislate.

In fact, I hate it so much I'm going to change it. What shall I do then? Change the life of the world or change my life in this world? Surely, those who die are born: why can't we accept this singular truth? All who believe in Jesus and work his God's word are the children of God for whom God saves the world, even their world. Nevertheless, the kingdom is God's, and our hells he destroys.

If any man serve me, let him follow me; and where I am there shall also my servant be: if any man serve me, him will my Father honour.

Whom has God honored since these words first were spoken? How does God honor a man?

Now is my soul troubled; and what shall I say? Father, save me from this hour; but for this cause came I unto this hour. Father glorify thy name.

Why should Jesus' soul be troubled? Death is distasteful: but he chose to taste it, feed in it, become involved with it, and destroy it.

We should confess our sins, not hide them. But we hide them and pretend we did not disobey God. This is hypocrisy. I love God's chastisements, his rebukes, his ways. He illumines faults so they may be seen for what they are and destroyed. Let us confess our death so we may enjoy eternal life. Surely, the princes of the world are bores and all their laws are vain. Why should we continue believing in them or being one of them?

What is death? Death is what we experience when we separate ourselves from the God of Life, even the Lord God of Israel. Do the dead move? Of course. The dead indeed do bury their dead: nevertheless, Pharisaical hypocrites with their love of man made laws and customs, continuously lead God's flock astray. My Father is greater than I, immensely so: but the priests of babble deface my image beyond recognition. The poet of love is despised in God's garden of delight. And men who have been transformed into mice by the witchcraft of the whore of Babylon and deceived by the image of the State mock me and make sport of my words. The original sin is idolatry: men worship the idols of their own mind and would rather taste of death and of hell then enjoy the presence of the living God.

I have life in myself: I have knowledge of good and of evil; of death and of hell; of pride and of Satan. I know of Man and his image; of the State; of Religion, Christless, barren, vain, foolish, stupid: and devoid of flesh and blood; titless, sexless, without penis or pussy. As I draw these things to myself, what shall I do with them? What shall I do with the pope and with my neighbor who pleases me in her bikini and whom I truly love? Obviously, death is a process of transformation, of assimilation, of judgment, of selection, of bondage; of rebirth. Death is an enemy we overcome and eventually destroy with the powers of life. How? By following Jesus. For he told us to love our neighbor, our enemies, our God of Love, and commanded us not to commit adultery with the whores of State and Church and Mammon. But men who adulterate and truth hate it: for if they loved it they wouldn't strive to pollute it.

God saves your world with the spirit of his truth which he sends into the world with the Word Jesus gives to you. The Lamb's book of life is real: so is yours. Let's stop being stupid. Let us worship God, not idols. How do we worship God? By giving the Spirit, pleasure. In this, our paradise is found.

Money satisfies all things for it is the oil of the animated idol men term Man, the miracle worker extraordinary, and the false prophet of the present hour: the ridiculous beast of the earth crowned with the twin powers of Death and of Hell. It's hard to refrain from laughter: difficult to take its creators seriously.

I must confess this work has an end. Men are known by the words that come out of their mouths; the work they do; the way they sell their talents and goods to whoever has money to buy. For truth, God charges nothing. But bullshit has a dear price. I marvel at men who still stand in awe of their own idols. Don't fear death. The soul returns to the God that gave it: dust returns to dust, but the resurrection of the body is as real as the return of the truth. I am that truth: nevertheless, I would have God father you, instruct you, delight you.

God's glory is within you: discover it for yourself. The State, the Church, Money itself, are the creatures men created. Surely this is simple fact, plain truth, an easily made and distinctly clear observation. There are no statesmen, churchmen, and money changers in heaven. If you doubt me, come and see.

Then came there a voice from heaven saying, I have both glorified it, and will glorify it again.

How? By judging each person's world and casting out its prince: for a world wherein I am not is full of abominable things.

So God not only creates the world, he also saves it. Rule with God your own world: thus are all these foreign princes seen for what they are, the mindless profiteers of their own proud self-interest. God is a king because he has made himself so to war against the princes of this world who afflict you. God created you: this is his original glory: God shall save you: this is his coming glory.

Nevertheless, for those who cannot believe the first coming, the second coming has no meaning. For those who cannot rejoice in God's past glory, his future glory is nothing to them. And for those who cannot believe in the God that was, and the God that shall be, the God who also is, cannot be their God. Whom then do they believe? They believe the liar, the accuser, the prince of this world. They are overcome by the world and are the world's bondmen and slaves and servants. They believe in the power of darkness and have made themselves children of darkness. They believe in the power of death and have made themselves the apostles of death. They believe in the power of money, of Democracy, of the State, of the government, of their party, of their church, and reject the commandment of that bold Jew of old who said, Follow me.

Let God declare his glory howsoever it pleases him. There is more to God than men have seen. Even Moses, who wrote of God's beginnings, saw only his back parts. What then shall the pure in heart see? Men who commit adultery with the Whore of Babylon and fuck around with laws, and states, and armies, and churches, and money, cannot see what the pure in heart plainly see. What is that? How two are joined and made one by the Spirit of Love during an orgasm of pleasure. What does the Lord of hosts, the Lord God of Israel know of pleasure? Plenty.

What do chief priests, Pharisees, lawyers, and scribes know of pleasure? We forget God's glory: he glorifies his name so that we might love him. In this is both our pleasure and his pleasure realized. But men who take pleasure in titles and various authoritarian roles, are the cause of the curse which afflicts the world. I am astonished, amazed beyond all measure, at the means used by lawyers to rule men. They are so blind to the glory and power of God that they set his worship at naught and despise his commandments of love and everlasting life.

No wonder they require votes and titles and money and arms and public applause and vain words and foolish myths and laws numerous to promote their own glory. Their blindness to truth has enfeebled them: thus are they incapable of sensing God's glory, or adding to it. They are too weak to draw the light yoke of love: too powerless to transport one stone of truth to Jerusalem.

My God is my glory: without him I am only what I am, the son of perdition seeking heaven in earth. Surely my God shall come to me and bring his kingdom with him. How do I know this? How do I know anything? I glory in my God and await her sweet pleasure.

The people therefore, that stood by, and heard it, said that it thundered: others said, An angel spake to him.

Men have forgotten what this voice from heaven once said. Has the name of Jesus' Father been glorified again? Yes, in Jesus: for God chose to glorify his name in Jesus. No wonder then that those who reject Jesus reject God.

Jesus answered and said, This voice came not because of me, but for your sakes. Now is the judgment of this world: now shall the prince of this world be cast out. And I, if I be lifted up from the earth, will draw all men unto me.

The voice came for the sake of those who sought Jesus. Even by worldly standards God has glorified Jesus. How is Jesus lifted up? If men love him, they lift him up into their highest heavens. He only commanded our belief, but I know he desires our love. The power that sent Jesus into the world is love: there is no other Word for the power of God. If then God loves us, why do we refuse him our love? We see men entranced with the prince of this world who rules us in the place of God. Who is this prince? Our self. Men love the things and devils they create more than their own Creator. Our love of self plays the devil with us. Let me cast out the prince of this my little world and receive the king of heaven.

This he said, signifying what death he should die.

Obviously, Jesus lost his life and found it again.

The people answered him, We have heard nought of the law that Christ abideth for ever: and how sayest thou, the Son of man must be lifted up? who is this Son of man?

Good question. Yet how might one who doesn't even understand man, understand his Son? The question is hard to answer: for the Son of man who has been lifted up is Jesus, the Christ: nevertheless, what can be said of him that John and Matthew and Luke and Mark and Paul and others who saw him and handled his doctrines have not written? Yet what am I to think? In almost two thousand years' time Jesus had done nothing else? God forbid that his death should have proved so fruitless. Who then is this Son of man? You tell me for obviously although Jesus owns his own soul what you believe him to be is also part of his spiritual body. Yet I suspect few men are ready for these metaphysical subtleties: so why should I bore them?

Then Jesus said unto them, Yet a little while is the light with you. Walk while ye have the light, lest darkness come upon you: for he that walketh in darkness knoweth not whither he goeth.

Men should walk with God: even the God Jesus reveals and knows and witnesses: even that same God who reveals and knows and witnesses to Jesus. There is a trinity in our world: God, Jesus and our holy self, working within us to lead us into all truth. Men, who also may rightly be called the sons of man, who walk in the darkness of their own mind, are blind to God. They do not know him: consequently, vanity abounds, evil multiplies, and hot loves wax cold as Martian winds. A man's holy spirit is no more holy than the spirit within him.

While ye have the light, believe in the light, that ye may be the children of light.

By believing, we be what we believe in: we are fathered by our beliefs. I believe in man: so am I fathered by man: I believe in perdition, so am I made a child of hell: I believe in Jesus and so am I enlightened and see the presence of God.

These things spake Jesus, and did hide himself from them.

There is a time to speak, and a time to hide: a time to be crucified, and a time to come down from the cross. Jesus' body was removed from the cross: but his coming down is strangely within his own power. We don't carry our cross to our crucifixion: for that's masochistically gross. We carry it away from the hill of death and fashion it into something else: for why should we waste good wood?

But though he had done so many miracles before them, yet they believed not on him: that the saying of Esaias the prophet might be fulfilled, which he spake, Lord who hath believed our report? and to whom hath the arm of the Lord been revealed?

Obviously, to the Jews and then to the Gentiles: which is as much to say, to all men.

Therefore they could not believe, because that Esaias said again, He hath blinded their eyes, and hardened their heart; that they should not see with their eyes, nor understand with their heart, and be converted, and I should heal them.

Who has blinded them and hardened their heart? Satan. Who is Satan? One who makes blind the eyes and hardens the hearts of men.

These things said Esaias, when he saw his glory, and spake of him.

Where is Esaias now? I suppose wherever Jesus is: for once the star is sighted, wise men follow it. But really, it's all so plain, it's getting a bit corny.

Nevertheless among the chief rulers also many believed on him; but because of the Pharisees they did not confess him, lest they should be put out of the synagogue: For they loved the praise of men more than the praise of God.

Few men take pains to publicly confess what they believe: yet because of the very nature of our selves, men reveal at times appointed and at times spontaneous what is within themselves. Hypocrisy is a lie against ourselves. Men enter hell because they oftentimes get caught lying to themselves.

I loathe the standards and morals of the world. The world is Satan's house divided seeking to make itself a house united. Men madly seek the praise of men: what some men applaud others loudly condemn. What praise is in this? What god could possibly knowingly seek it?

Jesus testifies of the evil in the world: men hate the truth: they therefore condemn Jesus or hypocritically flatter him and then are astonished to find no God in their world of experiences except the prince of the world.

What have I to do praising God? Surely I rejoice in the beauty of naked and loving women: in this God reveals his glory and rightly praises himself. The Spirit creates in flesh and blood: and I, composed of flesh and blood, create in spirit. My father is more than my Father: and there are parts to God's nature of which I know nothing.

But men praise men and seek the vain approval of their household, and the love of those they dearly love. Yet God loves his enemies and showers blessings upon the good and evil alike. I hate man's vain and enfeebling abstract idols: I hate communism and the State and the utter stupidity of Lenin's doctrine: but what of Lenin and Lincoln, Kennedy and Khrushchev, Manson and the Mafia's current chief assassin, unnamed and hidden though now he be, what of these souls, the living slaves of the idol of Murder? Surely, let them repent, for the kingdom of heaven is at hand and why should they be kept from it by their own pride and disbelief?

Yet, if I can find it within my heart to love Lenin, who surely is my enemy, how readily do I find pleasure in loving Ludmilla T., communist though she be? We are all victimized by the State, whereby divine love is transformed into human hate. So, pardon me, if I condemn your party: for nothing ugly has an eternal place in me.

Besides why fear being put out of the party? Getting one's ass kicked out of the synagogue is the best thing that ever happened to some men for how else might they have been drawn up to God's heaven?

Jesus cried and said, He that believeth on me, believeth not on me, but on him that sent me. And he that seeth me seeth him that sent me.

If we can see Jesus, we can also see God: and if we can see God, we can also see Jesus. But if we can't see God, our heart is impure and must be cleansed. Thus are we baptized, immersed in the Word of truth, and born again. It's really no different in act than those trifling procedures we follow to join either a synagogue or the communist party.

I am come a light into the world, that whosoever believeth in me should not abide in darkness.

Who abides in darkness? Children of the State, the blind followers of the blind leaders of the world. For such cannot see even though light is in the world sent there by God. Why did He send it into the world? To save your world from the powers of darkness.

In a spiritual sense, men are blind. It's so obvious, I'm embarrassed.

And if any man hear my words, and believe not, I judge him not: for I came not to judge the world, but to save the world.

How many men have judged the world and then condemned it? How many men set out to destroy the worlds of others? My world is attacked by communists and democrats alike: churches and nations rise up against me. I am rejected and despised. Tough shit on my part.

He that rejecteth me, and receiveth not my words, hath one that judgeth him: the word that I have spoken the same shall judge him in the last day.

And what is the judgment of that word? And when is the last day? Today. And what is the judgment? God is going to save your soul alive whether you like it or not for when God sets out to perform a work he desires to finish, he finishes it.

Nevertheless, there are many of your enemies yet to be destroyed, not the least of which is mental idol worship and bodily death.

For I have not spoken of myself; but the Father which sent me, he gave me a commandment, what I should say, and what I should speak.

God has given us a few commandments which we in our curiously perverse fashion have broken. Nevertheless there is one commandment we cannot break: no, nor can God.

What is that commandment? Life everlasting.

And I know that his commandment is life everlasting: whatsoever I speak therefore, even as the Father said unto me, so I speak.

Surely, Jesus has the biggest pair of balls in all of Creation. No wonder he delights so much in life and in love.

The world itself is too small to contain the growth of his seed. No wonder a new heaven and a new earth are required, and supplied.

How do I know a new heaven has come? Obviously, because Ludmilla is of the new heaven for I knew her not in the old.

Eternal life is as real as this passing moment. The words are recorded, the thought of the heart is made known; yet the moment, though past, is still with us. These everlasting truths are ours to enjoy:

the gift to us from the God of life. We do return: we have returned. In this we should rejoice. We drink of the fruit of the new wine as well as of the old. Does wine bear fruit? Delight is the fruit of its own seed: and joy is the product of its own created power.

Our Father is greater than all his created works, which works we are. We have grown: when men have reached heaven they ought not to deny the reality of the dust of the ground from which they have been raised. How much less so should they deny the power and glory of the husbandman of paradise!

What is good is good: what is evil is destroyed by the good. Dung nourishes the tree of life as well as the tree of knowledge. I have been crucified on the tree of knowledge of good and evil and found the experience unpleasant. If you doubt me, carry your cross and make a naked exhibition of yourself for all the world to see even as I have and as my Father has allowed. But after it is finished, and done with, let's continue in the pleasures of life. What I have done, you also can do, if it pleases you and our common Father.

Who is our Father? The bride of our soul, the mistress of our delight, the mischievous goddess of our dreams. Is God both male and female? Can a spirit be sexy? Of course.

"I don't believe it." So say most of Jesus' disciples. Perhaps Mary will understand and one day prove the point to them. I marvel at men who can believe God created the stars and who also believe, most wickedly, that God delights in forever having their tits concealed, and their breasts unsucked.

In the kingdom of heaven love rules as king and truth is the comely spirit which dissipates the foolish fears generated and sent forth from the many caves of little minds.

Let all the thieves now in paradise judge whether what I write be true or false, fact or fiction. Man, as Adam, is lonely and is in need of a wife, a comely mistress, a handmaiden, a goddess of pleasure fit to transform all his lively desires into flesh and blood.

"But. . ." But the beast is many butted as well as many headed: and you've surely known by now it's more blessed to believe me rather than super machine. Believe me, not your wife; not the beast, not the liar, not the accuser; not Satan, not the State, not Man, Mankind, nor any one, great or small, of his false prophets.

"And who are you?" A god created by my God: even by that God, who, if you will have it, also created you.

"I don't believe you." I know. But what is that to me? I cannot deny myself: it is impossible for me to deny my God.

Shall we go in to supper and discuss these things further?

"I don't believe this is happening to me! I've eaten so much bullshit I'm wary of all invitations concerning life and love and God." I know: but if you don't like what's being served, don't eat it.

"And what is being served?" Truth. "What is truth?" Myself.

"How can I know that for a truth?" Come and see, and judge for yourself. For all men are judged by the contents of their soul, and the words that come out of their mouths.

"I shall judge you." Of course: and thereby you also judge yourself.

CHAPTER 13

Now before the feast of the passover, when Jesus knew that his hour was come that he should depart out of this world unto the Father, having loved his own which were in the world, he loved them unto the end.

Jesus is the beginning and the end of God's written book of life. Our beginning is with him in Adam: our end is with him as Jesus, the Christ. Man created the world even as each man creates his own world: a world of beliefs, opinions, theories, facts, half-truths and lies. Jesus' world is a world saved by the truth. We have seen his beginning. We witness his end.

The battle of Armageddon is fought in the valley of decision. A man is forced to decide whether he be for God, even the Lord God of Israel, or for the Beast of State and for the false prophet Man given power for a time by the spirit of error, even Satan itself, the self-sustaining beast of the world.

I am born to enjoy the kingdom of heaven and why should we be kept from its joys by the violent servants of the prince of this world who know nothing except to despise God and serve the idols of their own mind? Whom do I serve? The Lord God of Israel: none else. But who really knows that God?

In the end, all shall meet the God they war against in the valley of decision. Truth shall slay them: and love shall resurrect them. Yet how do these mindless idiots weary me and tax my patience, nevertheless let me bridle my tongue and say no more. It is really over.

And supper being ended, the devil having now put into the heart of Judas Iscariot, Simon's son, to betray him; Jesus knowing that the Father had given all things into his hands, and that he was come from God, and went to God;

(For he knew that he was to come again with God.)

He *riseth from supper, and laid aside his garments; and took a towel, and girded himself.*

Jesus cleansed the dirt of their own worldly adventures from off their feet while girded only with a towel.

After that he poureth water into a basin, and began to wash the disciples' feet, and to wipe them with the towel wherewith he was girded.

A gentle, even pleasant, washing. Far better to be so cleansed than to be cast alive into a lake of fire. I marvel at men who make Hiroshima's possible, and know somewhat of its horrors, who blandly continue to serve the beastly systems they have created because of their service to Mammon.

We cannot serve God and Mammon: Mammon should serve us; serve us, that is, in this world.

There are other worlds: but this one which the Word creates and Jesus saves, is the immediate concern of Jesus. Men are so grossly insensitive to the impulses of love, the light of beauty, and the power of truth, that I constantly marvel at their capacity for foolishness. At times, I find myself so contemptuous of their earthly idols that I am troubled beyond all measure. They delight in doubt: they wallow in pride: they lust after hell.

We need to wash: but we refuse to be cleansed by the spirit of Jesus' Words. It is as if we refuse God's desire to serve us. With the words and actions of many men, I am disgusted; myself included. Shit: God is perfecting me: it is his business, his work, his task: why should I deny the obvious? Yet what do I receive from men? The irrational conclusions of their own proud minds. Let God come to me: I am too weak to ascend to him. Let my God cleanse me with her own self: my soul is polluted: I also must be made clean. I wash in my own words: bathe in my own dreams.

But what of worldly men? They are confusedly striving to reach heaven by building a tower of babble. Their work is immense and replete with vanities. Anyone who has ever walked up this structure gets dirty feet. I am no exception.

Yet there is more to it than this simple story suggests. Our soul is bathed in fire: we are cast into a furnace of affliction and yet we are unharmed even by hell's own fire. This is not true of all men: for some perish in the hate they themselves kindle.

Hell is real: so is its destruction. Creative energy is found within the Word. Yet men use words to suggest something can be fashioned with words which is beyond the beginnings created by the Word.

The Sons of God are real: but men are deceived by their own creations into making themselves the slaves of their own systems of world government, psychological myth, literary fantasies, and religious idolatry. We have been given dominion over the earth: we have multiplied and filled it: and, in spite of our powers to kill, murder, deceive, and destroy, our problems are overpopulation and a plethora of knowledge which has increased beyond our power to measure. Death, and its apostles, constitute an enemy to be overcome. How do we destroy death? With the Word of life. Any other method is unprofitable: and, oftentimes, ridiculous.

But men refuse to be cleansed in the stream of truth. For reasons far too many for me to number, they prefer to wallow in the slop of their own intellectual garbage. I speak not of all men: surely the poor in spirit are not victimized by the subtleties of law with which the lawyers of the world constantly occupy themselves. Men, who have the power to resist the Spirit of God, won't utter two words to rid their souls of the weakest of devils.

What is a devil? A spirit created by the evil use of words. What then are we? Living souls so created by the Spirit of God's Word.

Then cometh he to Simon Peter: and Peter saith unto him, Lord, dost thou wash my feet? Jesus answered and said unto him, What I do thou knowest not now; but thou shalt know hereafter.

Knowledge, even as the tree of life, grows within us. We learn in many ways. We are instructed by priests, angels, devils, our own selves, even by our own creations: our words, our works of genius; even by our computers.

Peter yet lacks knowledge of what Jesus is doing: you can't walk in the world without getting dirtied by it.

Listen to Peter's resolution.

Peter saith unto him, Thou shalt never wash my feet. Jesus answered him, If I wash thee not, thou hast no part with me.

Men who reject the cleansing of Jesus' word have no part in him: no, nor do they possess any part with him. They have their own doctrines, received from the men of the world who busy themselves with the affairs of the world.

I judge not the world: the Spirit of Truth judges the world: and if I say I judge the world it is the Father who speaks, not I: for what do I know of the world?

Simon Peter saith unto him, Lord, not my feet only, but also my hands and my head.

Who is Peter? What man has drawn the net of the kingdom of heaven to himself and found in it one hundred fifty and three great men? Obviously, Peter has drawn many angels of intellect and great geniuses to land. Upon these and with these, Jesus, some of his disciples, and many lambs and sheep are fed. Yet whom does Peter love more? Plato, Shakespeare, Gibbon and other such like great men are ours for the taking. Nevertheless, so is the bread of life Jesus provides. And what is one without the other? Who then does Peter love more? Let us examine once more Peter's reply.

Simon Peter saith unto him, Lord, not my feet only, but also my hands and my head.

Peter herein recognizes a deep truth.

Jesus saith to him, He that is washed needeth not to wash his feet, but is clean every whit: and ye are clean, but not all.

The need for baptism, even a fiery baptism of many tongues, is real. Yet God supplies all our needs: for even the stupidities of Marx and Lenin are available to us in another tongue. The miracle of translation is real. And I feel grateful for the industrious angels and devils alike who have spared us the pains of resolving the babble of hell. I know a rose by any other name would smell as sweet: and I trust the bullshit of Lenin is as noxious in Russian as it is in English.

We, even as Peter, would do well to have our head and hands washed after thinking and handling the doctrines of men. Nations are transformed into hell when they reject the doctrines of God and accept the doctrines of men. I love the Russian people; but in all truth Lenin is a fool, Marx is a bore, and the State is as much an oppressor over here even as it is over there.

Nevertheless, it is well to remember these words of Jesus, when we feel muddled by the turmoil's of the world's great men.

Jesus saith to him, He that is washed needeth not save to wash his feet, but is clean every whit: and ye are clean, but not all.

And sometimes those that have been made clean get dirty again: it is well to remember the Word is always freely available for another cleansing. I marvel that men are able to survive so long in their filthy states without it.

For he knew who should betray him; therefore said he, Ye are not all clean.

When I consider all the men throughout the ages who kept this supper in remembrance of Jesus, and yet who, like Judas, were not cleaned by the spirit of Jesus' word, I can appreciate the need for Jesus to depart and the Spirit of Truth to come. Surely, Judas need not despair, nor need Jesus lament this lost son of perdition, for what Jesus could not clean, the Spirit of Truth shall clean, in its own invisible way.

Men forget that Jesus chose Judas for a special purpose. And what is that? To have a friend in hell: for Jesus also is a son of perdition. Where is Judas? I don't know: that's part of the hell I must presently suffer. I desire none should be lost: absolutely none.

So after he had washed their feet, and had taken his garments, and was set down again, he said unto them, Know ye what I have done unto you?

I doubt that they realize it even to this very day which is February 15, 1977.

Ye call me Master and Lord: and ye say well; for so I am.

Shall love ever master us: and beauty, rule us? Shall God's king ever come?

If I then, your Lord and Master, have washed your feet; ye also ought to wash one another's feet. For I have given you an example, that ye should do even as I have done to you.

This is to be done by speaking the truth, one to another. If you find sin in me, cleanse me of it.

Verily, verily, I say unto you, The servant is not greater than his lord: neither he that is sent greater than he that sent him.

My God is greater than I: immensely so. How can I deny this single truth? And if I could not abandon any in hell, how much less so could my God? Hell is consumed; destroyed by God's fiery truth. There is nothing fit for the lake of fire except a deceiving devil, the beast and the false prophet, and death and hell and whosoever was not found written in the book of life.

And what is the lake of fire? God's truth fallen to earth, even to the bottom of all our earthborn conceits. And who is this devil? Satan, the social beast of the princes of the world; super antichrist in all its godless totality; the filthy fiction men energize with their own minds; my ridiculous tempter. And what beast? The State: even Man's pathetic substitute for the kingdom of heaven. And what false prophet? Man, even mankind's animated image of itself. And what is death? The foolish fiction sustained by those who cannot enjoy the resurrection of the body. And what is hell? The playground of evil men.

Nevertheless, whosoever is not found written in the book of life shall also remain forever in the lake of fire.

And who are these?

Nobody. For all are now written in the book of life.

And if ye know these things, happy are ye if ye do them.

And I also would be so if you would cleanse yourselves of the bullshit doctrines of eternal damnation.

My God is greater than I. His understanding is not inferior to my own. His love cannot be less than mine. His persuasive power of spirit cannot be less than mine. His love of truth cannot be inferior to mine.

But men are not all clean. They pollute the kingdom of heaven and hold themselves sinless. I love those who hunger and thirst after righteousness; who love truth, beauty, genius, and all the ways of God. I am nevertheless astonished at angels who despise God's Word and mock the longsuffering God of Israel with the very gifts, the very talents, he has given them. They use his talents to lure men into rebelling against him.

Happy all of us would be if we would wash one another of all the filth and foolishness of hypocrisy with which this world abounds. There is no law but love: all else is vanity, In the world we have tribulation: in the kingdom of heaven we have love, and therein none can disturb its awesome power. Our peace is of the God within: not of the Doubt without.

Do you understand these things? How many Words must be spoken, how many things must be done, before you believe in what I tell you?

I speak not of you all: I know whom I have chosen: but that the scripture may be fulfilled, He that eateth bread with me hath lifted up his heel against me.

Satan and Christ consume the doctrines of God. Satan is a beast, a social mechanism of extraordinary power: Jesus, is the Son of God; a god sent by God to overcome the powers of Satan. God created the world: Satan corrupted it. Who created Satan, the ephemeral spirit of this present world? This programmable computer of technical and emotional power? I did.

Nevertheless, the subtle beast of the world has within itself the seeds of its own destruction. In fact, Satan, of itself, can only tempt and accuse and threaten. His power to execute is limited.

Many who eat bread with me rise up against me: my enemies vary from the likes of Lenin to the daughters of Charles Manson: from George Washington to Ed Davis: from Muhammad to Muhammad Ali. And many of those near to me have been overcome by Satan and his own corrupted world.

The evil in the world and of the world is real: what also is real are worlds wherein evil is overcome, love triumphs, and the spirit of God prevails.

Men, especially great men, writers, politicians, churchmen, military men, corporate men, men of the organization, are the creators of the system they glorify, praise, and honor with their lives: the job they work at becomes their lord.

Nevertheless, is this not true of us all? Work is made for the man: man is not made for the work. The Pharaohs greatly erred: the pyramids are a technological joke, and a spiritual obscenity. They are about as useful for the liberty of the human spirit as the modern Soviet State: they are about as instructive to human genius as any one or all of the divided United Nations combined.

The builders of such things have become the very slaves of their thing. I created Satan for my pleasure: but what has resulted? My children have revolted against me and have worshipped the idols of their own mind, and the creations of their own hands, and despised my Word. Satan is a fucking beast: a toy, intricate and spiritual though it be.

How can they possibly be impressed by it, or overcome by it, or serve it? Mammon is a product of the Satanic world: must we pay to drink water, to read words, to witness foolishness, to applaud mediocrity, to wipe our own ass? I can scarcely believe it. Mothers pay to have their children born; families pay to have their loved ones buried; we even pay for things that do not occur, that shall not happen, that exist only in the minds of insurance agents and their corporate masters.

A pay toilet on the moon is ridiculous: but no less a financial corporate beast than AT&T, craves to charge a fee for information on how to use its slot and dial machines.

Excuse me. I must leave off. It's all so funny, I'm a bit beside myself.

Anyway, the point is simple: we've all eaten of the doctrines of God: I've created the kingdom of heaven by planting its seed: and the princes of this world have created the kingdoms of this world.

But the power is in the Word. Do you now understand? When you lose your life for the kingdom of heaven's sake, you've only lost your life in the world: what you find is life, even your life with God, within an eternal kingdom. Anyone who has ever been within the New Jerusalem, the city of truth, knows these things to be true. I've kept you in the world, even in your world, to overcome it. Every child of God needs a world or two to play with. The salvation of your world, even the world, is accomplished when you receive the kingdom of heaven brought to earth by God for you.

Observe carefully what is of God and what is of Satan. The fallen sons of God have corrupted the beast almost as much as they have marred my image. Nevertheless, know that I am what I am: I am not my image.

Eat my words: don't play the part of Judas: he has already played the part for you. There is more fitting work to be done than forever reliving the same old story.

Do you have any questions?

Now I tell you before it come, that, when it is come to pass, ye may believe that I am he.

I know it is hard for you to believe in me. It also has been difficult for me to believe in my own words. My past, at times, is as hard for me to believe in as my future. But the times are long yet eternity is without end. Yet, it really hasn't been that long, has it?

Verily, verily, I say unto you, He that receiveth whomsoever I send receiveth me; and he that receiveth me receiveth him that sent me.

If you cannot receive me, you cannot receive the Son of man: if you cannot receive him, whom can you receive? The products of Satan are many: don't be deceived by humanoids.

Receive the spirit of truth which spirit is of God. Try the spirit: question it: ask of it: seek for it. If it deceives you, then you'll know it for what it is, a spirit, not of God, but of yourself. But if it leads you into all truth, know it for what it is, even the Holy Spirit of God.

When Jesus had thus said, he was troubled in spirit. . . .

At this point, what god wouldn't be?

and testified, and said, Verily, verily, I say unto you, that one of you shall betray me.

To be betrayed is to be troubled. Yet, as God once told me, Imagine the deep shit you'd be in if you hadn't been betrayed. Judas and Satan kept Jesus from herein becoming a false prophet.

Men cannot easily understand Satan: as a consequence they allow it to enter into them. Yet the process is quite plain. A man hears a lie, confirms it within himself, and makes it part of himself. Why do we fear the Lord God of Israel? Because woe is our portion if we disobey him. (Or her, as she gently reminds me, at this time.) But men who do not fear God lose their proper perspective in this universe of light which encompasses us all. Consequently, they are victimized by Satanic myths, visions, beliefs, emotions, fears, and feelings. Those who do not fear to piss on a live, high-voltage wire, may be in for a shocking experience. It is best to fear God and despise idols. Yet, for most men in the world, the reverse is true. Why? Because they are open to everything that impresses them. They do not let their no mean no: they don't let their yes mean yes. Consequently, even though the treasure house of their own knowledge is full, they have no means left whereby to discern what is good and what is evil. The Greeks seek Harmony: the God of Israel has provided judgment.

Surely, we should desire cleansing, purging, judgment. The thing we should never desire is to capture all our shit within a bag and carry it around with us. Yet is this not what the men of the State constantly do? From the tapes of presidents, the encyclicals of popes, the memoirs of generals and secretaries of state and war; to the voluminous records of trials criminal and trials civil the products of the ultimate computer are found. And there is so much else besides that we can readily identify with Solomon when he said: all is vanity.

Is this not all one to Jesus? Of course: for those that are not with him are against him. Love is love: truth is truth: forgiveness, mercy, and beauty are what they are. So also is it with Roman justice, Roman law, Roman righteousness, Roman iniquity. It is what it is: and what is it? The feet of the powerful image of Man.

Let us fear God: lest we begin to fear Man and make fools out of ourselves. Our enemy is one, yet it shall be smashed into pieces innumerable and ground into dust.

Men produce monsters out of their own minds. Plato would ban all poets for they are full of myth. So also today science fiction occupies the fancies of many. Take that which is small and make it large and one has a monster. The little ant becomes a formidable foe: the gorilla becomes King Kong, and a lowly lizard becomes Godzilla. Take that which is little and make it smaller, and Lilliputians and little people in the land of giants and a man fighting a spider with a pin, are horrors to enjoy. Take that which is future, make it past, or that which is past, and make it future, and much fiction is generated. Take that which is distant and make it near, and destroy the bounds of space and time, and again much fictional fantasy is possible. Make that which is slow, swift, and reverse the process, as it pleases you, and again the fictional products are many. Also parts may be interchanged; and mice may talk, and walruses expound like politicians. What instruction is found in all this madness? What profit in making machines men and men machines? What pleasure is found in conceiving of. . . but why should I go on? I weary of it all.

Let God cleanse me: free me from the gross foolishness I have allowed to enter my kingdom. I have not taken Plato's course: nothing is hidden: all is brought to light and may be seen for what it is. The world of ideas and the world of images are also sources of tribulation. My God has never lied to me.

This life I live is also a dream, a nightmare from which I pray to wake.

We are all betrayed by those who also having received the doctrines of life, betray us to those who hate Christ and worship Rome. They would rather participate in a public trial than exercise private forgiveness. They do what Satan encourages them to do. Men have killed for Washington; for Lincoln; for Wilson; for Roosevelt, Truman, Eisenhower, Kennedy, Johnson, and Nixon: pray tell me, will they kill for Carter too? I pray they won't. One day the madness must end and the God of life shall rule over us forever. Men must one day realize this truth: that which is highly esteemed among men is abomination in the sight of God.

The State has overcome all who do not worship the God of truth. Let us not turn even our enemies over to the powers of the State: how much less so then should we deliver our own children to its Satanic power! What truth is found in *Judas*? Even this: Jesus *understands* Satan. It is well for us to cultivate that understanding ourselves lest the spirit of evil find its way into our own heart.

Then the disciples looked one on another, doubting of whom he spoke. Now there was leaning on Jesus' bosom one of his disciples, whom Jesus loved. Simon Peter therefore beckoned to him, that he should ask who it should be of whom he spake. He then lying on Jesus' breast saith unto him, Lord, who is it? Jesus answered, He it is, to whom I shall give a sop, when I have dipped it. And when he had dipped the sop, he gave it to Judas Iscariot, the son of Simon. And after the sop Satan entered into him. Then said Jesus unto him, That thou doest, do quickly.

Each time we receive a portion of God's truth, Satan struggles to enter us. It oftentimes succeeds. In the beginning God created the heaven and the earth.

"I don't believe that. What heavens? It's an evolutionary product, this earth of ours. Shit! Science proves it. There is no God." So saith Satan. Many men never get beyond this simple statement of creative fact: God created. I am no longer amused by it. The programmers have done me a great disservice by keeping secret from men the fact that they have power to say no to Satan. Beware of false doctrines: the world is drowning in them. There is as much bullshit in Science and Religion as in Politics.

Now no man at the table knew for what intent he spoke this unto him. For some of them thought, because Judas had the bag, that Jesus had said unto him, Buy those things that we have need of against the feast; or, that he should give something to the poor. He then having received the sop went immediately out: and it was night.

I know the feeling of being lost. We follow the promptings of the beast within and a dark night envelops us: no stars, no moon, can be seen: and we are alone with ourselves and with the lie we have received from some devil.

Carter has all the gadgetry to wage an atomic war: would an angel of light so equip himself? No. But we need such things to keep us free from our enemies! Bullshit.

283

What can I say? Take a little scripture and a great army and in God's name kill those he loves? So always have these great men always done.

Therefore, when he was gone out. . . .

and here many must depart for if they love the world and its great captains more than me, I can have no part in them.

Jesus said, Now is the Son of man glorified, and God is glorified in him.

It is the Son of man rather than man or the son of perdition who is hereby glorified. And how are we glorified? By allowing the Lord God of Israel to glorify himself in us. And how do we do that? By believing in those who hear and do the words of Jesus. In this way do you receive Jesus and do the will of God.

If God be glorifed in him, God shall also glorify him in himself, and shall straightway glorify him.

The world cannot overcome Jesus. He has reigned for a thousand years: that reign has ended. Satan again has deceived the nations of the world. Once again tribulation in the world is the common experience of those who know Jesus as Lord and Master: and those who know him as a friend suffer persecution for righteousness' sake. But what does that mean? What does it really mean? It means the kingdom of heaven suffers from the violent who take it from us with the forces of Mammon, law, politics, religion, statesmanship, Roman idolatry and barbaric ignorance. The State, the very beast of the sea, a sea of wicked and restless men, is their substitute for the kingdom of heaven.

How shall God be glorified in you? By having you overcome the world, and all its nations and states combined, and entering into the kingdom of heaven. Shall the kingdom be born at once? Of course. You've been pregnant with it for so long it is about time you let it come forth. Every child of God is born into his own kingdom and witnesses his own birth. For as it is with me, so also is it with you. For I seek your glory and the Father's and not mine own.

Little children, yet a little while am I with you. Ye shall seek me: and as I said unto the Jews, Whither I go, ye cannot come; so now I say to you. A new commandment I give unto you, That ye love one another; as I have loved you, that ye also love one another.

Love opens all doors within the mansion of your own soul. Learn to love yourself also.

By this shall all men know that ye are my disciples, if ye have love one to another.

If you love one another you will discover truth in others as well as within yourself. For your own treasures are within you.

Simon Peter said unto him, Lord, whither goest thou?

After Judas.

Jesus answered him, Whither I go, thou canst not follow me now; but thou shalt follow me afterward. Peter said unto him, Lord, why cannot I follow thee now? I will lay down my life for thy sake.

It is really easier said than done as all these who call Jesus Lord and do works in his name, yet do not do the will of his heavenly father, illustrate with their lives.

Jesus answered him, Wilt thou lay down thy life for my sake? Verily, verily, I say unto thee, The cock shall not crow, till thou hast denied me thrice.

Let Peter be comforted. To have denied Jesus only thrice is much easier to bear than those who have denied him thrice three million times.

CHAPTER 14

Let not your heart be troubled: you believe in God. Believe also in me.

(This is really very good advice.)

In my Father's house are many mansions: if it were not so, I would have told you. I go to prepare a place for you.

What place? Surely the place where you are now.

And if I go and prepare a place for you, I will come again, and receive you unto myself; that where I am, there ye may be also.

Well, here I am still hanging round this earth. I know heaven has been brought to earth. But men forget, I never left them as they thought I left them. For what advantage have I more than they? I am here and so are they. Nevertheless, so weird are the religious and scientific fictions produced by the priests of Babylon, and so gross are those idols of the mind worshiped in hell, that I can sympathize with your dilemma.

And whither I go ye know, and the way ye know.

It's really much easier Jesus' way. How do I know? I tried many other ways while God laughed at the difficulties I got myself into.

Thomas saith unto him, Lord, we know not whither thou goest; and how can we know the way? Jesus saith unto him, I am the way, the truth, and the life: no man cometh unto the Father but by me.

Jesus said man, not angels. Sorry, for the confusion generated thereby: nevertheless what angel has ever taken a man to the Father?

If ye had known me, ye should have known my Father also: and from henceforth ye know him, and have seen him.

Who is my Father? God. The Spirit of Truth is my heavenly father because he so conceived me. I am his child, his first begotten son. I frankly can't understand why so many get so heated over this simple fact. Even my own loved ones deny me. Yet I am born of his Word. Why? To make it visible. I know this input drives the computer bananas. Yet I never said Satan could explain this mystery. We know God, our heavenly Father, by knowing Jesus. The Lord God of Israel is not known by the law and prophets alone. Men need his Son to show them God in himself. But men wish to find God visible in some other way. There isn't any: and Satan can't create a true image of God because it's a liar. It was designed that way: there is no truth in it: it provides the needed contrast: that, and nothing else. True, it's been used for other purposes, but only because it's so handy and flexible. It's a large machine.

And yet, let me leave off. I don't want to create another parable.

Men are ignorant and know not what they do: yet they will not confess their ignorance to one another. Thus their pride insulates them from the spirit of truth and the waters of repentance cannot cleanse their souls. God's Word is not only clear water but cleansing fire. We are all forgiven: all saved: but what horrors are endured by many as they stray so far from the city of truth!

They know nothing of God, little of Jesus, and yet boast themselves wise. The writers, the scribes of this present generation, constitute a class or nation of people united in this one task of putting images on matter. I write with ball point pen on ruled paper: or with pencil on vellum: or with inked ribbon on plain bond using the characters available on typewriter balls and keys: or with the spoken word modulating and energizing electrical impulses across plains of moving magnetic tape. In all this, I find different methods of scribing images on matter. Whether it be sharp lines on clay tablets, or simple images on papyrus; or chiseled stone, or whittled wood, or sculptured steel; or electron beams striking patterned dots, or brushed patterns of paint on canvas, or mathematical arrays of colored lights, or various letters of various type on various pages of various books—the idea is the same: in all this nations of scribes are at work. And yet there are still other ways to scribe matter, using a variety of chemical techniques for example, but I won't continue to bore you with an extended enumeration.

Nevertheless, all these constitute what I envision when I herein use the word *scribes*.

Satan has its scribes, and I have mine. I also am mine own scribe. Yet does not God write upon our heart, enlighten our mind, speak within the deepest interiors of our soul? Surely, *Ludmilla* and *Brigitte* are but scribed words: to confuse these with the supernatural beauties which they are is madness.

Men are mad because they confuse images with realities: and the source of much of this madness in this modern world is caused by the ignorance of those scribes who have set themselves against the Lord God of Israel. I do not say that all those scribes who have departed from God do evil: nor do I say that those who remain with him do good. What a scribe does, he does; nevertheless, the goodness of God is such that he overcomes the madness and ignorance of men with his own creative genius. Satan is to be used, toyed with, commanded, manipulated, programmed, analyzed, repaired, refurbished, and destroyed. To worship it, or induce others to worship it, or serve it, or idolize it, is human madness.

If you know me, whom my Father has created in flesh and blood, you know my Father, even the Lord God of Israel, not because I am the Father, but because the Father is in me and I am in Him.

There is much more within me than what angels reveal: I also know there are things I learn of angels. Nevertheless, what do you think, I learn nothing of Satan, nothing of men, nothing of the heaven and earth God has created? Believe me when I say to you, I have life within me.

There is no appeal from truth: it is intolerant: it cannot forgive: it is the source of its own judgment: it is one of many spirits sent into the world by Jesus to comfort those who mourn, to satisfy the cravings of the righteous, and to bring everlasting life to men.

What is death? The state of confusion in which those who hate eternal life find themselves. How do I know? Because I have been there. If you don't believe me, or accept my witness, believe the witnesses my God has sent into the world, even into your world, to proclaim the same truth.

There is more I have to say, but I cannot bear it now: no, nor could a whole nation of scribes. Prophets also are required: and the fulfillment of their prophecy is found in you if you can find it in your heart to love me, even as you so obviously love one another.

If you see me you see the Father, because I am that which he created me to be: even his son. If you doubt this of me, how can you believe it of yourself? I am only one witness; the Spirit of Truth within you, is the other. Shall we remain dead forever? I think not. Nevertheless, let us see what results: let us see what really happens.

There are nations of scribes, nations of lawyers, nations of Pharisees gathered together before you in the world of your own mind. To whom shall you give the kingdom of heaven grown within you? Which nations are on your right hand, which on your left: Whom will you gather to yourself, whom will you reject?

Don't let Mankind deceive you: don't let the State mark you, number you, use you as a piece of money, a mere commercial item of insignificant worth. Don't let a Religion of babble transform you into an intellectual mouse or a hooting owl or a dumb jackass. Why? Because it's much more fun to be born again as a child of God than as a child of Satan which system produces all these others.

It should be obvious that from the time Jesus first spoke of himself as he who enables men to know and see the Father, until this very present time, the disciples of Jesus have both known and seen God. Can we honestly believe that John, who wrote these words Jesus spoke, saw not his own Father? Or that, he did not see God? If so, how is it that his gospel is read and loved and kept and used and quoted by so many men, great and small, and so many children, both the innocent and the wise? Surely, the gospel has been published among all the nations, and men, with John's words, have preached the good news of the kingdom to the uttermost parts of the world.

But those who do not love Jesus, keep not his words: no, nor do they keep his commandments: nor do they believe in him, nor do they do the will of his Father. They are the children of the lie, and must be freed by us: for they cannot free themselves. Their dreams are short-lived: their desires are limited: their life is mortal: their way is worldly. What then? shall they be forever cursed; forever eternally bound to death and hell and the varied products of the super bullshit machine? Not if I have my way: not if I successfully end this war I have started.

Jesus gave us the sword of truth to be used in this world. The Word of God shall overcome Satan, the beast, and the false prophet, and all their host.

What is the source of their power anyway? What is the spring of their devilish energy? Shall Pride and Covetousness forever devour men? No. For God has determined to save your soul and woe to those who oppose him with their own ungodly ways! Their power to deceive you has an end.

When men obey God and reject the promptings of their own serpent-deceived spirit, even the wife of their own soul, paradise is open to them.

But what do you think, now that we have come this far and the work is finished? Is it finished? Of course, for you already know the outcome.

You have seen Jesus. You have known God. You have seen God. So once more we eat of the fruit of the tree of life, and drink again of the fruit of the vine God planted. Shall God plant the seeds of a god? Why not? do not men plant seeds of themselves within a woman? Surely they even plant the ejaculations of their own evil ideas into those souls who give birth to their idolatrous conceptions. Yet, though they conceive themselves otherwise, men are gods. And so am I.

Philip saith unto him, Lord, shew us the Father, and it sufficeth us.

Men take their earthly fathers in stride. They first crawl and then walk about in life until one day they come to see and know their father. Yet when do they really see their father? When can they really say they know their father? Even our earthly fathers' claim on us must be taken on faith: for how can we really know our mother wasn't balled by a traveling salesman?

Who really is our father? Who really first conceived us? God. But since that time many of us have taken many strangers to be our father.

Jesus herein shows us, plainly reveals to us, our Father.

Yet does this manifestation suffice?

Jesus saith unto him, Have I been so long with you, and yet hast thou not known me, Philip? he that hath seen me hath seen the Father; and how sayest thou then, Shew us the Father? Believest thou not that I am in the Father, and the Father in me? the words that I speak unto you I speak not of myself: but the Father that dewelleth in me, he doeth the works. Believe me that I am in the Father, and the Father in me: or else believe me for the very works' sake.

I know more of my heavenly Father than I do of all my earthly fathers combined. The Son of man is explanatory only of his earthly birth. I can understand that the flesh of my brain is so formed that I write in English. Surely, the past of my life is present with me now making possible my second coming. I said I would come again: I said, I knew not when. Now that it is done, what shall I say? The Father did not lie to me: the times are reserved to himself and my work is to learn them. My Father created and I created because I was with him in the beginning.

I am also a son of perdition: a prodigal son: yet a father in my own right. God fathers gods: men father idols. Of what are men so proud? Why should they deny me a place in God's heaven?

If men cannot believe in Jesus, and in his words, and in his witnesses, and in his book of life, and in his flesh and blood reality, how can they believe in me or in the God within me?

Men hate Jesus because he testifies of the evil in the world and of the evil works of the world. But is his testimony false? And if it is true, why then do not all believe in him? Because they never heard of him? Surely, they kill him so they alone might enjoy the vineyard of God. Men know not what they do: yet they despise the widsom of God. Nevertheless, wisdom is justified of her children, from the least even to the greatest; even all of them. But men are proud: they know not how to choose the good and reject the evil. Surely the history of Man, and the signs of the times are plain: men despise God and worship Satan.

Men are so slow to believe, yet so quick to deny, and judge, and condemn.

Verily, verily, I say unto you, He that believeth on me, the works that I do shall he do also; and greater works than these shall he do; because I go unto my Father. And whatsoever ye shall ask in my name, that will I do, that the Father may be glorified in the Son. If ye shall ask any thing in my name, I will do it.

No shit? Jesus is within God. Somehow, God provides the power to accomplish this in a way which baffles me. Do I ask too much if I seek to understand what these words mean? Yet, surely, we know of men whose works and words, given of God, were greater than the works and words of Jesus. Somehow, God through his Son empowers us to accomplish the creation of the kingdom of heaven within us. What a man sows, he reaps: yet, his most abundant harvest is in that field wherein the treasures of heaven, prepared for him by Jesus, are found. Jesus has clothed men with his Word. What have they accomplished with it? And yet how can one separate Jesus from his Word?

I must confess my God works within me and that God is the God of Jesus. There is no other. I know of no other. There is Satan, and gods, and false Gods innumerable: But these I count of little worth. My God astonishes me: and the gods of this world are also astonishing: I am astonished at their pride, at the hardness of their heart; at their ignorance, and cruelty, and foolishness.

Let me try Jesus on this most singular point: let me ask this one thing of him and of his Father, even the God of whom he boldly declares so many other things. And what is that? Let him come again, with all his clouds of witnesses, and all his angels, and all his saints, and cover the ends of the earth, even all of it, with the kingdom of heaven, for so I ask it even in his name.

Now let us see whether he will do this one little thing for me or not.

If ye love me, keep my commandments. And I will pray the Father, and he shall give you another Comforter, that he may abide with you for ever; Even the Spirit of truth; whom the world cannot receive, because it seeth him not, neither knoweth him; but ye know him; for he dwelleth with you, and shall be in you.

Truth is found within us: and not in books. We should believe the gospel: but many men believe they should only read the Bible. They invert their priorities: thus the kingdom must come to them since they refuse to be born into it.

The Spirit of truth is also the Spirit of Jesus reconciling the world to himself. In this manner is the world, even your world, saved from those violent forces which otherwise would destroy it. What are these forces? The mechanisms of spiritual creation: even the words of gods, devils, angels, and men.

The words of Jesus are his spirit dwelling within us. His is the truth, for what other truth is there? I know truth is immense: that it grows: that it fills an entire city. That it analyzes hell, empowers angels, defeats devils, enlightens the lives of men, rebukes the world for its evil, and separates fact from fiction: reality from imagination: death from life.

Yet it also dwells with those who receive it from the Father. Truth is the great Comforter. The kingdom of heaven is yours: your fit inheritance: let no man keep you from it.

Do you know this Spirit of truth of whom Jesus speaks? If not, why not ask him for it? you might find that spirit eternally comforting. Nevertheless, what do you think? can this spirit be found in the world? No. But it can be found working within you. Why not receive it? It is free: without price: yet precious.

I will not leave you comfortless: I will come to you.

Here again, Jesus testifies that he will come. Surely, to preach we shall die and go is madness.

Yet a little while, and the world seeth me no more;

True.

but ye see me: because I live, ye shall live also. At that day ye shall know that I am in my Father, and ye in me, and I in you.

Space is the unbounded sensorium of God. We are within this universal space. But what is within Jesus? His disciples? You? But what is in you? These words, for symbols of themselves are dead. Only you can see them, hear them, and bring them into yourself to give them life.

In a few words, the Word comes within to give you life.

He that hath my commandments, and keepeth them, he it is that loveth me: and he that loveth me shall be loved of my Father, and I will love him, and will manifest myself to him.

Has any one loved us more and worked so hard to manifest himself to us so that we might love him? Jesus obviously delights in love as much as he lusts after truth.

We have to look into Jesus to see the Father for in this manner does God show himself to us.

Judas saith unto him, not Iscariot, Lord, how is it that thou wilt manifest thyself unto us, and not unto the world?

The world is full of its own numerous manifestations. How is the world to receive another? It cannot: it is too full of its own images. It has no place for God's Son. There simply is no room within it to receive Jesus, even as a child. Therefore a new world is created, wherein the kingdom of heaven is found. It is the world within you transforming the world without. For the kingdom of heaven is like treasure found in the world of your own experience of life.

The world keeps the words of the world, and buries the Words of Jesus. I speak only of Jesus' Words: for the world cannot bury the least of God's stars, let alone, Jesus, the Christ of the Lord God of Israel.

The world does not even realize the goodness and truth and beauty of God fermenting within itself.

Jesus answered and said unto him, If a man love me, he will keep my words: and my Father will love him, and we will come unto him, and make our abode with him. He that loveth me not keepeth not my sayings: and the word which ye hear is not mine, but the Father's which sent me.

All our talents are given us of God. Jesus gives us not his own word, but God's. Do we believe this? If we believed it, we would keep them: but men love their own word more than God's. Thank God then for Jesus, who preserved his word by giving it to us again. We receive the word in the manner we receive it. But God's word is like seed and bears fruit in its season. To keep Jesus' word is to keep God's word: even a creative power forceful enough to have created flowers as well as stars.

These things have I spoken unto you, being yet present with you. But the Comforter, which is the Holy Ghost,

i.e., God's host

whom the Father will send in my name, he shall teach you all things, and bring all things to your remembrance, whatsoever I have said unto you.

John, if nothing else, has a remarkable memory, for how else could he have remembered all these words? And Matthew is a scribe in his own right and without equal in all the history of heaven. If the Holy Ghost did not teach Matthew and John to write these words of God, and if that Holy Spirit did not bring these words to their remembrance, and to mine and yours as well, who did? Surely, not the world: not Satan: not any single man who loved not Jesus.

Peace I leave with you, my peace I give unto you: not as the world giveth, give I unto you. Let not your heart be troubled, neither let it be afraid.

What peace has Jesus left with us?

Ye have heard how I said unto you, I go away, and come again unto you. If ye loved me, ye would rejoice, because I said, I go unto the Father: for my Father is greater than I.

If we knew the greatness of God, and understood it, I doubt the whole world could ever trouble us, or disturb our peace, if we desired not to be troubled, nor disturbed. I am troubled: and oftentimes at war: yet my peace returns: In quiet I possess my soul.

Listen to this:

And now I have told you, before it come to pass, that when it is come to pass, ye might believe.

How much has come to pass since first these words were spoken? Few men saw Jesus: fewer still heard these words directly from him. Yet, even though he left his disciples, did he leave them to go to the Father by dying on the cross? Strange way to go to the Father.

We have been told many things Jesus both said and did in the presence of John even by John, Jesus' beloved disciple. But what of John, one of Jesus' angels? Those who cannot comprehend that John and Jesus are both Sons of God as well as angels of God probably never question themselves as to where David, the Son of Jesse, and Jonathan, the Son of Saul, presently are. The dead have a weird way of looking at life: even mortal life. The plain truth of everlasting life is hid from them since if they had it, they'd corrupt it and this God surely does not allow. We leave the world and go to the Father, and leave the Father and come into the world with rejoicing.

Belief in the Word is the key which unlocks the mysteries of John's gospel. Jesus' work is to quicken our belief. Prophets are useless if none believe them. Even false prophets are rendered impotent if they can deceive only themselves. Could Hitler have precipitated so much hell if none believed in his gospel? Would the people of China have suffered so much evil if they didn't believe in the words their warlords spoke? Whether Sun Yat-sen or Chiang Kai-shek or Mao Tse-tung or any other puppet of the godless state did them good by dividing themselves against themselves to murder themselves, let their children judge. God's command is clear: don't kill and hate lest you become dead and hateful.

Those who believe in devils are overcome by devils and become devils. But what do you think? Are the peoples of Asia insensitive to the powers of love? Are they untouched by it? Are they blind to beauty? Have they no desire for truth? Can they not learn how to choose the good and reject the evil? I think not: God knows his work. The power of liars, murderers, and the foolishly proud has an end. Hell is the product of those who create it. Do you believe this?

Let the Lord God of Israel be your king: serve him: worship him: conduct his business righteously and well. What is his business? To get you to believe in the Word, his first begotten son, Jesus, the Christ, gave us a long time ago: even in that same Word which has grown to be what it is today.

The God that shall be knows what shall be: the power of the God that only is, is limited. I have planted the seeds of the kingdom of heaven in your hearts even as I said I would. Has it not grown? Has it not been harvested? Has it not been separated from many other hurtful growing things? Did I not tell you these things before they came to pass, so that when they would come to pass, you would believe God and despise idols?

What is God? The Creator of heaven and earth, for openers. What else has God created? Me, for one example. You, for another. How has he done this? With his Word. What else can you tell me about God? She is the voluptuous goddess of your soul, the loving bride of your dreams, the very husbandman of paradise.

I know the thoughts of many of you. You find my doctrine far out: it is too much for you. Nevertheless, it needs must be far out, for My God is the boundary of this boundless universe I sense, and enjoy, and in which I live. The stars are mine to sense and love and use and enjoy. For why else were they created? Indeed, they were created for God's pleasure, and our pleasure, and their own pleasure.

We have been told many things of God by Moses, by Jesus, by John, by Paul. Have the things they speak of come to pass? Yes. The evidence is overwhelming. The world cannot accommodate God: God is simply too immense for the world. Indeed, the world is really too small to house even your soul. I find tribulation in the world: I find, the kingdom of heaven, as treasure hid in the world, as secret joys found within the field of mine own experience. What Jesus tells us has come to pass; much of it is already past. Yet, we still find it hard to believe. Why?

Satan is an awesome power, a formidable beast, an intricate machine capable of accomplishing many wonders. It is the beast of the field, the mechanism of the world, the image the sons of God worship, yet dare not name. Carter serves Satan, yet he calls it by another name. World leaders serve the State, or the people, or the government, or law, or Man: they know not what they do. Love of our enemies, love of our self, love of our neighbor, and the universal forgiveness of sins and the sealing up of the righteousness and mercy of the God of love within our heart, is too much to ask or expect of those pathetic men who have made themselves the bondslaves of mediocrity. Satan is an imperfect machine, and I am disgusted with it.

The beast and the false prophet shall be destroyed by God's truth. I have told you these things before they come to pass so that when they come to pass, you will not be frightened by the spectacle. Frankly, I am disappointed in myself. I thought by now the truth would have accomplished its work.

Is their faith on the earth? Faith in the truthfulness of the Word of God? No. Even in heaven, atheists and agnostics abound and proud angelic intellects of many shapes and forms and colors delight themselves with their God given talents: and yet these same children of God despise my word.

As for me, at this moment, I can only confess that I enjoy such peace as my God has given me: which is as much to say that I don't give a fuck what you believe anymore. My work has an end, and I am seeking it even as I now am enjoying it.

Things pass in time and remain still within eternity. Love is eternal, but it is not an eternal object for unobjectively speaking, love is full of life and motion. Philosophers rarely consider it, but a hard-on, a pussy, and erect nipples, followed by an orgasm of pleasure, often precede the birth of a child. To strip the word of flesh and blood, is to mock God and praise the machine. Men do worship the sterile, lifeless, and barren ideas they themselves create. These fools must be answered according to their own folly lest we become like them. Men who are too pure to consider the joys to be experienced in sucking an angel's ass never consider the disgust God experiences as they blaspheme his holy name with their own verbal bullshit. Heads of State are heads of state, the great men of the world who serve the state: which is to say they serve the abominable image set up within their own heart.

I require the Word of God: for without it, how could I clearly see the beast and false prophet set against me? I am the Son of man, not Man's son. For what is Man? Another abstract idea produced by the Satanic computer to confound the idiots who are worshipping their thing.

Whom do I worship? The Lord God of Israel, even my heavenly father, the voluptuous goddess of my flesh, the bride of my soul: even that spirit of love who is the source of my eternal pleasure.

"Slow down, baby, or you'll lose all of them."

Belief is necessary: I take no pleasure in those who murmur and fret and complain and trouble themselves needlessly. I must confess there are many in the world who can fear, at one time or another, almost any thing: yet they fear not the Lord God of hosts. Why? They've lost their initial wisdom: they know not what God is working and are frightened by all the creative forces his spirit has set in motion.

God laughs at me. I chose the strait way, the shortest route, the most direct approach to bring men everlasting life, and lost my own portion of it in the process. You can't see the stars from within the cave: thus men fear to travel through my time tunnel. Frankly, at times, so am I.

The problem with eternal life is its reality. I am who I am, and I am the same that I was at the beginning: this then is also my ending: my God is drawing me to his own self. Where is Jesus now? Within the tunnel, reviewing scenes from his past and future. What's outside the tunnel? God. Our beginning and our end is with God. But those who can't believe in the words of Jesus, won't believe me.

Men hide from God: in caves of unrealized desire: in dens of iniquity: in graves of wickedness: in tombs of mediocrity: in the prison cells of hell: within seas of wicked and troubled men: in the womb of a church: in the house of a whore. Why? They are too proud to confess their foolishness, their incompetence, their blindness, their sins. Forgiveness frightens them and God's greatness and love and mercy is more than they can bear.

There are things within me that I cannot reveal: there are seeds within me, even many new beginnings, which cannot take root in earth; no, nor could all these earthly worlds together even hold one of them.

What shall I do? I am also pregnant with possibility. Let me be drawn to my God and be brought before him. Let him tell me, what the fuck is going on, for the varied babble of men constitute words without power and their fables are not even amusing.

It is March 2, 1977: what next shall come to pass?

Hereafter I will not talk much with you: for the prince of this world cometh, and hath nothing in me.

Why? Because I have rejected his bullshit.

But that the world may know that I love the Father; and as the Father gave me commandment, even so I do. Arise, let us go hence.

What is that commandment? Sit at my right hand until I make your enemies your footstool.

Surely Jesus must rejoice in the fact that so many of his enemies are powerful, and beautiful, and skilled and talented. Jesus learns of his enemies: they support him in ways they know not.

Nevertheless, let's leave this Jewish passover and its doctrines and realizing we've passed from death to life, let's consider what the future holds for those of us who grow within the kingdom of God even as the kingdom of heaven grows within us.

CHAPTER 15

I am the true vine, and my Father is the husbandman.

Are there other vines? Of course.

Every branch in me that beareth not fruit he taketh away: and every branch that beareth fruit, he purgeth it, that it may bring forth more fruit.

Surely, this is not only true of Jesus, but myself, and yourself as well.

Why should we lament the loss of a few fruitless experiences which never did bring us joy? The poor in spirit have yet to realize the sorrow God has kept from them by banning them from the councils of learned ignoramuses. In some committee meetings so much shit is hurled about the place it's impossible to come away unspotted.

Now are ye clean through the word I have spoken unto you.

Does the word clean? The words Jesus speaks do clean: other words dirty us.

Abide in me, and I in you.

Herein Jesus rests: even within us. His spirit is more desirable to have than that of Lenin. Why do I pick on Lenin? Because such liars and their disciples anger me.

As the branch cannot bear fruit of itself, except it abide in the vine; no more can ye, except ye abide in me.

We see two worlds: a world before Christ and a world after Christ. What is a world before Christ? Even this world of communist Russia and China, and pagan India, and Roman Europe, and divided Africa, and Mammon-ruled America. And what is a world after Christ? The kingdom of heaven brought to earth by the God Jesus worships.

Those who abide in Jesus abide in God wherein all things are possible if you only believe in the Word. And if you don't believe? It doesn't matter much to me, because you're destined for paradise anyway. Nevertheless. . .

What fruit have those men yielded who have not abode with Jesus?

I am the vine, ye are the branches. He that abideth in me, and I in him, the same bringeth forth much fruit: for without me ye can do nothing.

The world is governed by men who, having not Jesus, accomplish nothing. If you doubt this, look carefully at the world and its great men. What did Hitler do? Even his own generals count him something of a nut. What have the popes accomplished? Even *Penthouse* magazine is read more avidly by Catholics than any one or all of the popish encyclicals combined. What has the Congress of the United States accomplished? They've written more laws, recorded more vanity, funded more wars, collected more taxes, and given birth to more bureaucratic nonsense than their computers can be programmed to accommodate. And what does it all amount to? God has blessed America in spite of them for within it are many poor in spirit who enjoy life without having the slightest idea of what their representatives are doing or have done: the poor in spirit possess the kingdom, even though their leaders strive to take it from them.

If a man abide not in me, he is cast forth as a branch, and is withered; and men gather them, and cast them into the fire, and they are burned.

Where are Caesar's branches? Where are Napoleon's? Where are Nixon's? Where are Stalin's? Where are Muhammad's? Where are Mao

Tse-tung's? In the world, awaiting the fiery judgment of those who have the God of truth within them. Don't be deceived. If the bigger dummies are purged within the domain of your own soul, so also can you be purged of all the teensy weensy, itsy bitsy accusers who abide not in the heart of the lord of love.

God's word is a consuming fire. It can destroy that which even an H-bomb cannot.

If ye abide in me, and my words abide in you, ye shall ask what ye will, and it shall be done unto you.

Now here's a campaign promise which even I get skeptical about, in spite of the fact that God has already granted me much. Why do I doubt? Because of the impossible dreams within me. After all, with me, heaven come to earth is just for openers.

How does one abide in Jesus? The Son of man has no place to rest his head. How then can he abide in us and we in him? Obviously, through the power of the Word: for the words are spirit and the spirit makes all things possible. I am comforted in this: the Word of God is in battle with the beast, is at war with the Antichrist and its many spirits. And where is this man of sin to be found? Where shall the Antichrist appear? In Western Europe? In Rome? In Russia? On Mars? No. But within ourselves. The keepers of my God's vineyard, even the very husbandmen of paradise, deny me, reject me: they have killed me. Even God is denied the fruit of his own vineyard. Those who do this are of Antichrist. There is no flesh and blood in any of their doctrines: they reject the resurrection of the body, despise the teachings of angels, are unmoved by the impulses of love and untouched by the loveliness of naked flesh. Neither art, nor science, nor literature, nor Nature itself holds any wonder for them. The universe of stars, and the magic within a lover's eyes, is closed to them. The kingdom of heaven is shut up against them through the powers of lawyers, who will do anything for Mammon and nothing for God. And the hypocritical Pharisees will cover heaven and earth in hot pursuit of those souls whom they can gather into their churches, or into their political camp, or into their self-righteous organizations, or into their gang, or into their family, or into their selfish little arms.

My words cannot abide in them: they have their own words, their own inner source of enlightenment, their own darkened vision of what my God is like. Who are these? Look about you, the world is full of examples. Mammon, the State, and the Whore rule earthy men and have overcome them.

This then is my request. That God make them see, so that I might heal them. And why should I heal them or even desire to do so? Because I delight in the impossible and joy in what they shall become.

All of Jesus' words abide in me. Do all my words abide in him? And where is he, this friend who said we wouldn't see him and yet would never leave us alone? Where is the sinless man who is supposed to bear our sins? Where is this fellow who, having been born among us, having lived with us, supped with us, believed on by us, has gone to the Father and yet promised to remain with us until the end of the world? Is this Jesus still hanging around? I suppose it must be true for his sign has surely been raised up before all the nations of the world.

But so has the hammer and sickle of Lenin, the words of Mao, the religion of Muhammad: and what can we judge of these false prophets and great deceivers whose spirits stir up strife and controversy even to this very day in the worlds of men? They are footnotes in the life of Christ, for he foretold their rise and fall even before they came to be.

How do I know these things? Because the words of Jesus abide in me. He is my teacher.

Herein is my Father glorified, that ye bear much fruit; so shall ye be my disciples.

What fruit have I borne? To what have I, even I, given birth? The words that I speak, the words that I write, the dreams within me. As it is with all other men, great and small, male and female, so also is it with me. Moses has his words: Elias has his words: Jesus has his words: and you have yours. What my God gives me, he gives me: what he denies, he denies. What has he denied giving me? The kingdom of heaven covering the earth, even all of it, and all the souls of men, even all of them, enjoying the fruits of paradise—yet.

And what have I received? The religious and commercial Whore of Babylon in all her idolatrous splendor: the State, Man's One World Government, even the very beast of the sea, with its wounded head of pride, and its envy and its causeless anger and its covetousness and its sickening spiritual sloth: and its powerful horns of worldly power, even the government of the United States and Russia with their nuclear-tipped absurdities and their armies of bureaucrats and militarists alike, and the horns of India's and China's governments with their incompetent lords of mass organization and mass deception. And Man, glorious Man, with his prophecies great and small, and his knowledge and his many books, and his apologists great and small, arming themselves as it were with the twin horns of Death and of Hell.

Surely, such spiritual realities confront me in this my valley of decision. And what are they really? In all truth what are these things? Can man create hell? Of course. Can man deceive? Most certainly. Can man blaspheme my God? Of course. Can Mankind or Humanity or Man or the Human Race be believed in and worshiped in spite of the incredible horrors of Death and Hell that spring from its own head? From whence come wars, and prisons, and hate, and communism, democracy, laws vain, various, and oppressive? From man's mind or brain?

Man is numbered: he is covered with six hundred three score and six talents of gold stolen from the treasure house of Solomon's wisdom. He stands sixty cubits tall, six cubits broad, and is sunk six cubits into the earth. He is the great image before whom and by whom the kings of the earth wield power over frightened men. He is the false prophet of the earth animated by the fallen sons of god who worship it, delight in it, make music before it, and praise it. Such are the adulterers of truth and the whoremongers of idolatry: such are the writers who have despised the Word of the Lord God of Israel. Such are my fallen brethren. From them I receive Mammon, law, the states of the world, lies, and false prophets numerous, Babylonian absurdities, Egyptian bondage, and the God of Women.

And from my God? What have I received from my God? Up to this point in time, the spirit of truth, even that comforting spirit which makes all earthly furnaces of affliction cool by comparison. Can the spirit reside within a tabernacle of flesh and blood? Yes.

As the Father hath loved me, so have I loved you: continue ye in my love. If ye keep my commandments, ye shall abide in my love:

even as I have kept my Father's commandments, and abide in his love. These things have I spoken unto you, that my joy may remain in you, and that your joy may be full. This is my commandment, That ye love one another as I have loved you. Greater love hath no man than this, that a man lay down his life, for his friends. Ye are my friends, if you do whatsoever I command you. Henceforth I call you not servants; for the servant knoweth not what his lord doeth: but I have called you friends; for all things I have heard of my Father I have made known to you.

I have laid down my life and taken it again. Let this not appear strange to you: for surely, you have done likewise. Much has come and gone: much has been done: much remains to be done. But eternity is long and full of many great works of God. You have overcome the world, and its evil, even as I. Truth cannot fail: no, nor can it ever prove itself false. God is truth. Believe in it and thereby become his child.

My work is near its end. Really, what more can I say? My God has given me a little book, a revelation of things that were and are and shall be. Let me enjoy my kingdom, and you enjoy yours. I cannot kill: I crave no such power. The lie and its prince are my adversary: the idols of the mind are many: the rulers of the mob and the marketplace worship their own selves. I serve the God that created me, even the God within me, and the God in whom I am. I am not God: that spirit is greater than I, immensely so. Yet I am one with that spirit, for truth conceived me and love bore me. If you cannot believe these things of me, believe them of yourself: for my God is not mine alone, but yours. My God is your God: and Satan is what it is, a social beast to be used for good, and to be destroyed when it leads men astray. I know its works are many, and its products varied. But it is only a toy, a product itself of God, a thing no longer needed, nor amusing, nor useful. Destroy it. Surely, the word which can divide leviathan and rid the earth of dinosaurs can also destroy Satan.

The Word is in battle with Satan and its products: the godless governments of this world, created as they are by the vain lawyers of the world, are no satisfactory substitute for the kingdom of heaven. So proud and vain and hypocritical are these grand deceivers that they covet to rule you in all your ways. It is plain to see how they accomplish this. Mammon is served: the Lord God of Israel is despised. The whole earth is his: yet they divided it up among themselves for their own use. His laws are simple, and his vengeance is within his own power to execute. Yet what do these lawyers occupy themselves with except it be their own laws with which they make you their bondslaves? Know the truth: continue in the words of Jesus and be free: free of their senseless rules; free of their petty conceits; free of their trust in wars, in armies, in prisons; in clever methods of taxation; in public opinion; be free of their trust in money, in the prestige of office, in image making, in law. God's law is love: if you have that law within your heart, there is no other law which can bind you. Trust God: in time, truth will cleanse these hypocrites and make lovers of them all. If I ever am troubled it is with them: for their ignorance is vast, their vanity is colossal, and their faith in themselves is almost beyond the power of God to understand.

Money is the great beast of social inequality: law is its shepherd: and with it, men create idols of the spirit, and make bondslaves of us all.

Have I told you anything new? Or taught you anything which you do not already inwardly know? Is this not all ancient scripture, long-established fact, common sense, simple observation? Of course. Be my friend and understand these matters lest I find you guilty of violently assaulting my kingdom with your laws, your pride, your theft; your deceit, your ignorance, and your foolishness. The kingdom of heaven is mine: it is God's gift to those that have made themselves his sons. You cannot prevail against it: for at the last day it shall win your heart, and conquer your pride, and destroy your ignorance, and make you the blessed bondslaves of love.

You have been given God's Word, without which all my words are nothing, so that you might know what both my God and I are about and what we are doing. The kingdom of heaven has come, is with us today, shall destroy all other kingdoms. Why fight needlessly against this truth? Many of you are so faithless, so perverse, so slow: and what joy can I find then in you? Shall those without faith suddenly believe? Shall the perverse meekly submit themselves to the truth? Shall the slow instantly become quick? Why not? With God, all things are possible and why should I, created thing such as I am, set bounds to his power?

Ye have not chosen me, but I have chosen you, that ye should go and bring forth fruit, and that your fruit should remain: that whatsoever ye shall ask of the Father in my name, he may give it you.

God chooses: we often forget this. Some fruit remains: other does not. We who sin bring forth good and evil. Why can't we always bring forth good? Because we have knowledge of both good and evil within us, and about us, and we are dead to the voice of God who alone can teach us how to choose the good and reject the evil.

The good we do remains: this, because of God. The evil is destroyed. Jesus chose us, even as he chose himself, to bring forth good things and to cleanse himself and others of evil things. Jesus is also baptized of the fiery spirit of truth as well as with the belief John commanded. Belief is as water: truth is as fire. The parables and proverbs are what they are. They speak directly to our heart and mind as to what God is doing with us, doing to us, doing for us. God is giving us what we ask in Jesus' name. What is that? The kingdom which is neither found here nor there, but within us, about us, and among us: even the kingdom of the Father come to earth: the kingdom of love, of Jesus; we know it as the kingdom of heaven. This is what we have asked of our Father: and this surely is what we receive.

Yet men still doubt this simple truth. Why?

These things I command you, that ye love one another.

If we loved one another, we would not shut up the kingdom against ourselves.

If the world hate you, ye know that it hated me before it hated you.

The world hates Jesus because his kingdom is of universal love, truth, forgiveness, compassion, mercy, judgment, wisdom, and life. It is an everlasting kingdom. Here we are, removed thousands of measures in both space and time from the words spoken by Jesus, recorded by John, and translated and kept by multitudes of God's host, and his kingdom is still with us. So is the world wherein courts of law and prisons mock forgiveness: wherein national governments and military powers delight themselves with the weapon systems of death: wherein religions numerous beautify the tower of babble and despise God's house of wisdom: wherein hate and vengeance is applauded and love and mercy is despised. There are nations of people who are on God's right hand: and there are nations which he has placed on his left. But I speak of nations as groups of living souls and not of the governments and nations of the world. For these latter are nothing but the delusions of cartographers, lawyers, politicians, and vain persons in high places who are forever dividing up a united world. How is the world united? In its opposition to Jesus Christ, God's appointed king of the Jews: the same king the Jews reject and the world hates.

If ye were of the world, the world would love his own: but because ye are not of the world, but I have chosen you out of the world, therefore the world hateth you.

What is the world? the sphere enclosing our life. Each man lives in his own world. He becomes a Son of God by overcoming that world and enjoying heaven with God, even the creator of his body and the redeemer of his soul. But our worlds are invaded by devils, and angels, and men; by lies, foolish hopes, groundless fears, and idle advice. I marvel at men who can allow so much evil to enter their world and reject that which is good.

But all these words, of themselves, are sterile judgment, bloodless psychology, a way of viewing the world in an abstract manner.

Yet, what has God wrought? Are you not composed of flesh and blood and bones as well as hope and dream and thought? How can I have a place in your world except it be through these words? Surely, there is no other way. If this is true of myself and my words, it is also true of you and your words, and of all other men, great and small, who enter into your soul with their words. Search for and seek the God within you working the works of paradise and the salvation of your world. And cast out all those thoughts and impulses and accusations which reject the God of truth, judgment, love, and beauty. Many writers, many wise men, many great men; many of your own family, and household, and nation; many of your own party, many of your own loved ones may despise the God that loves you. Be not deceived by their ways, and works, and words. In the end, love triumphs and the kingdom of heaven is formed within those who seek it.

My God is capable of satisfying all my desire: which is even this, heaven come to earth for you.

Endure the hate of the world. In such endurance, God works the miracle of your eternal life. Love my God and that spirit's ways. To surrender your love to any other is vain: for why should you despise the father of your soul and the creator of your heaven? Come out of your world and get involved in the ways of the kingdom of heaven.

Remember the word that I said unto you, The servant is not greater than his lord. If they have persecuted me, they will also persecute you; if they have kept my saying, they will keep yours also. But all these things will they do unto you for my name's sake, because they know not him that sent me.

If men knew Jesus they would know God, who is love. It surely is obvious that the world is ruled by men who love not God but who love power, law, and money. They know not Jesus, nor his father. But they know much about law, much about power, much about money: for with such things they rule those that fear and covet these things. And yet what type of power is the power to kill, to imprison, to legislate, to tax, to deceive, to babble bullshit? Is it a power to be sought by gods? Hardly. Rather such power is the power sought by devils, analyzed by angels, and destroyed by love.

If men knew who sent us Jesus, they would not ignore Jesus, nor defame him, nor gamble for his coat.

If I had not come and spoken unto them, they had not had sin: but now they have no cloke for their sin. He that hateth me hateth my Father also.

Those who do not allow the words of Jesus to enter their heart, are sinners. Love is the great commandment: there is no greater commandment given men by God. Yet how can we know love unless we hear his word and see his works and sense her beauty and proclaim her glory?

The key to the mystery of God is that there is no mystery. We are Adam. We are created by God, even the creator of heaven and earth. We do eat of the knowledge of good and evil. We cannot become wise by doing this no matter how gluttonously we indulge ourselves with its fruit. We do die because of it. We sin greatly because of its prolific effects. Yet we are saved by God through his angel Jesus who guards the tree of life and leads us back into paradise. Yet how proud are men! How foolishly vain! How grossly incompetent to handle the doctrines of everlasting life! Judge for yourself what is good, what is evil, what is true, what is false. Everyman is judged by the words that come out of his own mouth; by the works he does with his own hands; by the place he occupies with his own feet; by the throne he sits upon with his own ass.

Those that love Jesus love his words: love his victory: love his ways: love his Father also.

If I had not done among them the works which none other man did, they had not had sin: but now have they both seen and hated both me and my Father.

What works? Even his words.

But this cometh to pass, that the word might be fulfilled that is written in their law, They hated me without a cause.

Causeless hate, and causeless anger, are two great evils working within the world. Because we love, hate is not thereby justified. Because we seek truth, anger is not thereby justified. Nevertheless, our love of God and our desire for his truth causes anger in our fellow men and hatred of our ways before them.

We do not desire to kill. They draft us into their armies. We do not desire to lie; they pump us full of their Babylonian conceits. We seek no revenge: they entice us into their worldly courts. We seek simple truth concerning creation's beginnings: they pride themselves on their sophisticated premises, their abstruse logic, their brilliant deductions, their wondrous discoveries.

The truth is plain. They hate us without a cause, for the cause of their hatred is no cause at all.

But when the Comforter is come, whom I will send unto you from the Father, even the Spirit of truth, which proceedeth from the Father, he shall testify of me. And ye also shall bear witness, because ye have been with me from the beginning.

There are many who have not been with Jesus from the beginning. Yet the Spirit of truth is provided for all. I cannot see why men cannot accept Moses' record and writings as true, and accept Jesus' words as they are, and John's revelation as it is, and move on to explore the depths of eternal life, the glories of the starry universe, the wonders of God's creation, and the miracles of our own selves. The Spirit of truth is adequate for all these things.

But men are deceived by their own babble. No wonder atheistic communism and Tchaikovsky can enter the ear of the Russian soul and reside therein without judgment for such a long while. Stupidity and beauty, the issues of devils and angels alike, ought not to be spiritual comrades. Yet they are. Without the judgments of God, *Pravda* is truth, and bureaucratic ugliness is covered with the stolen mantle of genius with which God clothes his angels. The State is the usurper: Satan's creation and the soul's greatest enemy

The spirit of truth proceeds from God. It glorifies God and comforts the human soul. But the State proceeds from the souls of men who, having not the truth, reject the teachings of the Lord God of hosts and the witness of his angels and the testimony of his son. Thus czars, premiers, demagogues, and bureaucratic tyrants of body, soul, and mind are produced. In this manner is the individual enslaved and the slaves of systems encouraged to worship the State. For what purpose? To what end? To give all men the mark of the beast and make merchandise out of human lives. The Comforter is the spirit of truth coming out of those men who possess it within themselves. What is the truth? Communism is **a** bore and the Russian peoples are my most lovable enemies. If I loved them less I would flatter them for their foolishness. But the truth is plain: they tolerate the State and have rejected the intolerant God of truth.

Those who lie, imprison, murder, prepare for war; and control, confine, and restrict the lives of people are the idolaters of social slavery and the unwitting supporters of their own spiritual hell.

Men little note how great is Jesus' power: for he sent us the spirit of truth: even that same comforting spirit which reveals to us the hypocrisy, the incompetence, the imaginative and earthy blindness, of all governments of the world. Antichrist is the spirit which impedes the kingdom of God coming to the human soul and sets up in its place the insensitive bureaucracies of godless men.

Jesus comforts us with truth. Men who departed from Jesus long ago trouble us with the lie. What is the truth? Our souls are God's: neither Man, nor State, nor Church, nor Satan itself has any right to any of them. Nevertheless, the spirit of Antichrist is with us today. And men worship it to their own hurt.

Jesus is his own witness: but also his Creator testifies of him, reveals him to men, and, in addition, gives men a prophetic book of revelation about himself. Only the spirit of truth, only truth itself, can establish a foundation for its own justification.

I am vexed with each man's unholy Self: mine own included. The more my God gives me, the less I feel bound to the earth: my self becomes whole within God and in this I rejoice. But men without God are such pathetic and egoistic fools that my heart burns to set them free. But they shut me out: they love their own Self: their pride, I cannot penetrate. The world is insane and truly I am living on the planet of the apes. So many men ape Darwin, ape Freud, ape Jung, ape Caesar, ape lawyers, ape Rome, ape priests, ape each other, that I pray they might evolve into a higher nature.

They despise the Word and create their own word. I find so little that is socially redeeming in lawyers and worldly scribes and ignorant religious zealots and servile military men that I scarce know how to judge.

If it were not for the poor in spirit, and the meek, and those who mourn, I would have long ago gone. At times even I forget that I am not of the world.

Let the spirit of truth comfort me. I am not alone. My God is my strength. I had best rest in this knowledge for a time: for I am weary.

CHAPTER 16

These things have I spoken unto you, that ye should not be offended.

Jesus did depart. The spirit of truth does comfort. The New Jerusalem is real. Wise men, such as Augustine, and prophets such as Francis Bacon, and scribes, such as those unknown believers, and writers, and keepers, and printers, and translators, and publishers, and distributors, of the Word of God, did come into the world and did manifest with their lives that they thought the Word of God worthy of their attention. Are we offended by this? Most surely I am not offended by it: I rejoice in it.

Those who bear witness to Jesus even to this very hour are in the world saving the world from its own lies by the power of the comforting spirit of truth dwelling within them.

But are these witnesses found in the synagogue? No. Have these witnesses oftentimes been killed by those inquisitors who thought they were doing God service? Most certainly yes, they have been so killed. And if we expand the meaning of God to include the God of Muhammad and the God of Lenin and the God of Truman and the God of Lincoln and the God of Communism and the God of lawyers, and police officers, and generals, and popes, and kings—can we honestly state that the witnesses of Jesus' Word have not been killed by those who think they were doing God service? And if we expand the meaning of the word "killed" to include those who deaden our lives to sexual pleasure, and the power of love, and the beauty of nature, and the glories of music, and the goodness of God's children, what can we think of those who kill us and think they do God service? Can we be offended because they do these things to us? I think not. They know not the Father, and it is our glory to show them the Father of Jesus. Listen to Jesus' words.

They shall put you out of the synagogues: yea, the time cometh, that whosoever killeth you will think that he doeth God service. And these things will they do unto you, because they have not known the Father, nor me. But these things have I told you, that when the time shall come, ye may remember that I told you of them. And these things I said not unto you at the beginning, because I was with you.

Now what? What shall we who have seen not only the beginning but the end of Jesus say about these matters? Did he give us the truth or bullshit? Did he tell it plain or did he embellish fact with worldly hypocrisy and angelic pride? Did he glorify Rome and its lawyers, religion and its priests, Herod and his soldiers, the synagogue and its rabbis? Did he glorify himself, or Israel, or the gentiles, or those who would believe in him? No, he did not.

But now I go my way to him that sent me;

He's really very independent since he chose to go his own way.

And none of you asketh me, whither goest thou? But because I have said these things unto you, sorrow hath filled your heart. Nevertheless I tell you the truth; It is expedient for you that I go away:

How often, how very often, men who believe in Jesus forget this important truth: it is expedient for us that he does go away.

For if I go not away, the Comforter will not come unto you; but if I depart, I will send him unto you.

Men need the comfort of truth: we mourn for it, and receive it. Truth is a comforting flame, a cooling lake of fire, a soothing and intolerant judge: for it tolerates no lie.

315

We may dwell in heaven with our Father, or we may reside in the world wherein not God but the prince of the world rules. Who is this prince? Our self, incomplete, earthy, ignorant, selfish, proud, foolish, and, oftentimes, silly.

Thus heaven is the throne of God: the world is the throne of our self. The world, even our world, is saved by God through his spirit, his word, even Jesus himself, working within us.

I suffer tribulation in my world: it is a world I overcome daily. God is my strength: this is simple truth. Without God, I become the self-sustaining image of my self. With God, I become even what I am, the created Son of the eternal God. Yet men, in their conceited wisdom, wish to make of me that which surely I can never become: namely, nothing. As it is with me, so is it with all those that love me and suffer tribulation in the world. Such are pregnant with truth, alive with eternal possibilities; such are the woman, taken out of myself, who in simple truth is the mother of all becoming.

We are sons of God: sons of men: male and female: we are gods. Thus, problems arise. The Lord God of Israel is a god of gods. But devils, from the bottomless pit of their own imagination, produce Zeus, a mythical God of gods, whose spiritual existence is as about as real as Uncle Sam, John Bull, and Mother Russia.

The most lovable thing about Jimmy Carter is his wife, Rosalynn. The most abominable thing about Jimmy Carter is his relationship with the United States Government: for this government is one horn on the beast of the sea. China is a horn: as is Russia: India is a horn. There are six others. Let Man choose and name them. Why? Can't I name them? No. For the names change depending upon the perspective of each soul's world. Nevertheless, let it be remembered that I speak of State governments, not of nations of peoples. For although I endure the mark of the beast on my body, it cannot be placed within my heart, nor within my soul, nor within my mind; for my strength is sufficient to keep these powers safe within the kingdom of God. Again, what I say here of myself, I say of all those who love me and have made themselves mine. Who are these? In this each soul must speak for itself: for in plain truth, at this moment, except for my knowledge of my God, I stand alone.

Truth is knowledge of God and his ways: in this manner, those who know the truth, know their heavenly Father, and possess eternal life.

I am filthy with the shit of Israel, of Man, of earthy men, of angels. Why? Obviously, because in examining them and judging their prince, I have looked upon all their parts: the good and evil alike.

I need to be baptized even after I am born again. As it is with me, so is it with those I love. And I love all men. I am fighting to save men from the sinful products of their own selves: the idolatrous images of their own heart and soul and mind. Men give their strength to idols and consider it not.

What is a nuclear weapon system? The ultimate absurdity in the armory of fools. And what are all these heads of State? Heads of the beast of the sea of wicked men who continuously preach peace and equip themselves for war: they are what they are: the self-appointed substitutes for the Lord of Heaven and Earth, even God himself. And what is the State? Man's pathetic substitute for the kingdom of heaven. And what is money? The devil's substitute for love, genius, joyous work, and the impulses of the heart wherein God seeks to dwell. And what is Law? Mankind's personified hypocrisy whereby righteousness, mercy, forgiveness and common sense are mocked.

And who am I? The one who knows the things he herein writes are true. I judge no man: only the Satanic prince of his own world.

But what are these things of which I write? Surely, they are those things given to Jesus by his angel John in the book of revelation given to all of us by God. Nevertheless men have added to those words and taken away from those words much to their own hurt.

And what of me? Am I not doing likewise? No. I am only opening the book my God has given me to read. Nevertheless, all that I have is yours for the asking.

But let me continue this commentary, for there is much in John men have yet to perceive.

And when he is come, he will reprove the world of sin, and of righteousness, and of judgment;

Sin, righteousness, and judgment are the principle concerns of all the intellectual angels of God: Paul is concerned with it: Augustine is concerned with it: Thomas Hobbes is concerned with it: and even such Greeks as William James and Alfred North Whitehead concern themselves with it, although, admittedly, these scribes prefer to use their own terminologies and categories of thought and metaphysics. But what is that to me? The Lord God of Israel, and the heart and soul and mind and strength of man, by any other name, remain eternally what they are. By now, most angels must acknowledge God is not greatly moved by their philosophical compliments. The barren idols of abstract thought are the curse of every intellectual age. Nevertheless, there is virtue in this: not every abstraction is barren.

Truth is found in these men, these angels who have made themselves the Sons of God by overcoming the world. The spirit of truth worked in Thomas so that he could envision Leviathan as the beast of the sea: and even esoteric Alfred could proclaim, the kingdom of heaven is with us today. And what did James explore save the sins and judgments and righteousness within the soul and mind of his self and thereby, within all men? Nevertheless, I marvel at angels who can find so much in themselves, and in the world, and in other men, who yet find so little in Jesus and his disciple John. Yet, if Jesus were not in John, how did his gospel come to be written? And if John were not within me, how could I know of his love for Jesus?

Let the Comforter come to you and answer. We know that which is within us and know not that which has no part in us.

Of sin, because they believe not on me;

The only reproveable sin in your world of eternal importance is your belief in Jesus. Sins against truth are never forgiven: our penalty is just: namely, to be told the truth. In this angels rejoice, and devils piss, and moan, and fret, and wail, and weep, and gnash their teeth. Become an angel: don't persist in worshiping Satan and his priests adorned, as they are, with fool's gold. The world's sin is unbelief in Jesus.

Of righteousness, because I go to my Father, and ye see me no more;

Without Jesus in our world we require the spirit of truth to lead us, and explain to us, the righteousness of God.

Our world is a world of good and evil. As Adam we are full of the poisonous effects of our knowledge of evil. We yield evil with our lips and think it good. We lie, and think we speak truly. We appear wise, but are only exposing our own foolishness. When I am evil, when I am foolish, when I spout nonsense, the truth reproves me. This is then the salvation of my world: this is how my kingdom is husbanded: this is how my bride cares for me. But if this is true of me, it is true of all who receive the truth. Who receives the truth? Few. Nevertheless, God has poured it out over all the world.

Of judgement, because the prince of this world is judged.

Who is the prince of this world? How is he judged? Who is the prince, the spiritual authority, behind this world? Is this world, not your world? You have not been taken out of the world: not permanently, anyway. There is another world, a world to come wherein these simple questions find ready answers. But I'll consider that world elsewhere.

Let truth judge the prince of this your world and cast him out of it. Nevertheless, this prince is legion and takes many forms. It is not easy for one to cast out Satan from the world, as the history of the world, written so doggedly by the devils themselves, so laboriously testifies. If you doubt me, read the history of the world: or if this is too much for you, review the statistics of the world in any of the world's almanacs. In this manner the spirit of truth uses the devils themselves to provide their own body counts.

I have yet many things to say unto you, but ye cannot bear them now.

A characteristic understatement. When shall they be able to bear them? Probably, when it is all over: for the greatest hell is endured by those who understand the kingdom of heaven.

Howbeit when he, the Spirit of truth is come, he will guide you into all truth:

How is this done? With the Word of God.

for he shall not speak of himself; but whatsoever he shall hear, that shall he speak; and he will show you things to come.

God's still, small voice is heard within us. We reason, we think, we pray, we create, we dream, we sense, with words. The words of God are not strange words: we hear the spirit responding to our prayer, to those words we speak to it. The spirit responds in kind.

"Why am I a bit overweight?" "You eat a bit too much." Amen. But an evil and adulterous man fucks his mind with such a multiplicity of thoughts and dreams and images and fantasies, that quiet truth is not conceived.

Once, after agonizing over the evil of the world's works, I began to toss and moan and groan. At which point, the spirit told me to be still since I was annoying him.

We are gods. But we don't believe it and oftentimes howl like lonesome dogs. Our God is longsuffering and his patience, when you really think on it, is most astonishing.

Has the spirit shown us things to come? If the Spirit of truth, is not a true prophet, who is? Men live in such small and troubled worlds and the universe of truth is so immense that tragedy, and melancholy, and despair are the themes of many angelic dramas.

Am I the only one who knows the end of the story? Of course not: for many had been told long before it ever came to pass.

He shall glorify me: for he shall receive of mine, and shall shew it unto you.

To speak the truth is man's greatest glory. Yet how can one separate truth from the man speaking it? Jesus is the truth, for without this one man of truth, what could the spirit of truth ever give us concerning times past, present, and yet to come?

All things that the Father hath are mine: therefore said I, that he shall take of mine, and shall shew it unto you.

Jesus has the Spirit of truth within himself: he confesses that the truth he is, is given him of the Father. Jesus is with God as his Son. In this way, does the Son of God do the works of God which is even this: to enable men to believe the truth they have been given. Men are evil: it is not good for them to be alone. God is their spiritual companion. Men's words are the words they speak and write. And what is the worth of each man's words without God's Word? Nothing. What is the worth of each man's word with God? Men with God are a precious treasure, a storehouse of possibility, a power within the Universe in which God delights.

The things of God are God's: yet they are also ours. Our inheritance is of truth and love and beauty: ours is the kingdom of God, for so has God decreed. Our world is saved by the universe of God bringing it light. What is earth without the stars and sun and the vast stretches of interstellar space in which it moves? A little planet revolving around its own dying ego. Why dying? Because it cannot long exist without the universe of which it is a part. But scribbling fools, the writers of this present age who forsake the God of Jesus, even the Lord God of Israel, war against the scripture of truth with their own words. Where are such found? Everywhere within the world: in councils of government, in religious congregations, in the publishing houses of modern magazines and newspapers, in scientific libraries.

In the spiritual sense brother wars against brother: *Penthouse* and *Playboy,* as corporate entities, attack the pornography of law and religion: those in law and those in religion attack the pornography of these and such-like corporate publishers. I am astonished at the stupidity of it all. Every naked man and woman is a joy before God. Sexual expression is meant to be an expression of love. And those who nakedly and unashamedly declare the truth of God's word are a joy before God. What displeases God is the hypocrisy we adulterers of the truth generate when we fuck the world by scribbling our own lies.

Jesus is the Son of God: a God in his own right, to be sure: a God who glorifies his Father, the Word, and the Spirit which makes the Word flesh through the creative provisions established by God. Jesus knows God and declares him. But the scribes of the world are wise in their own conceits: pride and mammon overpower them. Thus do they condemn their brothers, their fathers, their mothers, their children to that hell which is made possible by those who, having asked nothing of God, even Jesus' Father, have nothing of eternal worth to give men except some bits and scraps of truth they stole from the angels of God.

Decide in whom you believe. Choose your beliefs. Act upon them. Follow them. Evaluate the results. Try God. Don't tempt him with self-righteous nonsense, feeble judgment, puerile sentiments.

All I have is God's: if he rejects it, what is that to me? All that God has is mine: why then ought I to refuse to use my portion? With Satan, the social beast of this sinful world, the opposite is true. All I have to give it, is nothing: for I owe it nothing and moreover I have nothing left to give it. Yet it tempts me often: it desires my attention: my time it lusts for: it craves my worship: it seeks my fear, my talents, my love. Nevertheless, it is only a machine I have built within my own mind and I no longer have need of it nor its products. I cannot worship that which I myself created to be only an earthly beast.

I have created other things for heaven, however: I do not say I do not require these things, for they were made for my pleasure.

Don't be deceived: men are gods who war against God to their own hurt. They despise truth and love and beauty because of their disobedience to their Creator. Our spiritual death is real: we cannot handle good and evil without God: every scribe who wars against Jesus manifests to all with the words of his own mouth and hand, that he has nothing eternal to give us.

Heaven and earth have passed away. Yet my words remain: as do the lawyers, chief priests, scribes, and hypocrites who, having lost their own souls to the world's ways, strive to kill me and persecute those I love, including themselves. The gates to the New Jerusalem, the city of truth, are opened to those who love the Lord God of Israel, even that Lord God who is love. Therein, our adversaries cannot enter.

Yet all these words are without foundation in the hearts of those who cannot accept the fact that no scripture is of private interpretation: all scripture is public fact. God is the author of his own words, the creator of his own works: I am one of his works. Let each man judge himself with his own words. I judge the ridiculous prince of each man's world: I judge no man, except myself, and that with my God's help. He has made me a son of perdition: a man of sin: a son who has died because of a gluttonous consumption of the fruit of the tree of knowledge of good and evil. In this I am, as each man, male and female as they are, Adam.

Now what? God has undertaken my perfection. When shall he finish? Ask him, for there are mysteries I sense, but have not resolved.

Let's follow Jesus. His way is to give and receive of God. What things of Jesus has that Son of God given to his Father? What has the Spirit received from Jesus that he has shown us? What does the Spirit present show us? Has God received anything from Jesus? I think so.

What then of ourselves?

A little while, and ye shall not see me: and again, a little while, and ye shall see me, because I go to the Father.

Why would he go to the Father? To get the Spirit of truth, the comforting spirit of flesh and blood fact, and send it to us. How did he do this? With his Word. But if he got his words from God, then surely his Word is also the Word of God. Nevertheless, there are metaphysical distinctions in these truths we can seek out at a later time.

Now Jesus needs to do more. He must not only manifest himself again to his disciples: he must also quicken them so that they might see themselves for what they truly are: not only his disciples, but friends: not only his friends, but angels of God and sons of God and gods enjoying the mansion of their own souls within the kingdom of heaven established on this earth.

The expansion of the Word corresponds to the expansion of heaven.

Then said some of his disciples among themselves, What is this that he saith unto us, A little while, and ye shall not see me: and, Because I go to the Father? They said therefore, What is this that he saith, A little while? we cannot tell what he saith.

A little while with God is a long time with men. Yet, if men walk with God, even a thousand years is as a day. God has reserved the times to himself. Eternity is: times, and its measures, are images that pass.

My God is my Lord: I am his servant: the God who created the stars, created me. How do I know this? I know this because his Holy Spirit persuades me of this truth. Men have seen me in the past. In that past, a few men were present. They received my doctrines: they handled my words: they cultivated my ideas: they took my words into themselves and therein they grow. Light, water, and good ground, together with the right seed, and the right husbandman, produce a plentiful harvest of spiritual truth.

The words are true: there is no lie in them. The kingdom of God is within you: it is God's kingdom: nevertheless, you are also your own god. Why deny the obvious? Only gods can use words to create. Gods create idols of stone, wood, clay: idols of verbal nonsense: idols of scholarly vanity: idols of law, opinion, self-importance. The pyramids are idols of the mind produced by the ancient Egyptian rulers who conceived of them in their mind: cultivated their desire in their heart: and produced them with the power of their lying words. Men enslave each other with lying words.

The Lord God of Israel, the God in whom Moses lives, states the matter forcefully: I am the Lord thy God. Thou shalt not have strange gods before me. In times past, all other gods were strange gods. Today, many gods are not strange at all: in fact, some gods have been fighting against the truth for so long, with the same cursed results following their stupid actions, that they are not strange to us anymore. They are the same idolatrous fools we knew of old. Yet Dr. Strangeloves are real: they love their Minuteman, Thor, Jupiter, Poseidon, Atlas and other such idolatrous products of the Greek mind and the Roman hand: nevertheless, what Greece conceived and Rome brought forth is simply the ideal of the perfect state: one world empire: one beastly State. Strange it is to see men attempt to set up these things within the temple of my spirit: these strange gods shall not be brought before me except to be destroyed.

In a little while we can read the words of Jesus, given us because of the love and power found in John, even that scribe Jesus sent into the world to overcome the world. Yet, did not God receive the words of John, which words he received of Jesus, and plant them in his heavenly kingdom, which kingdom is growing within us? Of course. God receives of Jesus and of all who love him. God uses us: uses our faith, our hope, our love, our words to build the city of truth: even the New Jerusalem: even the capital of the kingdom of heaven within us.

We are within God. The universe is vast: eternity is without beginning or end. Jesus' gospel has a beginning: it also has an ending. This is its ending: even your belief in his heavenly Father, and in his power and in his glory.

The idols of gods fallen are vain. Satan is my beast: my created social mechanism: my created thing. Don't be deceived by its voice nor by the foolish and pathetic gods that serve it. I go to my Father; I stand before my God, naked and unashamed.

Men have mocked me. Doubted my words. Denied me and my God who sent me into their world. They have even set my own creation and creatures against me. But my love of the God of truth shall one day end this silly strife.

When is that day and when shall it occur? Even when Jesus returns to abide with you forever. And how can one spirit be within another spirit except through the power of the Word?

Jesus is with us when his words are with us. For wherein is the difference? True, he leaves us: we cannot see him, for a little while, he goes to the Father to receive from his God a kingdom. Yet, it is done in the way it is done. He returns on the day his Father decrees.

Without the Word of God what are all these words worth? We understand the truth because of the laws of God written in our mind and placed in our heart. Let God rule you: learn his ways. For the ways of the servile princes of this world are vain and oftentimes, cruel. Their doctrines are of themselves. Jesus is not their Lord: if he were their Lord they would serve his God and not mammon. They do not love their enemies: for if they loved them, they would tell them the truth. But there is no truth in them: they do what they do: they say what they say: their own words reveal to all who hear them and read their words exactly what they are: the spokesmen of the world, the self-appointed princes of the doctrines of man, the very servants of mammon, war, taxes, prisons; the lovers of democracy, communism, state, law, and Man. Love, mercy, forgiveness, patience, compassion, truth, and the righteousness of the Lord God of hosts is not in their hearts; nor are those things written upon their minds. Who are these? Judge for yourself.

Now Jesus knew that they were desirous to ask him, and said unto them, Do ye inquire among yourselves of that I said, A little while, and ye shall not see me: and again, a little while, and ye shall see me?

Those with Jesus saw Jesus. We have a record of what they saw. The Egyptians have their pyramids: the Babylonians have their tower of babble, unfinished as it is, since their babble is still adding to it: the Romans have their laws, and their ways, and their senators, and their idols of men, for these are still with us today: the Persians have their king: the Greeks have their philosophers, and poets, and dramatists, and myths: for the world is full of their products: and the Assyrians have Muhammad, their prophet, and Allah, their intolerant God of slaughter: and the world itself has its states, and nations, and kingdoms and principalities and powers and seats of wickedness in high places: and we have the gospel of Jesus Christ, the Son of the living God.

Because Jesus cannot now be seen, shall we despise his gospel, and follow the ways of the world? I shall not for my God will yet strengthen me in this my resolve.

Verily, verily, I say unto you, That ye shall weep and lament, but the world shall rejoice: and ye shall be sorrowful, but your sorrow shall be turned into joy.

Have you known sorrow?

A woman

even the woman taken out of Jesus

when she is in travail

even that travail experienced by those made pregnant by truth

hath sorrow, because her hour is come: but as soon as she is delivered of the child,

even the Christ child born within our kingdom of heaven

she remembereth no more the anguish, for joy that a man is born into the world.

Jesus is born into the world of our experience. In the larger sense, Jesus, the Christ, is already in the world planting the seeds of the kingdom of heaven within the hearts of those men who believe in him. But the kingdom has grown great in the world and the end of the use of these parables must also be seen. We really need to speak with new tongues for the earth itself cannot contain the kingdom forever: we require the heavens: even those heavens we now have, not those which have passed away.

And ye now therefore have sorrow: but I will see you again,

This is my great expectation.

and your heart shall rejoice, and your joy no man taketh from you.

(In spite of the fact many try.)

And in that day ye shall ask me nothing. Verily, verily, I say unto you, Whatsoever ye shall ask the Father in my name, he will give it to you.

We ask directly of the Father: in this, Jesus is only the door to our Father.

Hitherto have ye asked nothing in my name: ask, and ye shall receive, that your joy may be full.

God is our king: we ask of him directly. Yet, only in Jesus' name: not in the name of law: or Muhammad: or self-righteousness: or worldly power: or worldly ambition.

Let God bless America in the name of Jesus: and let Democracy, and the vain absurdity of its laws, fuck itself to death.

These things have I spoken unto you in proverbs:

Scientists have their parameters: Jesus has his proverbs.

But the time cometh, when I shall no more speak unto you in proverbs, but I shall shew you plainly of the Father.

Surely, Angie, and Brigitte, and Ludmilla are of my God, even of the Father of whom Jesus speaks. The world uses them for its own purposes: but I love them for what they themselves are: the children of the living God. And the kingdom of heaven is full of many of God's creatures who are even more excitingly beautiful than these. Nevertheless, can beauty be compared and love measured and truth calculated? I think not: what God creates, God creates: and who am I to measure the extent of his glory? As one of his sons, I can only rejoice in it.

At that day ye shall ask in my name: and I say not unto you, that I will pray the Father for you:

There is a time to pray and a time to recognize God has received the message. The effective fervent prayer of a righteous man accomplishes much: but repetitious and public prayer God despises: and I am greatly embarrassed by it. And herein Jesus illustrates that to pray for the saints is ridiculous: does not God himself love them?

And who is a saint? All who continue in Jesus' words.

For the Father himself loveth you, because ye have loved me, and have believed that I came out from God.

Men who know not God cannot believe anything ever comes out of God. They can fill their small worlds with the words that come out of themselves and refuse to believe God can bring something out of himself. From such farts let all keep a reasonable distance.

I came forth from the Father, and am come into the world: again, I leave the world, and go to the Father.

A man comes into the world by manifesting himself in the world. In this Muhammad, Lenin, Carter and all other world figures, great and small, foreign and domestic, play the same role. But where do they come from? Who sends them?

The world is the world: and the kingdom of heaven is the kingdom of God. We shall prevail in both realms: indeed, our world is saved when the kingdom of heaven comes. Nevertheless, who brings heaven to earth? The God of Jesus, even the Lord God of Israel.

Let us also enjoy this truth: we can also leave the world and go to the Father: and we can leave the Father and come again into the world. Multitudes do this even several times a day. But by now, we should realize that in earth there are two kingdoms: the kingdom of heaven and the world. The kingdom of heaven found in your world is your world saved. But saved for what? Saved for the pleasures of God: saved for the joys of love.

His disciples said unto him, Lo, now speakest thou plainly, and speakest no proverb. Now are we sure that thou knowest all things, and needeth not that any man should ask thee: by this we believe thou camest forth from God.

A man is born naked in the world: a man, sent by God into the world, hungers and thirsts in this evil world for the righteousness of God. Man lives by the words of God, even all of them, and by every one of them. I do not say James Clerk Maxwell's words must be read by all: nevertheless we live more abundant lives because of what this great angel of God accomplished. But little men are blind to the works of great angelic minds. Thus they confuse the stars of heaven with astrological nonsense. Genius and talent and good works are God's gifts to the human souls who receive them: and are those souls' gifts to those that use them righteously. But perverts, for money, use the gifts of truth to conceive wickedness, bring forth evil inventions, and conduct wars. No wonder Newton kept things secret from evil men.

Men should be clothed with the righteousness of God: this alone is protection against the cruel elements of this stormy world.

We are sick: we are imprisoned: we are strangers: what nations, of all the nations found within the world, receive us and accept our gospel? Those that come forth from God are of God. Be not deceived: those nations that receive us are those organizations of people who are governed by the forces of love and are armed with the sword of truth. The nations of the world, are governed by the forces of the world, even money, the laws of men, and military power. We live among them: but are not of them. They number us for their own pathetic purposes. Nevertheless, the kingdom of heaven is our inheritance. Can we honestly find a place within our heart for all the worldly vanities with which the leaders of the world constantly occupy themselves? If God is our king, his kingdom is our kingdom: we accept no worldly imitations. But why do we come into the world? To overcome it and thereby manifest to all we are the sons of God. In this manner is your world saved and in no other way. Yet why am I in the world? Because it pleases me to come again.

Jesus answered them, Do ye now believe?

Yes, God, I believe. But what next?

Behold, the hour cometh,

(But is now past.)

yea, is now come, that ye shall be scattered, every man to his own,

What is each man's own?

and shall leave me alone

For so did God decree:

and yet I am not alone, because the Father is with me.

Even as God is with all of us, for though he hid himself for a while, and though we put him far from us, he never did leave us, for he has always carried us and borne us and loved us even from our own beginning to this very day. But how many blind themselves to this simple fact!

These things I have spoken unto you, that in me ye might have peace. In the world ye shall have tribulation: but be of good cheer; I have overcome the world.

And that's a fact. Why not experience it for yourself? Believe in Jesus and live his Word: and, forgive me my vanity, but I know you'll enjoy it.

CHAPTER 17

These words spoke Jesus, and lifted up his eyes to heaven, and said,

When speaking to God we should lift up our eyes to heaven: it is vain to focus them upon ourselves. Men all too often close their eyes and minds and drop their heads in prayer. Heaven is the universal expansion of life, and beauty; of joy and love. As we look upwards we can see heaven.

I know the kingdom of heaven is discovered as growing within us. Heaven is God's throne and it is there the Spirit rules with the power of love.

Father, the hour is come; glorify thy Son, that thy Son also may glorify thee:

What is the purpose of this glory? Only this: to excite our love, to win our worship, to beautify our souls, to make perfect our lives. God glorifies himself with ourselves: yet how foolishly we, unlike Jesus, oftentimes find ourselves seeking our own glory.

As thou has given him power over all flesh,

The power given is over flesh: it is not over all things.

that he should give eternal life to as many as thou hast given him.

God gives men to his Sons. Why? So the Sons of God might give them eternal life. God creates men and gives these men to Jesus so that

331

he might give them eternal life. But the blind, the believers in devils, desire men to be as they themselves are: Jesus has also this desire that men become as even he is: a Son of the living God. Who are the Sons of God? Even those who have under Jesus' guidance overcome the world and presently enjoy the kingdom of God. Follow Jesus: make the blind see so they too may inherit eternal life.

And this is life eternal, that they might know thee the only true God,

We know the world is full of many false Gods. Allah is as false as Molech.

and Jesus Christ, whom thou hast sent.

The Father of Jesus Christ is the Lord God of Israel, the only true God. Jesus is not in this his own Father: and those who proclaim Jesus God, and not the Son of God who was created by his Father, instructed by his Father, sent by his Father, are those who prepare for him a crown of thorns.

I have glorified thee on the earth:

On the earth not in the heavens: for the heavens of themselves declare the glory of God as any astronomer open to the truth will readily admit.

I have finished the work which thou gavest me to do, and now, O Father, glorify thou me with thine own self with the glory which I had with thee before the world was.

Jesus had the glory of the Father even before our world, such as it now is, ever was. The phrase "before the world was" emphasizes the beginning of the world: even the world of each man who is created by God and then corrupted by Satan, the powerful prince of his own little world. Jesus saves our world by enabling us to overcome it. Our world is to be ruled by us: not by Satan. Jesus works with God to create heavens for us: we cannot enjoy the heavens unless they be there: God created them and they are there: nevertheless, we cannot sense and enjoy and live eternally within these heavens unless we are enlivened with the Word of God. In this manner, the Word creates. And what power in all the world, can prevail against Jesus and his Word of love?

God has glorified Jesus with his Word: this prayer of Jesus has been answered times innumerable.

I have manifested thy name unto the men which thou gavest me out of the world: thine they were, and thou gavest them me; and they have kept thy word. Now they have known that all things whatsoever thou hast given me are of thee.

Jesus receives from God. The wise men of the east bring him gold, even precious truth discovered in the earth and refined out of it. The truths of science, philosophy, and arts various, as well as the men who are wise in these things, are of God, and are not of the world.

For I have given unto them the words which thou gavest me; and they have received them, and have known surely that I came out from thee, and they have believed that thou didst send me.

What can we peacefully believe in if we do not receive the words Jesus gave us through his disciples? Let us ask those who have received his words, and believed in them, and believe hat God sent Jesus into their world, if there is anything in all the world that they would receive in exchange for those words. Perhaps their witness is true: perhaps God did send Jesus into the world so that we might inherit everlasting life. Nevertheless, Antichrists are many and, for such, simple witnessing is never enough.

I pray for them: I pray not for the world, but for them which thou hast given me; for they are thine.

The world, even as the men of the world speak of the world, is a source of tribulation. What are all the nations of the world, the armies of the world, the laws of the world, the hypocrisy, and vanity and sheer stupidity of the world—what are all these worldly things worth? Our contempt and condemnation for such things are man's substitute for the kingdom of heaven. Let us work God's will in earth: in this way does love's kingdom grow: in this way does the kingdom come: in this way is the nation born.

Zion is the stronghold of Jerusalem. *Zeal in our* own *n*ation establishes the stronghold of truth. *Zest in our* own *n*atures is what strengthens us against the onslaught of lies we receive from the world. Jerusalem is the city of truth which Jesus rules in peace. All tribulation is of the world and is found in the world.

God responds to Jesus' prayers for his loved ones by bringing them the city of truth, even the New Jerusalem, a fitting bride for man's own holy spirit. Fundamentally speaking these things are literally true as any angel of great literature must admit.

And all mine are thine, and thine are mine; and I am glorified in them.

If men cannot see Jesus glorified in the lives of such men as John, and Paul, and these great multitudes of poor in spirit who yet believe in him, perhaps they might see Jesus glorified in Augustine or Milton or Blake or Newton. Nevertheless, for the blind, neither sun, nor moon, nor stars impress them. LET the blind see, O God, so that they might be healed once and forever.

And now I am no more in the world, but these are in the world, and I come to thee. Holy Father, keep through thine own name those whom thou has given me, that they may be one, as we are.

God's name is hallowed by those whom he keeps one with himself. There are many sons of God, angels of God, prophets of God, wise men of God, whom God has kept one with himself. Such do not deny Jesus is the Christ. They rejoice in this fact. God also clothes them with his own glory and in his own name: for those who bring heaven to earth are many.

While I was with them in the world I kept them in thy name: those that thou gavest me I have kept, and none of them is lost, but the son of perdition; that the scripture might be fulfilled.

Who is this son of perdition? Me.

And now come I to thee; and these things I speak in the world, that they might have my joy fulfilled in themselves.

Their joy is Jesus' joy: their sorrow is his sorrow: their victory is his victory.

I have given them thy word; and the world hath hated them, because they are not of the world, even as I am not of the world. I pray not that thou shouldst take them out of the world, but that thou shouldst keep them from the evil.

Why? Because knowledge of evil makes one a son of perdition. Men are made fools when they glut themselves with corrupt fruit. They cannot handle knowledge of both good and evil: they cannot choose wisely among the branches of this tree.

No wonder idiots can boast: Truman shortened the war by using the atomic bombs to destroy Hiroshima and Nagasaki. Yet, in all truth, he did not shorten it: he enlarged it.

Nevertheless, although Truman has passed away, many other sons of perdition remain, wantonly disporting themselves with the mechanisms which could destroy all flesh.

Yet God keeps his beloved from this, as well as many other, great evils.

They are not of the world, even as I am not of the world.

Thank God Jesus is not of the world!

Sanctify them through thy truth: thy word is truth.

What is the truth? It is raining gently even during the State's greatest drought. In this way is the power of heaven brought to a dried up and lifeless soul.

The word makes us holy: it is done in no other way.

As thou has sent me into the world, even so have I also sent them into the world.

Governments various send ambassadors and armies alike into the world: the churches send missionaries into the world.

God sends Jesus and his prophets into the world. Whom has Jesus sent into the world? Even his disciples: those who continue in his word and know the truth. What truth? Even that God loves them and that the world hates them. The world hates the truth because if it loved the truth it would vanish and be no more. Yet I talk of the world that shall end: not of the world that God loves and which God saves.

Are there many worlds? Of course.

And for their sakes I sanctify myself, that they also might be sanctified through the truth.

Truth makes whole: the lie makes devils* of us all.

*Or, if you prefer, schizophrenics

Neither pray I for these alone, but for them also which shall believe on me through their word. That they all may be one; as thou, Father art in me, and I in thee, that they also may be one in us: that the world may believe that thou hast sent me.

When the world believes, the world is saved. The world that does not believe is destroyed. Why? Because it's not worth saving.

And the glory which thou gavest me I have given them; that they may be one, even as we are one:

What glory? Knowledge we all are God's children.

I in them, and thou in me, that they may be made perfect in one; and that the world may know that thou hast sent me, and hast loved them, as thou hast loved me.

The world is a slow learner.

Father, I will that they also, whom thou hast given me, be with me where I am;

Where is this? Obviously, right here on this little planet earth, because when you really understand what Jesus is saying, you'll have to confess that he's been hanging around with us all these years. And for a purpose.

Father, I will that they also, whom thou hast given me, be with me where I am;

If men didn't have the scale of worldly pride covering their eyes they surely could see Jesus is still on this earth living and tasting of death with them.

that they may behold my glory, which thou hast given me: for thou lovest me before the foundation of the world. O righteous Father, the world hath not known thee:

(meekly put)

but I have known thee, and these have known that thou hast sent me.

Let each man examine carefully what he means when he claims he "knows": for belief is one thing, and knowledge is another.

And I have declared unto them thy name,

And so he did.

and will declare it:

And so he does.

that the love wherewith thou hast loved me may be in them, and I in them.

The love within Jesus is too great for his heart alone to carry.

CHAPTER 18

When Jesus had spoken these words, he went forth with his disciples over the brook Cedron, where was a garden, into the which he entered, and his disciples. And Judas also, which betrayed him, knew the place: for Jesus ofttimes resorted thither with his disciples. Judas then, having received a band of men and officers from the chief priests and Pharisees, cometh thither with lanterns and torches and weapons.

The thing I so greatly love about Judas is his willingness to quickly act out his beliefs. Money is powerful in the world: it energizes many sinful enterprises. Chief priests ensconce themselves in the social structure and feed themselves with the labor of God's poor: such succeed in acquiring the money necessary to sustain themselves in their opulent vanity. But who is a chief priest? Men who hold high office and conspire with the teachers of vanity to crucify Jesus. Yet, big deals are accomplished by little men only because of the steadfast determination of Satan's helpers. Judas is necessary because without him we'd still be arguing what to do on the Sabbath.

In all truth, I'm almost too bored to continue developing the point. Thank God for Judas. Satan tempts Judas with the thought Jesus is a mawkish messiah; and Judas, believing it so, betrays Jesus to the chief priests who hire such officers and men as they find in their deceitful world. Since men who serve Mammon, serve not God, the authority of our chiefs is incontestable. Taxes and tithes are the source of power with which chief priests, Pharisees, and lawyers control the lives of Mammon serving officers and men. And even the scribes, who at one time wrote for the hell of it, now charge ten cents a word and up. It takes a Judas, however, to set them all in motion.

Thank God for Judas, otherwise this story would have no end and Jesus would have perished in an endless circle of circumlocution.

Only Jesus, his disciples and the men Judas received have the courage to cross over Cedron.

Jesus therefore, knowing all things that should come upon him, went forth, and said unto them, Whom seek ye?

I hate to edit John, for his literary genius is impeccable: nevertheless, what Jesus is saying here is, What the hell do you guys want?

They answered him, Jesus of Nazareth. Jesus saith unto them, I am he. And Judas also, which betrayed him, stood with them. As soon then as he had said unto them, I am he, they went backward, and fell to the ground.

It's impossible to take Jesus the first time he reveals himself to those who are led by Judas.

Then asked he them again, Whom seek ye? And they said, Jesus of Nazareth. Jesus answered, I have told you that I am he: if therefore ye seek me, let these go their way.

It's the Jesus of Nazareth who is taken. The Jesus of Revelation cannot be taken. The teacher clothed with the wisdom of God's gospel is one aspect of Jesus' life: but it is only one facet of his personality: Judas, who understands Satan so well, only lately has begun to realize there is more to Jesus than what he originally thought.

That the saying might be fulfilled, which he spake, Of them which thou gavest me have I lost none.

Which is true since Jesus chose to wander within the wilderness of sin until I had found all who had been given him. Men are conceited: they do not take their own sins seriously. Jesus is Israel's scapegoat in spite of the fact they prefer superman. God is the giver: Jesus is the redeemer. God is the Savior: Jesus is also saved, albeit he, as do many who love him, also save: they also may be called saviors.

For those who can't see this clearly, let me add that Jesus saves our souls even as some men so cleverly save us money, time, and energy; to say nothing of jobs, reputation, and trouble. Men also save us very many other things: but let them boast of it.

Then Simon Peter having a sword drew it, and smote the high priest's servant, and cut off his right ear. The servant's name was Malchus.

His right ear? Let Malchus hereby be consoled: he lost his ear, but John preserved his name unto this very day.

Then said Jesus unto Peter, Put up thy sword unto the sheath: the cup which my Father hath given me, shall I not drink of it?

God pours us a powerful drink. No wonder so many of us so frequently get drunk. Yet how else can we fortify ourselves against the vanities of the coming weekend? Even Peter the Great could not control himself when it came to dealing with the Babylonian conceits of the Eastern Orthodox Church which is the puerile product of such Pharisees, chief priests, and scribes that produced it. I sympathize with Peter's zeal: nevertheless, their servants need all the help they can get to understand the hypocrisy of their master's babble. They need both ears.

Then the band and the captain and the officers of the Jews took Jesus, and bound him.

Good. We're finally getting down to the flesh and blood reality of this story. Angels of intellect are anemic. We are saved by water and by blood. Our pain is real: our suffering is real: our bodies are real. But men who have been overpowered by the machine, but who nonetheless pride themselves on punching a button now and then, confuse the Satanic response with the actions of God. Judas went to the high priests, as every Judas does, since he could not receive armed men from any other source. Yet it was Peter who first drew the sword and poor Malchus was the first to suffer the consequences of such actions. Peter, even as Judas, has his trouble with the machine. The machine, the ultimate social computer, is to be used, not obeyed. To obey it, is to become, as so many men have become, an automaton.

Contrast is necessary: alternatives are presented for our thought: there do exist many intricate things for fools to do. But why do them? Knowledge of evil is knowledge of what the Pope, the President of the United States, and the Chairman of the Communist Party are doing. And what are they doing? Violating the commandments of God. How so? By worshiping the idols of their own mind. These chief priests are the deceived deceivers of the present hour. Solomon himself put the manner plainly: all is vanity. Why? Because without God all is vanity: our wisdom, as heaven and earth itself, passes away.

It is good to eat of the tree of life and nurture the kingdom of heaven growing within us. Those of us who believe in the words of Jesus are the kingdom of heaven. But chief priests desire to rule us in the place of God. They desire to make us the bondslaves of their own laws, and ways, and silly doctrines.

Am I my brother's keeper? Of course not: yet so many silly asses will conspire to mark us, number us, buy us, and sell us, so that their images of law, religion, and money may be worshipped. And they do this in terms of brotherly love, or world peace, or revolution; or they boast of how they're going to preserve and guarantee our rights or our energy or our life or our freedom or our health or our water or our environment and many other such things which we freely receive from God but which they hypocritically take unto themselves.

Know men by the fruit of their lips: if they speak truth and sacrifice their bodies to God, they will not shut up the kingdom of heaven against you. But with lies, vanities incredible, money, and law, the high priests of mammon and the disciples of bureaucratic bullshit, flood the earth. From the many, one: such is their motto.

I delight in the many mansions of my Father's house. What he parts, and singly approves, none may sunder. What he joins, none may part. But those who generate evil pollute and adulterate God's work with their own additions and subtractions. They add to it: they take away from it. Don't let the chief priests take Jesus from you. The last time they took him, they defaced him beyond recognition. Accept the words for yourself: then the Spirit of Truth can teach you how to enjoy everlasting life. The words of Jesus are without price.

Why keep yourself from such a great treasure? All Judas had to say is simple to understand. Jesus is not the Son of God. Jesus Christ has not come in the flesh. In this lie, both Judas and the high priests confirm themselves. Satan is too much for them: so why not reward them good for evil? How? By telling them the truth: the kingdom of heaven is ruled by the God within you and you have no need of their works, or words, or feeble ideals. They also must learn of Jesus.

Did Jesus tell them this? Of course, but they've hardened their heart against him. Their God is Satan: their king is Caesar.

Jesus is bound and taken away. Let's observe what men who bind him to themselves with the power of Jewish custom and worldly hypocrisy and Roman power do with him when he submits to them.

And led him away to Annas first; for he was father in law to Caiaphas, which was the high priest that same year.

Many men make themselves fathers-in-law to high priests. The State and Church fathers conceive laws: and many men marry themselves to their pathetic doctrines and make themselves high priest for a year or some other term of office.

Now Caiaphas was he, which gave counsel to the Jews, that it was expedient that one man should die for the people.

Caiaphas herein is a true high priest of the living God. With God, one man is enough. But Washington requires thousands: Lincoln requires multiplied tens of thousands: Roosevelt and Churchill and Hitler and Stalin and Chiang Kai-shek and Mao Tse-tung each required multiplied millions. The warlords with us today, however, require billions of dollars to provide for the destruction of billions of people. Man, as Man, is a false prophet: for in all their expedient slaughters nothing good is ever accomplished.

Jesus beat his sword into a plowshare a long time ago: and even I disdain to create a hydrogen bomb and hide it in my garage. We are disarmed. But hypocrites who have at their command the weapon systems of death preach disarmament. The hypocrisy of it all is astonishing.

Three cheers for Caiaphas and the wisdom of his counsel!

And Simon Peter followed Jesus, and so did another disciple: that disciple was known unto the high priest, and went into the palace of the high priest.

For those of us, who, like Jesus and John, enjoy life within the atmosphere of earth, in which air of life, many creatures live and move and declare the glory of God, the shack of the high priest is a letdown. Little men require a palace in which their tiny voices might be amplified. Those who love the uppermost places are with us today. Cathedrals, temples, mosques, and the many Roman arenas dot the landscape of God's earth. Devils, like Mao Tse-tung, who roam from cave to cave, and from hovel to hovel, are apt to end up eventually in some high priests' palace. And then they take from these little men all the trappings wherein they trusted.

Why are men so blind to their vanities?

But Peter stood at the door without. Then went out that other disciple, which was known unto the high priest, and spake unto her that kept the door, and brought in Peter.

It is easier to get Peter into the high priest's palace than it is to get him to enter into the kingdom of heaven. Why? Because he is awed by the temples of men and feels uncomfortable in the universe of God. The trappings of priestcraft still impress him: angelic vanities still delight him: and though he eats the worldly fare of both Gentile and Jew, he's more fascinated with the great men he has caught within the net of his own kingdom of heaven, than he is with those sheep who follow Jesus.

Then saith the damsel that kept the door unto Peter, Art not thou also one of this man's disciples? He saith, I am not.

Indeed, he speaks truly. For he is not: not yet, anyway. Why? Because he's occupied with his own business.

And the servants and officers stood there, who had made a fire of coals; for it was cold: and they warmed themselves: and Peter stood with them and warmed himself.

The servants and officers of the high priests of Mammon abound in the land. We dwell among them: warm ourselves with the fires they provide. All who have never stood in God's lake of fire, those who really haven't been subjected to God's fiery judgment of truth, must warm themselves in this way or else experience the cold discomfort of the world's cruelty. The angels of intellect are anemic, however; and we ought not to begrudge them the manner in which they warm themselves. Nevertheless, I despise lukewarm opinions: be hot or be cold. Believe the gospel and become a disciple: or reject it. You can change your mind later. But these brilliant minds who think, and examine, and analyze, and collect, and compare, are used by devils and Pharisees alike to prove whatsoever it pleases them to prove. With such, I can do nothing except reject their words. In fact, whenever I find myself becoming ill with their tepid messages. I vomit: have I not better things of which to drink?

The high priest then asked Jesus of his disciples, and of his doctrine.

Jesus speaks openly to the world. The gospels may be read in a single day: the gospel believed in a moment of time. The high priest of your religion, however, handles Jesus in his own way. How does the pope inquire of and ask of Jesus? How does Luther handle Jesus? What does Sun Myung Moon or Mary Baker Eddy or the president of the Mormon Church, or Joseph Smith himself, ask of Jesus? What does Jimmy Carter ask of Jesus, for is he not a high priest of the system, this Democracy in which so many lawyers and law-abiding citizens place their trust? What does Muhammad ask of Jesus? A high priest is a high priest and even though many of them are blind to their own priestly role, since they continuously ask for sacrifices various and yet know not what they do, let us, who even in this night enjoy the inner light of truth, know them for what they are. Surely, their sacrifices of lives, of money, of talent, of work, of people, are vain.

I rejoice in the wisdom of Caiaphas. He knew what to sacrifice, and did so. But all these others are the blind priests of ancient

Pharaohs, corrupting themselves with Egyptian technology, Greek wisdom, and Roman law. The only sacrifice of heavenly worth is to offer our body to God, even the God of life, of joy, of pleasure. High priests have nothing to do with us, except to learn of us.

Jesus answered him, I spake openly to the world; I ever taught in the synagogue, and in secret have I said nothing.

Contrast this with the methods used by the governments of the world: their secret councils, their secret organizations, their secret lists; their secret police, their secret weapon systems, their secret prophets and operators; their secret intelligence agencies, their secret commercial transactions, their secret processes; their secret documents; their secret industrial and literary patents; their secret scientific discoveries.

No wonder they're so fearful! The world is so full of secrets they really don't know what the hell is happening. Nevertheless, God shall bring all things to light; and even our secret prayers shall be publically answered.

From those whom Jesus taught, the chief priests have much to learn.

Why askest thou me? Ask them which heard me, what I have said unto them: behold, they know what I said.

A snotty answer, to be sure: yet it is really good advice. Pity, so many high priests still refuse to take it.

And when he had thus spoken, one of the officers which stood by struck Jesus with the palm of his hand, saying, Answerest thou the high priest so? Jesus answered him, If I have spoken evil, bear witness of the evil: but if well, why smitest thou me?

Poor servants of poor high priests: they regard not the truth, but only the high priest. We tell them the truth, and they strike us for it. Men are what they are: am I to be denied what I am because of their priestly delusions? God forbid.

Now Annas had sent him bound unto Caiaphas the high priest.

Jesus is still bound up in the mentality of many and ill-treated there.

And Simon Peter stood and warmed himself. They said therefore unto him, Art not thou also one of his disciples?

So asks the social machine of us all: it is really Satan who inquires of us, our beliefs. A yes ends the matter. But a no will prompt yet another inquiry. The time shall come when the question will prove profitless and the usefulness of the machine will end. Yet men are still deceived by it. They know not how great they are destined to become: indeed, many even this day know not how great they are. For they can overcome it if only they believe in the Christ who commands them to do just that. Really, Satan's power is a bit of a joke. Muhammad, Lenin, and Mao Tse-tung are great false prophets, for they are greatly false. If that pisses off a billion or more souls, what is that to me? They have to learn the truth sometime. In some things men have no choice whatsoever: this is one of them.

He denied it, and said, I am not.

I hope Peter will understand: but at this point it's really kind of funny.

One of the servants of the high priest, being his kinsman whose ear Peter cut off, saith, Did not I see thee in the garden with him?

What garden? The Garden of Eden, wherein we enjoy the paradise of delight the spirit of truth has prepared for us.

Peter then denied again: and immediately the cock crew.

What cock? Even the *c*ouncil *o*f *c*ruel *k*ings who constantly review evil and wickedness. Why are they cruel? Because in so doing they wrongly accuse us and condemn us for doing what God intended us to do. We believe in the prophecies of Jesus, even all of them, and in his words, even all of them, and they call us fools. There are kings who are of God: and there are kings who serve Satan and use us cruelly. We are of heaven: and they are full of so much knowledge of good and evil, that they poison the world with their products. And what is their product? a world wherein Jesus, and the Word of God, does not rule. A world of controversy: of divided opinion: of deceits: of laws many and vain: of crusades, of wars, of babble, of money, of taxation: the world of the lawyers: the world of religious teachers, the Pharisees of the present hour: the world of silly scribes who pollute the world with the vain products of their own godless imagination.

Nevertheless, let us forgive them their trespasses, root up and destroy their silly ideas as they rise within our own kingdom of spiritual life, and move on to enjoy what the Spirit who makes his word flesh gives us.

The kings of pride crow only to wake us to God's morning.

Then led they Jesus from Caiaphas unto the hall of judgment: and it was early;

Early judgments are oftentimes unrighteous: men glory in the dawn of a new truth, and angelic wisdom is transformed into human pride. Let God save us all from our own selves. The Sons of god should love their creator: from whence comes pride? From ourselves. We are born to be commanded of God and to manifest his glory. Nevertheless, what do we do with God's first begotten son when he is brought before us in the judgment hall of our own minds?

and they themselves went not into the judgment hall, lest they should be defiled;

In this, the Jews acted wisely. The judgment halls of Rome defile men. Vengeance is God's; ever does it belong to the righteous Lord God of Israel. Jesus commanded love, forgiveness, mercy, and truth. But the Romans, the lawyers of the present age, are full of defilements: for these proud hypocrites judge according to their own selfish interests. Beware of courts of law and those who love to serve Satan within them. Judge with God, not against him.

but that they might eat the passover.

When we Jews eat the Lamb of God, even when we consume his Word made flesh, and drink the bloody truth contained within his own cup of life, we pass over from death unto life. Let us then pass over the tribulation, and the sorrow, and the wanderings we experience in a land wherein God is not and enjoy God with us. Is God with us? Of course he is: for he is either cursing us or blessing us: for he is always perfecting us.

Pilate then went out unto them, and said, What accusation bring ye against this man?

The pilots of the ship of state are always seeking accusations, for they are our accusers and guide us into their courts for their own selfish and monetary purposes. What we drink: what we smoke: what we speak: what we refuse to speak: what we publish: what we see: what we produce: what we have: whom we obey, and whom we don't obey: are some of the many matters with which these babbling founts of wisdom occupy themselves.

I love these Jews for the genius of God abides ever with them for they know that any Roman procurator, as any prosecuting attorney today, can find something with which to accuse, and condemn, and persecute, any man. The servants of Rome are full of accusations against us and surely need not receive any more from the poor Jews.

Then said Pilate unto them, Take ye him, and judge him according to your law.

This is really good advice: yet even Pilate couldn't see any profit in judging Jesus.

The Jews therefore said unto him, It is not lawful for us to put any man to death: That the saying of Jesus might be fulfilled, which he spake, signifying what death he should die.

There are, of course, many different deaths. To taste of some, is not unpleasant.

Then Pilate entered into the judgment hall again.

I wonder where he went in the meantime.

and called Jesus, and said unto him, Art thou the King of the Jews? Jesus answered him, Sayest thou this thing of thyself, or did others tell it thee of me? Pilate answered, Am I a Jew?

Of course he is a Jew since he is also a *Jehovah's witness*.

Thine own nation and the chief priests have delivered thee unto me: what hast thou done?

The truth is Jesus had done a lot of things, but Pilate really wasn't interested in receiving an answer.

Jesus answered, My kingdom is not of this world:

True. The kingdom Jesus received is the kingdom given him by his God; even our Father, our Lord, our husbandman; the Lord of Hosts and the Lord God of Israel. And that kingdom is not of this world: for this world is a world of money, hypocrisy, manmade laws, accusations, senseless strife, vanity, Pharisaical delusions, and Jimmy Carter. Nevertheless, let all of Jesus' adversaries rejoice in this fact: the cunning Jesus has planted the seeds of his kingdom even in their own fields although they still don't understand the simplest of facts concerning how it grows and how it is harvested. They are choked up with the cares of their own perishing world and really could not care less about Jesus and his kingdom of love. How are they then his adversaries if they ignore him and care nothing for his kingdom or his ways? Only in this: he has brought a sword against them: even the sharp word of truth. They are so full of councils, and committees, and bureaus that they don't even realize a war exists between God and the State. They probably referred God's declaration of war to some junior officer serving the Council of Foreign Affairs who inadvertently round-filed it while he was eyeing the ass of his secretary.

if my kingdom were of this world, then would my servants fight,

Sounds ominous since if the Romans ever begin to see Jesus' kingdom coming of this world, the friends of Caesar might not have so easy a time handling Jesus especially in light of the fact that Jesus identifies himself with even the least of his brethren.

that I should not be delivered to the Jews: but now is my kingdom not from hence.

If the kingdom of Jesus was not to come from either the world of the Romans or the world of the Jews or the world of that time, from whence is it?

Obviously, from God, our Father. We receive it from him and not from the world. But what can we say to the world that judges Jesus and scourges him, and mocks him in a purple robe; and deals with him as the soldiers of Rome and the soldiers of Herod treat him?

Bye, bye. (Be ye enlightened, an acronym with double meaning.)

Pilate therefore said unto him, Art thou a king then? Jesus answered, Thou sayest that I am a King. To this end was I born,

His end is to be a King.

and for this cause came I into the world, that I should bear witness unto the truth.

Truth requires witnesses?

Every one that is of the truth heareth my voice.

Do you hear the voice of this King?

Pilate saith unto him, What is truth?

Too bad, as one angel expressed it, he didn't stay for an answer.

And when he had said this, he went out again unto the Jews, and saith unto them, I find in him no fault at all.

What did he find in him?

But ye have a custom, that I should release unto you one at the passover:

Let each soul release itself from custom's control on its own passover.

will ye that I release unto you the King of the Jews?

What say you Jews, shall you accept this man as your King?

Then cried they all again, saying, Not this man, but Barabbas. Now Barabbas was a robber.

And what have the Jews done with Barabbas? I am not widely read: but if they have done anything at all with him, I would be glad to hear it: for the scribes are silent on this matter.

CHAPTER 19

Then Pilate therefore took Jesus, and scourged him.

A typical Roman custom: it has nothing to do with the Passover: or any other feast day, for that matter.

And the soldiers plaited a crown of thorns, and put it on his head, and they put on him a purple robe.

Soldiers often crown Jesus king then go out and kill for the hell of it. Christians who kill their enemies, instead of loving them, clothe Jesus in a purple robe of mock authority.

And said, Hail, King of the Jews! and they smote him with their hands.

It's hard for them to do this today, however, since their hands are full of rifles, automatic weapons, hand grenades, the controls of a variety of weapon systems, and the latest orders from some officer confirmed by the senate. In this Protestants, Catholics, and Jews are all alike sinners. One noteworthy thing about Muhammad is that he preached death to the infidels: yet he is as mocked as Christ, since his servants don't kill Christians anymore, they sell them oil. The hypocrisy of the world is astonishing: and so is this notable King of the Jews who suffers it all.

Pilate therefore went forth again, and saith unto them, Behold, I bring him forth to you, that ye may know that I find no fault in him.

Obviously, Pilate is not a man to find fault in appearances.

Then came Jesus forth, wearing the crown of thorns, and the purple robe. And Pilate saith unto them, Behold the man!

And so we have, all these centuries.

When the chief priests therefore saw him, they cried out saying, Crucify him, crucify him. Pilate saith unto them, Take ye him, and crucify him: for I find no fault in him.

And so the masses do: for Christ is sacrificed daily not only in the Sacrifice of the Mass but in the mass media: for they crucify his brethren without cause. But the masses are deceived and know not what they do. But what can we judge of those Pharisees and scribes who feed the masses with their own doctrines and writings instead of with the Word of God?

Let us feed upon the word: and let those who feed upon Babylonian bullshit and constitutional crap submit themselves to God for cleansing for how else might they be saved from the folly of their own pride and hypocrisy?

The Jews answered him, We have a law, and by our law he ought to die, because he made himself the Son of God.

Let all those who have overcome the world, and know themselves as the Sons of God, ask the Jews where they got this law.

When Pilate therefore heard that saying, he was the more afraid; And went again into the judgment hall, and saith unto Jesus, Whence art thou? But Jesus gave him no answer.

Jesus came from God, Pilate.

Then saith Pilate unto him, Speakest thou not unto me? knowest thou not that I have power to crucify thee, and have power to release thee?

From whence did Pilate receive this power? In fact, from whence do these present heads of state receive their power?

Jesus answered, Thou couldest have no power at all against me, except it were given thee from above: therefore he that delivered me unto thee hath the greater sin.

Who is this? Who delivers Jesus to Pilate? Who delivers Jesus to this friend of Caesar? Who delivers Jesus to this newly found friend of Herod?

Let me keep Jesus to myself: let me keep his words to myself: let me obey his commandments of love. For they are not grievous: some of my enemies are a bit gross and hard to love: yet some of my enemies, to say nothing of my bikini-clad neighbors, are so beautiful it is impossible not to love them instantly.

And from thenceforth Pilate sought to release him: but the Jews cried out, saying, If thou let this man go, thou art not Caesar's friend: whosoever maketh himself a king speaketh against Caesar.

In this, the genius of the Jews is seen. For Caesar, as all Caesars, are the petty kings of the earth who keep God from being King over the souls he has created for his own pleasure. A man is born to be a king over his own soul and a priest expressive of his own doctrines. But various Caesars violently assault the kingdom of heaven given to us of God and rob us of our pleasures and joys in life so that they may enjoy being lords, and rulers, and chief priests, and dictators, and captains, and princes, and kings over us.

Yet God never intended it so: no, not from the beginning, nor even to this very day. The Lord God of Israel is our King: we have need of no other. When Love rules us and we are guided by the Spirit of Truth, we cannot be seized and taken captive by the kings of earth and pride. What then is Caesar's?

When Pilate therefore heard that saying, he brought Jesus forth, and sat down in the judgment seat in a place that is called the Pavement, but in the Hebrew, Gabbatha.

God, having seen how the Hebrews had made of judgment seats thrones for gabblers, allowed the Romans to pave the place over with their own hard laws. True, the Roman way is cruel and hard: yet it leads somewhere: to a cross, to a battlefield, to an arena. But whoever got anyplace arguing with a duck?

And it was the preparation of the passover, and about the sixth hour: and he saith unto the Jews, Behold your King!

Poor Pilate! Even today his descendants can't get the Jews to take a good look at Jesus. All they see is his marred image.

But they cried out, Away with him, away with him, crucify him. Pilate saith unto them, Shall I crucify your King?

I think Pilate is here being sarcastic rather than incredulous or hard of hearing. But I offer my opinion only since those who today assume Pilate's role are weird and hard for me to understand.

The chief priests answered, We have no king but Caesar.

In this, the chief priests and the servants of Rome are in agreement. Popes and presidents, or chief priests and emperors, or wizards and pharaohs, are all fashioned of the same mold. They all want to rule God's people so that they might retain their seat in some organizational pyramid of state or church. They divide a man in half: his body to the state and his soul to the church. I marvel we are not all schizophrenic.

Then delivered he him therefore unto them to be crucified. And they took Jesus and led him away. And he bearing his cross went forth into a place called the place of a skull, which is called in the Hebrew Golgotha:

(Which is an acronym for Gods only love going on to heaven always—and always also means all ways.) Even by way of the cross? Why not? Beats getting quacked to death by a foul-mouthed gabbler.

Where they crucified him, and two others with him, on either side one, and Jesus in the midst.

The thieves who stole their way into heaven, (for do they not live also in my heart), have yet to tell us their story.

And Pilate wrote a title, and put it on the cross. And the writing was, Jesus of Nazareth the King of the Jews. This title then read many of the Jews: for the place where Jesus was crucified was nigh to the city: and it was written in Hebrew, and Greek, and Latin.

This was in the beginning. In the end it is also written in many other tongues.

The sign of the cross is a sure sign. And what does the sign say? Jesus Christ is the King of the Jews? For those who can't accept Pilate's writing, namely, This is Jesus of Nazareth the King of the Jews, God has written through his angel another message: Jesus Christ is the King of the Jews. Perhaps they can accept that.

Then said the chief priests of the Jews to Pilate, Write not, the King of the Jews; but that he said, I am King of the Jews.

A nice distinction: nevertheless, did Jesus say that? No, he did not. Jesus bears witness to the truth: and the truth is he is king over those who love him. When will he be king of the Jews? When Jehovah's Witnesses become Jesus' Witnesses, and the dead body of believers which are Moses' body, together with the dead body of believers which are Elias's body, ascend up into the heaven of eternal life; and when these dead witnesses of God no longer stink up the city streets of Sodom and Egypt. But why haven't the Sodomites, those who accumulate salt without savor, those tasteless potato heads of this unbelieving modern era, buried the body of Moses? Because they rejoice in dead carcasses and tasteless topics of religious babble and priestly bullshit. And what of the city of Egypt, the city where evil gods yearly pollute truth with silly ceremonies, technological absurdities, idolatrous images, and other such burdensome tasks with which they enslave both themselves and the new born children of Israel? Why don't they bury these two great witnesses of the living God? Because they love to embalm bodies rather than resurrect the dead. But I speak of cities of people united by a complex bond of commercial and cultural activities and not of surveyed parcels of land. Pyramids of waste are produced by the priestly dullards who oversee the miracles of modern technology.

Man is a miracle worker. No doubt about it. But men of technological skill and genius who worship serpents are idolaters. But who are serpents but Pharisees: and who are *Pharisees* but *Pharaoh's* industrious and self-enlightened emissaries bringing the gospel of Pharaoh and the fear of serpents (for they generate their own fears) to many nations of the earth?

If men would focus their attention on the evolution of ideas instead of on the multiplying creatures of God, perhaps they could begin to understand some plain truth about their foolish priests and wise men and sorcerers.

Moses, as Elijah, is dead to the truth of his own body and his own resurrection. In this, they share with Jesus a common fate. And what is that? To discuss these matters in heaven. Nevertheless, for those who cannot see that Jesus is anointed by the prophet of God to be the King of the Jews, these words have no meaning. Yet Jesus is not dead to these truths: why then should these other two witnesses be dead to them?

Pilate answered, What I have written I have written. Then the soldiers, when they had crucified Jesus, took his garments and made four parts, to every soldier a part;

One part for the Catholic: one part for the Muhammadan: one part for the Protestant: and one part for the Jew. Are such soldiers of Rome? Today they are, for surely they delight in Roman law, Roman justice, Roman ways, and Roman gods. Yet they can't understand what Rome is, or was, or can never be. But that's not the point. The garments of Jesus are found where they are found.

and also his coat: now the coat was without seam, woven from the top throughout. They said therefore among themselves, Let us not rend it, but cast lots for it, whose it shall be: that the scripture might be fulfilled, which saith, They parted my raiment among them, and for my vesture they did cast lots. These things therefore the soldiers did.

Who won the lottery? The pope.

Now there stood by the cross of Jesus his mother, and his mother's sister, Mary the wife of Cleophas, and Mary Magdelene. When Jesus therefore saw his mother,

Who is his mother? Those who hear the word of God and do it for in this the will of God is done.

and the disciple standing by, whom he loved,

What disciple doesn't he love?

he saith unto his mother, Woman behold thy son!

What woman? Even that woman ravished by the spirit of truth and out of whom the Son of man came.

Then saith he to the disciple, Behold thy mother! And from that hour that disciple took her unto his own home.

What disciple? And where is that disciple now? And where is his home?

Continue in the word: become a disciple: and answer for yourself: for I find Jill St. John more exciting in living flesh and blood than all these saintly riddles combined.

After this, Jesus knowing that all things were now accomplished, that the scripture might be fulfilled, saith, I thirst.

I know the feeling.

Now there was set a vessel full of vinegar: and they filled a sponge with vinegar, and put it upon hyssop, and put it to his mouth. When Jesus therefore had received the vinegar, he said, It is finished

Why did it end with such a sour taste? Because of the answer God gave to his cry, My God, my God, why have you forsaken me?

I think so. And what was God's answer?

You are your own God.

and he bowed his head, and gave up the ghost.

God's host left him. He commended his spirit to his Father. And who is his Father? I would to God I knew.

The fruit of knowledge has increased: many run to and fro even within the world of their own minds. The flood of nonsense produced by Satan is incredible: had it not been foretold, I could scarce believe the report of mine own ears and eyes. And yet here I am: cut off, helpless, alone. Men minister nonsense to one another and the greatness of God is despised. Sour grapes on my part, I know: but thus must it be. I cannot deny the truth.

When we finish one life, God receives our spirit back to himself and plants it again withersoever she desires. God also has her ways: God is the bride of our soul. Our fears are vain. Let us even in this death enjoy life abundantly, for why should the pleasures of paradise be scorned? What is pleasure? to love one another within the garden of delight.

The *story* of *one* is finished: one more stone added to the new Jerusalem: the city wherein I enjoy the peaceful reign of my own soul. Yet now am I troubled. In death I experience the ferment of many ideas: words produce visions, thoughts, possibilities, questions. This is my cross: to endure that which my God makes of me.

The story of one Son of God, Jesus of Nazareth, is finished. It is true that the stone, even the living stone of that life, is mine to enjoy and to share with those who know me within the walls of truth which separate fact from fiction: reality from myth: the wisdom of God from the foolishness of men.

What next? I dream my dreams: cultivate my desires: harvest my thoughts: enjoy the truth and fruit of mine own tree of life. Yet the universe of my God is wonderful and I have no more time to discuss the mysteries of life with those who love death.

I have a commandment to take up my life: and to lay it down: and a commandment to take it up again. My God is our refuge: we are his sons. Our greatest joy is found in giving pleasure to the Spirit which eternally enlivens us. Even in death we live unto him. But many, if not all, once were dead to these simple facts, these plain perceptions, these crystal clear truths. But what of that? I was dead but am alive forevermore.

Our Father works, and we work. Our Father creates, enlivens, perfects: we do the same. Our Father seeks his own, and so do we.

I witness to the God within me. Let the God in whom I am bear witness to what I am: for what I am, what man knows? My words are spirit: they are what I am: and I am one within my God. Be one in me, and I in you, and all of us one in God. For who can really make one from many and many from one except our God? Surely, I know of no other. The works of men are vain: varied and marvelous and wonderful though they seem. They vanish in a moment of time and are gone forever. We are within a new heaven: enjoy the fruits of a new earth.

What comes next? Another life. Another adventure within the kingdom of our God. You have your beliefs. I have mine. You have your ways: I have mine. Why should we strive one against the other forever? Surely, all strife ends within Jerusalem.

Jerusalem, the city of the great king: the city of truth within us: the city of peace Jesus rules: the city wherein righteousness establishes peace, for salem is part of Jerusalem, and the effect of righteousness is peace—this city is glorified by Jews, who witness to it with their lives, and by Gentiles, whose genius, talents, and inspiration given by God Almighty, are used by God to enlighten men's minds even to the saving of their souls. God is the light of this city which comes to us from heaven. In this city the Lamb of God and the Lion of Judah are at peace and lie down together. It is the city within me and the city in which I dwell. It is the city of God. One city in a universe so vast, I marvel at what is contained in the one word, heaven.

God's will is done in earth: for what is this city except it be our bride, even the bride of our soul, that source of universal love which we are? Why not come to it, glorify it, live within it? The invitation extends to all. We are all men: we are of earth, of flesh, of blood, of bone: yet the city is of truth and light and love: it is a city of the Spirit, even that spirit who is love. For love and truth and beauty and joy everlasting live within us and so shall they be forever. Heaven and earth pass away: but the angels of love pass over us only to come again: for the spirits of God ever return and are everlastingly the same. Be wed to one of them and live forever.

Who is my Father? God, the loving spirit of heaven and earth: and man in whom my Creator works. And who am I? the son of my Father and the father of my son. As it is with me, so is it with all God's children: for the sons of God are many and are gods in their own right.

The Jews therefore, because it was the preparation, that the bodies should not remain upon the cross on the sabbath day (for that sabbath day was a high day,) besought Pilate that their legs might be broken, and that they might be taken away.

Who are those Jews who seek after the procurators and Roman governors of Judaea to kill those thieves whose crucifixion and suffering on the Sabbath day is an embarrassment to them? In the spiritual sense, Jehovah's Witnesses, even all who witness to his intervention in the affairs of men, whether good or evil, whether Nebuchadnezzar or the Shah of Iran; whether Muhammad or Muhammad Ali; whether Jezebel or some silly pope who names himself a saint and marks himself with the number of a man; whether David or Goliath: all such witness to the glory of the Lord God of Hosts: all such are Jews. The thieves who suffer justly under Roman law, but not under God's law, are Jesus' Witnesses, and also Jews. Nevertheless, some are blessed: others are cursed. David and Jesus are both blessed and cursed: for they are blessed with the promises of God and cursed with the sins of an unbelieving world.

The Jews do right to seek the death of those who suffer: for the cruel Romans would prolong our suffering beyond the bounds of time if they could: nevertheless, this God does not allow. They can kill the body: then their power vanishes and the soul returns to the God who gave it life.

Yet men know not what they do. For the righteous rebukes and judgments of God they substitute the laws of men. Thus lawyers take away the key of knowledge and shut up the kingdom of heaven against men.

Some men are able to see this and like Abel offer their sacrifice to God in all righteousness. But these Canaanites are without shame and even slay the righteous with impunity. For the law of God which is love acquiring wisdom they substitute the law of themselves, which is lust after wickedness: these latter serve Satan and think themselves wise because they have some knowledge of good and evil. Lawyers are idiots, for they worship themselves and their self-made laws and reject the commandment of God.

But God is merciful to all, and in the fullness of time even these blind guides of the blind will see.

Then came the soldiers, and brake the legs of the first, and of the other which was crucified with him.

Many have suffered the pains of sin longer than Jesus. But all that is another story.

But when they came to Jesus, and saw that he was dead already, they brake not his legs:

Did not Jesus say, Whosoever lives and believes in me shall never die? How is it then that John herein tells us Jesus was dead? Can one be dead yet never die? Most assuredly.

Jesus' heart broke before his legs could be broken.

But one of the soldiers with a spear pierced his side, and forthwith came there out blood and water.

The soldiers of Rome even to this day pierce us even though we're dead.

And he that saw it bare record, and his record is true:

Roman writers bear record of Rome: and these are legion. We have John's record. It is enough.

and he knoweth that he saith true, that ye might believe.

All these things are done to engender our belief: yet so many meatheads still doubt that I, even I, know not what more to say concerning this matter.

For these things were done, that the scripture should be fulfilled, A bone of him shall not be broken.

Good thing the soldier's spear missed the rib cage, otherwise Cicero and his imitators would be condemning Christians as fools, since one broken bone to them is of more importance than an entire city of truth. Better to be thrown in the arena with lions than argue with morons.

And again another scripture saith, They shall look on him whom they pierced.

I take it the soldiers themselves, unlike the blind Pharisees and lawyers, could see what they themselves had done. I pray that one day they can see what they are doing and tell Pilate to stuff his orders up his toga.

And after this Joseph of Arimathaea, being a disciple of Jesus, but secretly for fear of the Jews, besought Pilate that he might take away the body of Jesus: and Pilate gave him leave.

Makes one wonder if Pilate ever issued an order on his own inclination: but then again, in those days, John had quite an eye for the broads and really wasn't too observant of Pilate's actions.

But where did Joe come from?

He came therefore, and took the body of Jesus.

Last time I saw Joe he was going bananas watching Ann-Margret, a luscious angel if ever God made one, do her special thing to him via that worldly commercial absurdity, (presently run by the Mammonites) called TV. However, since this is true of multiplied thousands of Joes, Joseph of Arimathea's secret is still safe.

And there came also Nicodemus, which at the first came to Jesus by night, and brought a mixture of myrrh and aloes, about an hundred pound weight.

Poor Nick. It was a bit of a waste: but when the Almighty God wants to bury us in symbolism, even a hundred pounds of it, what can we poor souls do?

Then took they the body of Jesus,

I wonder if Ann is one of those who believe in Jesus? If so, she is part of his body of believers.

and wound it in linen clothes with the spices,

There are things I know and things I don't know. Nevertheless, I know Ann-Margret spiced up Joe's life. But poor Jesus got his carcass wound up with Jewish custom and missed many an angel's performance. I do not say he missed them all, since he has a way of storing up treasures in his heart that would embarrass even a Jewish star like Barbra Streisand if she could read his fantastic scripts.

as the manner of the Jews is to bury.

Lazarus is carried by angels unto Abraham's bosom: thus did Jesus, a Jew, express, using customarily Jewish parables, certain facts relative to death and burial. Thank God for the customs of the Gentiles whereby, I, God willing and angels cooperating, might find myself in life, before this life is done, buried, for a few hours at least, in the bosom of Sarah Miles.

I really love that God who makes his word flesh: for with him, all things are possible if you believe. Ah Lord, I believe: help thou my belief!

Now in the place where he was crucified there was a garden; and in the garden a new sepulchre, wherein was never man yet laid.

Oh God how I love to get laid in your garden! Yet these hypocrites still don't understand!

There laid they Jesus therefore because of the Jews' preparation day; for the sepulchre was nigh at hand.

What's the significance of *aloes*? Angels' love of exciting sex? My God of love is full of acronyms: but so is the Satanic computer: nevertheless, the decisions are mine to make: for my God feeds me butter and honey so that I might know how to choose the good and reject the evil. And I weary of those who use the Word made flesh to make of Christ's flesh and blood body a spiritual myth: and who use worldly systems and earthy things and manmade doctrines to pollute his spiritual holy place, which is the heart and mind and soul of those children who love him: and before God all are children.

Yet what is the Jews' preparation day? Indeed, for what are all these peoples of Jehovah, Jew, Gentile, and heathen alike, preparing themselves? For the day of the Lord? I would to God they were: but in all truth, many religious teachers are preparing their people for a death they shall never find: wherein then shall they hide their vanities and pride and foolishness?

But let us live out the story of this one life of Jesus and watch what happens.

CHAPTER 20

The first day of the week cometh Mary Magdalene early, when it was yet dark, unto the sepulchre, and seeth the stone taken away from the sepulchre.

What is a sepulchre but a cave of unrealized desire: a place wherein the tree of life is not found and heavenly desires are not satisfied? Desire satisfied is a tree of life. The stone no longer blocks the exit from my tomb. Yet here I am wondering what will happen next. Today is March 24, 1977: all times are in the hand of God. I write what I write: dream what I dream: report what I report. I am alive, yet dead to much. The parable of my life ever unfolds. What shall be the end of these wonders, Oh God?

Come and see: I must admit, on occasion, my God speaks like a smartass: yet who am I to stand mournfully before the Almighty? Just the other day my wife asked me what I wanted and I told her, "I want God to get off his dumb ass and do something with me." She thinks me a bit blasphemous: yet who knows what tomorrow shall bring?

The true treasures are buried within us: our own stone must be taken away before others can look into our private burial vault. God buries us alone: each one apart. And now, I'm concerned not about my story, but Mary's. Who is Mary? Where is she now? There are many Mary's: but now I'm curious and am seeking out just one in particular.

Where is Mary now, Oh God?

I'd prefer you'd drop the Oh, Oh Son: and get off your dumb ass and find her.

Amen.

Then she runneth, and cometh to Simon Peter, and to the other disciple whom Jesus loved,

(John's really hung up on the past tense when it comes to describing himself.)

and saith unto them, They have taken away the Lord out of the sepulchre, and we know not where they have laid him.

No comment.

Peter therefore went forth, and that other disciple, and came to the sepulchre.

The only way to get an enlightened idea as to what is in another's burial vault, is to have God provide us with an angel or two to explain the circumstances of the body's absence.

There is a mystery connected with the way in which we live in one another: and another mystery in which we can view the treasures buried within each other's hearts. There is a spiritual world, of course: a life within ourselves: and yet a life in which we come and go, even as a spirit. There are two worlds: we live in both. We fly from place to place much more than we realize: at least, at these times.

But let me pass on: lest I get kicked.

So they ran both together: and the other disciple did outrun Peter, and came first to the sepulchre. And he stooping down, and looking in, saw the linen clothes lying; yet went he not in.

Many great men see the righteousness with which Jesus was wrapped, but they don't enter into his treasure vault. The gospel is too plain and unembellished for them. They prefer looking into pyramids and mausoleums and other worldly tombs and graveyards of the world's great dead.

Jesus left a few linen clothes lying in his tomb. The gospels are really very short. But what we have from the past of Lincoln and Hitler and Napoleon and Shakespeare (if the bard will forgive me the literary conceit of this unseemly lumping together), to say nothing of Churchill, is enough to fill a library shelf or two.

But I must move on since my God is questioning the wisdom of my wordiness.

We should remember these things occurred while it was yet dark. In darkness, Mary thought, they have taken the lord out of the sepulchre and so reported her feelings to John and Peter. But did she know this for a fact? She saw one thing, and believed another. But in the dark, this response is understandable.

John, while it was yet dark, stoops down, and sees the linen clothes lying, yet dares not enter the sepulchre where Jesus was laid. Why not? Somehow, fear is generated in the dark: the light within a man is not sufficient to guide him into another's burial vault.

Peter, however, stoops down, and goes in; yet Mary and John had, while it was yet dark, prepared, so to speak, the way for his entering.

Then cometh Simon Peter following him, and went into the sepulchre, and seeth the linen clothes lie, And the napkin, that was about his head, not lying with the linen clothes, but wrapped together in a place by itself.

The observation made is of that with which Jesus, in his death, was wrapped. The death of Jesus, like his resurrection, is shrouded in mystery. We examine the wrappings of religion, the trappings of priest craft, the weird windings of scribes who have become the morticians of mediocrity. But if we enter into the sepulchre, and boldly examine the evidence, even as Peter, we'll confirm the fact that the body of Jesus, even his dead carcass, is not in that place where men have laid him. Jesus is not in the sepulchre even in the darkness of that time of the Roman day John describes as the first day.

Irving Wallace, a modern scribe, wraps the Word of Jesus with the restrictive bindings woven in the bottomless pit of his own imagination. In this way, The Word is made myth, and not flesh. But that's Irving's story and he can have it for what it is. He has his reward.

Many other scribes, ancient and modern, wrap the carcass of Jesus in their own mysterious ways. But what is true is what John herein reports: namely, Peter went into the sepulchre, and saw the linen clothes, and the napkin, and little else worthy of report.

The poor in spirit, however, take little notice of these angelic conceits and Jewish customs. They simply believe and are alive to the truth and thereby possess the kingdom of heaven. Yet how these worldly scribes bind up the story with their own mystical nonsense, I leave for you to discover for yourself. The sepulchre is empty: if you doubt, come in and see for yourself.

Then went in also that other disciple, which came first to the sepulchre, and he saw, and believed.

Believed what? Believed only the carcass was not in the sepulchre: perhaps the eagles had taken it away: indeed, perhaps the Roman soldiers themselves had decided to trick the believing Jews. In fact, is this not the story of some scribes who make merchandise out of it even to this day? Believe what you will: But, the carcass is not in the sepulchre.

I cannot be bound up in the confining and restrictive imagination of those men who, with customs ancient and customs modern, wish to entomb me within the sepulchre of their mind. How much less so then can we expect to find Jesus within the earthly skull of their own meaty brains? Yet, is this not their boast? Let them confine themselves to the linen clothes and napkin: let them do know more, lest they anger God. They do not have Jesus within their heart: how much less so then do they have Jesus within their carnal minds? The brains of men without the blood of Jesus are as dust.

My body is my tabernacle: I care not for the graves men provide.

But, even if you can see all these things in the living light of this new day, will you believe? The beauty of everlasting life is ever victorious: is ever exciting. Don't doubt the Word: live it.

For as yet they knew not the scripture, that he must rise again from the dead.

So must we all.

Then the disciples went away again unto their own home.

Peter will return later, and stoop down, and look again into the place where Jesus was buried. Perhaps, in the light of early morning, he'll begin to believe that which he could not accept in the darkness of the first Roman day.

But Mary stood without at the sepulchre weeping: and as she wept, she stooped down, and looked into the sepulchre.

Mary now dares to look. But what will she see?

And seeth two angels in white sitting, the one at the head, and the other at the feet, where the body of Jesus had lain.

It is more enlightening to see and listen to God's angels than to observe useless shrouds, and graveclothes, and bindings.

And they say unto her, Woman, why weepest thou?

Let all who weep because they can't find the dead body of Jesus answer the question themselves.

She saith unto them, Because they have taken away my Lord, and I know not where they have laid him. And when she had thus said, she turned herself back, and saw Jesus standing, and knew not that it was Jesus.

In this lack of initial perception, Mary is not alone. However, we must turn ourselves back if we wish to see Jesus.

Jesus saith unto her, Woman why weepest thou? whom seekest thou? She, supposing him to be the gardener, saith unto him, Sir, if thou have borne him hence, tell me where thou hast laid him, and I will take him away.

God is the gardener: Jesus, the sensitive plant. And Mary has taken him away also: more times than she even now realizes. But in the darkness of a thousand year day, though much happens, much is not sensed nor seen.

Jesus saith unto her, Mary. She turned herself, and saith unto him, Rabboni; which is to say, Master.

There are many stars named Mary; many asters and roses in the garden of God. Why are we so blinded by our own tears to the everlasting beauty of this eternal day? We are raised up from the dust of the earth: inspired with life: planted in the garden of God: told the truth of our beginning, and even our end, by the spirit of love. Our book of life is full: the waters of delight are crystal clear and good: our tree of life yields its fruit within ourselves: and our tomb is no more frightening than a woman's womb from which all of us were born.

Jesus saith unto her, Touch me not; for I am not yet ascended to my Father: but go to my brethren, and say unto them, I ascend unto my Father, and your Father; and to my God, and your God.

And how is this done? With the power of the Word.

When this is done, surely Mary will also ascend, and the touches of love will not be denied. Masters are no more: only many stars, and many flowers blessed with youth and life and joy, and many angels who come again and cry out, Oh Jesus! Oh God! Oh lover baby!

But will the disciples believe this? Even those same disciples who found it not in their heart to believe Mary Magdalene the first time, and the second time, and even the third time she told them of these things?

Mary Magdalene came and told the disciples that she had seen the Lord, and that he had spoken these things unto her.

But if the disciples won't believe, perhaps Mary the mother of James will believe: and perhaps the two of them will see something even more startling than what Mary Magdalene alone saw in the garden, near the tomb, while it was yet dark.

Is there faith upon the earth? There's faith in so much nonsense: faith in the increase of knowledge, faith in Man, faith in the Church, faith in the State: but faith in the Son of man? What can I say? Those who believe are in heaven: those who do not believe are a pain in my ass.

Then the same day at evening, being the first day of the week, when the doors were shut where the disciples were assembled for fear of the Jews, came Jesus and stood in the midst, and saith unto them, Peace be unto you.

Why should the disciples fear the Jews? Who are they really afraid of? Why keep the doors locked? Are they locking the Jews out or are they locking themselves within?

Surely, it takes Jesus himself to come to them, stand in their midst, and say, Peace be unto you. Really, it's in this day rather ridiculous to see the disciples of Jesus and the witnesses of Jehovah fearing one another. Is our Father not the Lord God of Israel? Are we not all his children, prodigal though many of us be? Let's do the will of the Lord.

And when he had so said, he shewed unto them his hands and his side. Then were the disciples glad, when they saw the Lord.

What has Jesus got in his hand? The print of the nails? No. Just the print. And all the truth fit to print and to handle and to see. The nail fastened in a sure place had been cut down. But why? Because the disciples of Jesus and the Jews were at cross purposes: the pointless controversies engendered by the father of lies was causing children to rise up against their parents, and parents against their children. Each god was worshiping his own self much as it is even to this very day. Men become devils when they worship the works of their own hands: when they believe the beast of the world, created by God, to serve both men and God even within the garden of Eden, rather than God.

Death is dead earth: it is the nonentity which men fear to their own undoing. The death of the body is the collapse of a tent: the tearing down of a tabernacle no longer useful.

What was inside Jesus that came out of him? Blood and water. Believe good: despise evil. We are ignorant, vastly ignorant of so very many things that life itself is filled with pain, sorrow, and suffering caused by our service to Satan, the ultimate beast, the super social organism which tempts us. Our blood is needlessly spilled, wantonly sacrificed by egomaniacal simpletons who preach peace and equip themselves for bloody wars. Such believe the beast: in this all who kill and murder reject God's commandments to the contrary and boast of their knowledge of what is good and what is evil. Surely, we should learn a truth of everlasting life: even if we are slain, and our blood is poured out upon the earth, we have only received a wound: men have killed the body: but in all truth, what once God gave us, he can give us again. A resurrected body is just that: a common fact of everlasting life.

But the stupid, and foolish, and vain, and abominable ideas we receive from men who have forsaken God, must be destroyed by the fiery spirit of God's judgment. His Word refines. His Word destroys. Jesus of Nazareth has a wound in his side. We can see it: read about it: hear about it: write about it. But what is that to the God Jesus became? Our Lord and our God is Jesus, the God of the whole earth. If you deny this, argue the point with the Lord God of Israel, even the Father of David, of Jesus; of you, and of me. Yet whom do we worship? Whom do we believe and act and serve before? Church, State, Money, Man, Satan; things which are, and were, and yet are not. For Satan cannot live unless our idol of self animates it. The sons of God have made themselves as idiots by revolting against the truth: and I weary of it all. Have I not other things to do than engage in profitless controversies?

We can receive the water of Jesus' Word and the blood of his Word and the flesh of his Word by eating his book of life, and assimilating his teachings. We can also witness the spilling of the water and blood from his side. The wound is real. Why deny the obvious? We pierce each other with the spear of an unforgiving spirit: we execute bloody sacrifice and have refused to participate in the redeeming sacrifice of praise. No wonder the Lord God is pissed off at what his creatures have made of this earth: no wonder Death and Hell are our portion. Let the Lord God of Israel save us how he wills: surely this is my desire: for the desires of the world are madness and their satisfaction, vanity.

Let us be glad we have seen this one side of the Lord which the world in ignorance pierced.

Then said Jesus to them again, Peace be unto you: as my Father hath sent me, even so send I you.

Why is it so hard for the disciples of Jesus to realize that they have been sent into the world to save it? Not to corrupt it; not to create it; not to use it as a testing ground; not to love it, but to save it for those who can find the kingdom growing within the field of their own experience of life?

And when he had said this, he breathed on them, and saith unto them, Receive ye the Holy Ghost: Whose soever sins ye remit, they are remitted unto them; and whose soever sins ye retain, they are retained.

God's spirit is so holy, and so mighty, that it requires a heavenly host to lay hold of it: yet so comforting is the way of that spirit of truth, that it can speak to us within, even with a still small voice. We are comforted by the spirit within and amazed at the host without. If the Lord God of Hosts did not exist, neither would we: and neither would Voltaire, a skeptical, scoffing and sinful scribe whose sin I remit. For why ought not the genius of hell serve the God of paradise? What's in hell anyway? A host of puerile fancies, abominable forms, silly ideas, and such assorted verbal bullshit that I thank God for my own life in this lake of fire I presently enjoy. What then is hell? Something I've experienced and something you had best avoid. Those nations of people who forsake God are transformed into hell. Why deny his story, the story of the prince of this world, the history of the world in which the princes of this world gloat and in which they record their accomplishments? Much that is abominable is found in it. And at times, it is all so laughable, I find it hard to take these assholes seriously. Yet there they be: and here I am. Ho hum. God surely will destroy it, and liberate the souls within it, even as he promised he would, so long ago.

Jesus is a prophet: and the spirit of his Word is the spirit of prophecy. But the dead prophesy death and are somewhat embarrassed by their life and the fact that, really, according to their own doctrines, they are not supposed to be here.

But if the world rejected Jesus and his words, what will they do with mine? At this time, it doesn't really much matter, for eternity is full of time, and times; and seasons, and hours, and half hours, and acts. And I, who know this, am amazed at those clowns who refuse to believe it.

But Thomas, one of the twelve, called Didymus, was not with them when Jesus came.

Thomas, like Thomas Aquinas, missed receiving the Holy Ghost. Consequently, his objectors often make a better stab at truth than he himself does. Men pride themselves on tedious circumlocution:

Jesus enjoins: Believe me: believe God: but the original skeptics become intellectual dogmatists and sins which are to be remitted or retained only, are excused, condoned, analyzed, catalogued, discussed, dissected, and encased in such a literary closet of adulterous bullshit that I marvel at the longsuffering God who said, Thou shalt not kill. The poor suffer: and yet the proud intellectual monarchs of this present age condone their evil wars, ways, systems and prisons. Worship God: love Jesus and keep his words: and judge all these angels and devils, these wise men and fools alike, that assault your just inheritance, even the kingdom of God growing within you. Without the fiery judgment of the God of truth we burden our souls and pollute our kingdoms with religious and political hypocrisy.

Blessed are the poor in spirit for theirs is the kingdom of heaven. How hard is it for these intellectual giants to enter the strait gate! They must examine every wound, feel every bruised rib cage, doubt every report, believe nothing but what their own eyes see and their own finger touches and their own hand can grasp.

We believe and do: they doubt and examine. Let the unseen God visibly justify me: for what I know my Father to be, men cannot believe. Let men doubt: let men examine: let men ask. But let the dead bury their dead: surely, we living are to occupy ourselves with the affairs of life.

The other disciples therefore said unto him, We have seen the Lord. But he said unto them, Except I shall see in his hands the print of the nails, and thrust my hand into his side, I will not believe.

Believe what? Believe the testimony of his own brethren? Or believe that his faithless sin would be retained even to this day? Or believe that the Holy Ghost was not given to those who in fact did receive it? Let his sin be remitted: I weary of these dogmatic defenders of religion who can believe almost anything in the Word of God except the fact that the poor in spirit are blessed with the kingdom of heaven.

And after eight days again his disciples were within, and Thomas with them: then came Jesus, the doors being shut,

(How true since even this day the churches shut the door to him.)

and stood in the midst, and said, Peace be unto you.

(Obviously, they needed a second dose of it.)

Then saith he to Thomas, Reach hither thy finger, and behold my hands; and reach hither thy hand, and thrust it into my side: and be not faithless, but believing.

Would this suffice?

And Thomas answered and said unto him, My Lord and my God.

A remarkable perception for a skeptic whose condition for belief Jesus satisfied. I marvel at men: they are blind to a thousand miracles a day, and to a record extending over three and a half thousand years, and to a thousand times thousands of witnesses, and to the living presence of the kingdom of heaven come to earth, yet they can perceive that Jesus is their Lord and their God. Well, why should I piss and moan about this? It's better than nothing.

Jesus saith unto him, Thomas, because thou hast seen me, thou hast believed: blessed are they that have not seen, and yet have believed.

Why? Because the power of the Word is given to those who believe those things which are seen are sustained by those things which are not seen. Our belief is fundamental and skeptics are only useful to prove their uselessness. Satan is useful: and it is used until it is destroyed. But the skeptics prove hard for God himself to use. Yet he seems to delight in the impossible and I continuously marvel at his ways: for he can bring good out of Satan himself, if it please him. And even I am hard put to take all these nonbelievers seriously.

Nonetheless, what do you think? Are those who have not seen Jesus, yet have believed in him, blessed? I believe it: but I have my doubts about Thomas.

And many other signs truly did Jesus in the presence of his disciples, which are not written in this book:

Shall you believe this ever?

But these are written, that ye might believe that Jesus is the Christ, the Son of God; and that believing ye might have life through his name.

Jesus is the Christ: surely, this I believe. Jesus is the Son of God: Satan is the imposter: the system: the customary accuser: the liar: the machine that provides a tempting alternative. Jesus Christ is come in the flesh: but the Antichrist is the idol of proud men's minds. Do you believe this? Or are you one with Antichrist?

CHAPTER 21

After these things Jesus shewed himself again to the disciples at the sea of Tiberias; and on this wise shewed he himself. There were together Simon Peter, and Thomas called Didymus, and Nathanael of Cana in Galilee, and the sons of Zebedee, and two other of his disciples. Simon Peter saith unto them, I go a fishing. They say unto him, We also go with thee. They went forth and entered into a ship immediately; and that night they caught nothing.

Why? Because in the thick of a Roman night, especially on the sea of a dead emperor, no man can work. But some children will try anything: good advice to the contrary notwithstanding. What time is it now?

But when the morning was now come, Jesus stood on the shore: but the disciples knew not that it was Jesus.

A perennial problem, a daily dilemma, a mystery that extends over three thousand years of time and reaches to the uttermost ends of the earth: even to Long Beach, California. But why? Their vision is dim: their heart is busy about other matters: an unsuccessful trip has blown their mind, and they are not aware of what has happened to them: nor can they perceive what is happening.

Then Jesus saith unto them, Cast the net on the right side of the ship, and ye shall find.

The net of each man's kingdom must be cast into the sea of dreams and forms and possibilities: thus does each man from his ship of state, ship of fate, ship of life cast into the sea of his own worldly soul, the gathering power of his own kingdom. We draw to us what we love. Yet we must use the net found on the right side: the others are broken, and worn, and rotten and useless. What is this net? It is what it is: the gathering power of our own spirit: one facet of the gift of God to us: one spiritual truth descriptive of the kingdom's power.

The net is cast into the sea of Tiberias. At night, nothing is caught. Why? Because the Roman sea of wickedness is full of death and hell and the net of love can draw nothing out of it. Even Thomas Aquinas used the foolish powers of Church and State to justify the wickedness of men, rather than condemning it. Even John Knox who could thunder against a Catholic Queen, and King James, who could command a Church and State to do his bidding, could catch nothing of worth from the Roman sea. And Nathanael, sitting under the very boughs and branches of God's kingdom, could only regret that he had but one life to give: give to whom? To his country. And Peter wields the sword of truth to savor the things of the world, the intellectual greatness of worldly minds, who concern themselves with State and Church and Wisdom and books and fables and myths and opinions of the mighty prophet Man in plentiful abundance. And what results? Truth comforts: yet Satan overcomes. Thus men are led to slaughter: lies are justified: Man is extolled and God blasphemed. The sheep of God are slaughtered: Mammon is served: and great angels content themselves with the cold and lifeless goddesses of knowledge, and power, and fame. Men are deceived by their own self: and forget so easily whose image they are.

The net on the right side of this troubled spaceship earth, is the net of love. For so spoke Jesus of Galilee a long time ago. No wonder they renamed the sea that which God intended it to be. The sea of Galilee is of all nations and is among all nations. And in this morning of this new day, the net of love produces a mighty catch of great fishes. How do I know? Because Tchaikovsky is as great as Laplace and their works even to this day live with them and are transforming words and dreams into living flesh and blood fact. Ludmilla is as real as any Russian and even more real than the machine which brought her image to me. And what do I see? A living soul clothed in flesh and blood which the Lord God of Israel created for his pleasure, and our pleasure, and her pleasure.

Surely this is the message of the man from Galilee and who am I to silence God's great voice?

They cast therefore, and now they were not able to draw it for the multitude of fishes. Therefore, that disciple whom Jesus loved saith unto Peter, It is the Lord.

Those that are born of love are quick to recognize God is love.

Now when Simon Peter heard that it was the Lord, he girt his fisher's coat unto him (for he was naked), and did cast himself into the sea.

But the sea is more properly a lake of cleansing truth and fresh and soothing fact. Yet when Israel takes from its waters what it needs, the promised land is nourished. And what is left over is not worth having. Flowing water is required for life: for this is living water: water trapped and locked within the burning basin of worldly hypocrisy is worthless and from its waters none may drink repeatedly and live. Yet men store up power in their own worldly reservoirs and meter it out to the poor as the servants of Mammon see fit. Even God's angels are told how much to drink and how much to use for flushing their own shit. How bold are these captains of mediocrity! How utterly fearless! The minnows of man who escape the net of God's great love. Yet, every creature has its uses. Let them take heart: for the kingdom of heaven grows within us all: and someday, when we've outgrown these parables, we'll know ourselves for what we all really are: God's children.

And the other disciples came in a little ship; (for they were not far from land, but as it were two hundred cubits), dragging the net with fishes.

In this act, Peter plainly plays no part.

As soon then as they were come to land, they saw a fire of coals there, and fish laid thereon, and bread.

Jesus evidently has prepared a catch and a doctrine of his own.

Jesus saith unto them, Bring of the fish which ye have now caught. Simon Peter went up, and drew the net to land full of great fishes, an hundred and fifty and three: and for all there were so many, yet was not the net broken.

Are these great fishes for all? As men, how can we escape this truth? The great men influence all even in ways we know not.

But why a hundred and fifty and three great fishes? Because Peter counted them and that's how many he counted that day. Or so I believe: but if I am wrong, let Peter correct me.

Jesus saith unto them, Come and dine.

On what? Obviously, on what he had prepared.

And none of the disciples durst ask him, Who art thou? knowing that it was the Lord. Jesus then cometh, and taketh bread, and giveth them, and fish likewise. This is now the third time that Jesus shewed himself to his disciples, after that he was risen from the dead.

Yet where was he in the meanwhile? Catching fish? Firing coals? Preparing bread? Does Jesus work this way even in the night? Strange fellow, this Jesus. Yet perhaps Paul would understand, for many men entertain angels unaware of who they really are. Men simply do not believe the truth of the gospel. Yet truth is stranger than fiction: that's what so entertaining about it. A police woman is a fictional creation and easy to understand. But Angie Dickinson is a true angel of God and no stranger to the world of entertainment. But I am cursed: for I play with words only. When shall I be blessed? God only knows: for my delight is to see the Word made flesh, but this occurs at the times appointed. With God, there is a time for all good things to be used and enjoyed and loved as the Lord God of Love decrees.

Perhaps there is even a time for these boring theologians and churchmen and statesmen to cease from boring out their canons of ironic beliefs with which they threaten the green pastures of God. But these spiritual eunuchs have no balls for truth: no, nor did they ever. And now that they've used up all of earth's resources and since they have no heavenly truth to shower upon men, they have recourse to verbal bullshit and booming nonsense.

Jesus Christ, where did you get all this stuff?

So when they had dined, Jesus saith to Simon Peter, Simon, son of Jonas, lovest thou me more than these?

Why did Jesus ask? Did he have doubts? What's a great haul of fish beside Jesus?

He saith unto him, Yea, Lord; thou knowest that I love thee. He saith unto him, Feed my lambs.

Can lambs eat fish? Yes, if properly prepared.

He saith to him again the second time, Simon, son of Jonas, lovest thou me?

Who is the son of Jonas? Even he whose father was swallowed up by the great fish of the stormy sea: Leviathan, the Godless State of the World, which carries the prophets of God whither they would not. For all things are under God's power: even man's own evil creatures.

He saith unto him, Yea, Lord; thou knowest that I love thee. He saith unto him, Feed my sheep.

Are the sheep of Israel, even the men God created for himself to be fed? Of course. How? In the way it is done. Even Jesus' way, and no other. But even his disciples don't understand.

He saith unto him the third time, Simon, son of Jonas, lovest thou me?

This question is still valid even to this day: not only for Peter: but for all who can receive it unto themselves.

Peter was grieved because he said unto him the third time, Lovest thou me?

Do we love Jesus? Not really: for if we did we would keep his words within us and live them. Shall we love him really, even all of us? Of course, for the spirit of love shall conquer all: truth is the damnation of the sinful soul: yet love, mercy, and forgiveness is its savior. Have we all sinned? Of course. But as they are taught to ask in EST, so what? So learn the truth, free yourself from worldly delusions and the manipulations of vain teachers: continue in the Word and be free in deed.

Thomas Jefferson loves man and the state: and Mao Tse-tung loved to read of the heroes of the world, such as George Washington, the old pompous ass, himself. And the disappointing Lincoln go so worked up over the issues of slavery and his fucking precious union that the quiet commandments of love spoken by Jesus could no longer move his heart to do that which is righteous. Shit! Could not the Lord God destroy in an instant of time all flesh on this earth if he so desired? Idiots forget simple scripture: are ignorant of plain fact: quickly deny all obvious truth. With God all things are possible: even his patience to this very hour.

Let us love Jesus and understand with our heart his gospel. Let these lawyers of laws innumerable, learn of God's law. The Lord God of Israel is our lawgiver: we need not their puerile legislations: our God has placed his laws within our heart and mind. His covenant is with those who live to worship him. Love, and every act and expression of it, excites God and makes him come again, and again, and again.

We hunger for righteousness: thirst for truth: seek to clothe ourselves with beauty. Yet we are naked prisoners in a strange land: even upon a planet of apes wherein God is not found. Where therefore is God found? Within us and among us, husbanding our garden of delight, and increasing the yields found on all these trees of life. I am but one tree in the city of my God. My Father is your Father: my God is your God: that Spirit is greater than I, immensely so. I never said it was otherwise. Why is Jesus unloved? For the same reason we hate each other: for the same reason we hate ourselves: God forgives; without him, we cannot: and many are without God.

How many of the United Nations are on the right hand of the Son of man? How many countries justly deserve the kingdom of heaven? Not one: surely, I know of none. Who then shall inherit the kingdom of God? All of the nations of people among them: for God full well knows how to transform goats into sheep even if Man does not. Our punishment is everlasting: for truth is eternal: and what is this everlasting fire? The spirit of God, enflaming us with his words of truth, and cleansing us from the evil of our own idolatrous imaginations.

I love the second death: I enjoy this lake of fire.

He saith unto him the third time,

(Repeated herein a fourth for good measure)

Simon, son of Jonas, lovest thou me? Peter was grieved because he said unto him the third time, Lovest thou me? And he said unto him, Lord thou knowest all things;

Does Peter really believe what he is saying? all things? That's heavy.

Thou knowest that I love thee. Jesus saith unto him, Feed my sheep.

Has he done this? In his own inimitable way, he has.

Verily, verily, I say unto thee, when thou wast young, thou girdest thyself, and walketh whither thou wouldst:

Men are embarrassed by naked truth. Why, I know not: and at this time I am too preoccupied with the beauty of naked angels to diminish my ignorance by searching into these psychological matters.

With what do these great peters gird themselves? With the fig leaves of wisdom torn from the tree of knowledge. No wonder now that they get embarrassed when excited by love's call.

But when thou shalt be old, thou shalt stretch forth thy hands, and another shall gird thee, and carry thee whither thou wouldst not.

What the heaven does this mean?

This spake he, signifying by what death he should glorify God.

Is God glorified by death? Only by the second death wherein we destroy our own self-created fears and stupid mental idols and return to him in naked love. Now all this is hot stuff, and greatly to be desired for those who can take it.

And when he had spoken this, he saith unto him, Follow me.

Where? To a lake of fire, of course. For God's love is a consuming fire as those with hot lips themselves shall one day testify. What has